BREAKING THE BARRIERS STORIES THROUGH THE LENS

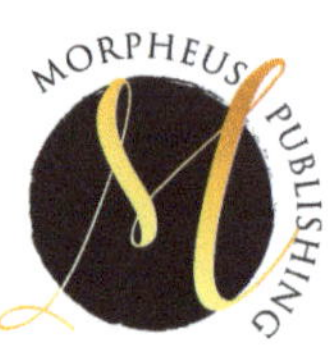

Copyright © 2025
First Published in Australia in 2025
By Morpheus Publishing
Geelong Victoria 3216
www.morpheuspublishing.com.au

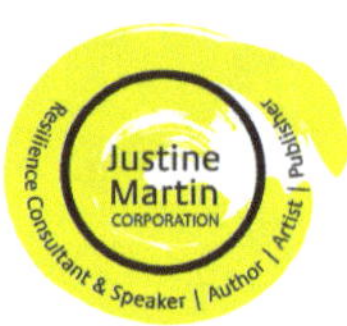

ISBN: 978-1-7636985-9-8

Author/ Interviewer: **Justine Martin**
Editor: **Justine Martin**
Cover Graphics: **Morpheus Publishing**
Photographer: **Golden Frame Productions**
Makeup: **Makeupartlis**
Hair: **Hair By Jo**

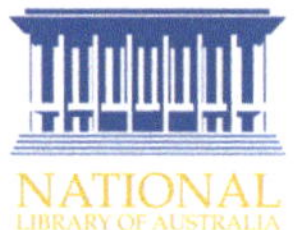

A catalogue record for this book is available from the National Library of Australia.

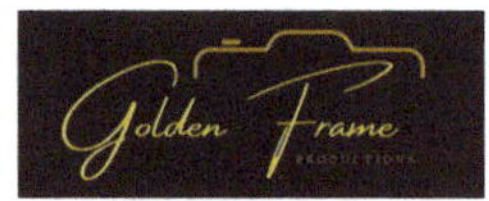

DISCLAIMER
The information contained in this book is for general informational purposes only. The author and publisher are not offering any medical, legal or professional advice. While every effort has been made to ensure the accuracy and completeness of the information provided, the author and publisher assume no responsibility for errors or omissions or any outcomes or consequences resulting from using this book's content.

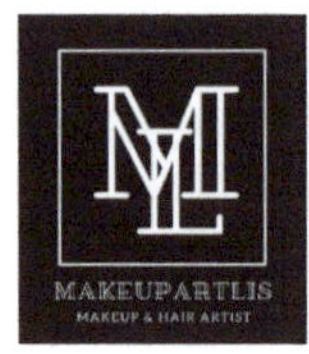

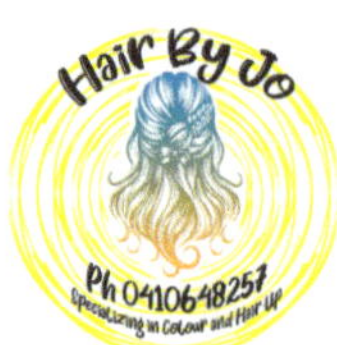

DISTRIBUTION
This book is distributed by Morpheus Publishing and is available through authorised distributors, booksellers, Morpheus Publishing website and Tory Trewhitt website.

PUBLISHER: Morpheus Publishing
www.morpheuspublishing.com.au || hello@justinemartin.com.au
|| +61403 564 942

INTRODUCTION

Welcome to *Breaking the Barriers Through the Lens*, a celebration of strength, resilience, and the transformative power of sharing stories. This book is a testament to the human spirit, capturing the journeys of individuals who have faced life's challenges head-on and emerged with courage, grace, and an unwavering determination to inspire others.

Each page invites you into the lives of remarkable people from diverse backgrounds and experiences, united by their ability to break through barriers—whether physical, emotional, or societal. Through vivid portraits and heartfelt narratives, these individuals share their journeys, offering insights into what it truly means to overcome adversity.

The idea behind *Breaking the Barriers Through the Lens* is simple yet profound: to create a space where voices are heard, stories are honoured, and resilience is celebrated. This project is not just about photographs or words; it's about challenging perceptions, fostering understanding, and amplifying the message that every individual has the power to make a difference.

From the young athlete defying expectations on the field to the artist finding healing through creativity, from the advocate raising awareness about invisible disabilities to the parent rediscovering life's purpose after a profound loss—each story is unique. Yet, collectively, they paint a picture of hope, determination, and the limitless potential of the human spirit.

This book would not have been possible without the passion, dedication, and collaboration of some extraordinary individuals. Justine, Simon, Julie, Jo, Lis, and Eden have poured their hearts and talents into making this vision a reality. Their collective efforts have brought these powerful stories to life, ensuring that every voice is heard and celebrated.

This book is also a call to action. It reminds us to look beyond the surface, to recognise the richness of every person's journey, and to champion inclusivity and compassion in our communities. As you turn each page, may you be inspired to see the world—and the people in it—with greater empathy and understanding.

Thank you for joining us on this journey of discovery. Together, we can break barriers, one story at a time.

Justine, Simon, Julie, Jo, Lis and Eden.

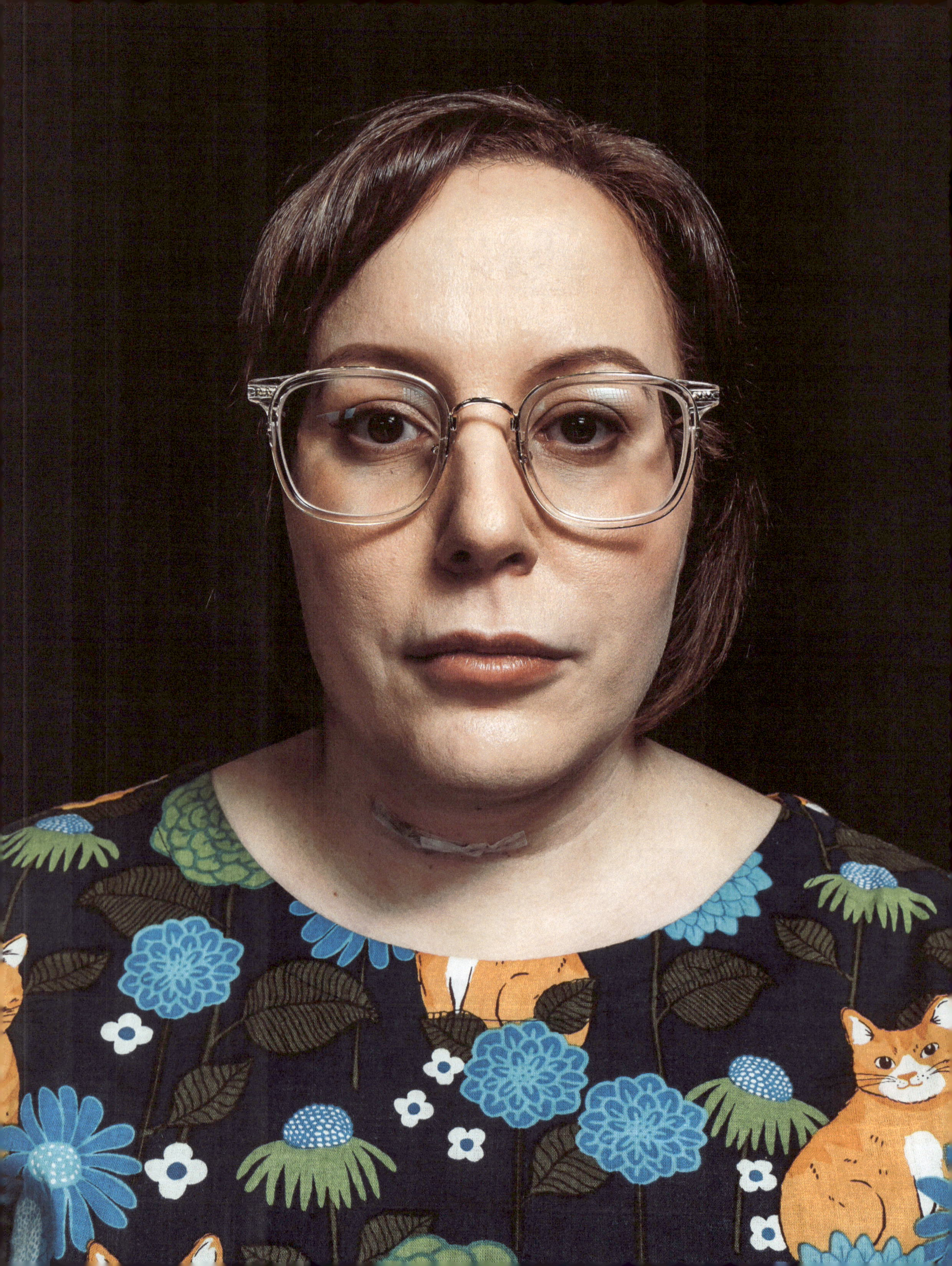

Alison Connoley

Navigating Adversity: Path to Advocacy and Impact

Alison is a proud mum, wife, and advocate who balances the complexities of life with cerebral palsy and other health challenges while managing a family-run business dedicated to supporting others with disabilities. Through her work and personal experiences, Alison embodies resilience and determination.

"I'm a mum and a wife, and I manage a business with my family called My Choice Group, an NDIS-registered provider in Geelong," Alison shares. "We started the business because of our combined lived experiences with disabilities. We're deliberately small, a boutique service, so we can really focus on meeting the individual needs of families."

Born with cerebral palsy, Alison reflects on how her disability has shaped her life. "It's been a journey of understanding and acceptance," she says. "In the early years, I didn't have a great awareness of how my condition impacted me. It wasn't until later in life that I started to embrace it and recognise how it could be a positive force, both for me and my family."

Growing up in the 1990s, Alison's parents faced a lack of resources and guidance when she was diagnosed. "My parents were young when I was born, and back then, the advice was just to 'get on with it.' There wasn't much support or understanding around what it meant to live with a disability."

Her journey of self-awareness was transformative. "Learning to understand my limits, why I felt tired or couldn't stand for long, was empowering. It helped me reduce stress and live a more comfortable and fulfilling life."

One of the defining moments in Alison's journey came when her son was born prematurely at 29 weeks, echoing her own early arrival. "He was in the NICU, and I was recovering from emergency surgery. The hospital was trying to discharge me without any support or even my wheelchair. I was sitting by his NICU bed, managing staff rosters for work, and I thought, 'We've got to do better.' That moment solidified my commitment to making a difference."

Alison uses a pink wheelchair, but her mobility varies. "Some days, I can stand or walk short distances. For others, seeing me get out of my chair is surprising. There's this misconception that wheelchair users are always confined to them, and it highlights the need for greater education about the diversity of disabilities."

Breaking barriers, for Alison, means challenging stigma and fostering inclusivity. "It's about breaking down the misconceptions people have about disabilities. Many barriers aren't physical; they're in people's minds—in their attitudes and assumptions. If we can shift those perspectives, we can create a more understanding and accessible society."

Her family has been a cornerstone of support. "My husband and three kids, aged 3, 8, and 11, keep me going. All my children have disabilities, so these values of acceptance and advocacy are part of our everyday lives. It's what motivates me to push through on the hard days."

Recently, Alison registered a charity, the Trevena Foundation, named after her maiden name and created to support people navigating the NDIS and accessing disability services. "It started as a small project helping others with paperwork and advocacy. Now, we're applying for funding to formalise and expand our efforts. It's about giving back and creating real change."

Despite her challenges, Alison finds joy and connection through hobbies like reading. "I love books, and they've become a way to stay connected with friends. We even swap recommendations and discuss our favourites—it's a small but meaningful way to keep spirits high."

Her role models include those who advocate for change and inspire hope. "The stories of others have deeply moved me, and hearing speeches like the one you gave last year really pushed me to share my own story. It's about stepping out of your comfort zone and realising that your voice can make a difference."

Alison's message to the world is clear and heartfelt: "Be curious and compassionate. There's no limit to what we can achieve for each other if we approach life with understanding. Disability isn't a limitation; it's a different way of living."

"

Disability isn't a limitation it's a different way of living.

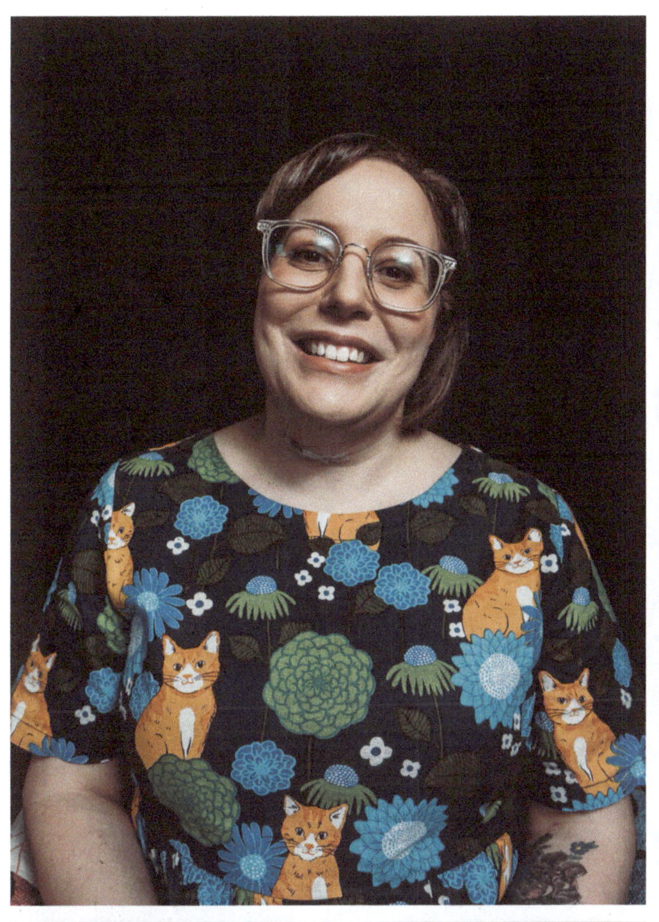

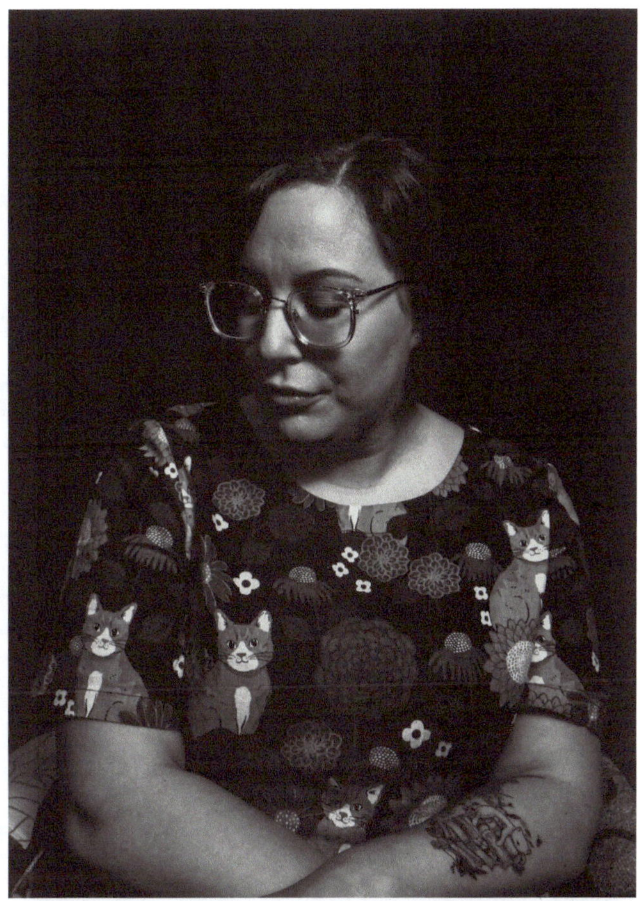

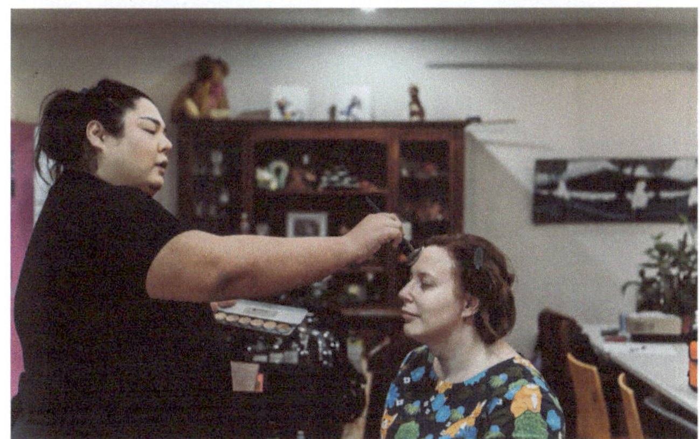

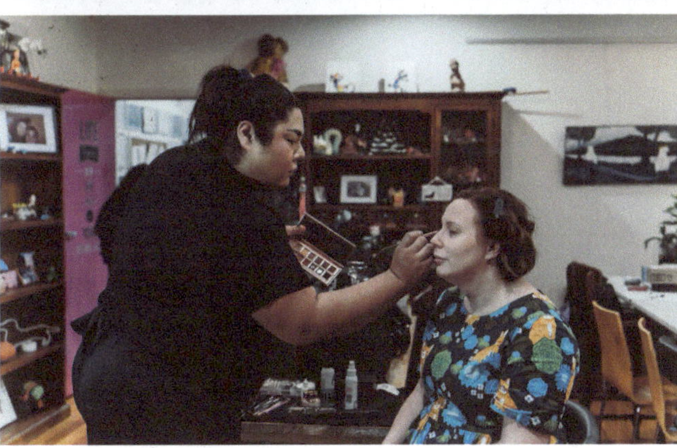

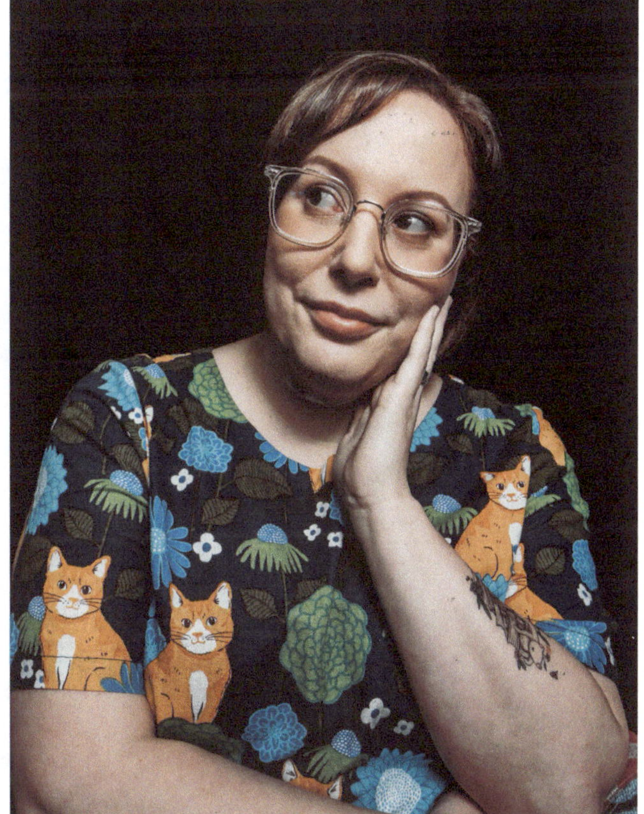

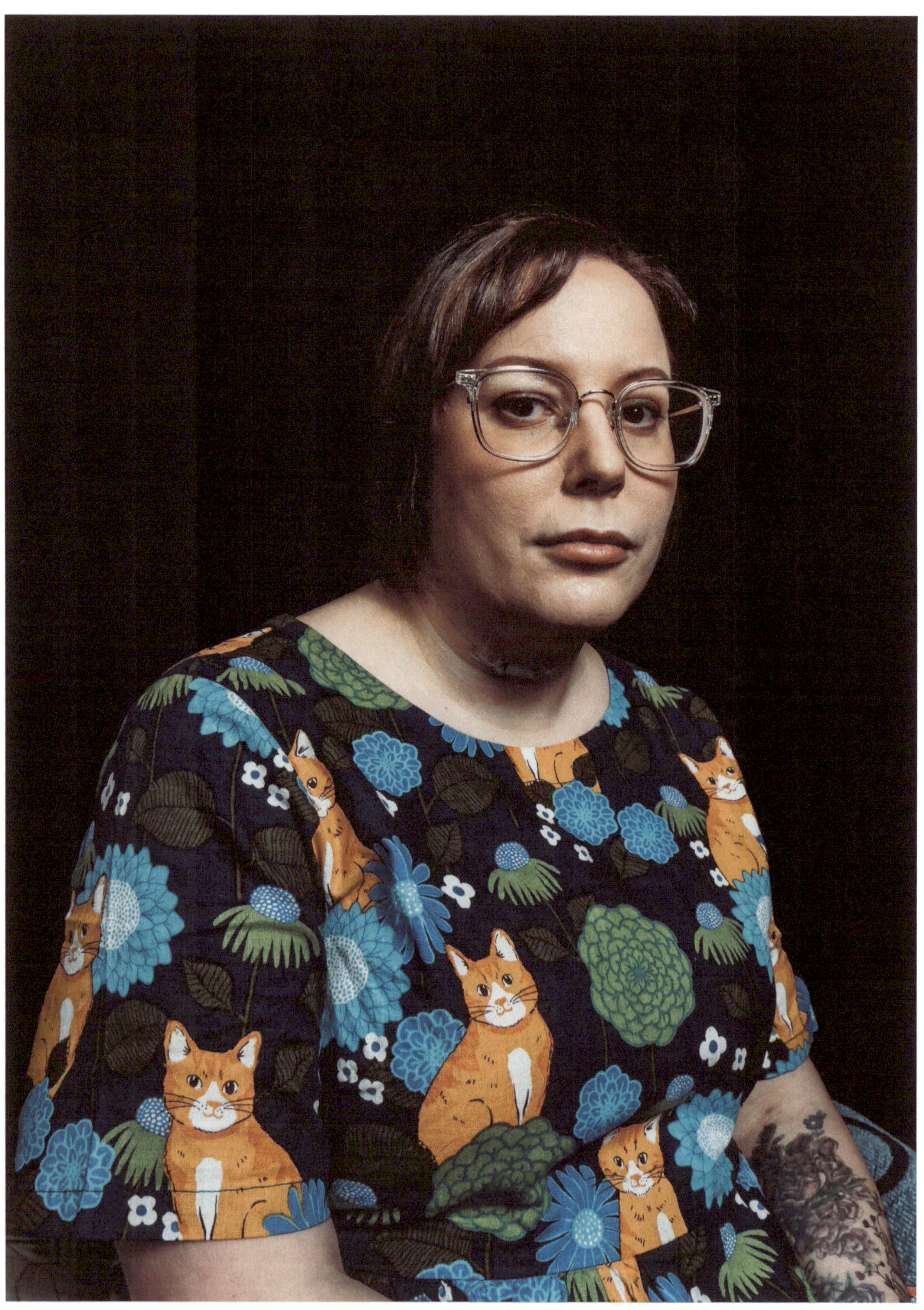

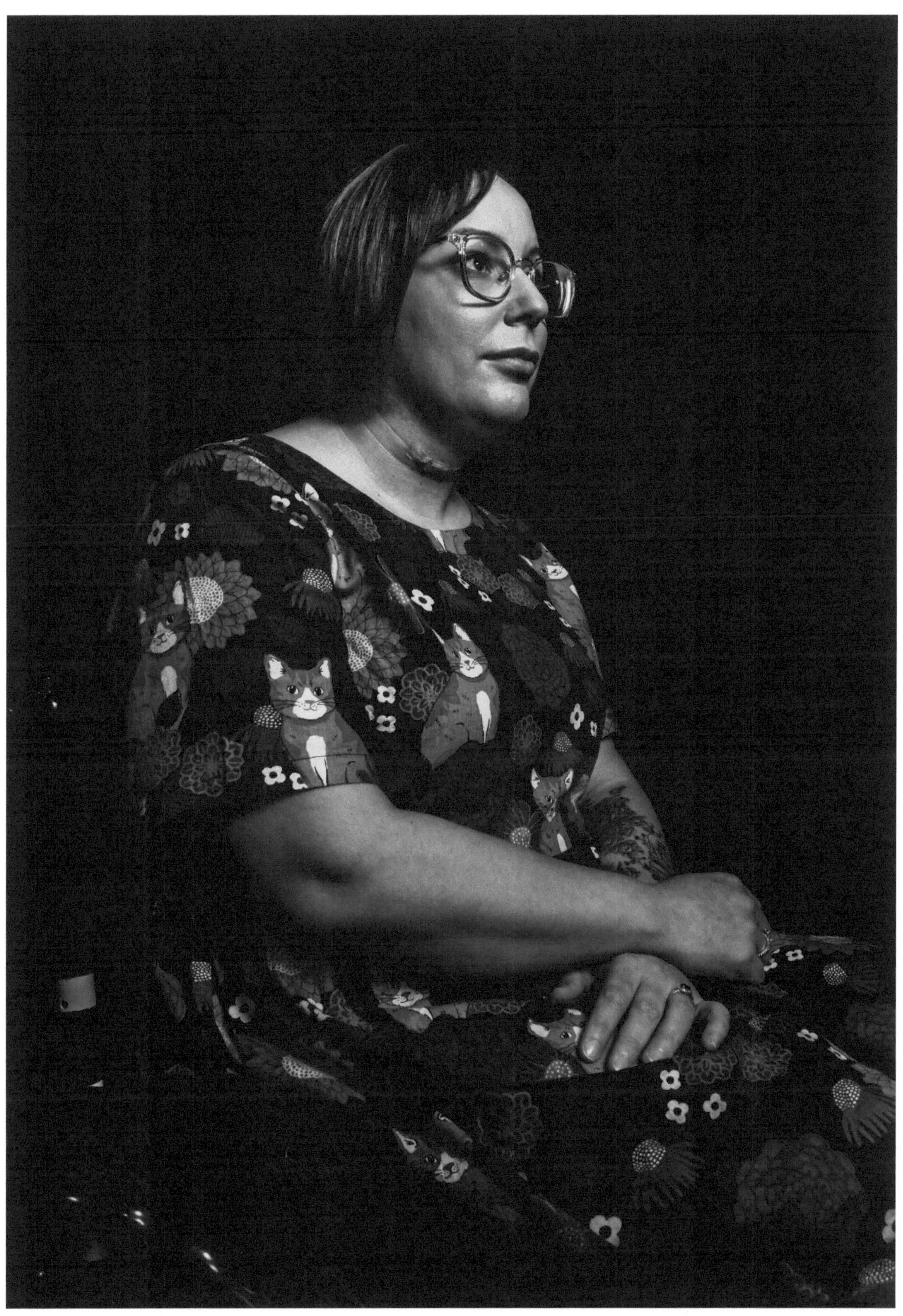

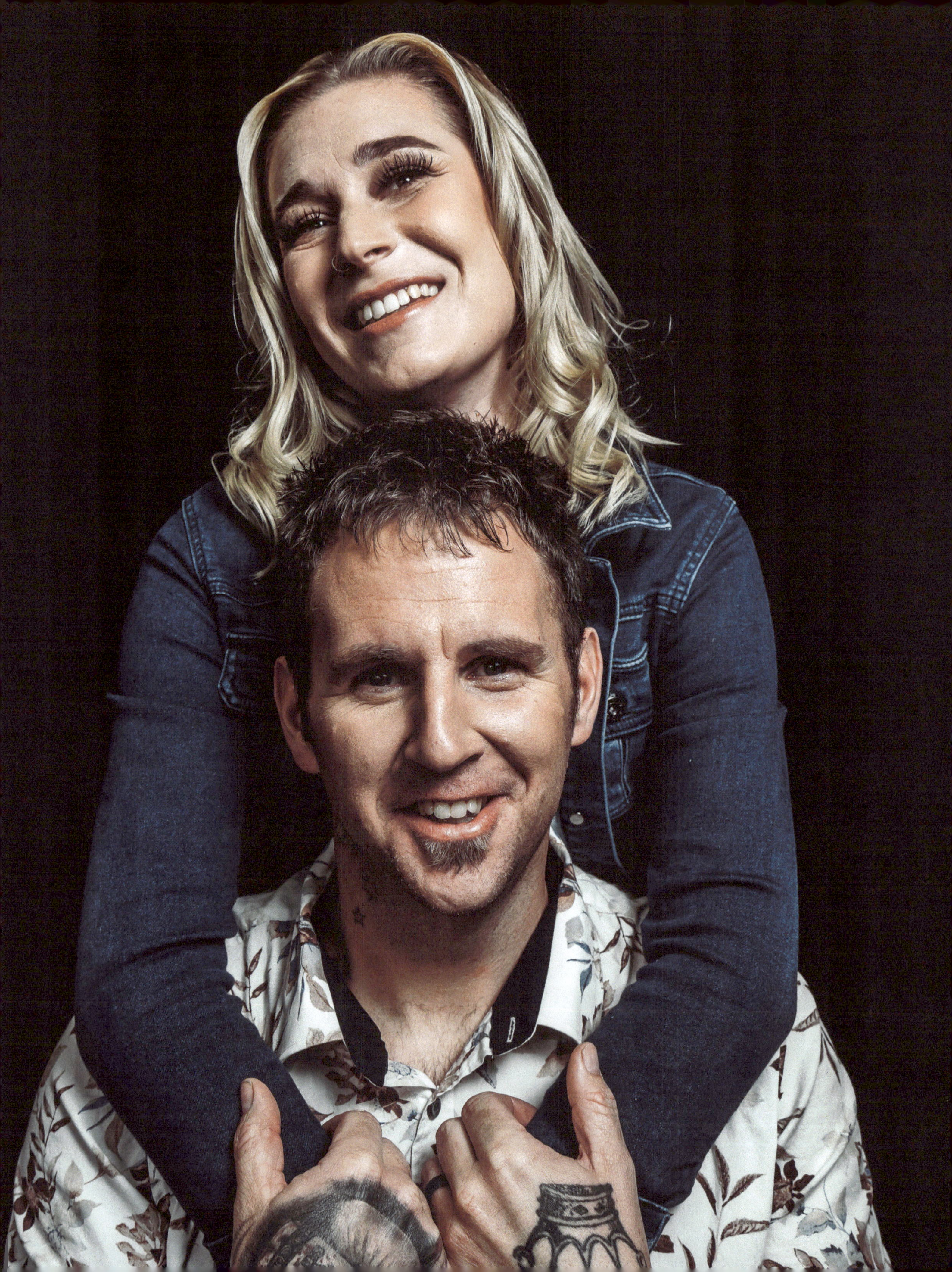

Ally and Matthew Wakefield

Together Through Adversity: A Journey of Love and Strength

Ally and Matt Wakefield are a dynamic duo whose journey is a testament to resilience, love, and determination. Married for just over a year, they have faced and overcome a myriad of challenges together, building a life that reflects their shared values of hard work, mutual support, and embracing differences.

Ally and Matt's story begins with their individual battles with disabilities. Ally was diagnosed with dyslexia, dyspraxia, sensory-auditory processing disorders, and passive ADHD, while Matt lives with ADD, which affects his emotional regulation, ability to focus, and sentence structuring. Both faced significant challenges in school and early adulthood.

"I didn't like talking about my disability," Matt reflects. "Growing up, was bullied a lot for wearing glasses and being different. I stopped wearing my glasses, refused my Ritalin, and tried to blend in. But deep down, I felt like I wasn't being myself. It wasn't until later in life that I started accepting my ADD as part of who I am."

> *Life is full of opportunities if you're brave enough to take them.*

For Ally, the journey was also fraught with difficulties. "I hated school. I struggled so much, and getting diagnosed wasn't easy. It wasn't just one thing—it was a mix of different conditions, and that made it harder for anyone to put a name to what I was experiencing. But once I was diagnosed and received the right support, things began to change."

Both Ally and Matt have faced barriers in the workplace, often struggling to find employment where their disabilities were understood and accommodated. Matt recalls working in and out of bottle shops but feeling trapped indoors. "I realised I love being outside. Gardening, mowing, landscaping—that's where I thrive."

Ally found her niche in cleaning and facilitating wellness classes, bringing structure and a sense of purpose to her days. "It's more than just a job," Ally says. "It's about building connections and helping others, which makes it deeply fulfilling."

Together, the couple is raising four children, including Chase, who has autism. “Chase is our biggest challenge and our greatest joy,” Matt shares. “He’s sensory-sensitive and doesn’t like getting his hands dirty. He struggles with certain foods and textures, and there’s never a dull moment with him around. But we’ve learned so much through parenting him—it’s taught us patience, empathy, and the power of love.”

Parenting with disabilities while raising a child with his own unique challenges has required immense strength and perseverance. Ally explains, “It’s not just about managing our needs; it’s about ensuring Chase and the other kids feel supported and understood. There’s no manual for this, but we figure it out as we go.”

Their proudest achievements are deeply personal. “Our kids are our greatest joy,” Ally says. “And getting married—that was huge for us. It wasn’t just a celebration of love, but also of everything we’ve overcome to be here together.”

As a family, they find joy in the simple moments: cheering on their kids at sports games, spending time in the garden, or just sitting together as a family. Matt has discovered a passion for helping others through his work, particularly with clients who have disabilities. “Seeing someone smile when I’ve made their garden look amazing, especially when they’re in a wheelchair and can’t do it themselves—it’s such a rewarding feeling.”

Ally reflects on how far they’ve come. “We’ve learned to set big goals for ourselves, like owning our own home one day. We’ve also learned to celebrate the small wins, whether it’s a good day with the kids or finishing a big project at work. Life is all about balance.”

When asked about misconceptions surrounding disabilities, Matt emphasises the importance of understanding and kindness. “Don’t hide your disability. Be proud of it. I used to think having a disability meant you had to look a certain way or act a certain way, but I’ve learned that disabilities are as diverse as the people who live with them.”

Ally adds, “Kindness goes a long way. People with disabilities are often underestimated or misunderstood. Treating everyone with empathy and respect is such a simple thing, but it can make all the difference.”

Their participation in this project stems from a desire to inspire others. “We wanted to be part of this to show younger people with disabilities that life doesn’t have to stop because of a diagnosis,” Ally explains. “You can have a career, raise a family, and achieve your dreams. Don’t let anyone tell you otherwise.”

Matt agrees. “It’s important for people to see that we’re not defined by our disabilities. We’re defined by how we choose to live our lives and the goals we set for ourselves. The world is your oyster if you’re willing to work for it.”

Looking ahead, Ally and Matt are excited for the future. They continue to set new goals, support their children’s dreams, and work toward building a home and life filled with love and possibility.

Their message to the world is clear and powerful: “Be proud of who you are. Don’t let your disability hold you back. Life is full of opportunities if you’re brave enough to take them.”

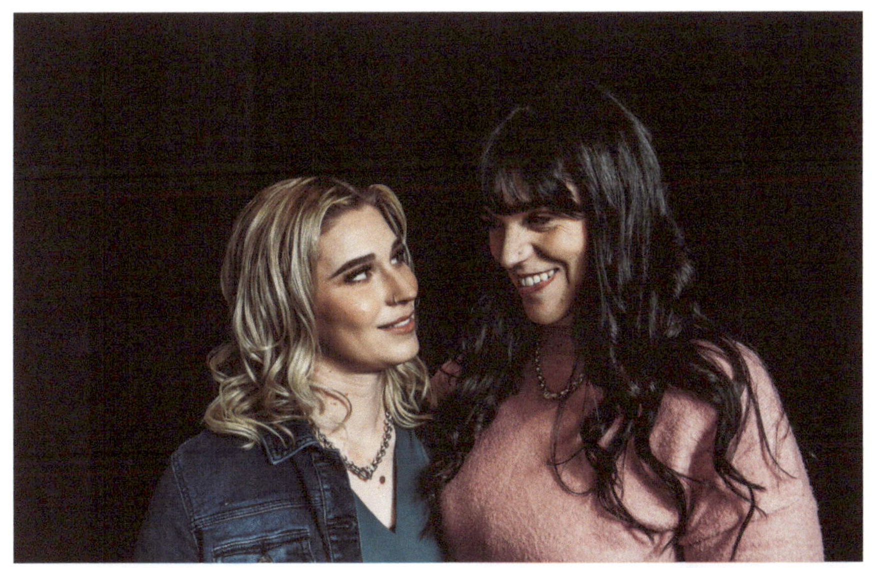

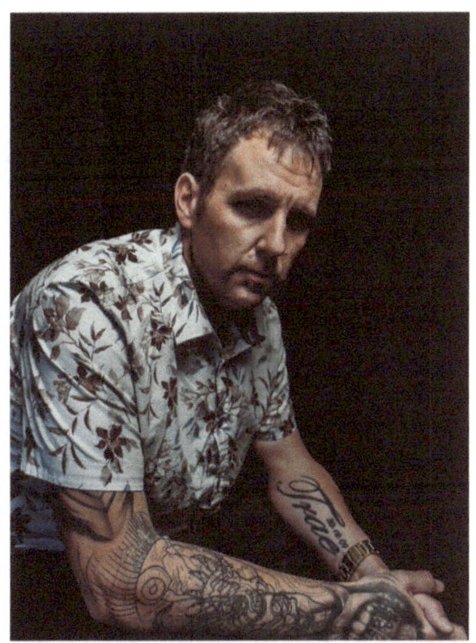

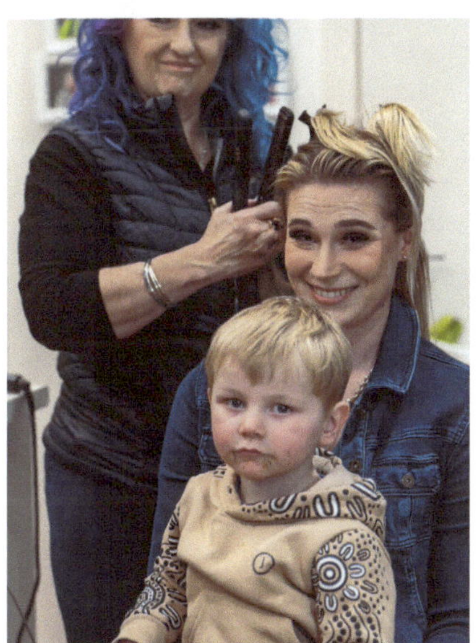

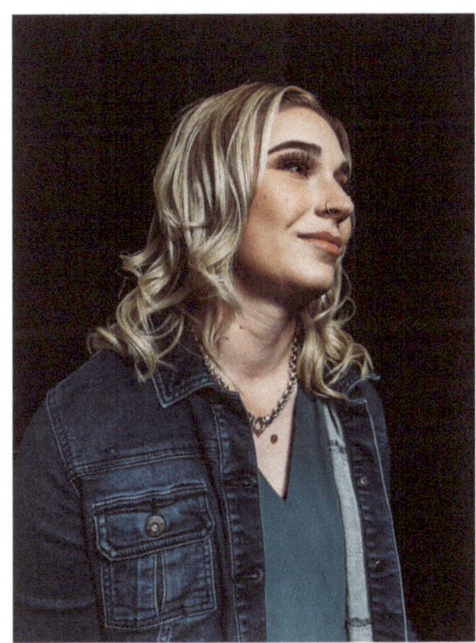

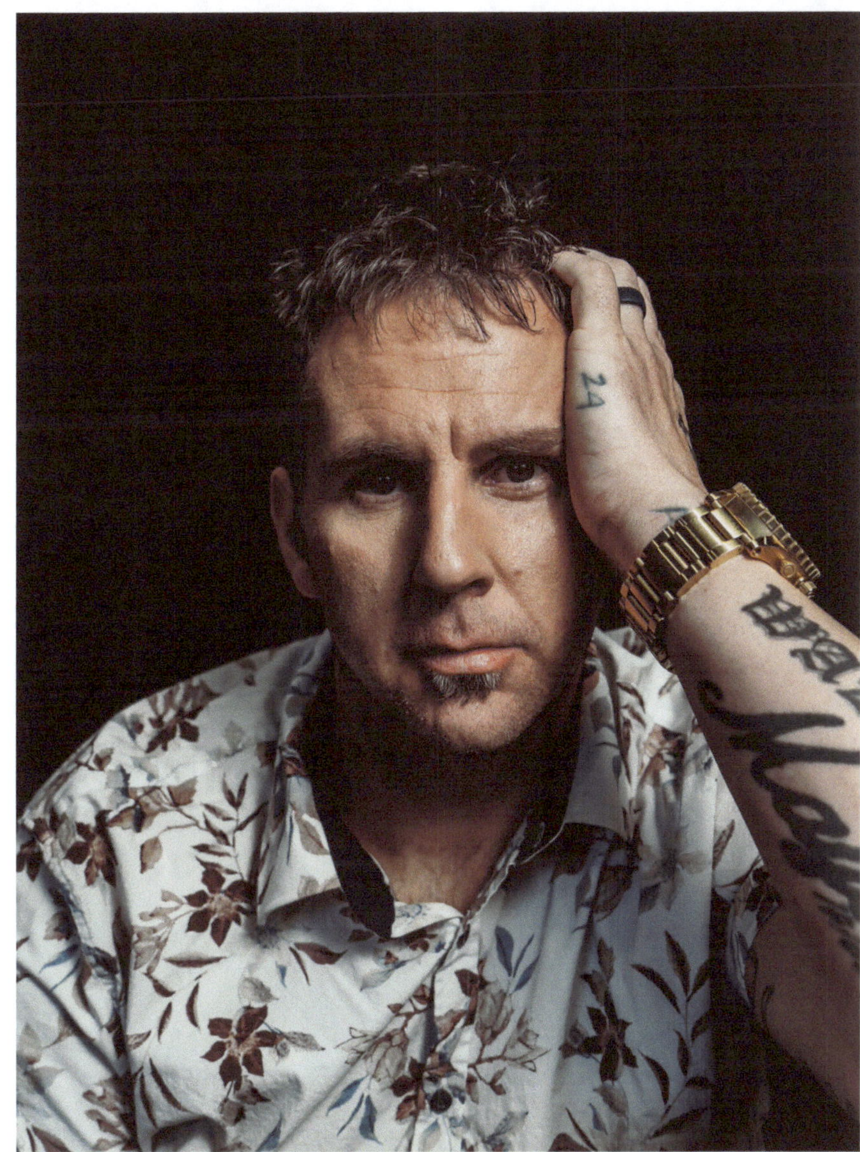
24

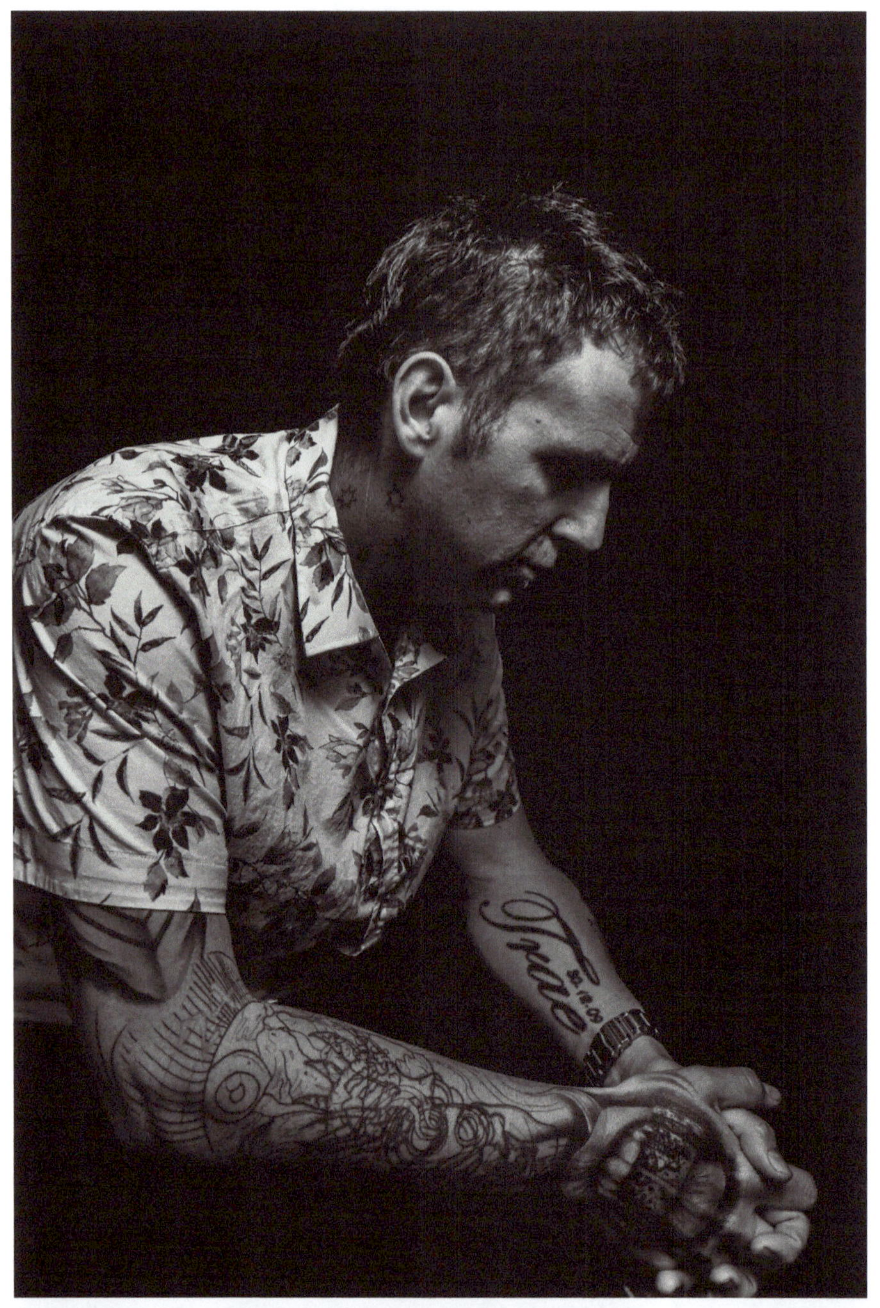

Kindness goes a long way. People with disabilities are often underestimated or misunderstood. Treating everyone with empathy and respect is such a simple thing, but it can make all the difference.

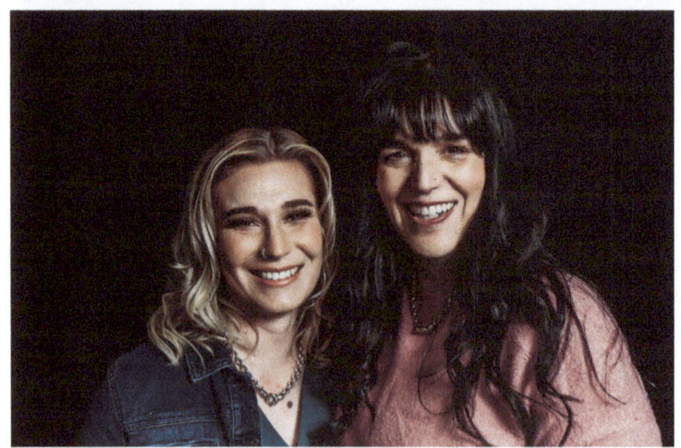

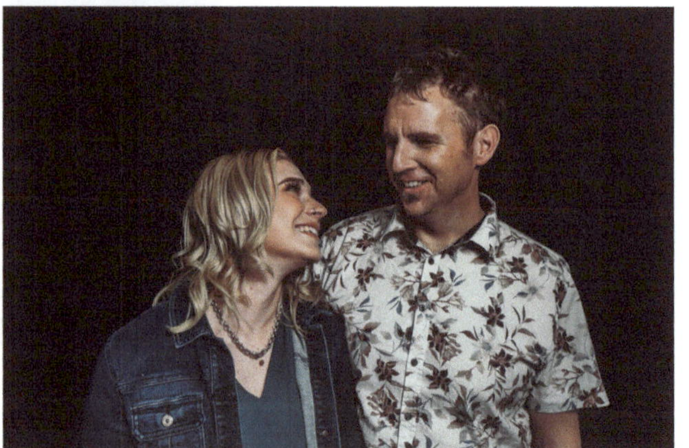

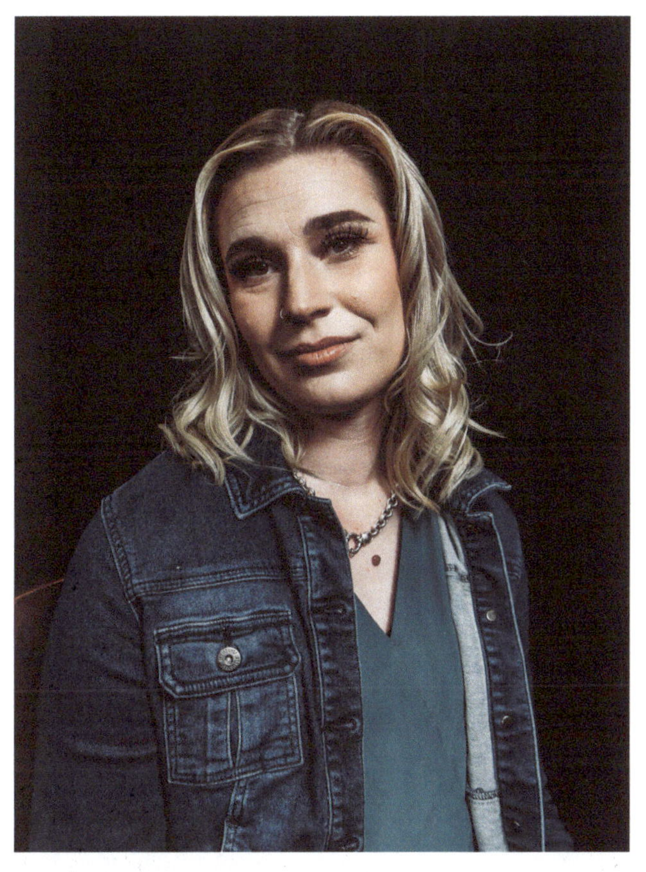
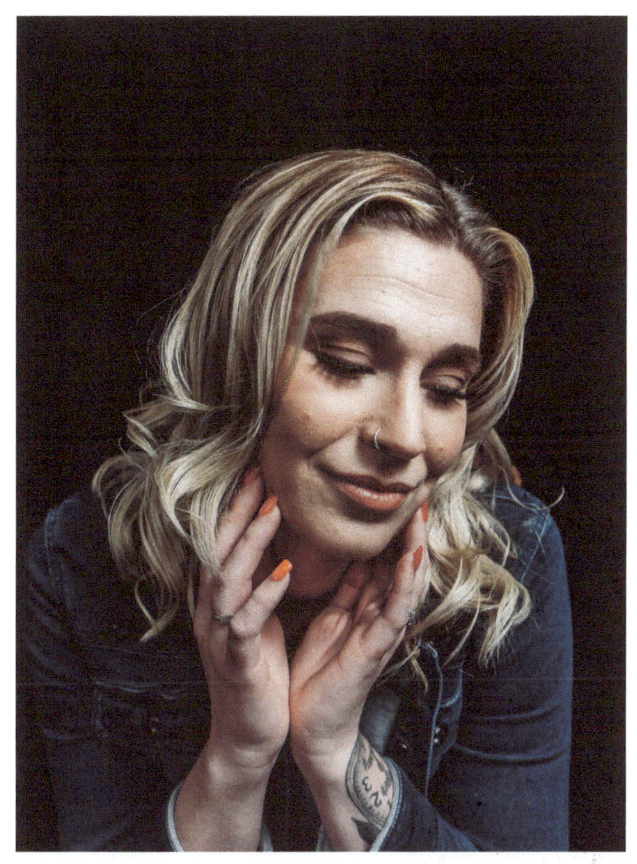
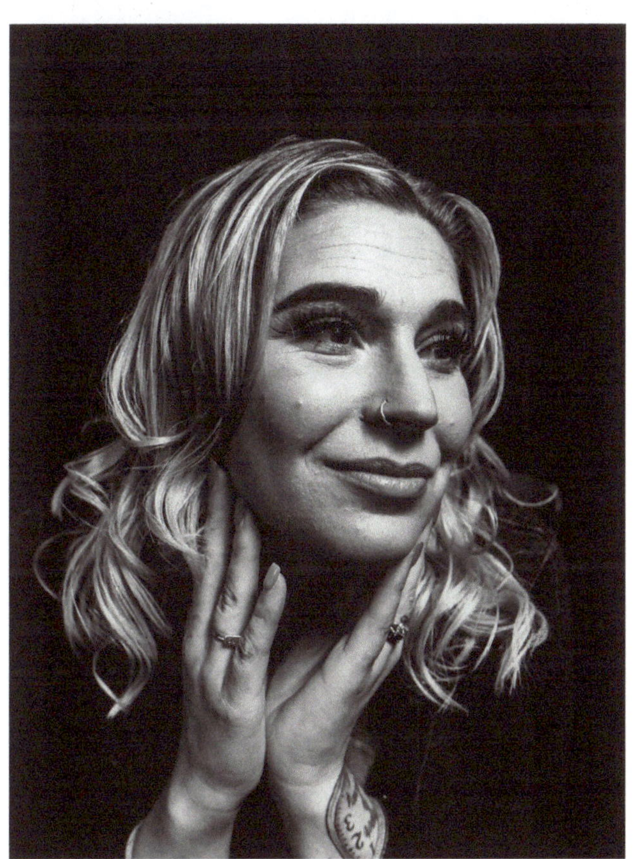
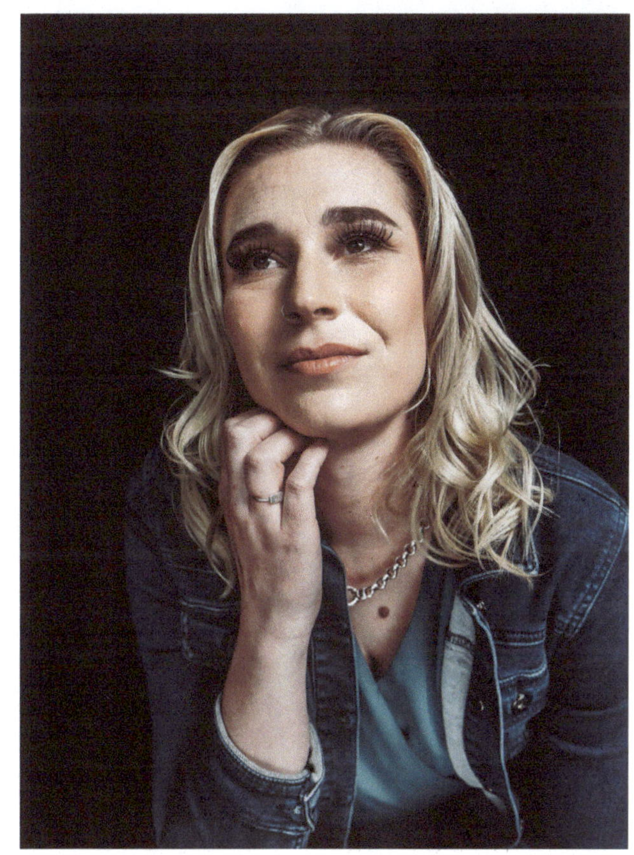

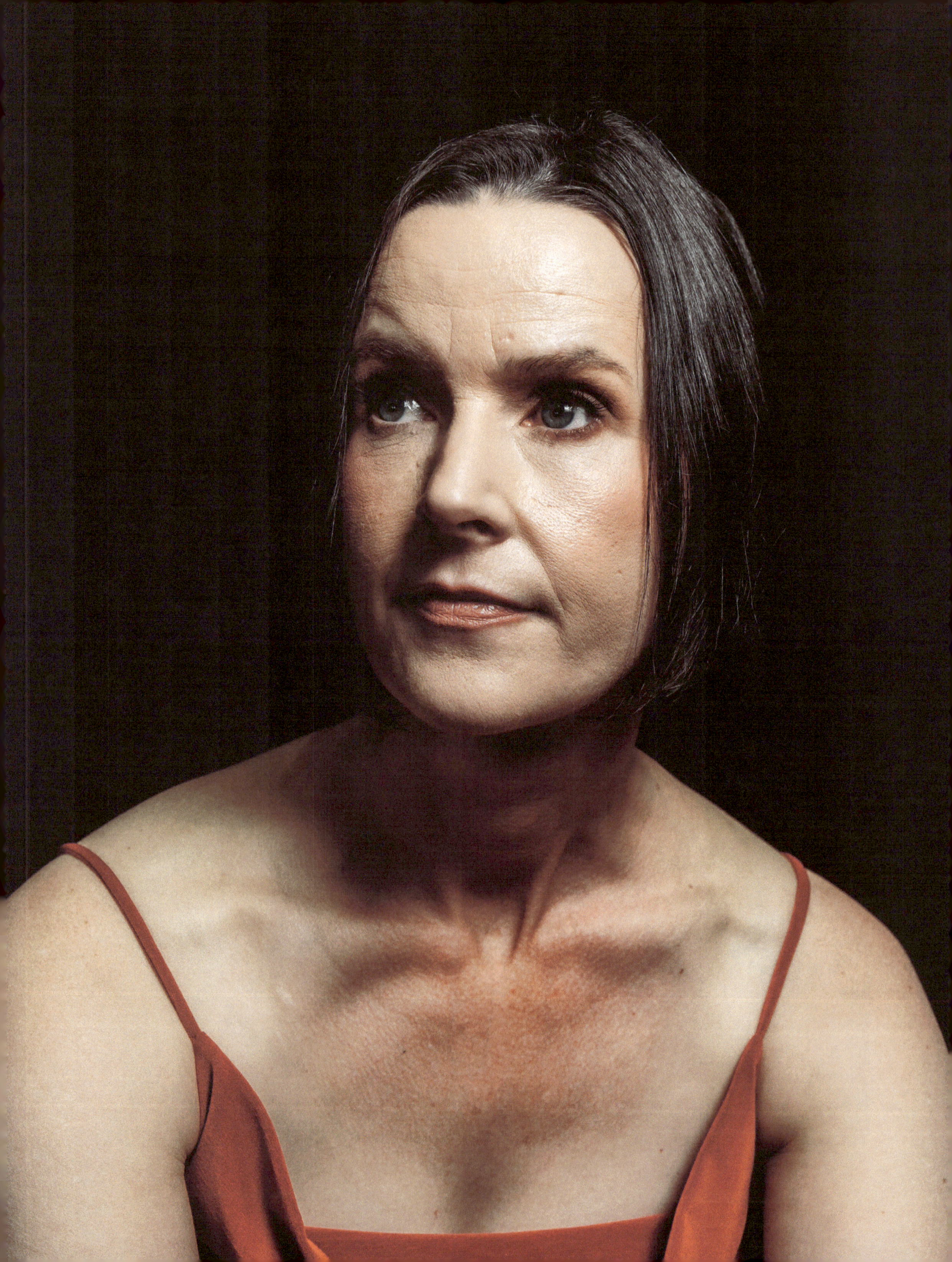

Allyson Brown

Challenging the Norm: Good Health and Purpose

Allyson Brown is a force of resilience, determination, and empowerment. Diagnosed with multiple sclerosis (MS) in 2005 during the second year of her PhD, Allyson's life took a challenging turn. Despite the setbacks, she has forged a path of self-discovery, health transformation, and advocacy, inspiring others to never give up on themselves.

"It was tough," Allyson reflects. "I was in a stressful relationship and dealing with the rigours of my PhD when the diagnosis came. It knocked me around a lot. I struggled with brain fog, fatigue, and the overwhelming reality of living with MS. But I made it through and finished my PhD despite everything."

Allyson's research was in forensic analytical chemistry, a field as complex as it sounds. "I studied how certain illicit drugs react with a reagent to produce light—think of glow sticks. It was fascinating but incredibly demanding, especially with my health challenges. Completing it was one of my proudest achievements."

In 2018, the symptoms of MS became too overwhelming, and Allyson made the difficult decision to resign from her corporate career. "I felt lost. But that's when I decided to take control of my health. I changed my diet, and within three months, my brain fog lifted, my energy returned, and I felt like myself again. It was a turning point."

Since then, Allyson has built a business helping others improve their health through diet and lifestyle changes. "I love seeing the positive impact it has on people's lives. It's incredibly motivating and fulfilling."

For Allyson, having a disability has shaped her life in profound ways. "At first, it felt like a curse, but now I see it as a blessing in disguise. It's taught me resilience, strength, and the importance of self-care. I'm healthier now than I've ever been because I've made changes I wouldn't have considered before my diagnosis."

Breaking barriers is a concept Allyson embraces fully. "It's about stepping out of the box society puts you in and showing the world what's possible. Disability doesn't mean inability. It means finding new ways to achieve your goals and challenging stereotypes."

Allyson's support network has been vital throughout her journey. "Early on, I had a lot of relapses. I couldn't walk or drive, and my mum was amazing, taking me to appointments and supporting me. My husband has also been incredible. He's always there for me, especially in the moments when I feel lost or overwhelmed."

Her hobbies reflect her zest for life. "I love painting, personal growth, and feeding local birds. Building trust with wild animals is such a beautiful experience. I haven't painted in a while, but it's something I want to get back to."

Looking to the future, Allyson has big dreams. "I want to deliver a TEDx talk, host wellness seminars nationally and internationally, and travel the world. I've visited 40 countries by 40, and now I'm aiming for 50 by 50."

Allyson's message to the world is one of hope and determination. "Don't give up on yourself. Aim high, follow your dreams, and remember that your disability doesn't define you. We all have something unique to contribute."

Despite the challenges, Allyson radiates positivity and strength. "I'm the most empowered version of myself today. I've stopped trying to be who others think I should be, and I've stepped into who I truly am. That's where real empowerment comes from."

Allyson Brown is breaking barriers every day, redefining what it means to live with a disability and proving that strength, resilience, and self-belief can create extraordinary outcomes.

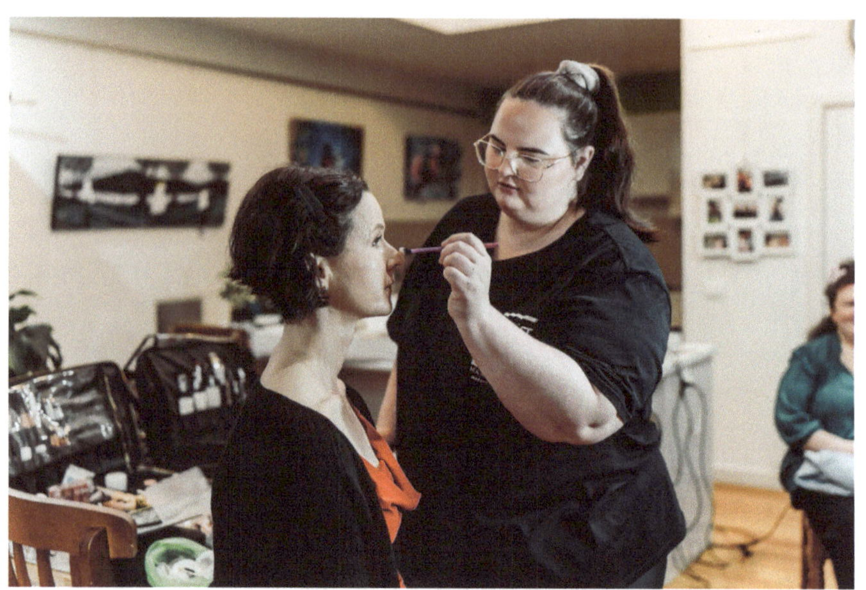

“

Step out of the box society puts you in and show the world what's possible. Disability doesn't mean inability.

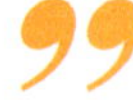

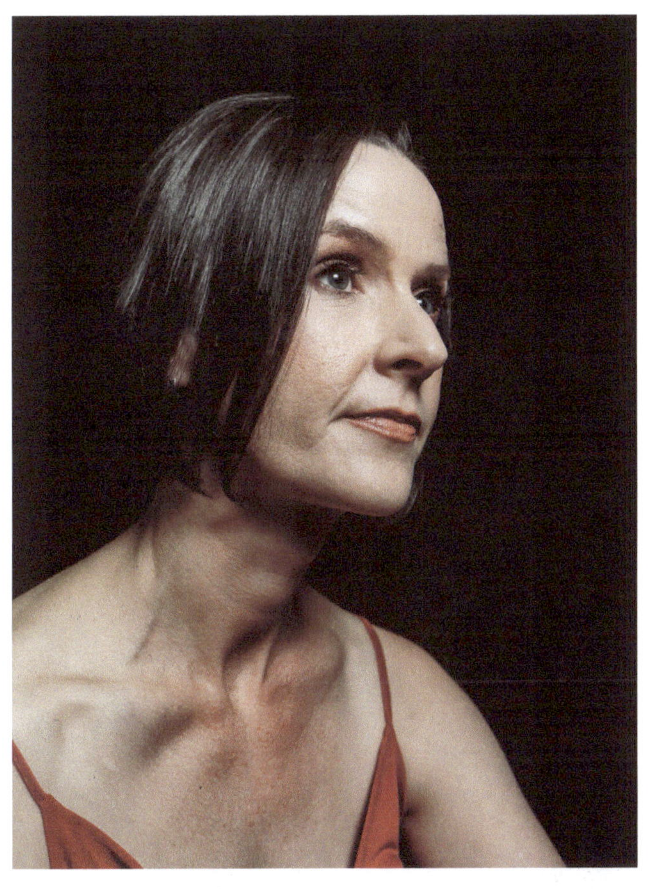
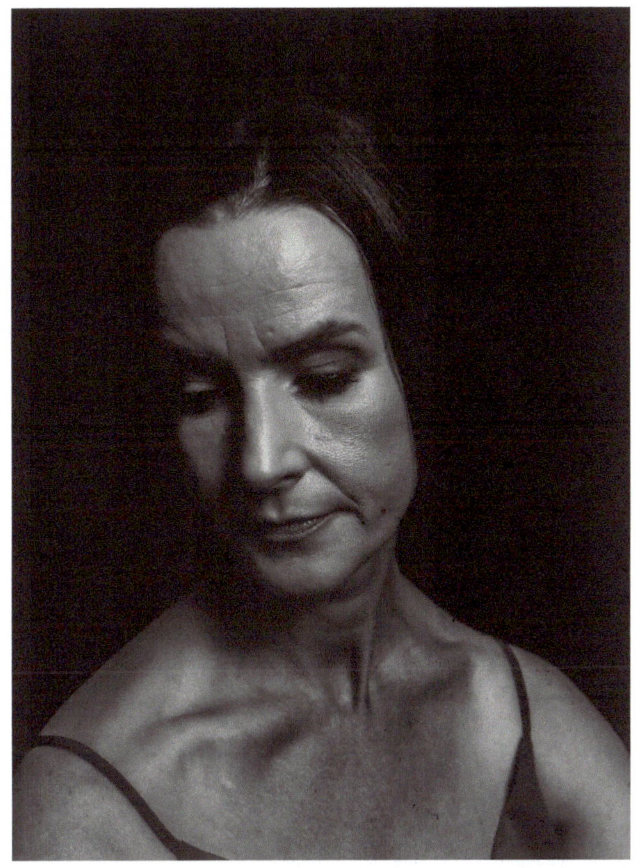
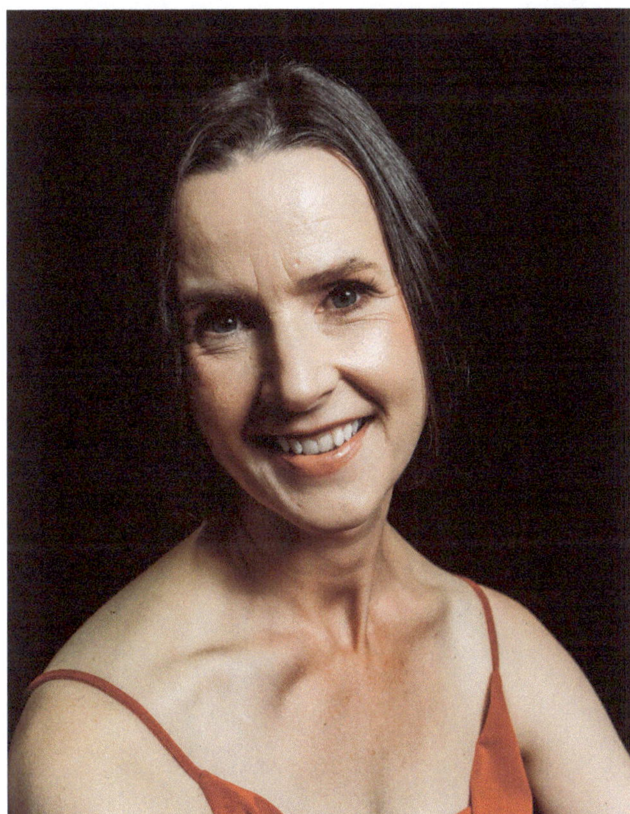
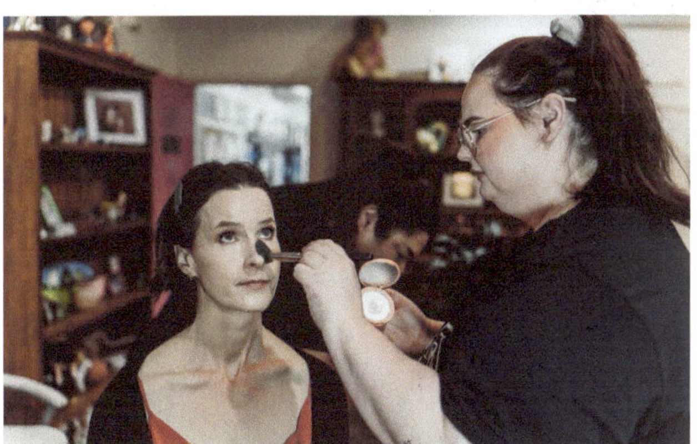
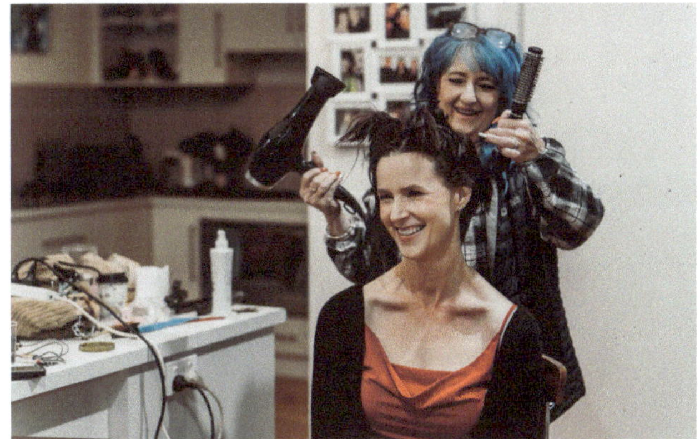

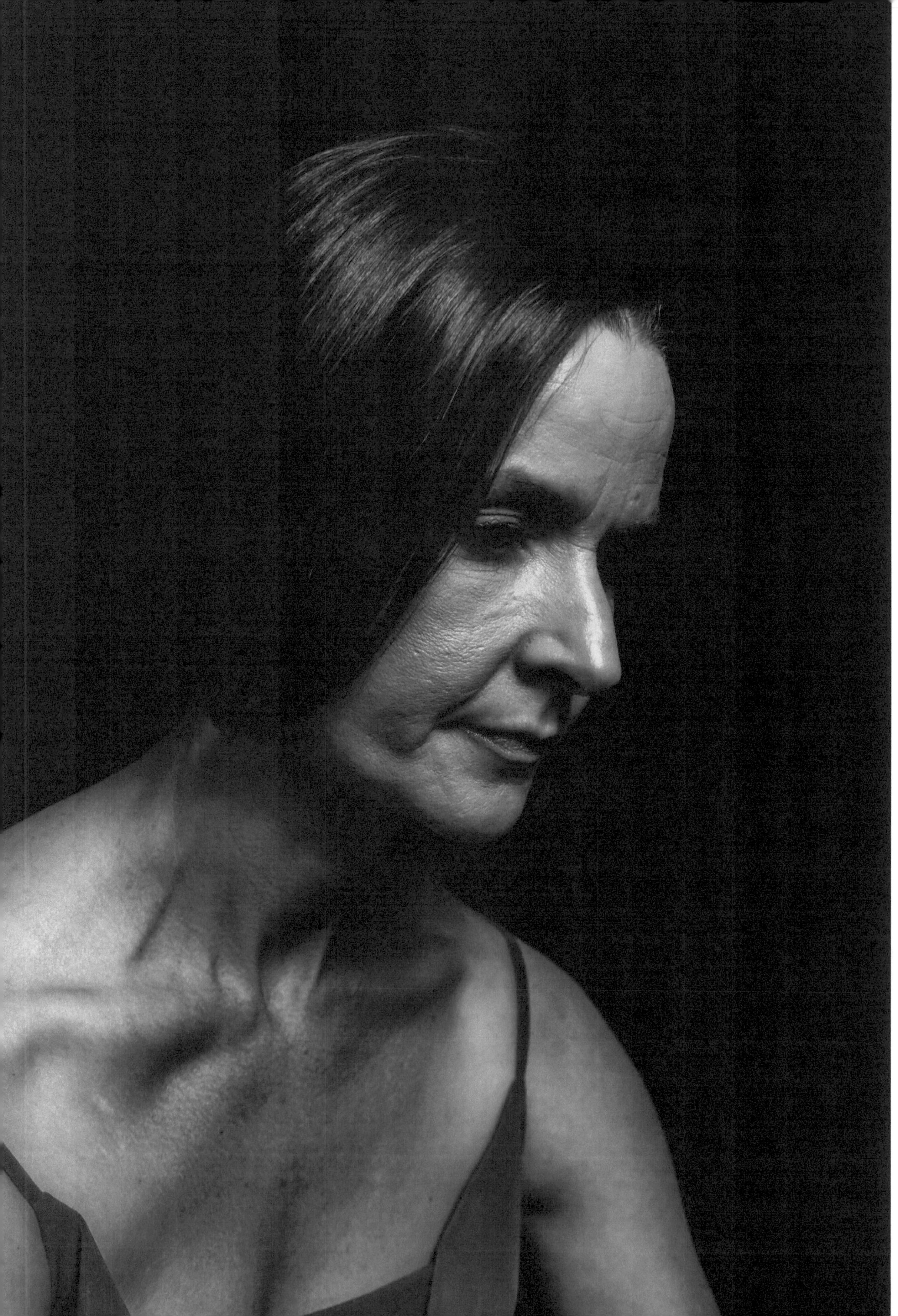

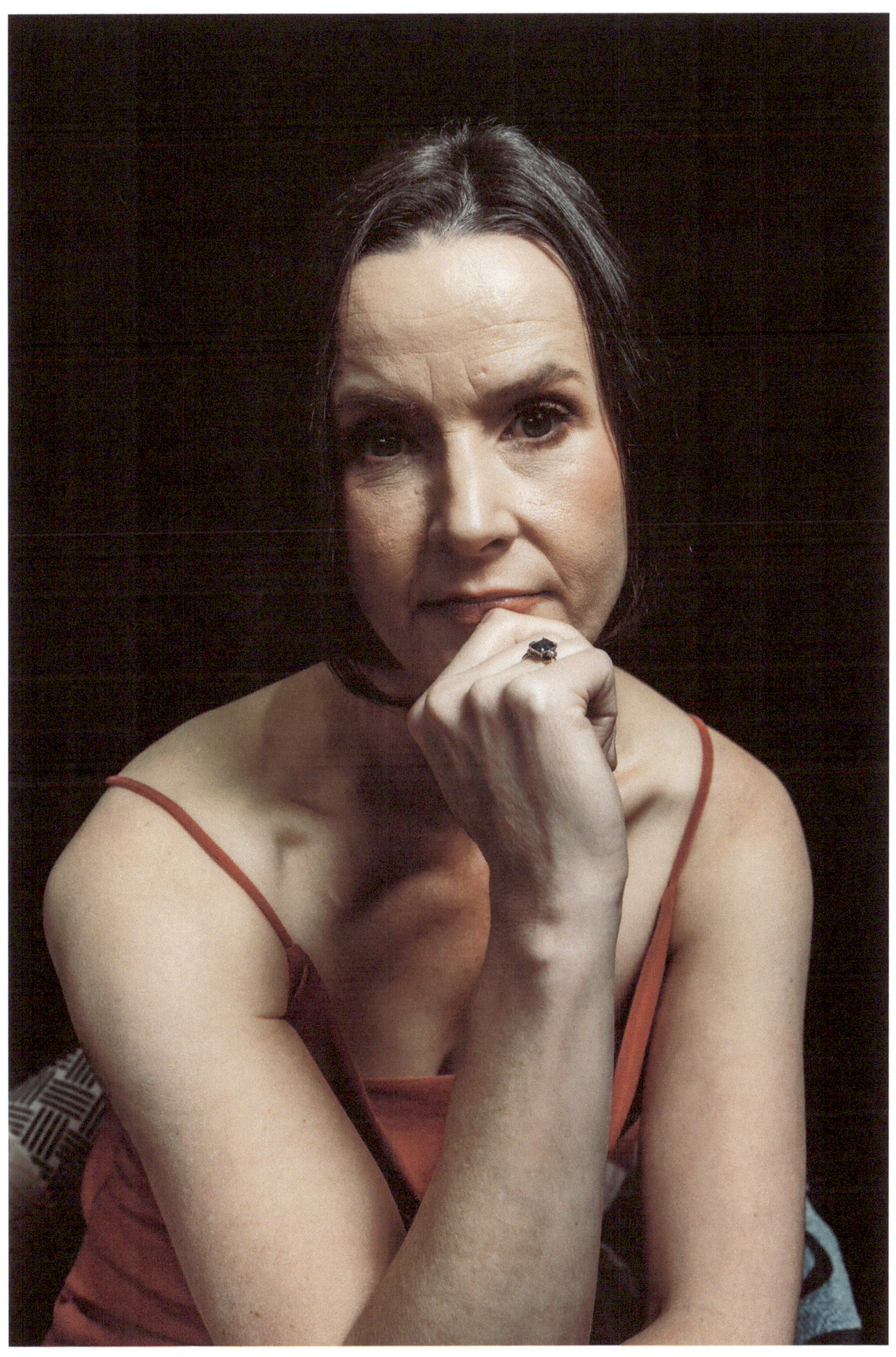

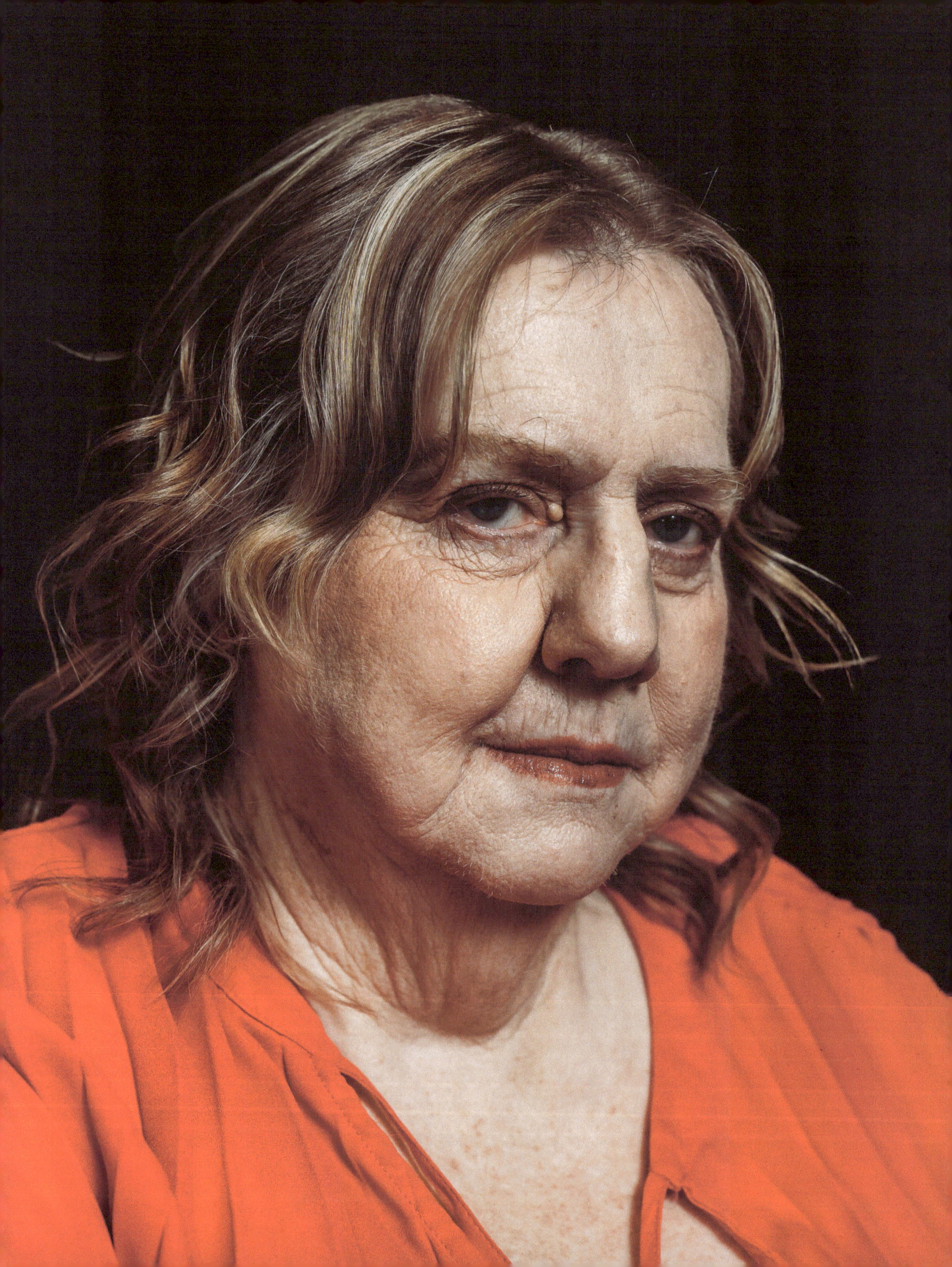

Christine Ducky Turner

A Litlle Bit Of Glitter

Christine Turner, affectionately known as "Ducky" by her friends at JUZT Art, is a proud mother, grandmother, and artist whose story exemplifies resilience, creativity, and determination. With a quick wit and a love for life, Christine has embraced her disabilities and turned them into a source of inspiration for others.

The nickname "Ducky" has become a term of endearment among those closest to Christine. "It's our little joke," she shares with a smile. "It's a sign of love and friendship here."

Christine's journey hasn't been without its challenges. Living with her disability has shaped her in profound ways. "I've had to deal with bullying for most of my life," she recalls. "People didn't understand me or my struggles, and it wasn't easy. But it's also made me stronger. I've learned to stand tall and prove to myself and others that I can achieve whatever I set my mind to."

Her support system has played a pivotal role in her life. "I rely heavily on my support workers," Christine explains. "Without them, I'd be stuck. They help me with shopping, going out for coffee, and attending my art and craft sessions. Those connections keep me going."

Art has become Christine's passion and a way to express herself creatively. "I love painting swans, dolphins, and sunsets. Adding a bit of bling is my signature style," she says, laughing as she recalls her love for glitter. "But we've learned not to let me have the glitter pot too often—it ends up everywhere, and I'm eating it for a week!"

Through art, Christine has found a sense of accomplishment and community. "Starting art and craft was a big step for me," she admits. "I don't like walking into spaces filled with strangers, but I took a chance, and it's been so worth it. This project is another step in that journey. I didn't think I could do it, but I did, and I feel so empowered now."

Christine's role models and sources of inspiration are her family. "My son, his girlfriend, and my four grandchildren mean the world to me," she says with pride. "There's Alex, who's just eight months old, Dominic, who's five, and Chanel and Simon, who are nearly 13. They're my heart and soul."

The photo shoot was a significant milestone for Christine. “I wanted to show people that I can do things, to prove that disabilities don’t define us. Seeing the photos afterwards—I couldn’t believe it was me. I looked like a supermodel! I think my son will be shocked when he sees them,” she laughs.

For Christine, breaking barriers means creating a society where everyone is treated equally, regardless of their abilities. “It would be so nice if everyone treated each other the same,” she reflects. “We all have something to offer, no matter what we’re going through.”

When asked what message she wants to share with the world through this project, Christine says, “I want people to know that anyone with a disability can do amazing things. You just need to take that first step, no matter how scary it feels. You can do it.”

Christine’s participation in this project is a testament to her courage and determination. “I was nervous at first—my anxiety was through the roof—but I pushed through it. Now I feel like I can take on the world.”

As she looks to the future, Christine’s goals are simple yet profound. “I want to keep going with my art, enter more exhibitions, and show others that anything is possible.”

Her journey is a shining example of resilience, creativity, and self-empowerment. “I’m proud of how far I’ve come,” she says with a smile. “And I hope my story inspires others to keep pushing forward, no matter what.”

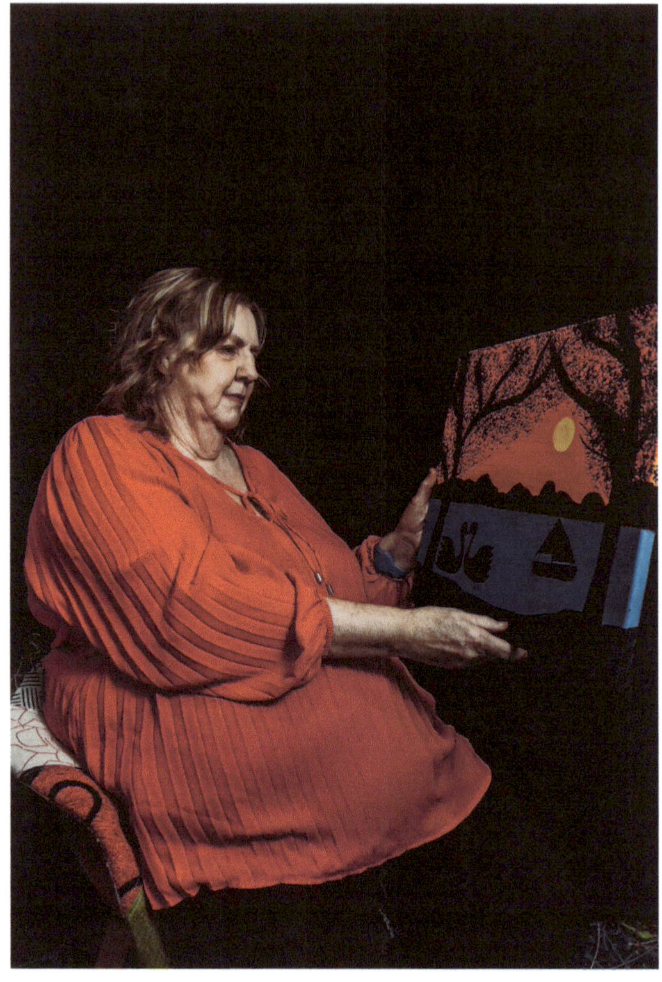

“

It would be so nice if everyone treated each other the same. We all have something to offer, no matter what we’re going through.

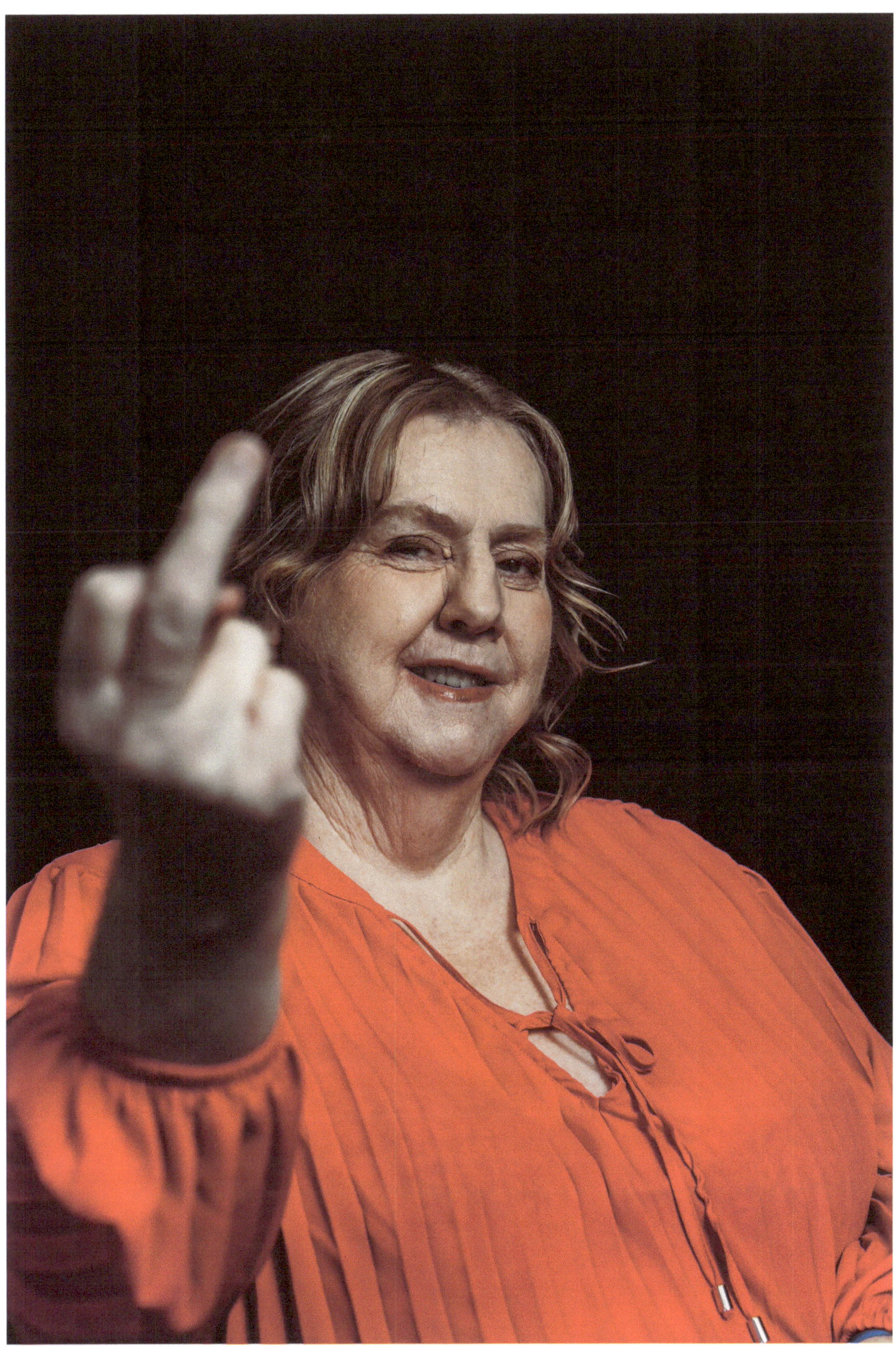

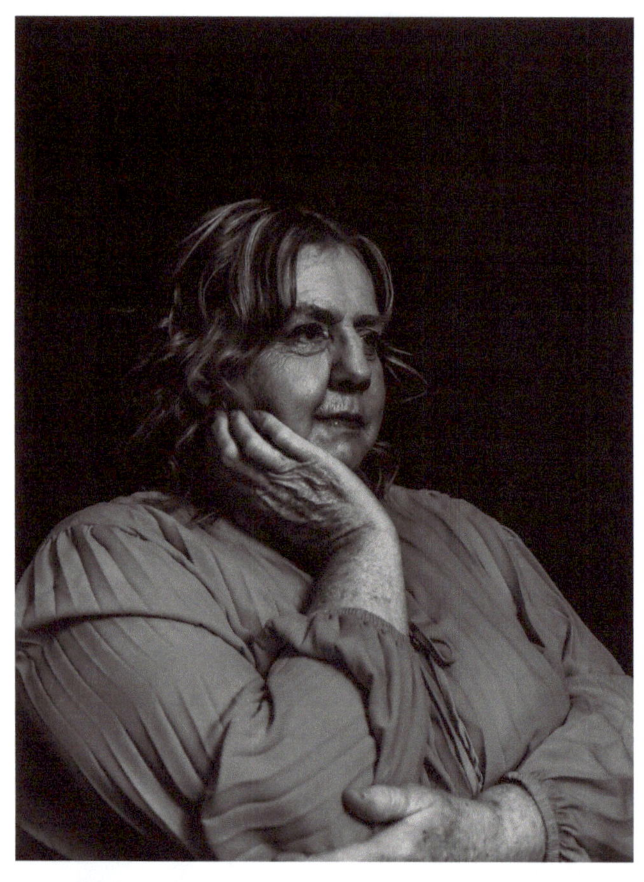

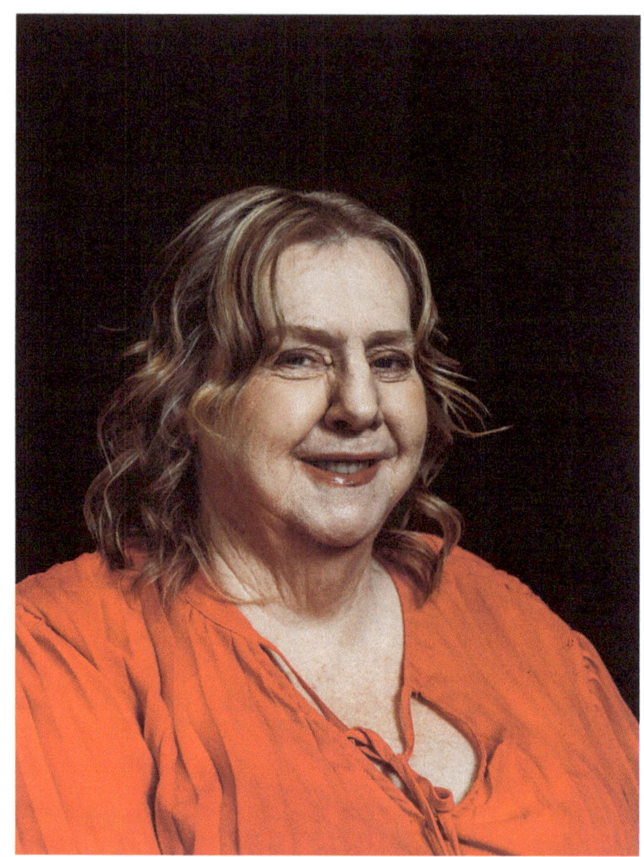

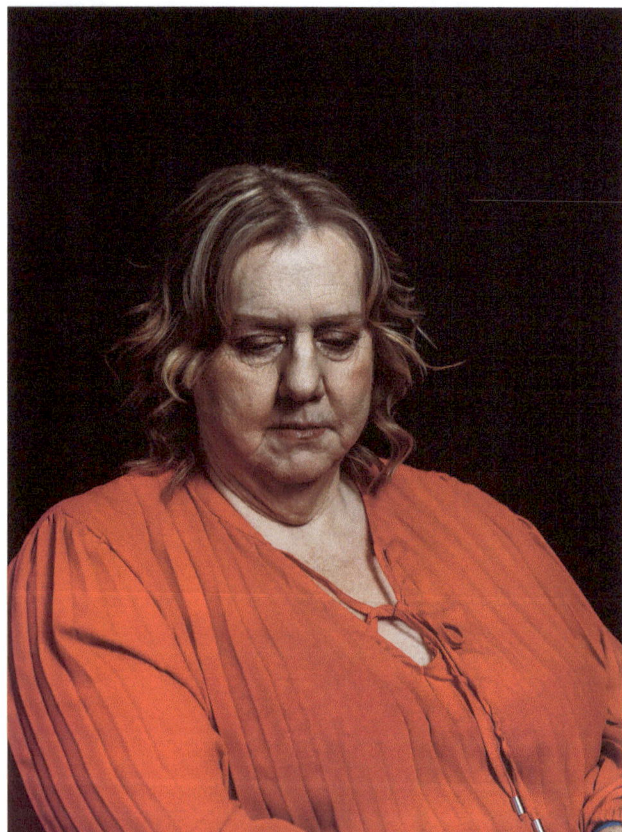

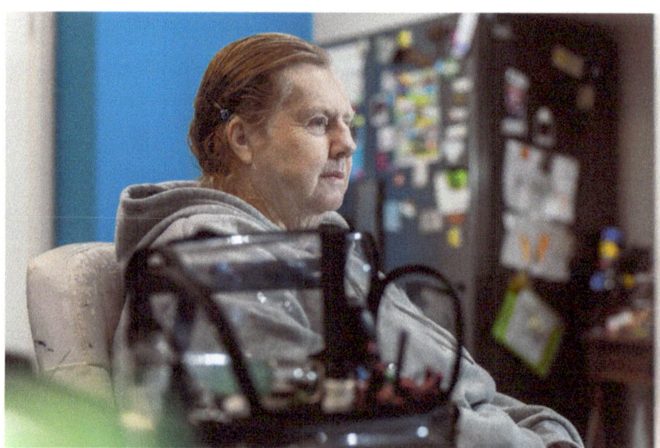

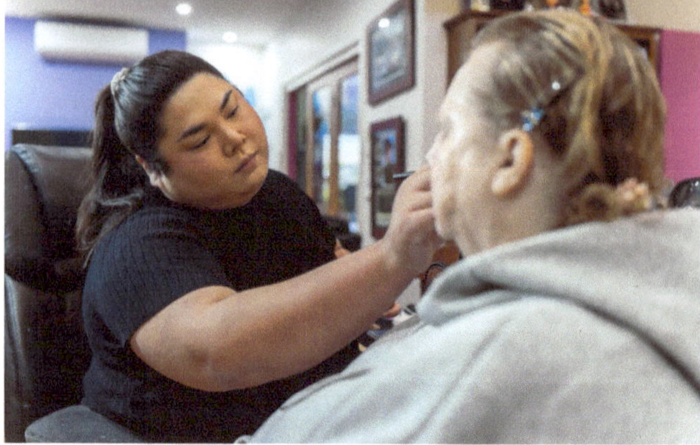

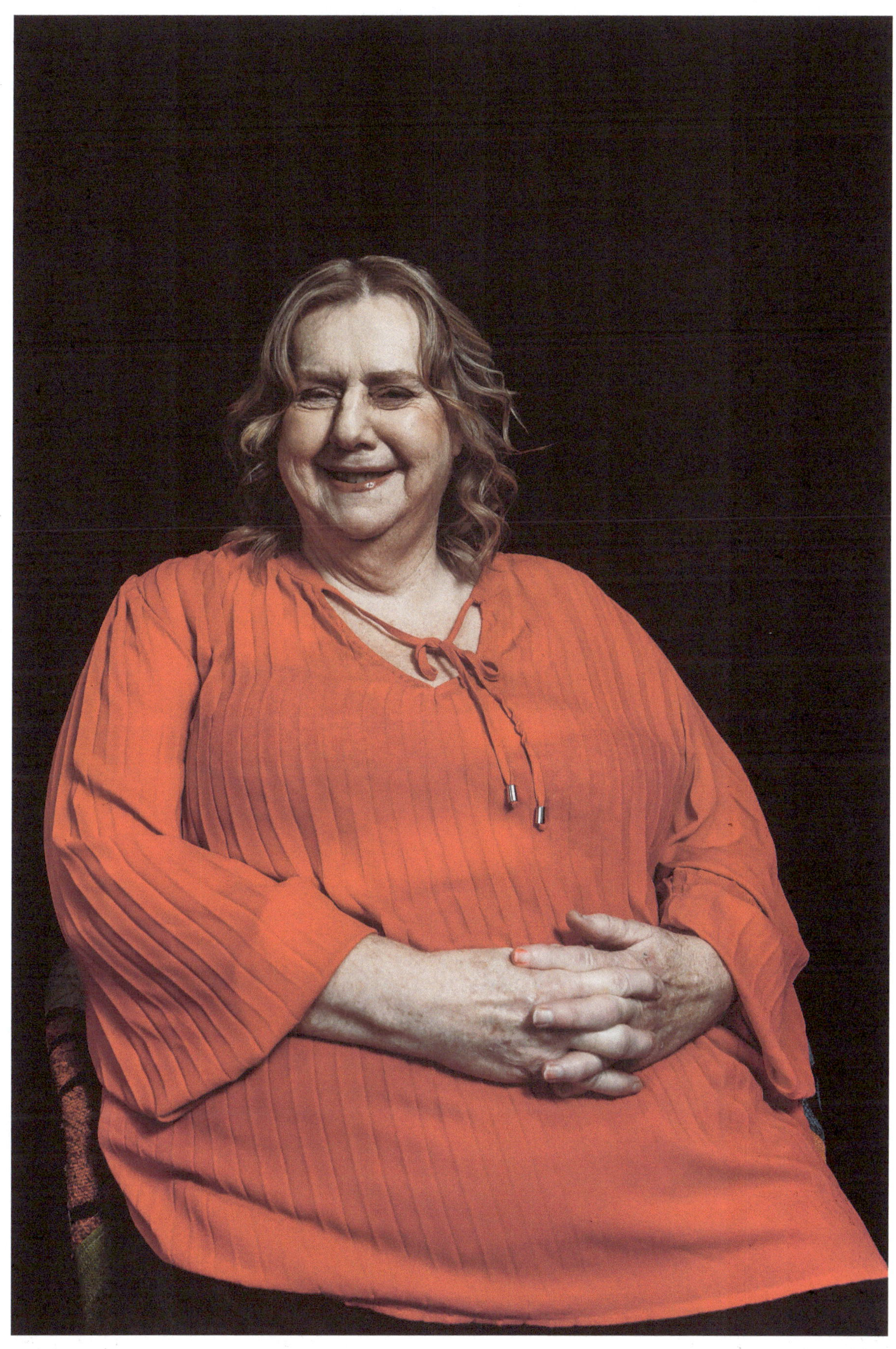

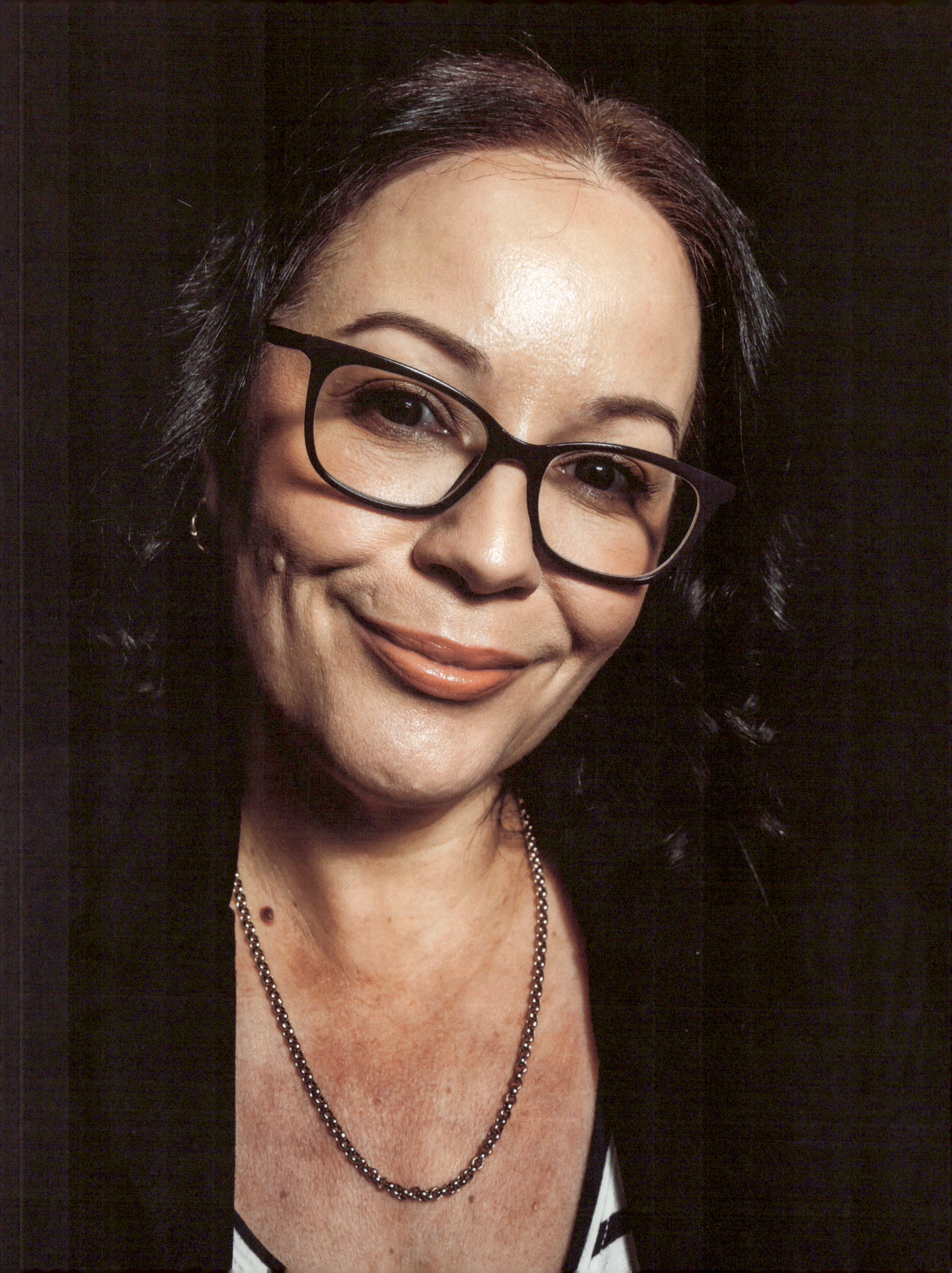

Claire Pritchard

Grace and Grit: A Journey of Strength and Adaptation

Claire is a spirited woman who embraces life with determination and grace, even as she navigates the complexities of living with multiple sclerosis (MS). A passionate traveller and former nurse, Claire has become an advocate for raising awareness about invisible disabilities and empowering others to live life on their terms.

Diagnosed with MS a few years ago, Claire reflects on how it has reshaped her life. "MS is unpredictable, and the fatigue can be debilitating," she shares. "One moment, I'm fine; the next, I can feel a wave of exhaustion wash over me, starting from my feet and travelling through my body. It's like nothing I ever experienced before."

> *"People often don't understand what they can't see."*

Despite these challenges, Claire refuses to let MS define her. Her love for travel has been both a joy and a test of resilience. "Traveling with MS requires a lot of planning," she explains. "Cobblestone streets, inaccessible public spaces, and the lack of disability-friendly facilities in some parts of the world can make it tough. But I refuse to let these obstacles stop me."

Claire's decision to prioritise international travel now while reserving domestic exploration for later in life highlights her practical and optimistic approach. "We've flipped our plans," she says. "Overseas adventures are for now, while I can still navigate them, and exploring Australia will come later when a car or caravan trip is more feasible."

Using mobility aids has been a personal and emotional journey for Claire. "There's a stigma attached to using a walking stick or wheelchair," she admits. "At first, I resisted them because it felt like admitting I needed help. But I've learned that these aids don't take away independence—they give it back. Without them, I'd be stuck at home."

Claire's work with the NDIS has been a source of support and fulfilment. "I'm fortunate to work for such an inclusive organisation," she says. "My workplace has made adjustments that allow me to work from home, giving me the flexibility I need. I encourage anyone with a disability to consider working for the NDIS—it's been an incredible experience."

Educating others about invisible disabilities is a mission close to Claire's heart. "People often don't understand what they can't see," she explains. "Fatigue, for example, isn't just feeling tired—it's an all-encompassing exhaustion that makes even simple tasks feel impossible. Raising awareness about these realities is so important."

For Claire, breaking barriers is about shattering misconceptions and creating a more inclusive society. "It's about adapting and modifying life so you can keep doing the things you love. Disabilities don't define us—they challenge us to find new ways forward."

Her family and friends have been instrumental in her journey. "My husband is my rock," Claire shares. "He knows me better than anyone and can sense when I'm struggling. My children, although grown, have also been incredibly supportive. And my friends—well, I've learned who my true friends are. They're the ones who stick around when times are tough."

Living with MS or any disability doesn't mean giving up on life. It means finding new ways to live it fully and meaningfully.

Participating in this project has been a meaningful experience for Claire. "I want people to understand that living with MS or any disability doesn't mean giving up on life. It means finding new ways to live it fully and meaningfully."

Claire draws inspiration from everyday people and public figures like Selma Blair and Christina Applegate, who have used their platforms to raise awareness about MS. "Their openness is inspiring, but it's important to remember that everyone's journey is different. We all face unique challenges."

Looking ahead, Claire plans to continue travelling, advocating for MS awareness, and embracing life with positivity. "Life is as good as you make it," she says. "Acceptance doesn't mean you have to like what's happening, but it allows you to move forward. That's the key to living fully."

Her message to the world is clear: "Never give up. Adapt, modify, and keep going. Disability doesn't make you weak—it shows how strong you are."

Claire's story is a powerful reminder that resilience, positivity, and self-belief can break even the toughest barriers, inspiring others to live their lives with courage and determination.

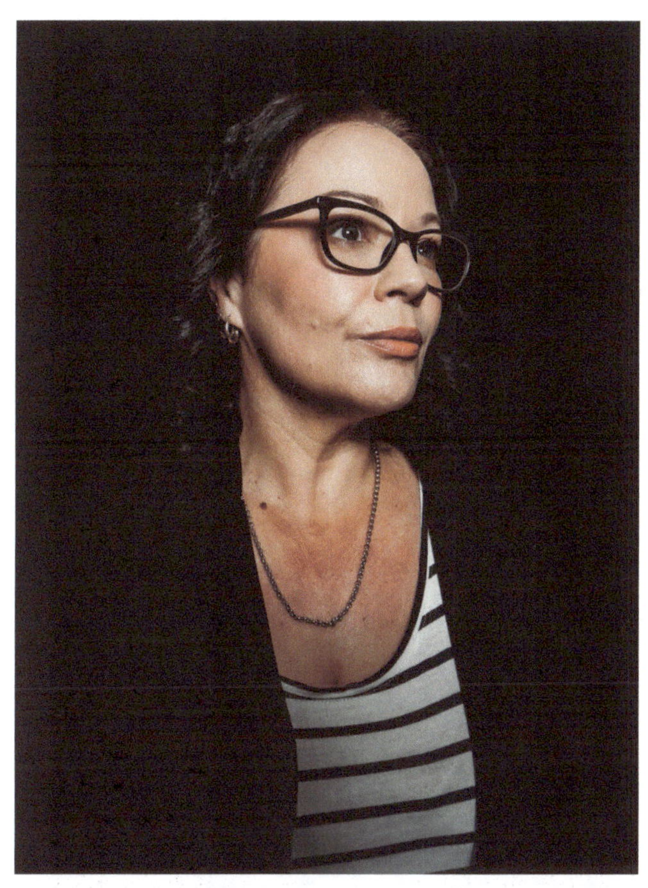
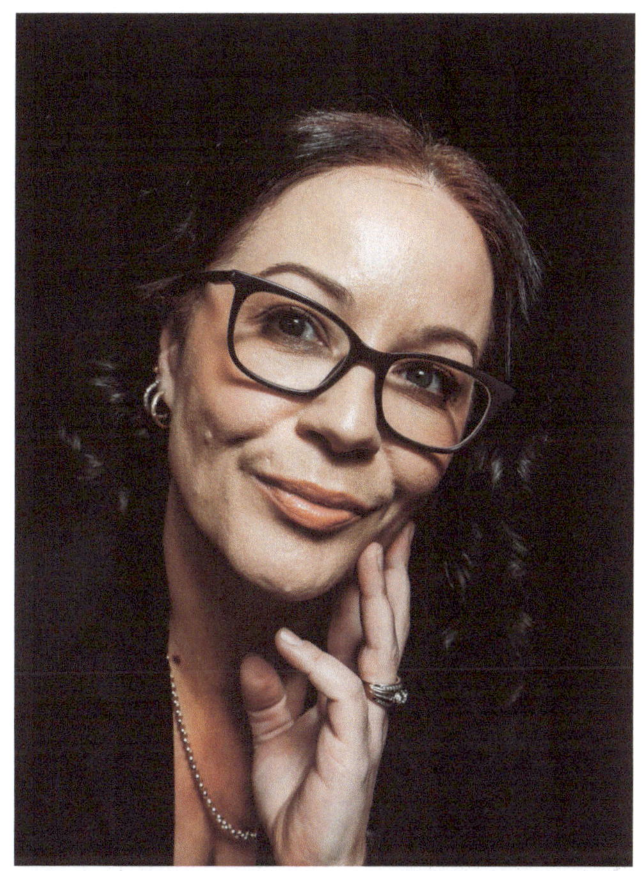
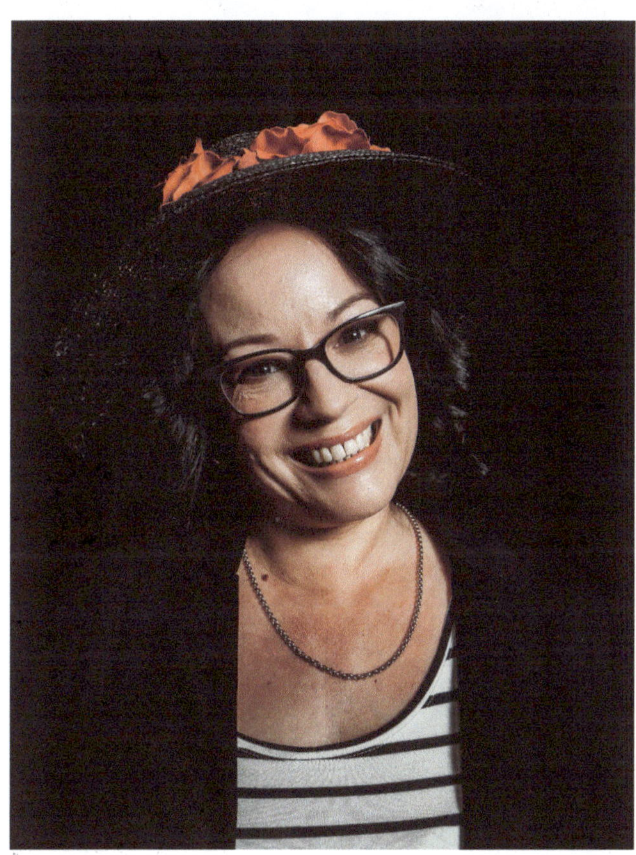
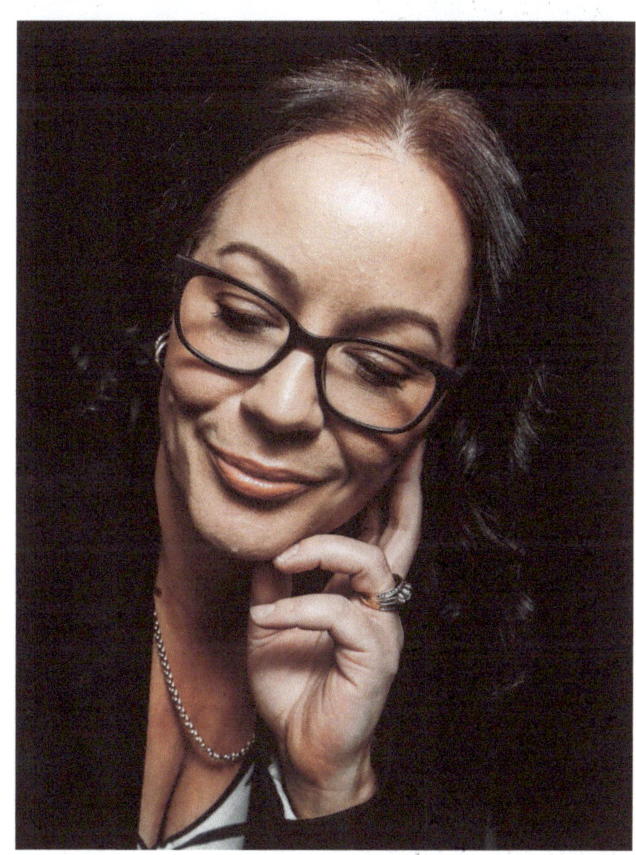

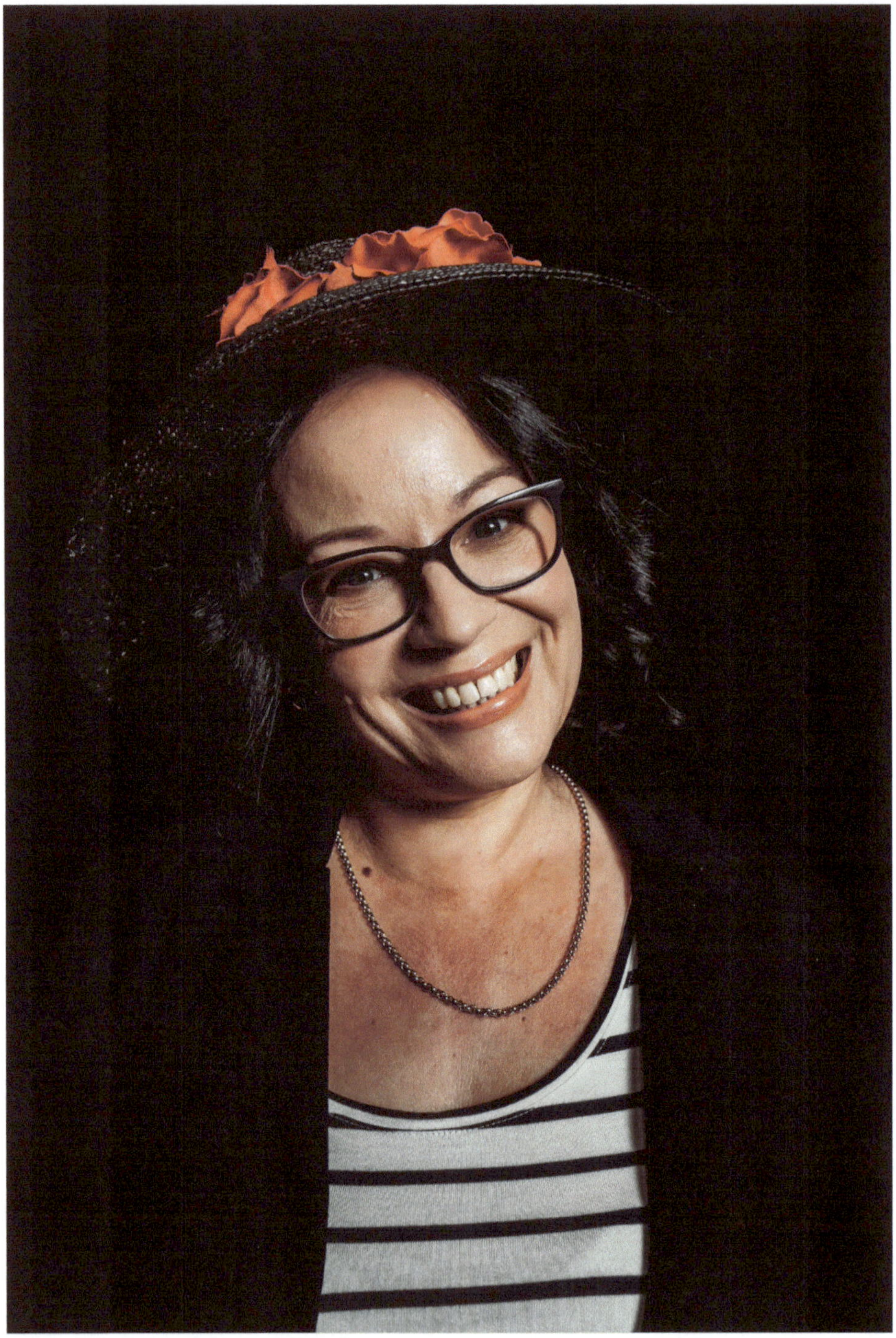

Never give up. Adapt, modify, and keep going. Disability doesn't make you weak—it shows how strong you are.

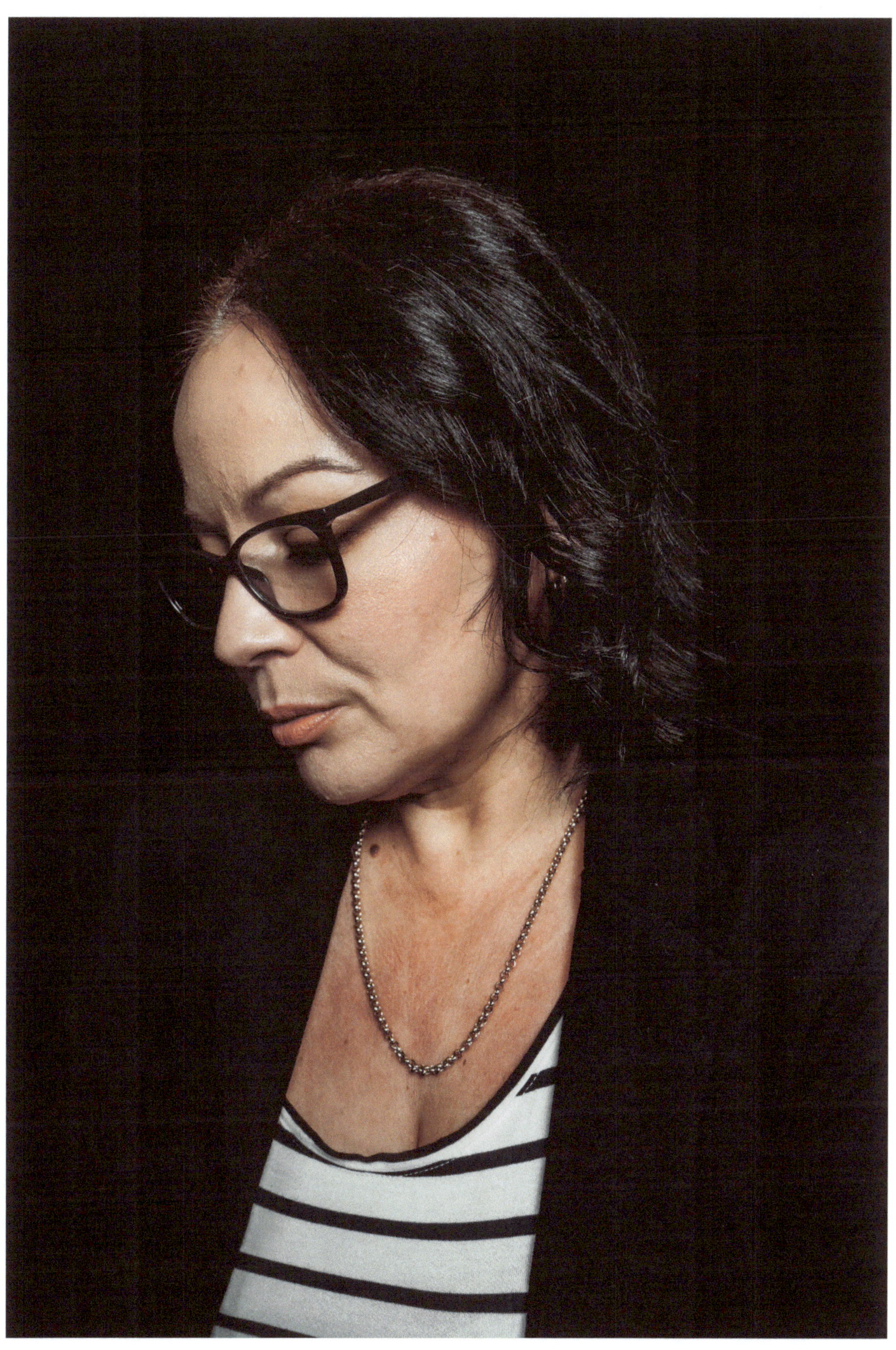

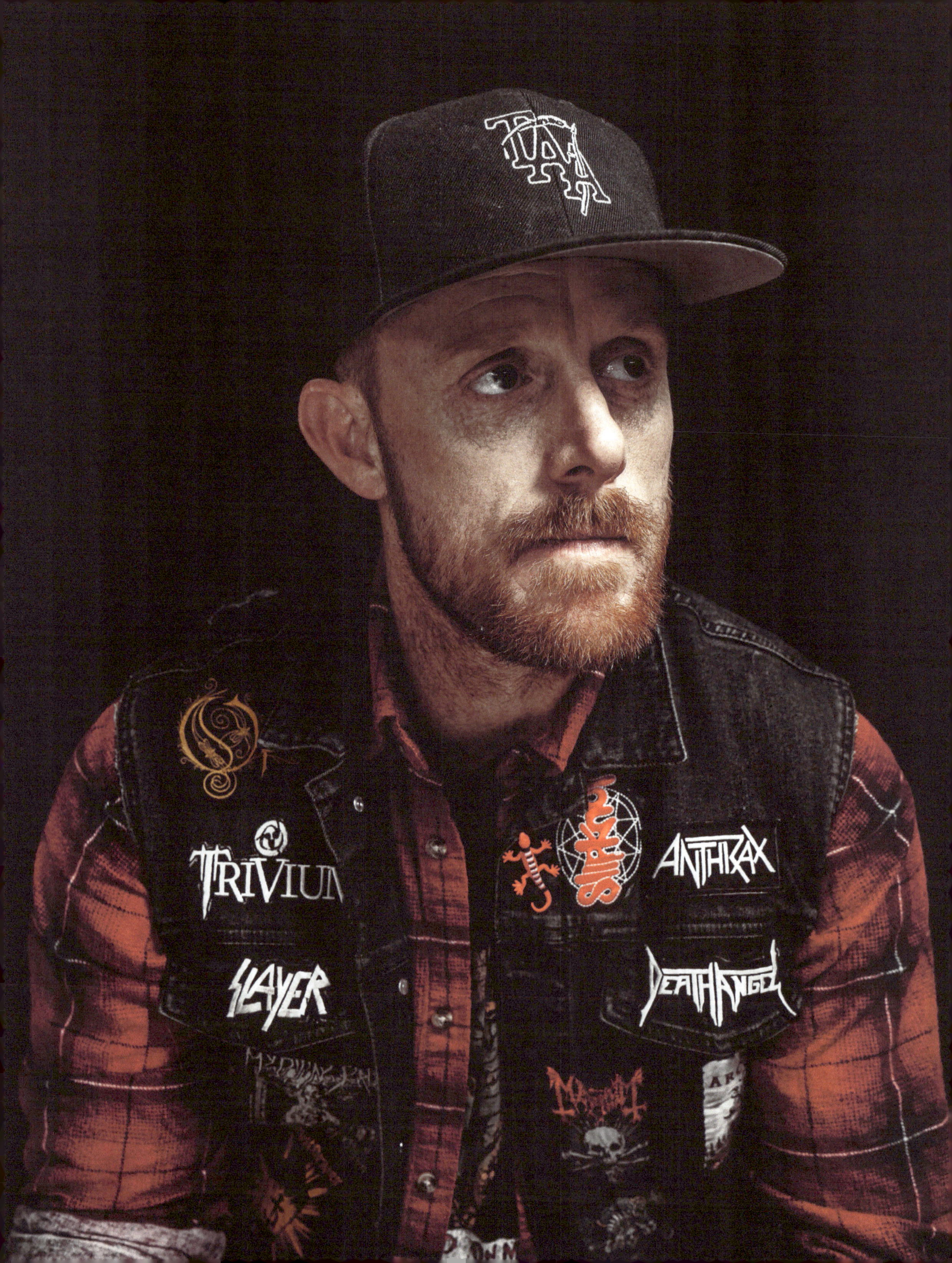
TRIVIUM
SLAYER
ANTHRAX
DEATHANGEL

Cory Schwarzkopf

Unstoppable Spirit: A Journey of Determination and Resilience

Cory is a 40-year-old man from Geelong with a passion for civil construction, fishing, and music. Married to Jo, who also participated in this project as a hairstylist, Cory's life recently took a significant turn when he was diagnosed with ankylosing spondylitis, a degenerative joint disease. Despite the challenges, Cory's resilience and determination have set him on a new path of self-discovery and advocacy.

For the past six and a half years, Cory has worked in civil construction as a manhole builder. "It's a physically demanding job, and I loved it," Cory shares. "I always put my aches and pains down to the nature of the work, but eventually, it became clear something more was going on."

When Cory received his diagnosis, it was a mix of relief and fear. "It was good to finally have an answer, but it was also daunting. Getting a label changes your life. It makes you realise you must rethink everything, from your career to how you look after yourself."

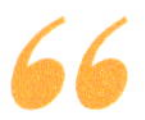

Check in with yourself and others. It's okay not to be okay, and asking for help is not a weakness. It's about caring for yourself so you can be there for the people who matter most.

Now, on monthly biologic injections to slow the progression of his condition, Cory is coming to terms with stepping away from his labour-intensive job. "I love what I do, but I can't keep pushing myself. My kids are 12 and 13, and I want to be there for them as they grow up. I've started studying for a Certificate III in Individual Care for Age and Disability. It's a challenge, but I know it's the right move."

Adjusting to a new career path is daunting, but Cory is motivated by his desire to support others. "I want to give back. Seeing what Jo has done to change her career inspires me. She went from being a hairdresser to working in a completely different field, and it's changed her life for the better."

Cory's proudest achievements include marrying Jo, being a father to his kids, and making the tough decision to prioritise his health and family. "Breaking barriers, for me, means not listening to what others say I can't do. It's about being stubborn in a healthy way and choosing what's best for myself and my family."

Cory has been on a journey to navigate societal expectations around disability. "People often look at me and don't see someone who's disabled. There's a stigma around invisible disabilities, and it can make it hard to explain what you're going through. But I've learned to focus on what I must do to stay healthy and happy."

Music and fishing are Cory's grounding activities. "Fishing helps me centre myself. It's my way of clearing my mind and resetting mentally. And music? That's my daily dose of happiness."

Cory's role models include his mum, kids, and wife. "My mum has been through a lot with her mental health, but she's incredibly resilient. My kids inspire me with their strength—especially after what they've gone through with their mum beating cancer. And Jo has opened my eyes to the power of supporting others and finding fulfilment in new ways."

Cory's message to the world is simple yet powerful: "Check in with yourself and others. It's okay not to be okay, and asking for help is not a weakness. It's about caring for yourself so you can be there for the people who matter most."

Participating in this project has been a unique experience for Cory. "This was my first photoshoot, and it was a lot of fun. Sharing my story is important because I want to encourage others to care for themselves and not let a diagnosis define their future."

As he looks to the future, Cory is focused on completing his studies, spending time with his family, and continuing to advocate for awareness around invisible disabilities. "Life throws you challenges, but it's how you face them that defines you."

Life throws you challenges, but it's how you face them that defines you.

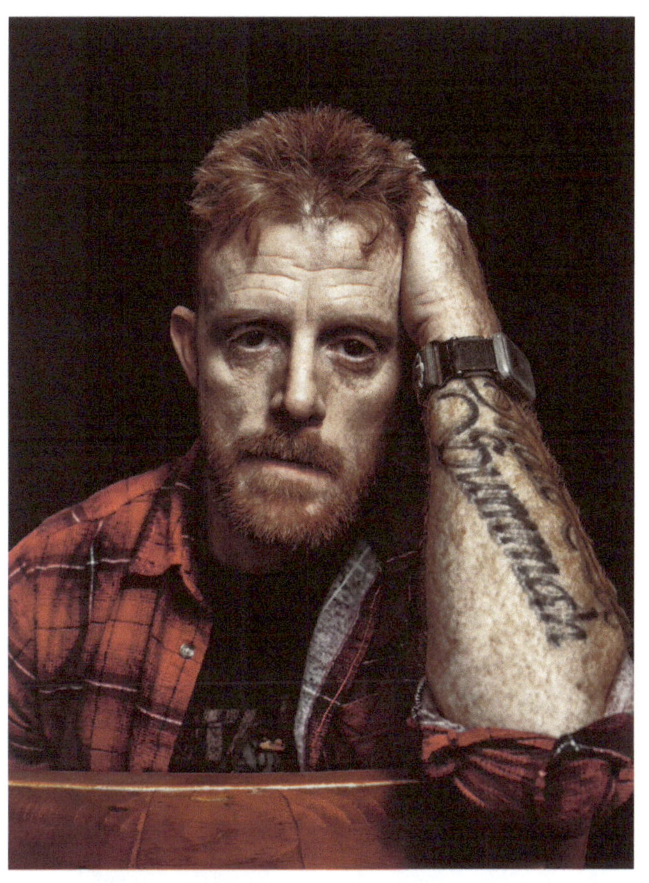

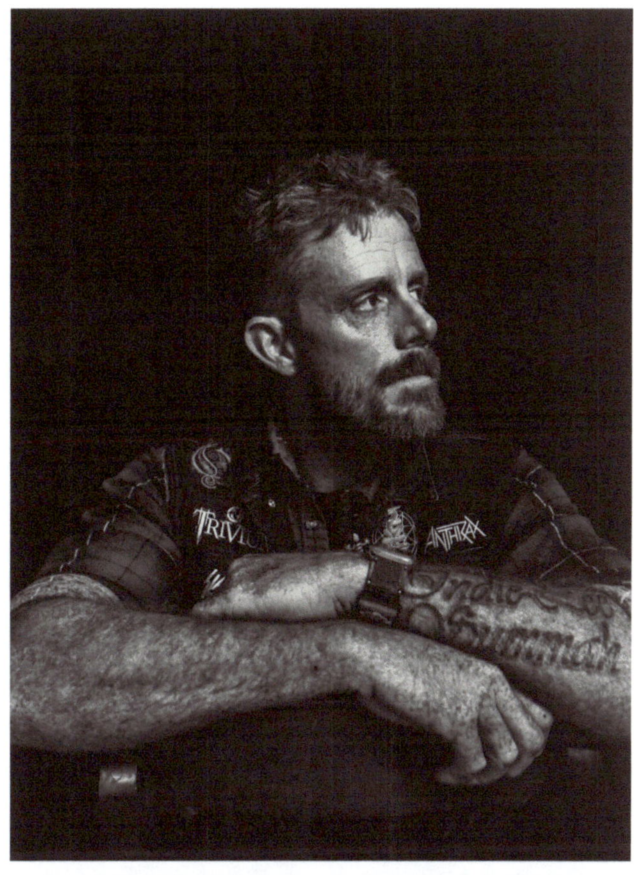
ANTHRAX

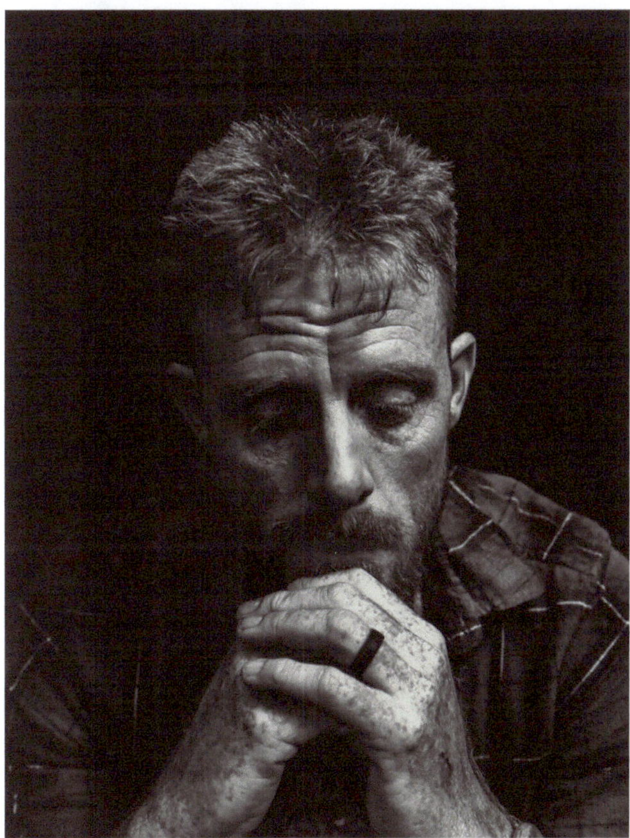

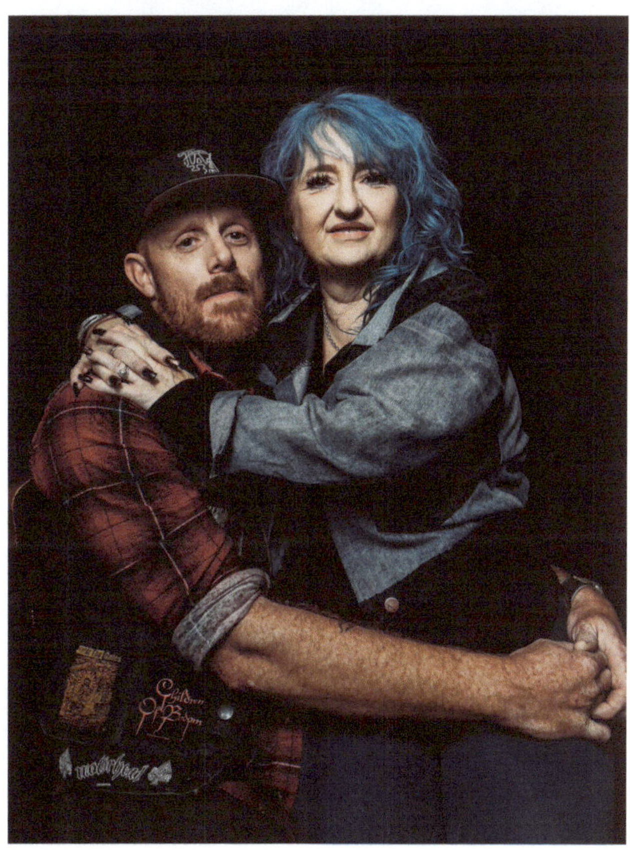

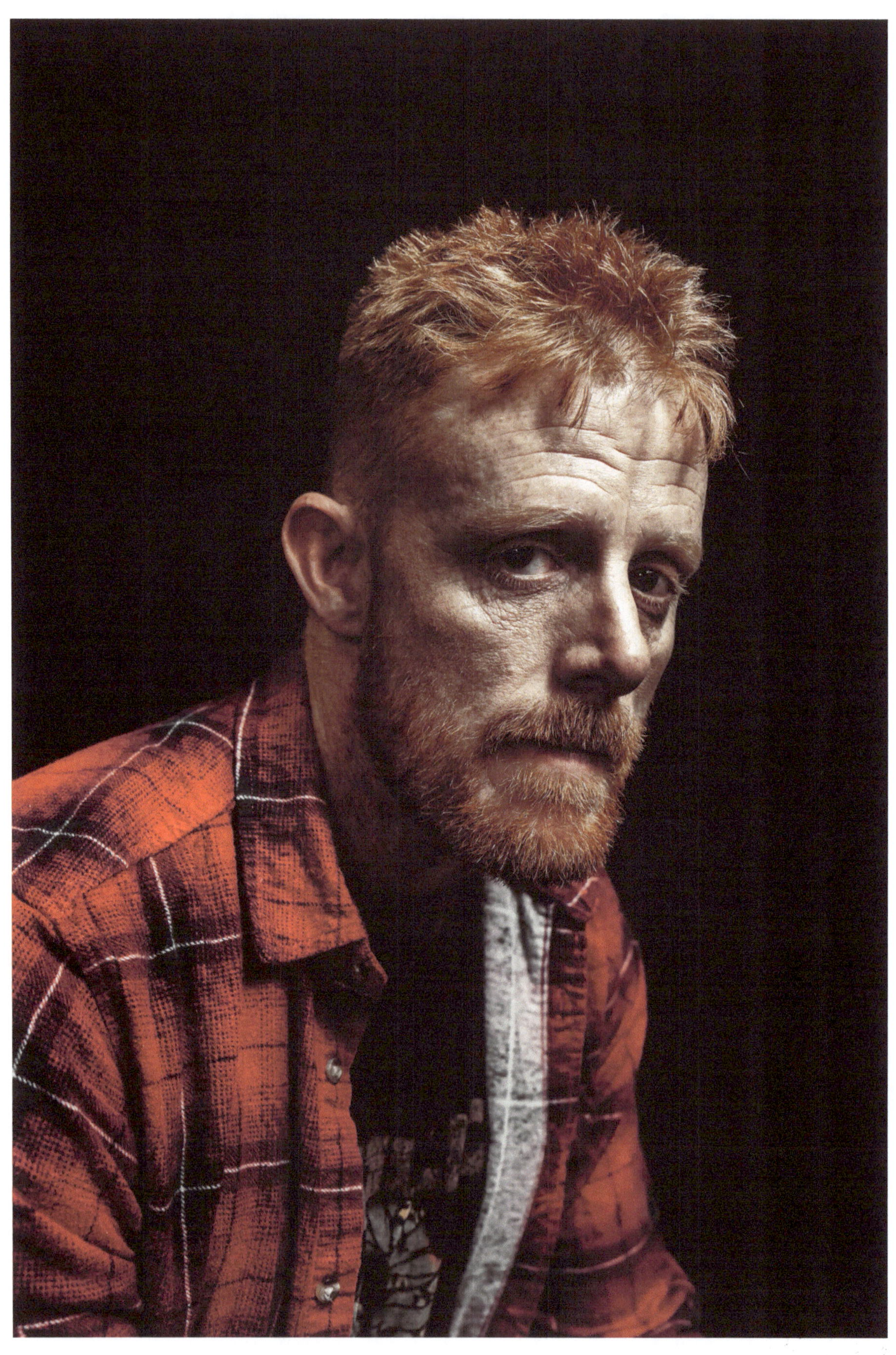

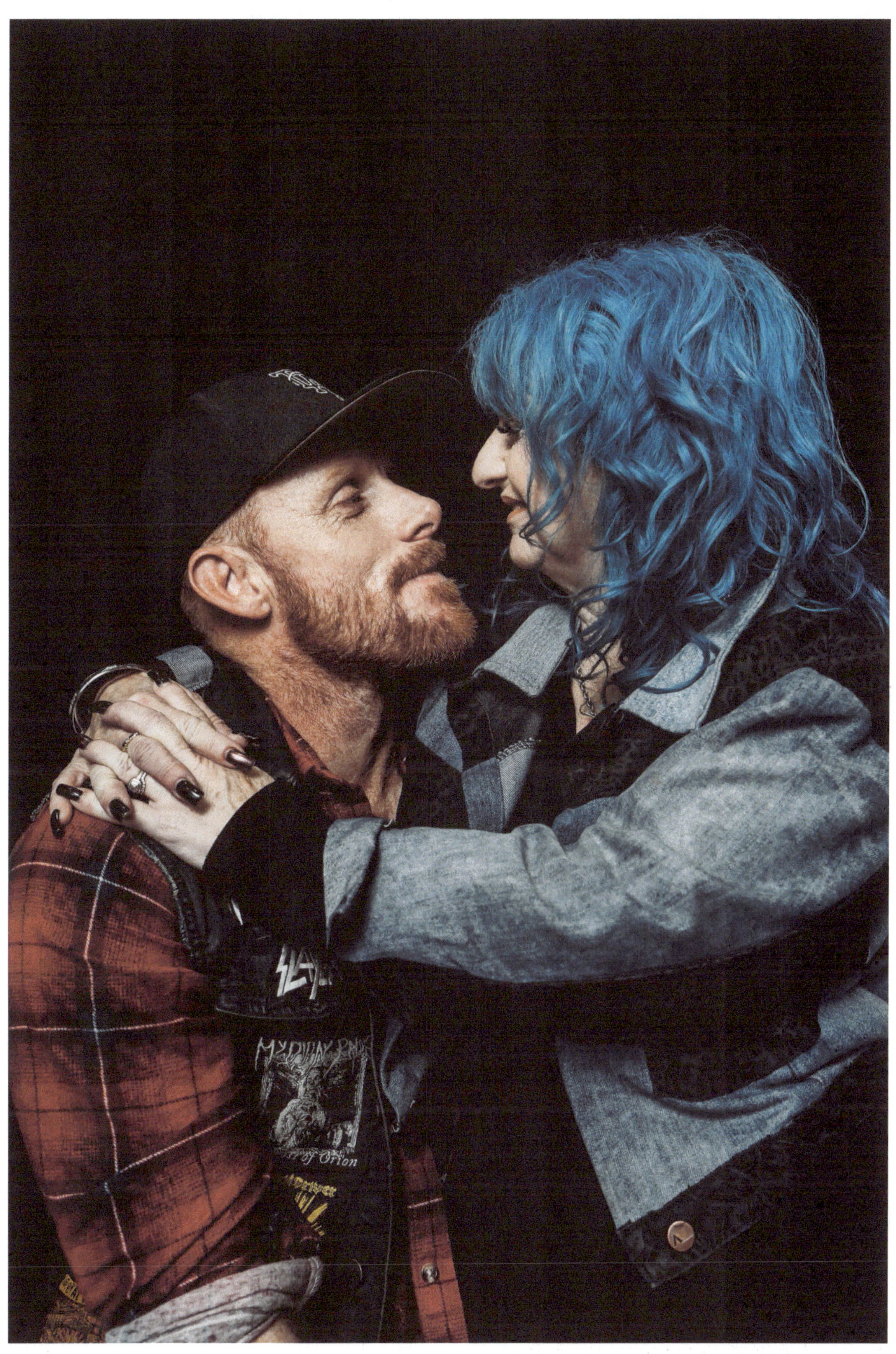
of Orion

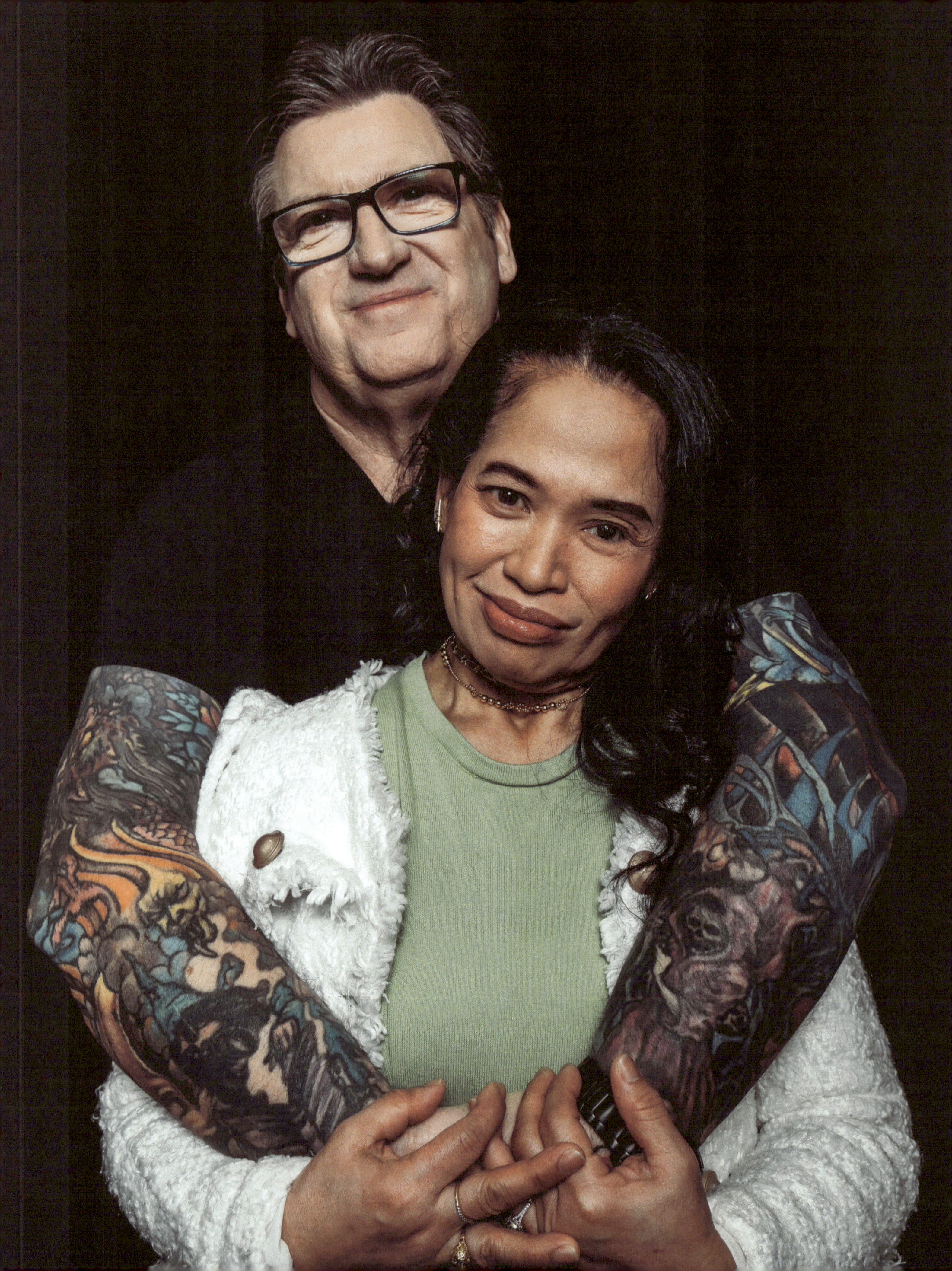

Craig and Rizza Young

Together We Rise: A Story of Strength and Unity

Craig and Rizza Young are a recently married couple whose journey of resilience, love, and faith serves as a beacon of inspiration. Together, they have faced their unique challenges with unwavering determination and a shared belief that disabilities are not hindrances but opportunities to prove their strength.

Craig, born and raised in Geelong, has lived with epilepsy since he was three years old. "Growing up in the 60s, people would tell me what I couldn't do instead of what I could," he recalls. "They tried to baby me, but I never saw myself as different from the other kids in the neighbourhood. I played sports and did everything they did."

Rizza, originally from the Philippines, was born with rheumatic heart disease, a condition she has managed since childhood. "When I was in high school, I also had eye surgery and lost clear vision in my left eye," she shares. "Living with these conditions shaped my perspective on life and made me more empathetic and resilient."

> *Don't worry about what you can't do. Focus on what you can do and embrace your strengths*
>
> -Rizza

For Craig, breaking barriers has meant proving he can do anything. "In 1985, I ran into a burning house and pulled a man to safety," he says. "Even with epilepsy, I showed that I could do what a firefighter does. It's about focusing on what you're capable of, not what others think you can't do."

Rizza, the eldest in her family, has spent her life caring for others. "In the Philippines, it's common for family members to work overseas and send money home. I've always helped support my family, looking after my parents and my siblings' children," she says. Her selflessness has been a cornerstone of her character.

The couple's faith plays a significant role in their lives. "We find joy and fulfilment through our church, the Church of Christ," Craig explains. "It's where we draw strength and build a sense of community. It gives us purpose and helps us focus on what truly matters."

Despite their disabilities, Craig and Rizza are active members of their community. Craig works in a customer-facing role and often challenges misconceptions about epilepsy. "People wouldn't know I have epilepsy just by looking at me," he says. "That's the thing about invisible disabilities—people don't understand what they can't see."

Rizza is an exceptional singer, surprising everyone with her talent despite her quiet and shy demeanour. "Put a microphone in her hand, and she transforms," Craig says proudly. Her love of music and her ability to express herself through song brings joy to those around her.

When asked about their proudest achievements, both agree that finding each other and getting married ranks at the top. "We've only been married for two years," Craig shares. "Rizza's kindness, strength, and support have been life-changing. Together, we've built a partnership based on mutual respect and love."

The couple acknowledges the progress society has made in recognising and supporting people with disabilities but believes there is still a long way to go. "Accessibility is a huge issue," Craig notes. "You don't realise how inaccessible the world is until you experience it firsthand. And there's still a stigma attached to disabilities—people make assumptions without understanding."

Their message to the world is simple yet profound. "Having a disability is not a hindrance," Craig says. "Everyone has abilities, and those should be celebrated. We're all human, and we all deserve to be treated with respect and dignity."

Rizza adds, "Don't worry about what you can't do. Focus on what you can do and embrace your strengths."

Through their love, faith, and determination, Craig and Rizza are breaking barriers and redefining what it means to live a full and meaningful life. Their story is a testament to the power of perseverance, the importance of community, and the beauty of embracing each other's unique abilities.

Having a disability is not a hindrance."Everyone has abilities, and those should be celebrated. We're all human, and we all deserve to be treated with respect and dignity.

- Craig

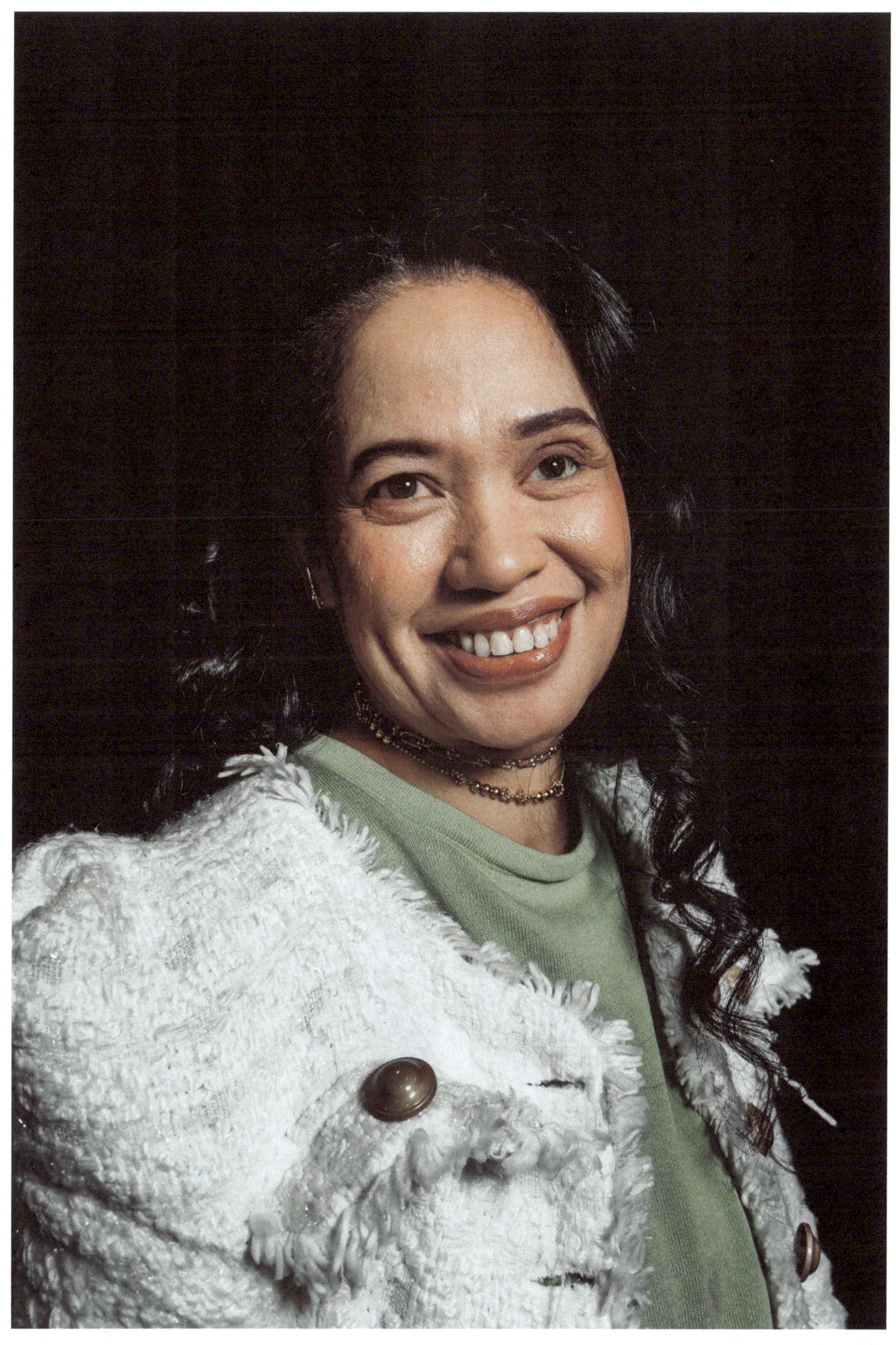

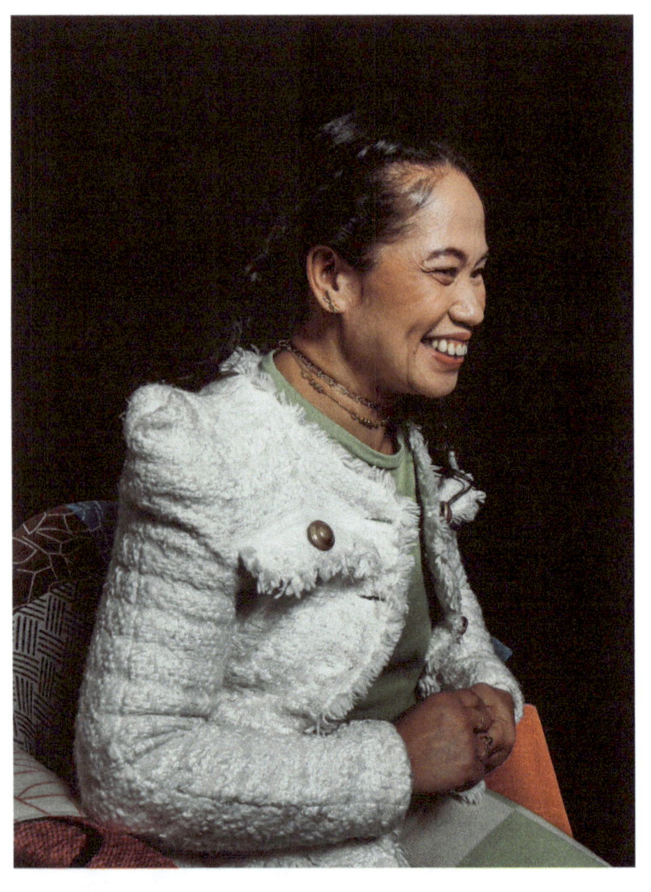

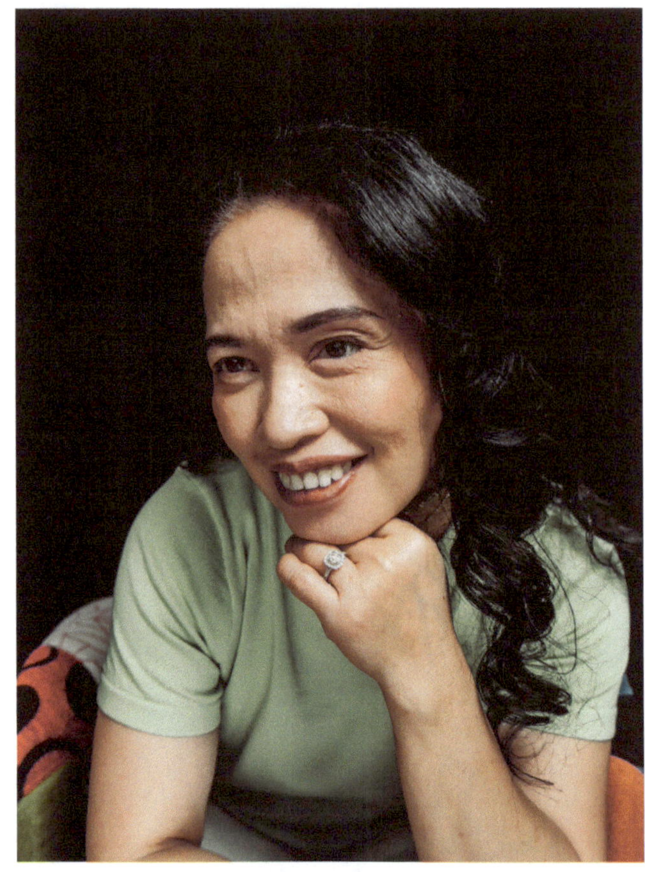

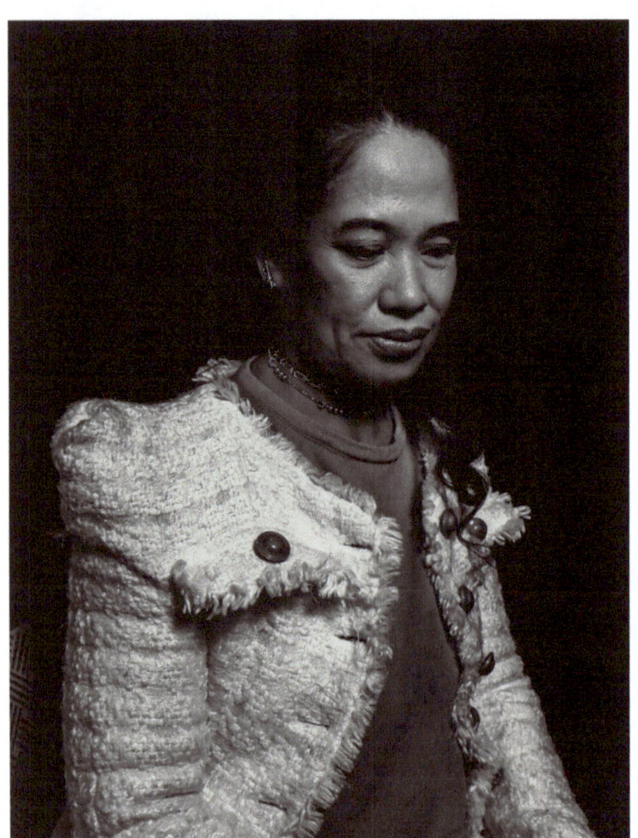

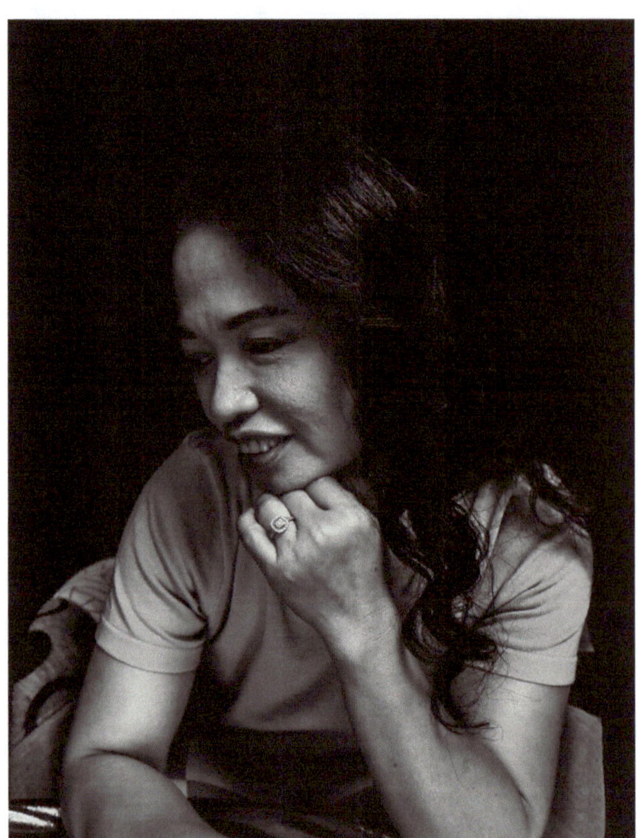

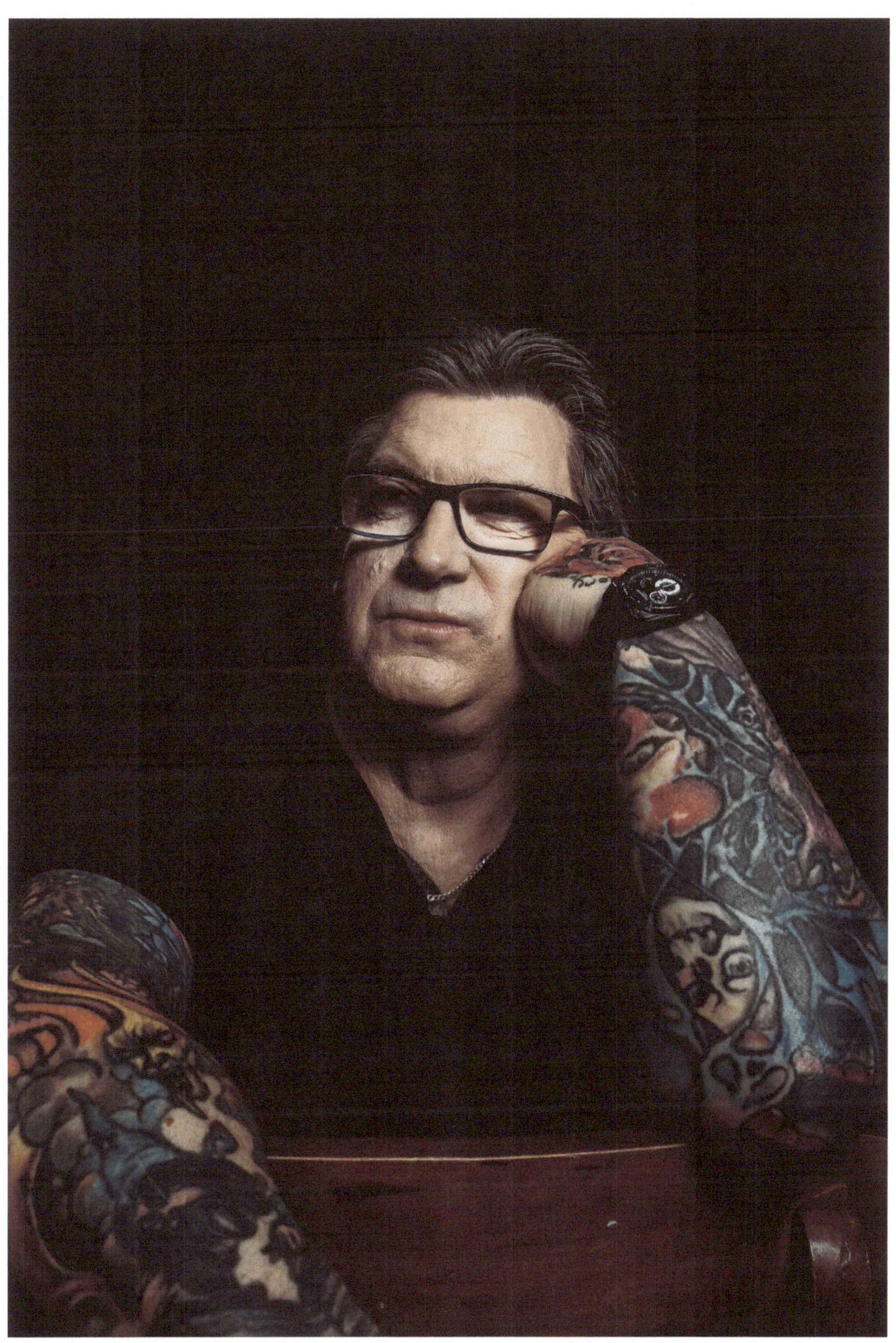

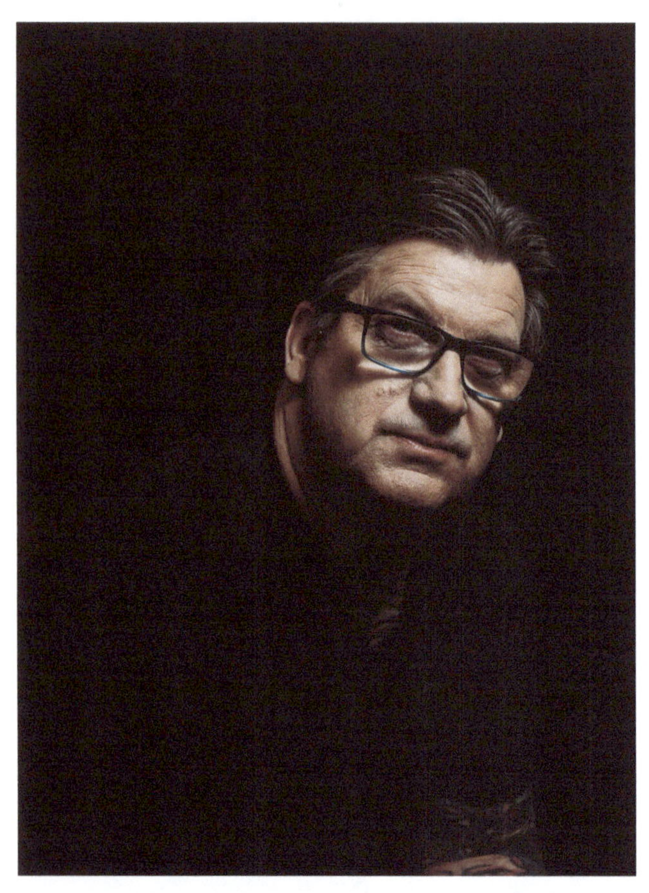

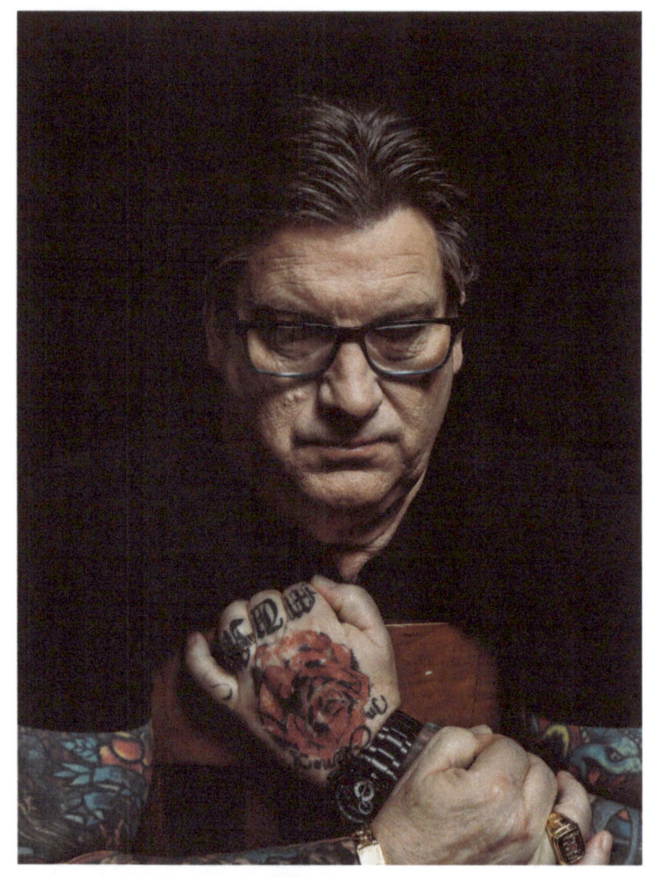

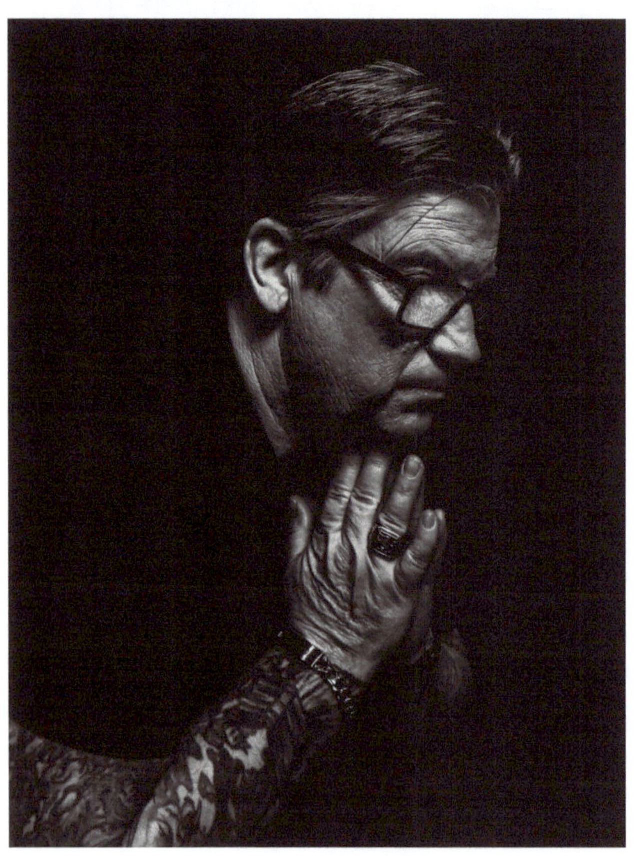

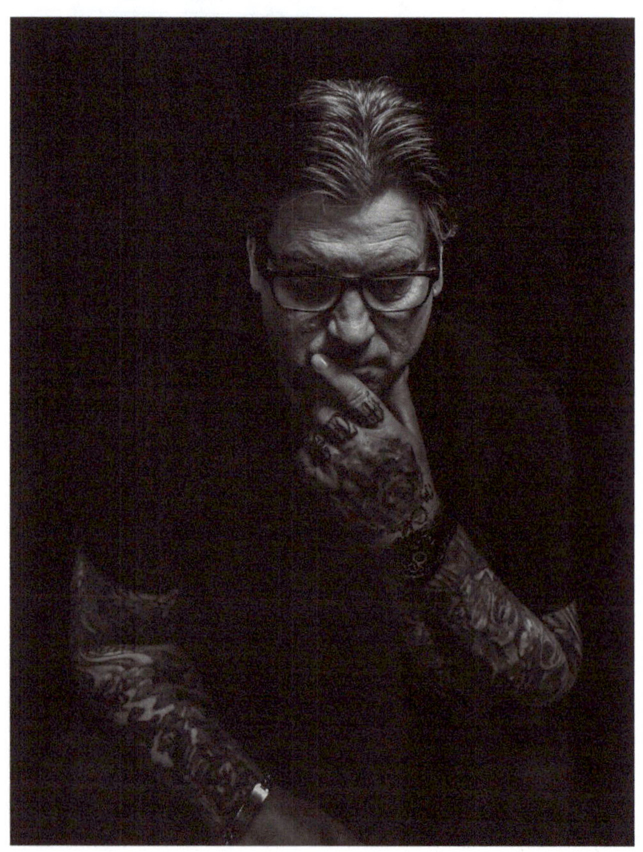

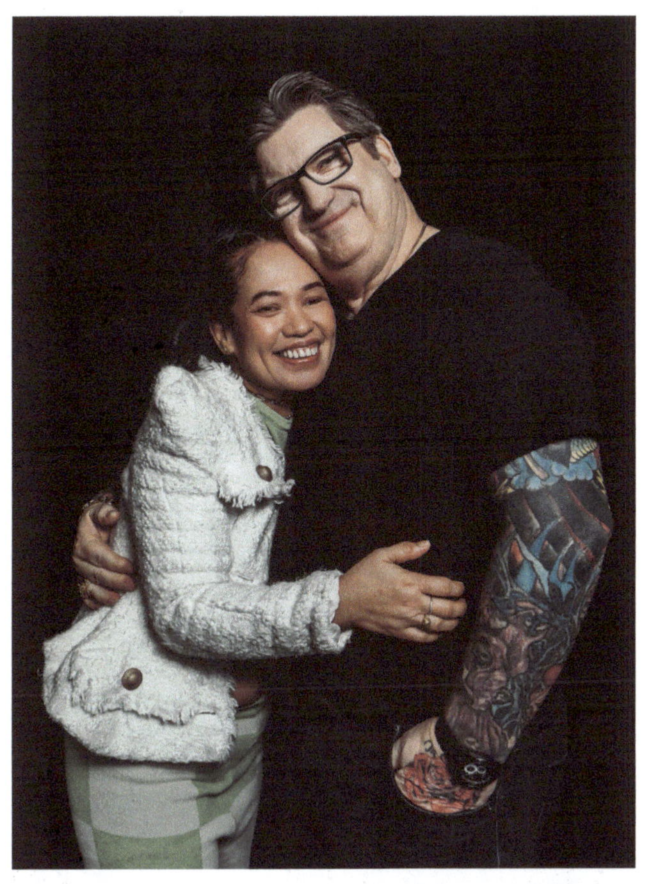
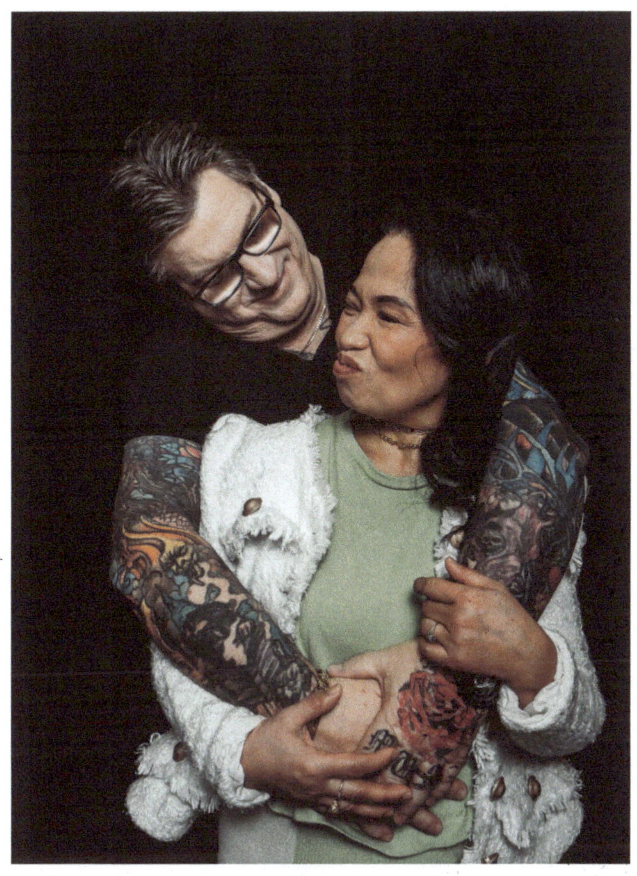
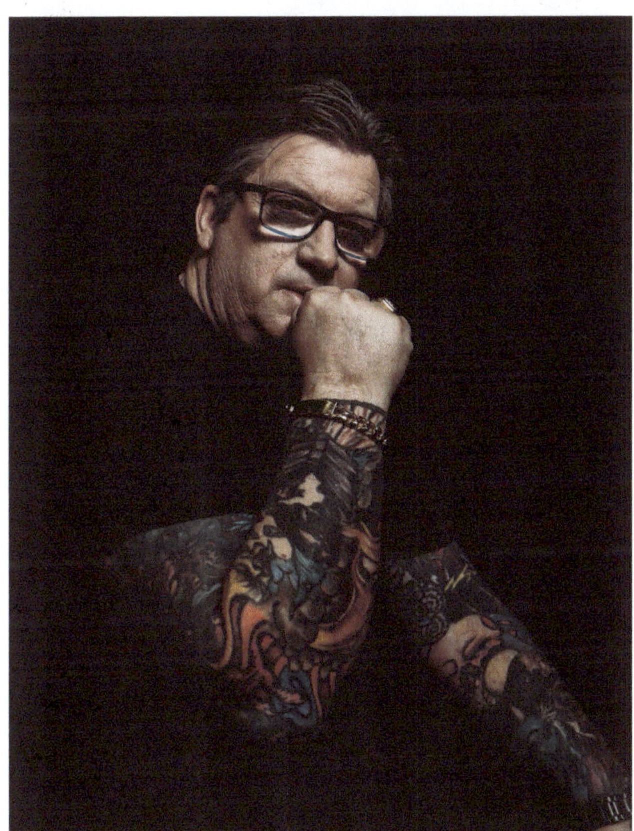
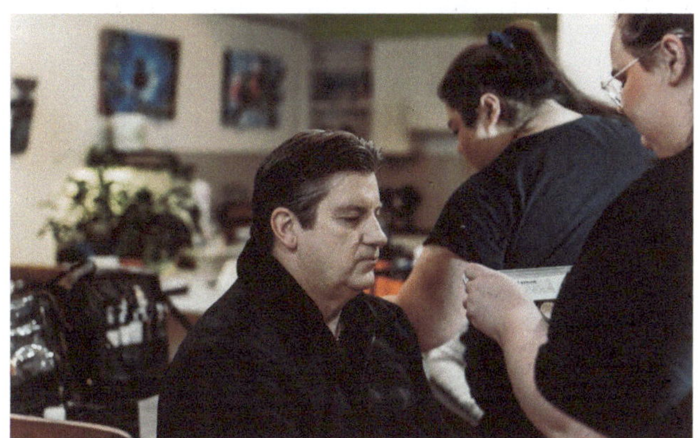
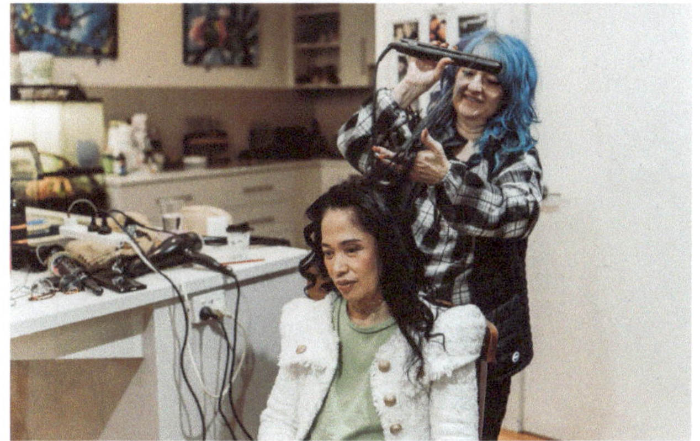

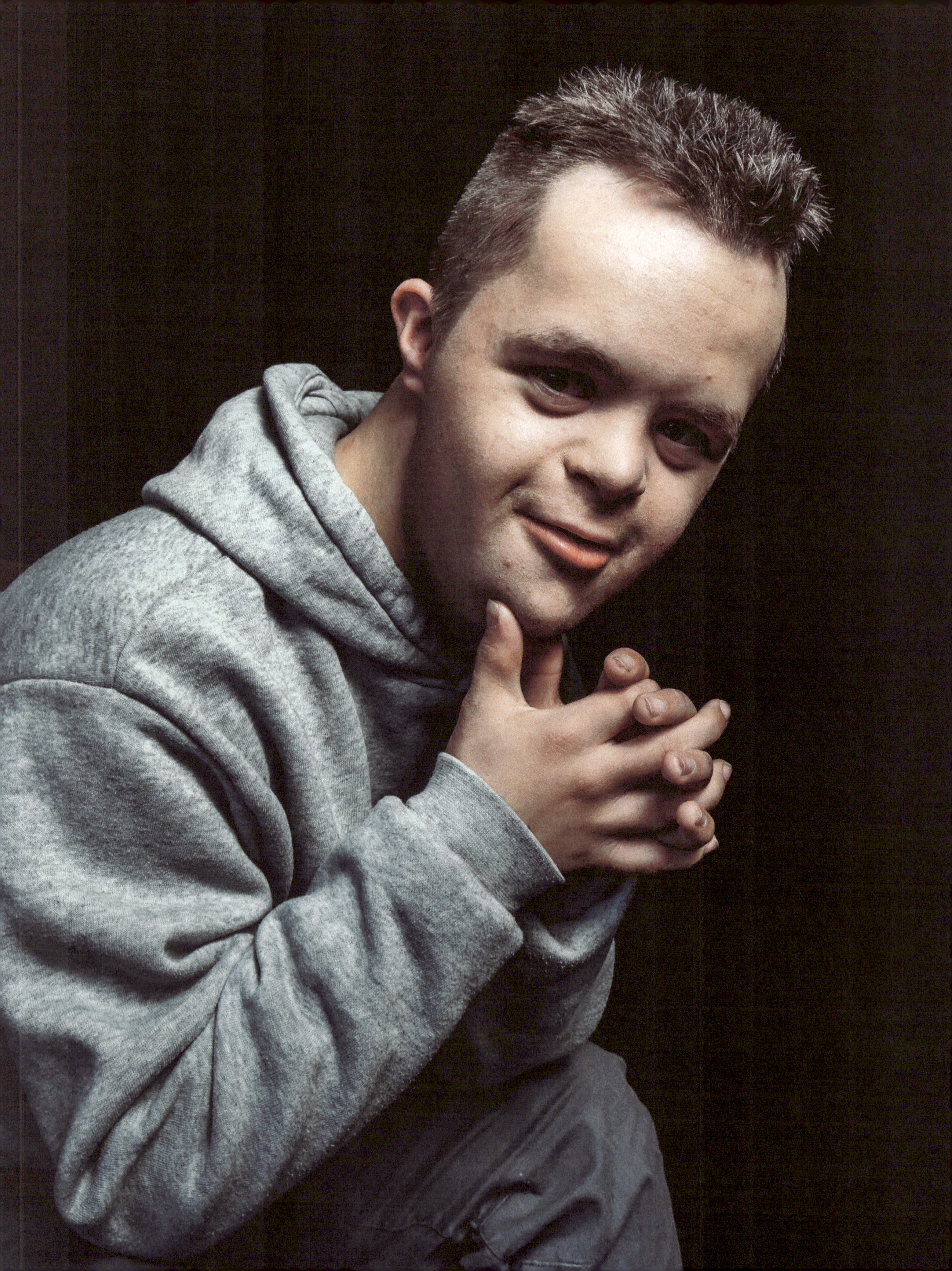

Darcy and Julie Fisher

Celebrating Strength: Darcy's Journey of Joy and Inclusion

Darcy is an 18-year-old who loves basketball, dancing, and music, especially *Sweet Child O' Mine* by Guns N' Roses. His infectious joy and playful nature light up every room he enters. His mum, Julie, supports him every step of the way, whose advocacy, resilience, and creativity have shaped Darcy's journey and inspired many.

Julie's commitment to advocacy began with Darcy's prenatal diagnosis of Down syndrome. It was a path she didn't expect but has embraced wholeheartedly. "Breaking barriers means challenging people's misconceptions about disability," Julie says. "It's about showing the world that Darcy is so much more than his diagnosis. He's human, with a full range of emotions, interests, and dreams."

People with disabilities thrive when they feel accepted and valued.

Darcy's vibrant personality shines through in everything he does. "He's incredibly loving and intuitive," Julie shares. "He has this amazing ability to sense when someone isn't feeling right. That's his superpower. He's also cheeky and full of life."

Julie's advocacy work includes writing books that share her family's experiences. Her first book, *The Unexpected Journey*, chronicles their story from Darcy's prenatal diagnosis through his teenage years. "It's an honest and raw account of navigating life with a child who has Down syndrome," she explains. "It covers the emotions, the friendships, the judgment, and the joy."

Julie's second book, *The Magic of Inclusion: Give People a Chance and Watch Them Shine*, focuses on the transformative power of acceptance and inclusion. "Inclusion isn't just a buzzword—it's a way of life," she emphasises. "When we include and accept others, the results are magical."

Her third book, *From the Hearts of Mums*, is a compilation of stories from mothers of children with Down syndrome in Australia, the UK, and the US. "It's a celebration of shared experiences and the incredible strength of mums worldwide," Julie says. "One story from a woman in California, who cared for an adult with Down syndrome for 21 years, is particularly moving."

Julie also wrote a children's book, *Big School*, inspired by Darcy's dual schooling experience in primary school. "It captures his first day at school, blending his experiences at mainstream and specialist schools. It's about teaching children to treat him like any other friend while understanding he might need a little extra help."

In addition to her writing, Julie organises an annual community expo that connects local families with disability service providers. "Not everyone can attend the big expos in capital cities," she explains. "I wanted to bring those resources to our community. The expo also highlights micro-businesses run by individuals with disabilities, showcasing their talents and contributions."

For Julie, advocacy is personal and powerful. "I've had mothers tell me that reading our story gave them hope and helped them decide to continue their pregnancies. Moments like that remind me why I do this work."

Darcy's interests reflect his love for life. He enjoys playing basketball, attending concerts, and participating in a dance group. His family, which includes two older brothers, a stepsister, and several pets, is a constant source of support and joy.

Julie's aspirations for Darcy are simple yet profound. "I want him to live a life where he feels safe, supported, and loved," she says. "I want him to be part of the community, pursue his passions, and have meaningful friendships."

Her advice to others is to approach people with kindness and curiosity. "A smile or a kind word can make a world of difference. People with disabilities thrive when they feel accepted and valued."

Participating in this project has been a meaningful experience for both Darcy and Julie. "It's about showing who Darcy truly is—a young man with so much to offer," Julie says. "Down syndrome is just one part of who he is; it doesn't define him."

Darcy and Julie's story is a powerful testament to love, advocacy, and the beauty of inclusion. Their journey reminds us that when we embrace diversity, we all shine a little brighter.

“

A smile or a kind word can make a world of difference.

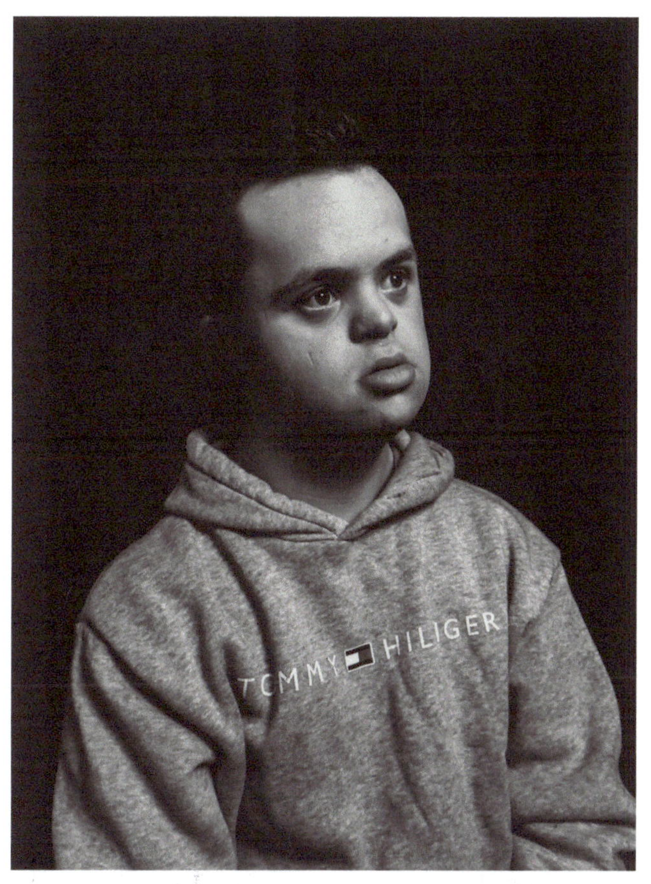
TOMMY HILIGER

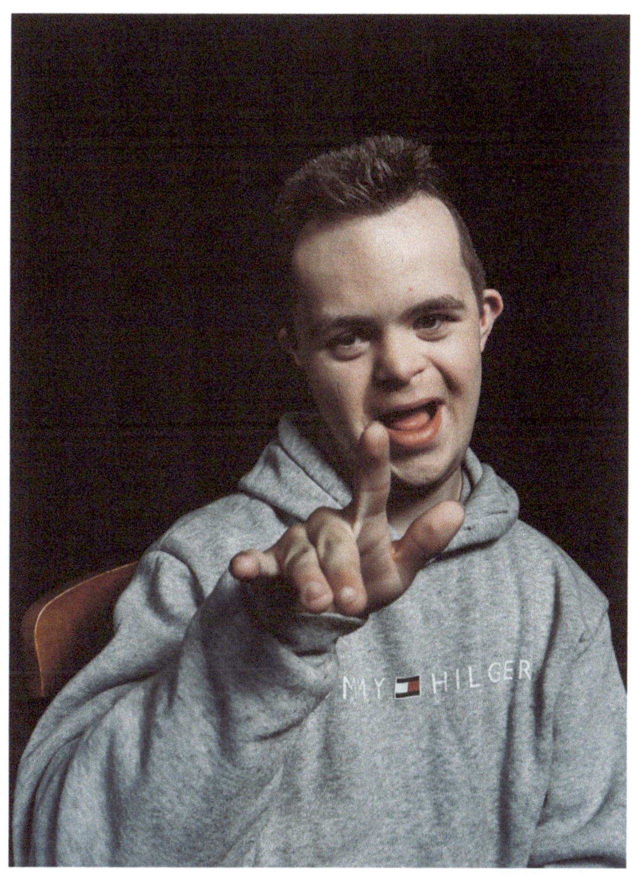
MY HILGER

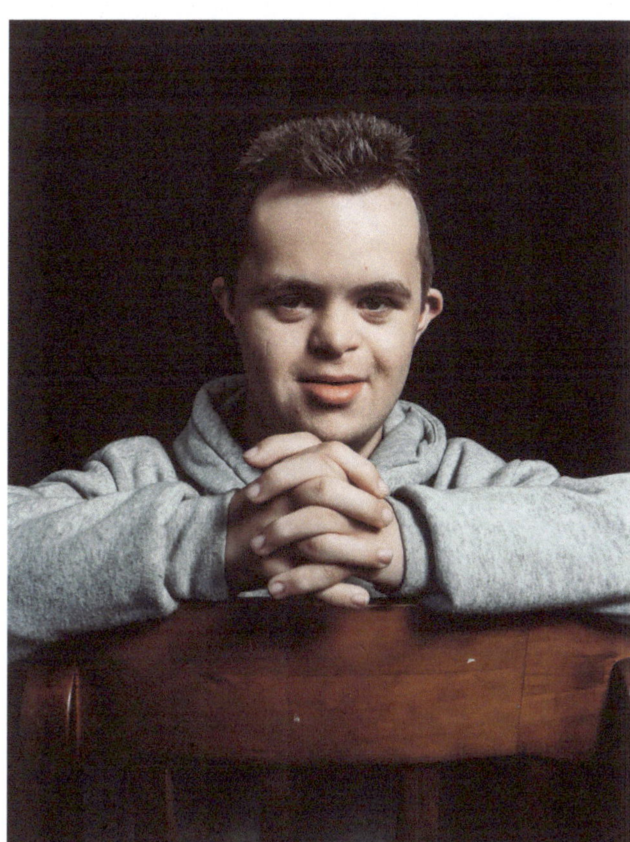

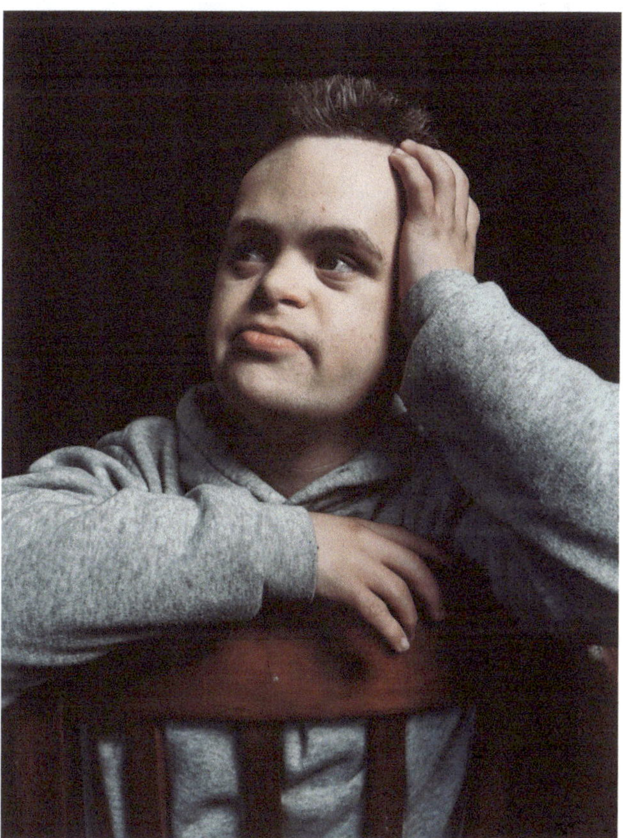

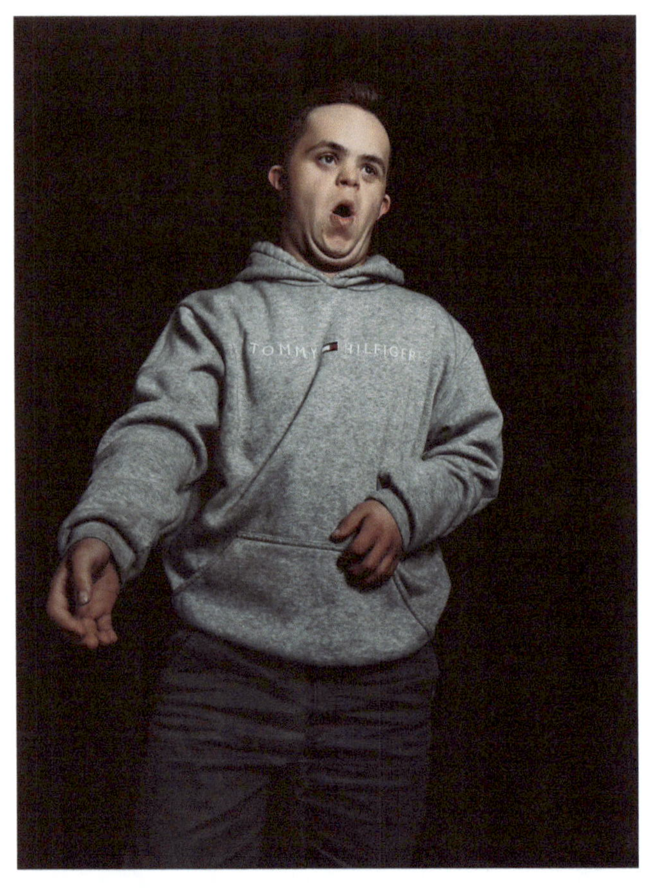
TOMMY HILFIGER
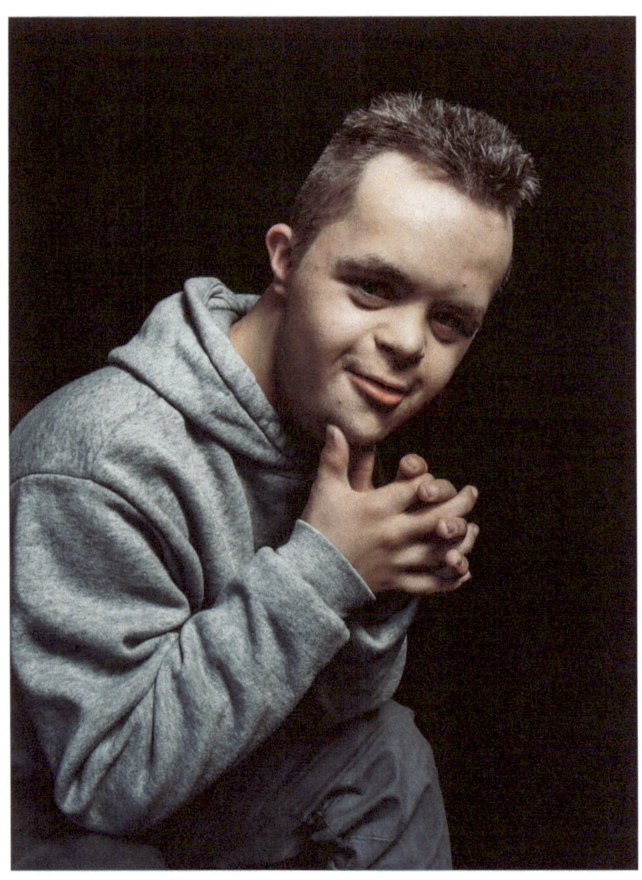
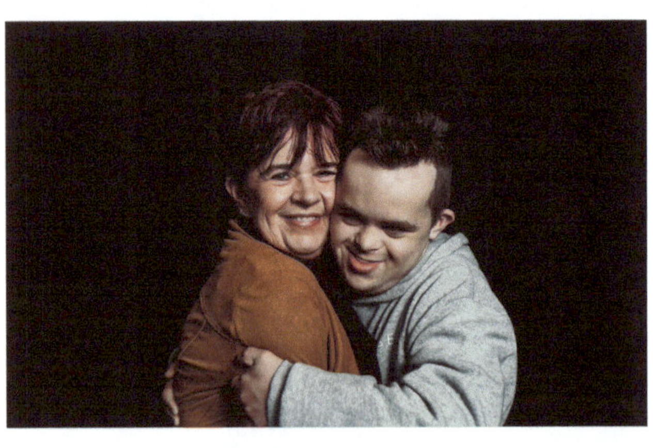
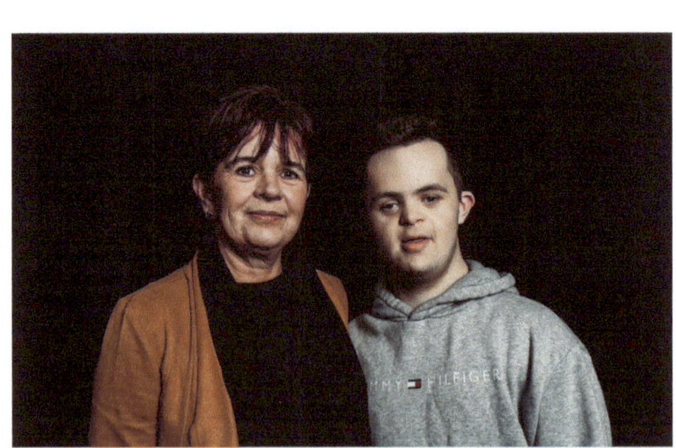
HILFIGER
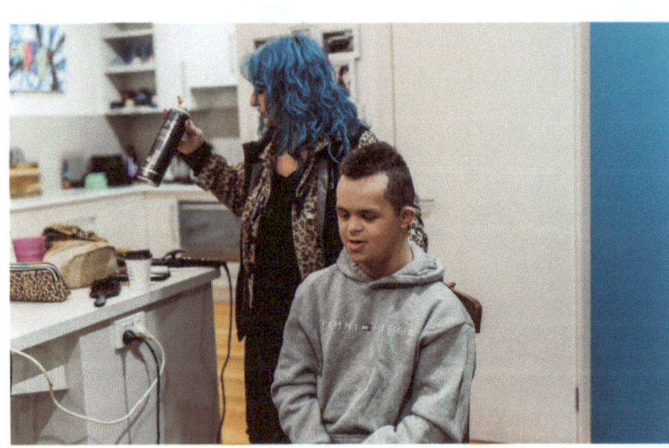
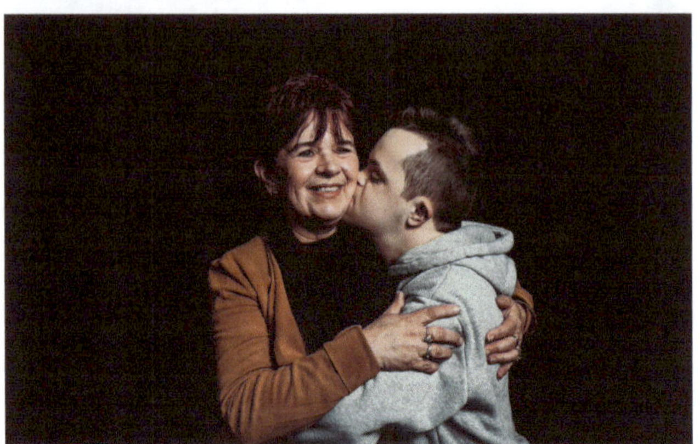

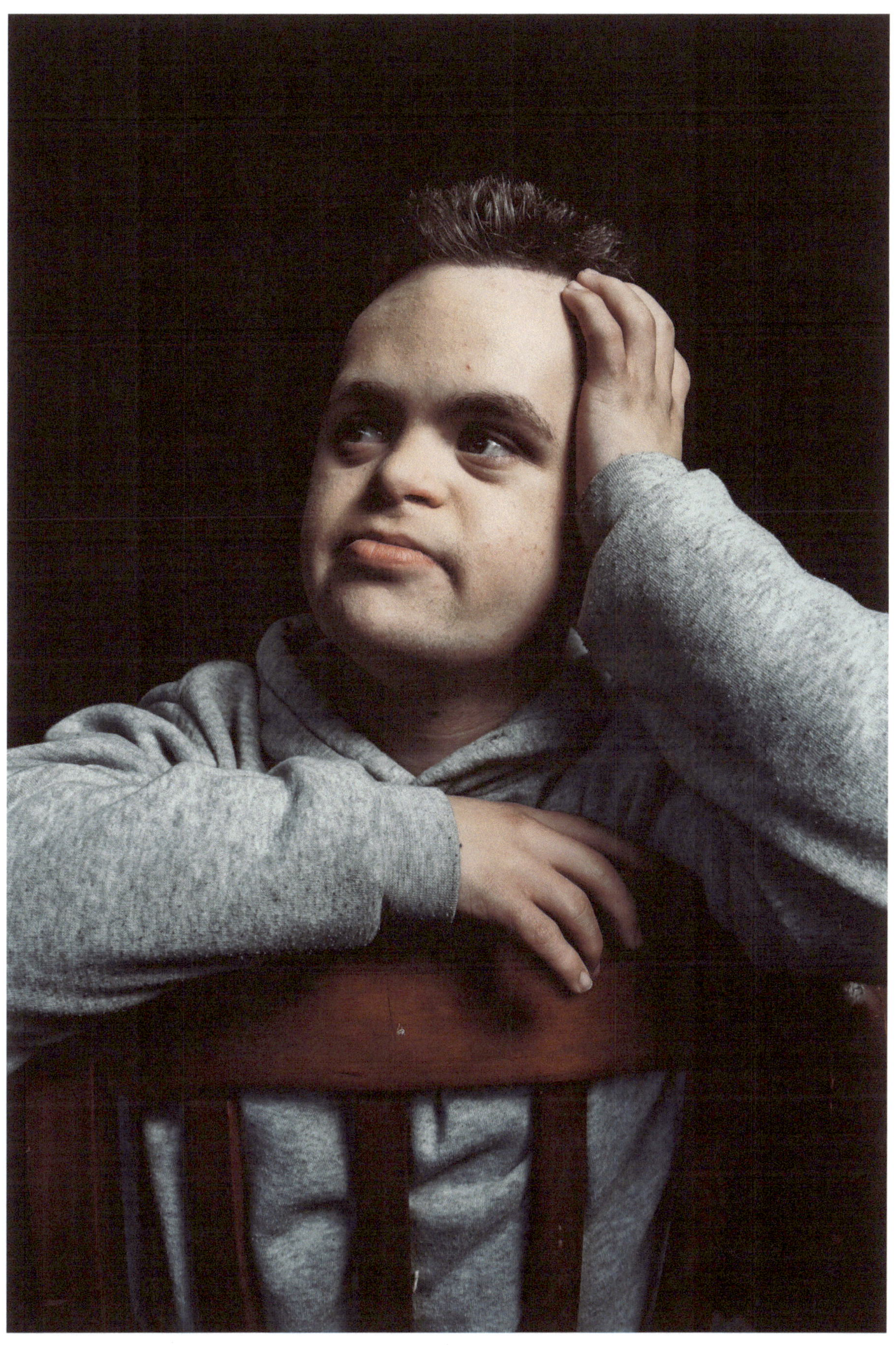

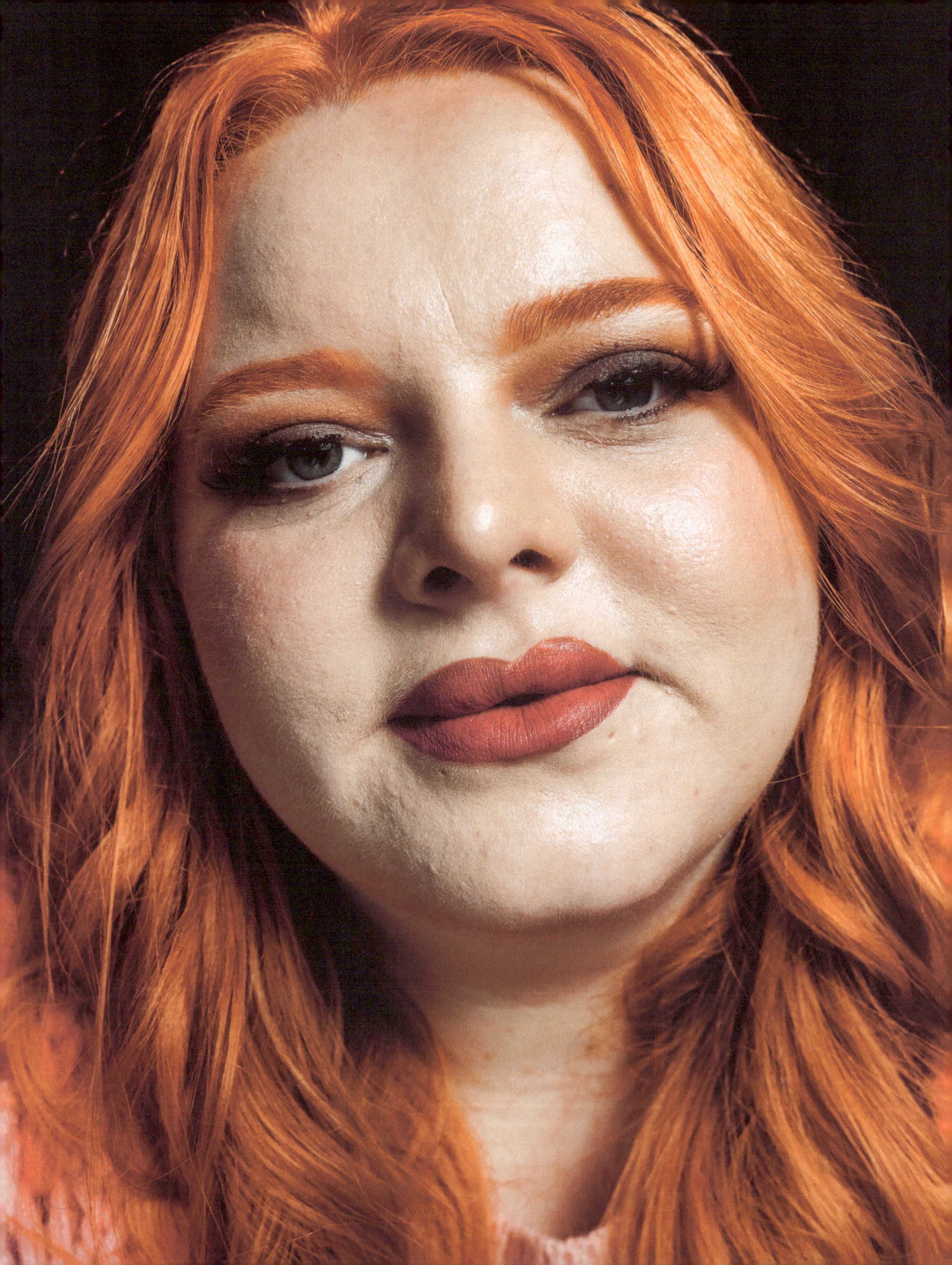

Darihan Mullenger

Finding Strength in Creativity

Darihan Mullenger is an artist from Geelong who has rediscovered her sense of purpose and joy through pottery after facing life-changing challenges. Living with fibromyalgia, autism, and various other health issues, Darihan's journey is one of resilience, self-discovery, and the transformative power of art.

Diagnosed three years ago, Darihan's chronic pain condition brought her life to a halt, forcing her to reevaluate everything. "The biggest challenge was losing my sense of self and living in a body that couldn't do what my brain wanted it to do," she explains. "I had to accept my new reality and find ways to accommodate my abilities."

This acceptance led Darihan to pottery, a medium that has become a lifeline. "I signed up for a pottery class at Roseville Community Centre in Corio, and it completely changed my life," she shares. "There hasn't been a day since that I haven't had my hands on clay. I even got my own kiln and started hand-building sculptures at home."

Her creations, ranging from doll sculptures to mermaids and cats, have brought her immense fulfilment. "Every piece I finish fills me with pride," Darihan says. "Having my work exhibited in Geelong this year was one of my proudest moments. Sharing my art with others is an incredible feeling."

Be yourself. Respect your body's capacity. And remember, you're stronger than you think.

Darihan's art also serves as an avenue to challenge misconceptions about disabilities. "There's so much stigma around what people with disabilities can or can't do," she explains. "I use a wheelchair, although I can walk, and I've faced judgment for it. But showing up and owning that reality helps empower others to embrace the mobility aids they need to thrive."

Her wheelchair, affectionately named Nina Flowers, reflects Darihan's vibrant personality. "She's pink and fabulous," Darihan says with a smile. "People are going to stare anyway, so you may as well give them something to look at."

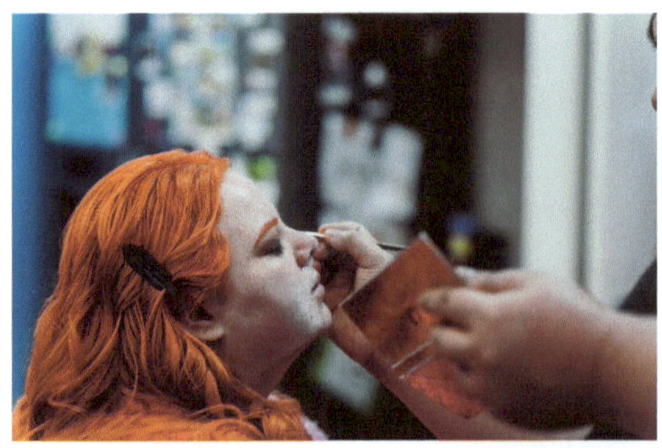

Breaking barriers is central to Darihan's philosophy. "It's about showing the world that disability doesn't mean inability," she says. "I want people to know it's okay to exist in the body you have and respect its capacity. Don't push yourself because of others' expectations."

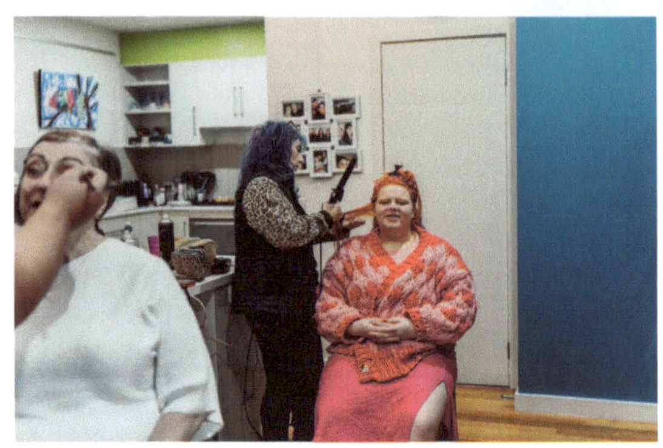

Darihan dreams of starting a clay community group from her home to bring people together through art. "Now that I've settled into understanding my capacity, I know working full-time isn't in the cards for me. But I'd love to create a space where others can find the same joy in pottery that I have."

Her advice to those facing similar challenges is rooted in hope. "Even when things feel unbearable, they do get better," she says. "Being disabled isn't the end—it's just a different way of living."

Darihan stays motivated through her connection to art, animals, and her belief in higher guidance. "I talk to angels," she admits. "It might sound unusual, but it helps me find gratitude and see the positive in life."

Her house is filled with love and creativity, from her French Bulldogs, Dolia and Mr Mki, to her four cats, Max, Edith, Pearl, and Myrtle. "Animals bring so much joy," she says. "They're part of my inspiration."

Darihan draws strength from other strong, independent women, particularly those in the arts community. "There's a local artist named Pinchy, part of Geelong Illustrators, who inspires me. She's passionate, ethical, and knows exactly what change she wants to make in the world."

> *Being disabled isn't the end—it's just a different way of living.*

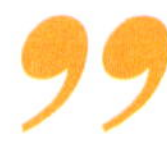

Participating in *Breaking the Barriers Through the Lens* was an opportunity for Darihan to contribute to a larger conversation. "When I was at my lowest, I had nothing to look to for hope," she says. "This project creates a sense of community and connection, showing people that they're not alone."

Through her art and advocacy, Darihan is breaking barriers and inspiring others to embrace their unique journeys. Her message is simple yet profound: "Be yourself. Respect your body's capacity. And remember, you're stronger than you think."

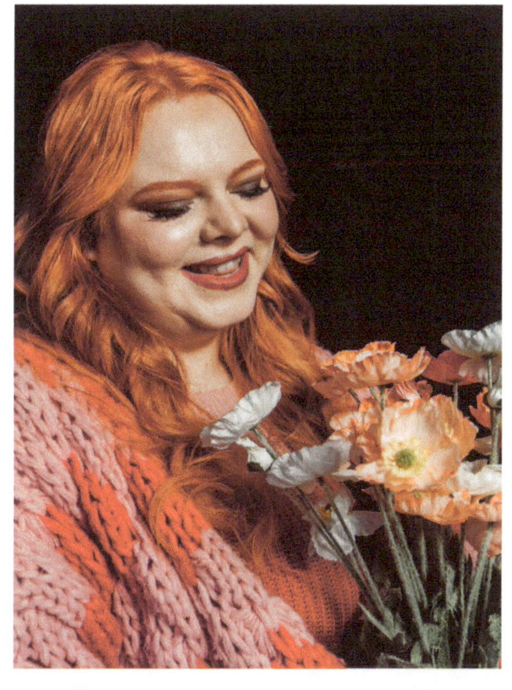
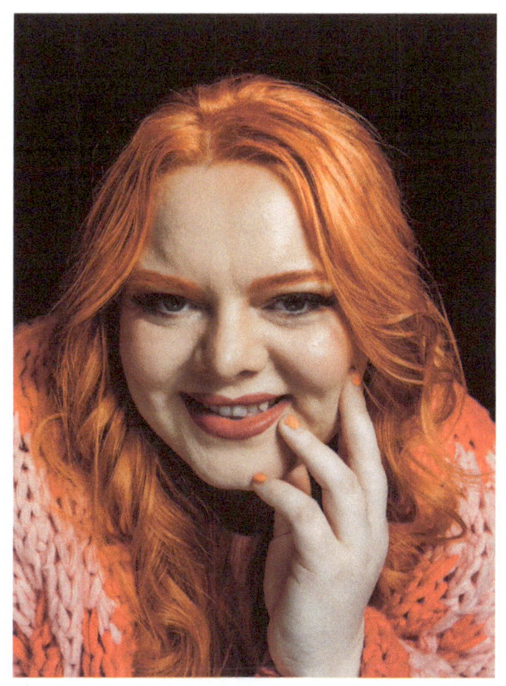
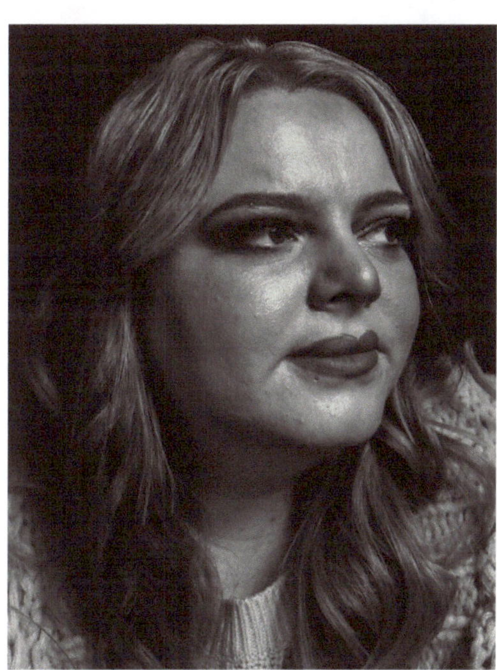
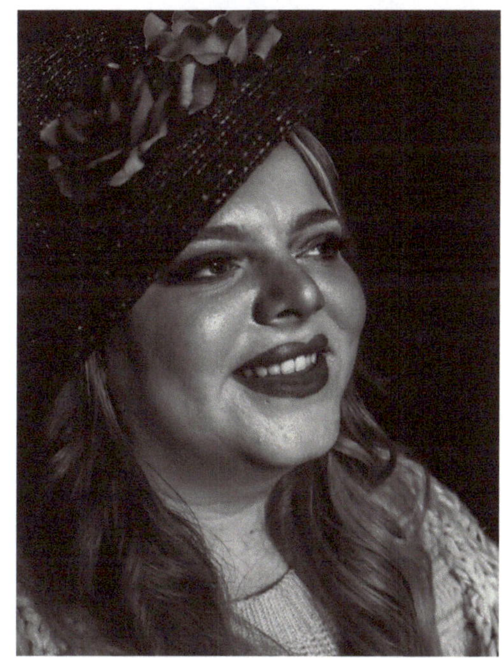

It's about showing the world that disability doesn't mean inability

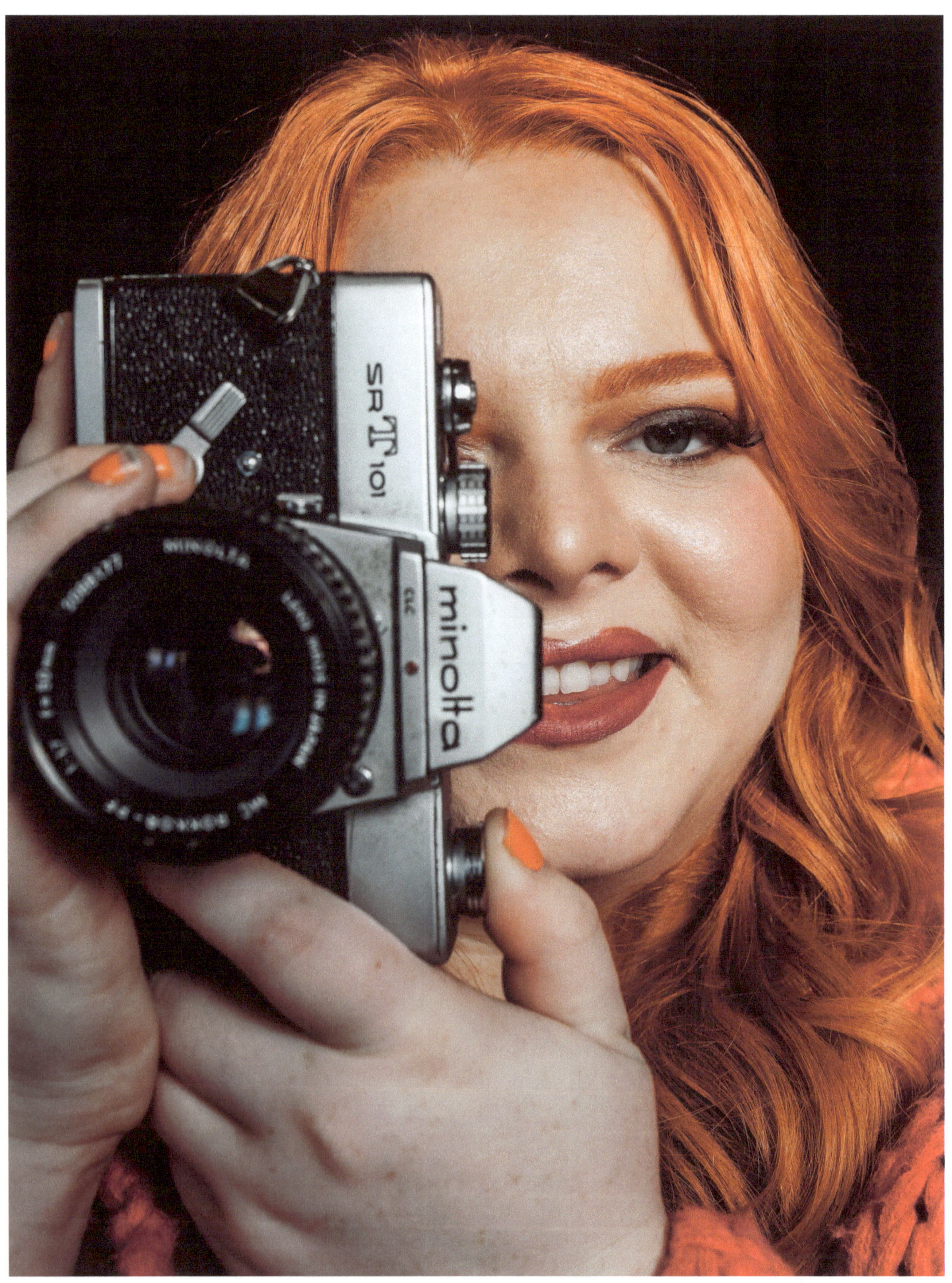
SR T 101
minolta

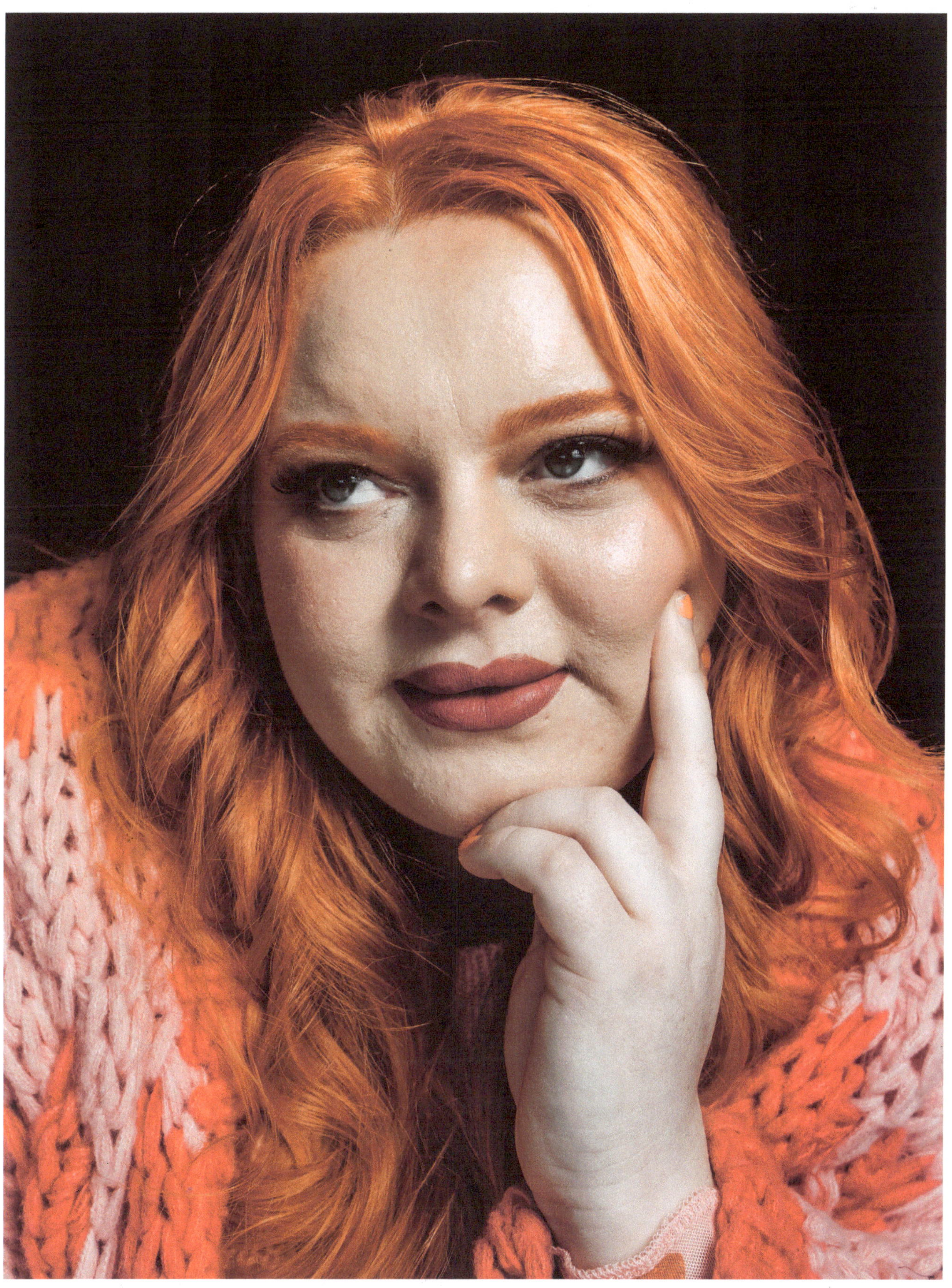

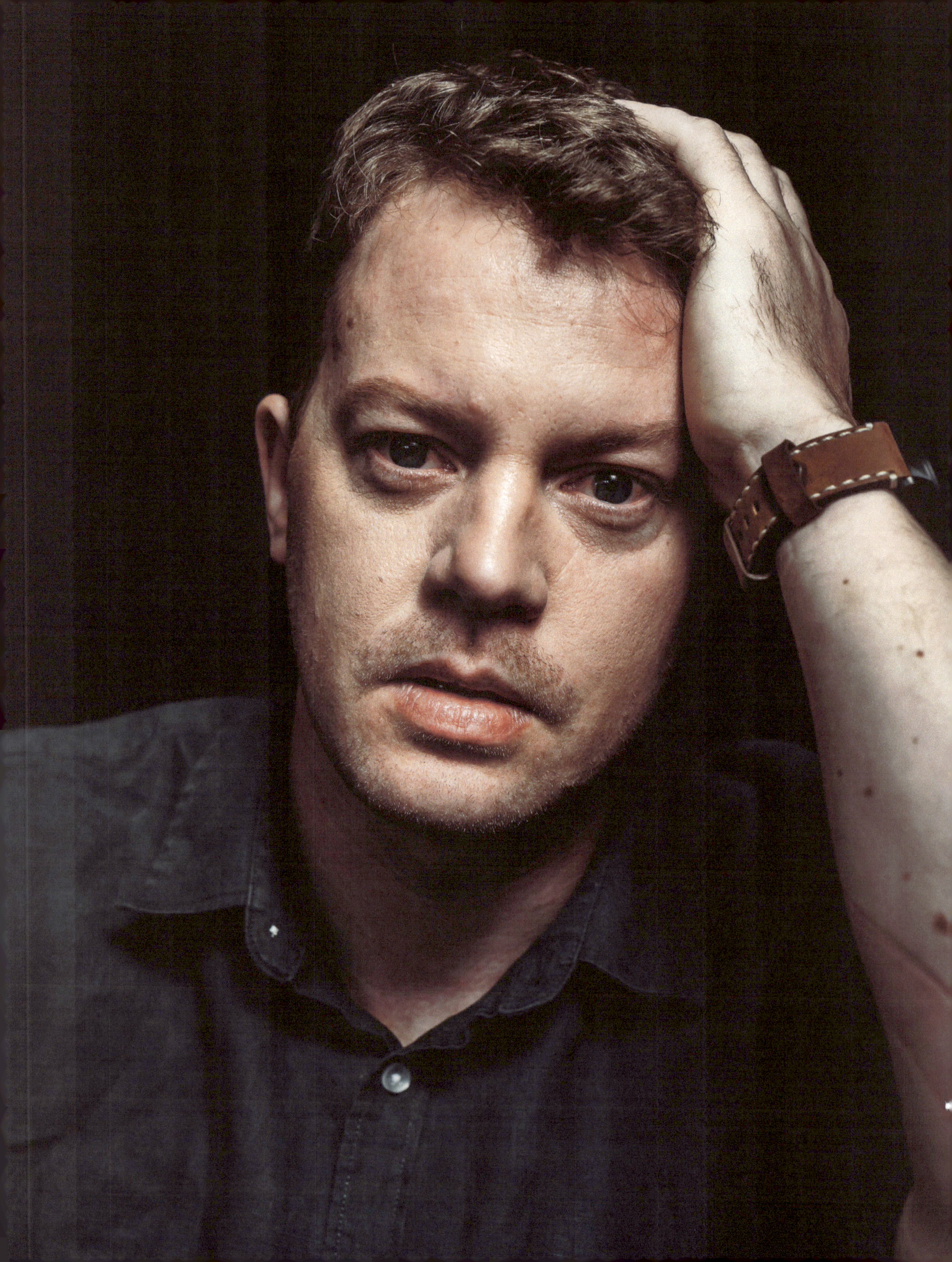

Dave Sayers

Rebuilding a Life: Story of Recovery and Renewal

Dave Sayers grew up in the countryside of Gippsland, Victoria, surrounded by farmland and the rhythms of rural life. His journey has been one of profound loss, resilience, and rebuilding, teaching him invaluable lessons about grief, mental health, and finding strength in adversity.

Life took a heartbreaking turn for Dave when his partner passed away in a car accident at just 21 years old. At the time, they had recently graduated from university and were making plans for a future filled with promise. "It flipped my world upside down," Dave reflects. "I'd faced death on the farm before, but this was a whole different level of pain."

Dave openly shares how the experience of grief was isolating. "What stood out the most was the silence, particularly from men. There's this cultural belief that being tough means keeping quiet, but that silence can be deafening. It left me feeling even more alone."

> *"Surrounding yourself with the right people makes all the difference."*

The loss took a toll on Dave's mental and physical health. "I lost weight, struggled to eat, and couldn't exercise. My mind and body just weren't the same. But I was fortunate to have support from family, friends, and programs like TAC, which provided access to counselling. That support was a lifeline."

Over the years, Dave worked through his grief, gradually finding a new sense of purpose. He reconnected with life, met a new partner, and now they share the joy of raising two young children. "It's a whole new world. We've even stayed close with my late partner's family, which has been a way to honour her memory and build something positive out of tragedy."

Today, Dave is a business owner and a passionate advocate for mental health awareness. His work often brings him into contact with elderly clients who face their own challenges with loss and grief. "I've learned to connect deeply with others because I know what it's like to go through something so life-changing."

Dave's involvement in the *Breaking the Barriers Through the Lens* project stems from a desire to challenge societal expectations around mental health. "People often don't consider mental health a disability, but it absolutely can be. It limits your ability to live, work, and connect. I want to break the stigma and show that it's okay to talk about these things."

He reflects on the importance of finding a support network. "I've been part of the Creating Success program for nearly five years, and it's been life-changing. You can't navigate grief or build a business without support. Surrounding yourself with the right people makes all the difference."

For Dave, breaking barriers means shattering perceptions about grief and mental health. "I want to encourage men, especially, to open up. Showing emotion isn't a weakness—it's a strength. We all go through loss, and talking about it helps us heal."

Dave finds joy in life's simple pleasures: music, hiking, riding motorbikes, and spending time with his family. "Living near the bush allows me to reconnect with nature, which is incredibly grounding. It reminds me to slow down and focus on what really matters."

Some of Dave's proudest achievements include his growing family and building a successful business. "Starting a business was daunting, but it's been rewarding. Connecting with customers and seeing the impact of our products has been incredibly fulfilling."

Looking to the future, Dave dreams of creating more freedom for his family. "We're planning to spend six months living in England in the next few years. It's a goal that felt impossible at one time, but now it's within reach."

His message to the world is one of hope and perseverance: "Don't let grief or mental health challenges limit you. Life might not turn out as you planned, but you can still find purpose and joy. Take it one step at a time, find your tribe, and never stop moving forward."

Don't let grief or mental health challenges limit you. Life might not turn out as you planned, but you can still find purpose and joy. Take it one step at a time, find your tribe, and never stop moving forward.

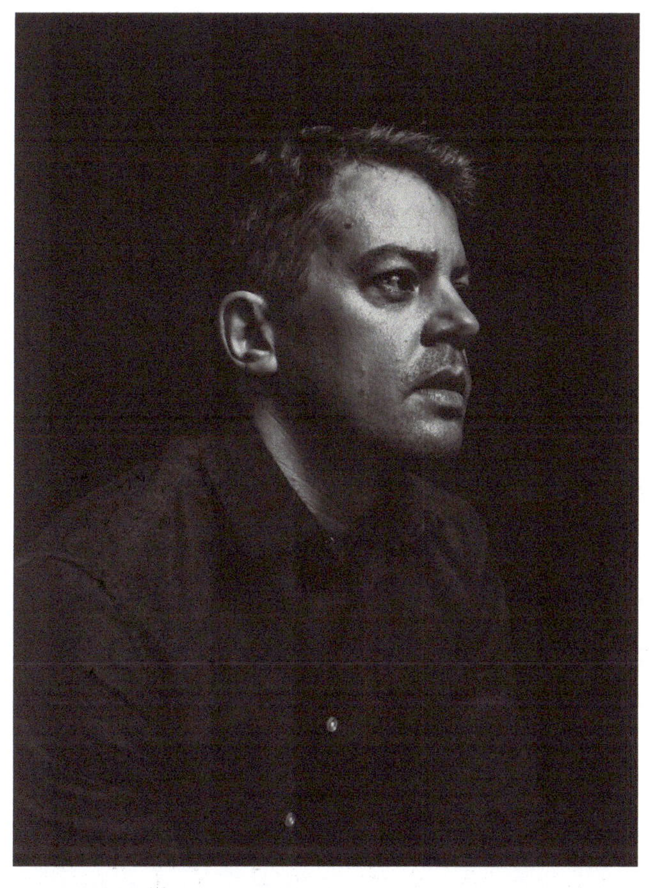

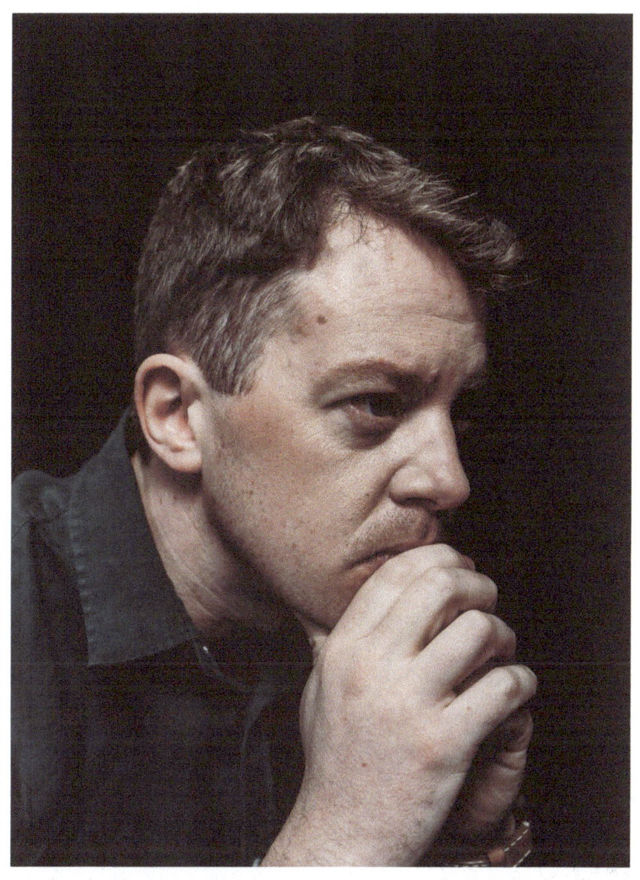

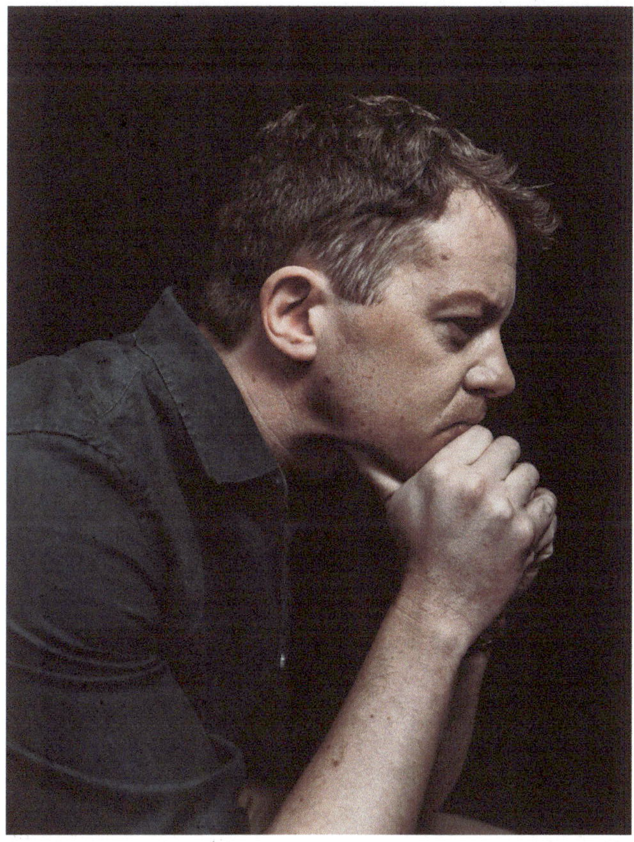

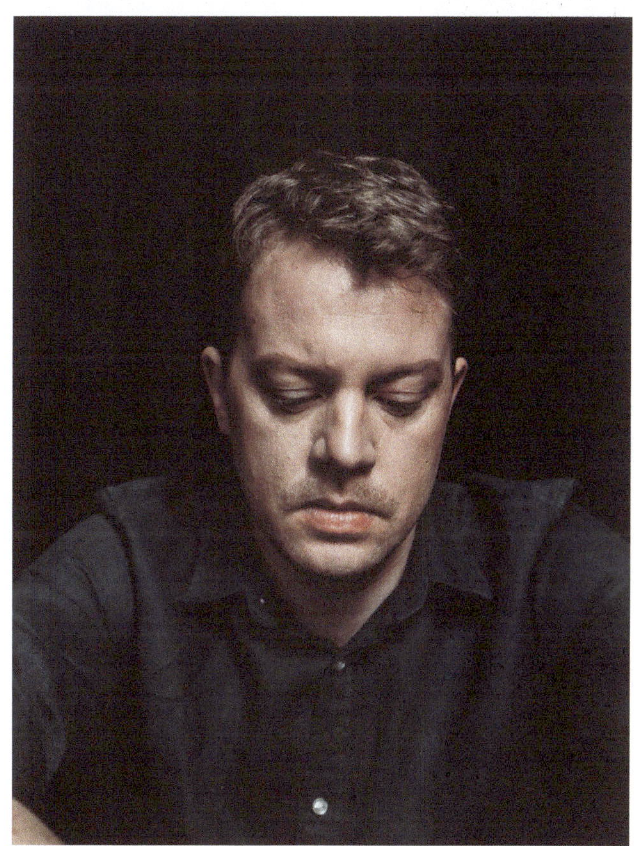

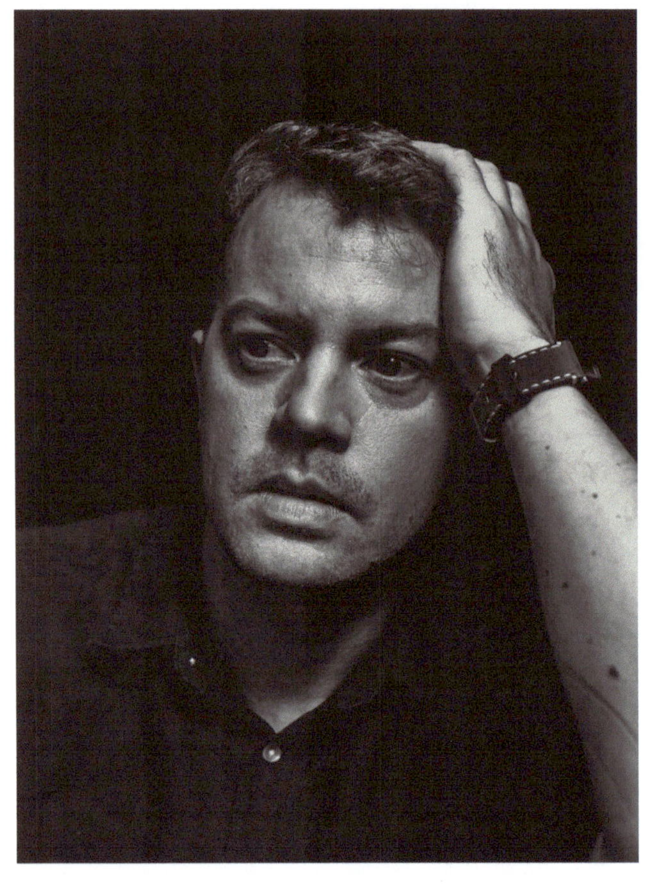
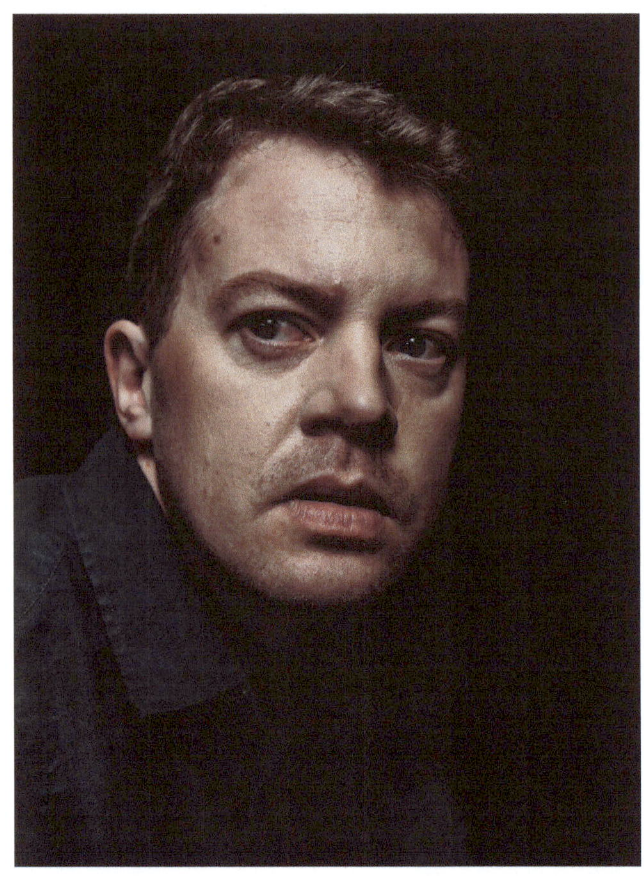
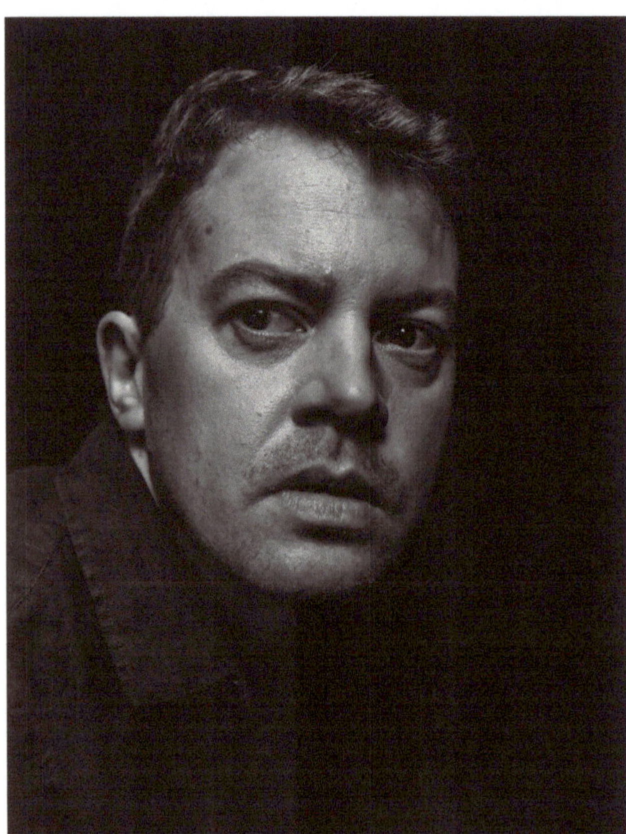
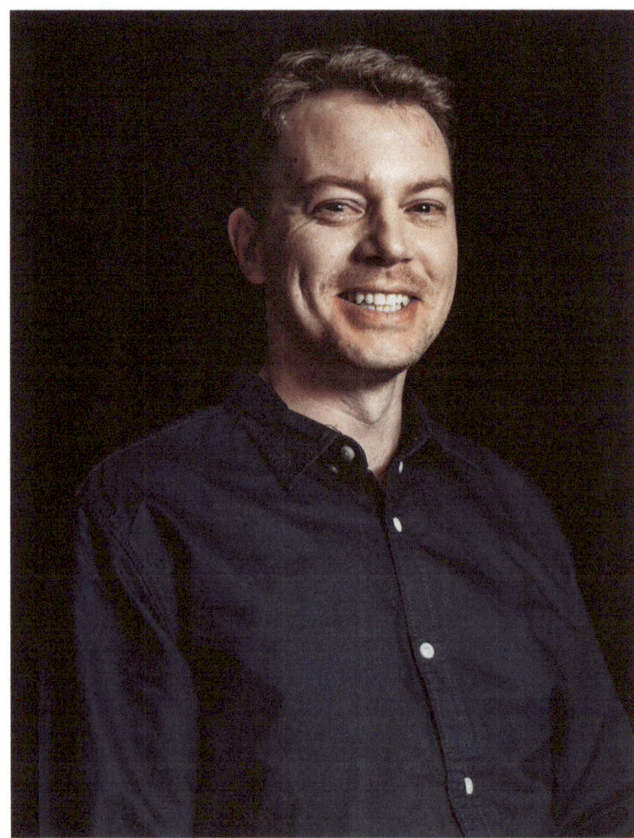

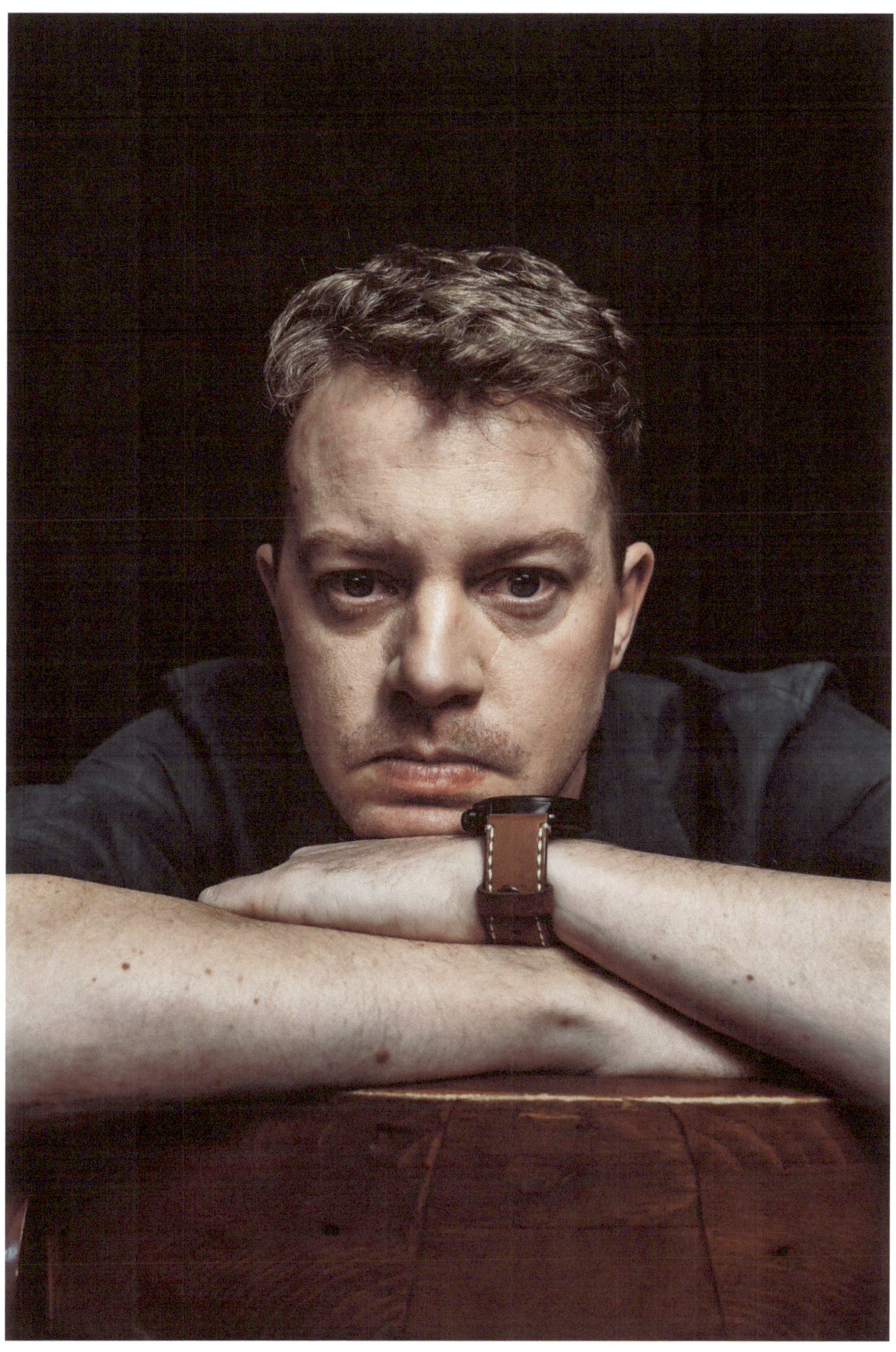

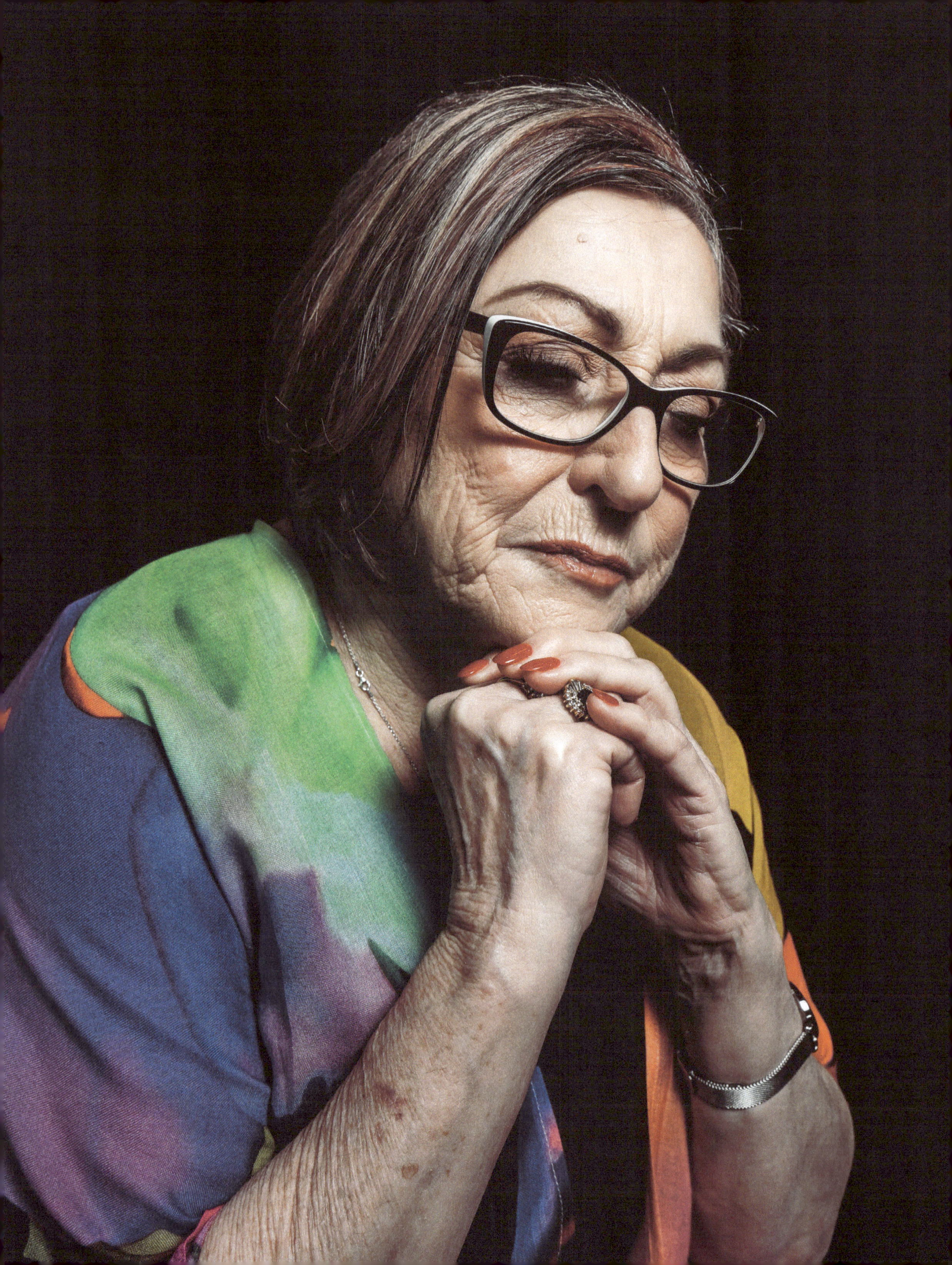

Deb Fribbins

Redefining Strength to Empowerment and Impact

Deb is a seasoned professional and passionate advocate who has spent decades breaking barriers in the workplace and beyond. Diagnosed with diabetes over 25 years ago, she has faced the challenges of her condition head-on, balancing her career, health, and personal life with determination and grace.

Originally from Adelaide, Deb began her career with Myer, securing a school holiday job that became a long-term opportunity. "Myer offered real training programs back then," she recalls. "I stayed for nearly 10 years before moving on to other retail giants like John Martins, David Jones, and eventually Target, where I worked for 26 years."

Deb's journey with diabetes started over two decades ago and was initially managed through diet. "For the first 15 years, it was diet-controlled, but as time went on, it became harder to manage. Diabetes isn't just a condition—it's a constant presence in your life, influencing every decision you make."

> *Education is key to breaking down these stereotypes.*

Her condition has impacted various aspects of her life, from weight struggles to stress-related complications like postural psoriasis. "Weight has always been a challenge," Deb admits. "It's not about eating huge meals but making the wrong choices when life gets busy. Working long hours in retail often meant skipping meals and relying on quick fixes like Coke and chips, which didn't help."

Despite these challenges, Deb has refused to let diabetes define her. "You make choices," she says. "Some people let a diagnosis stop them, but for me, it's about managing it the best I can and continuing to do what I love."

Breaking barriers has been a recurring theme in Deb's life. "I was the second-ever woman in South Australia to hold certain roles at Myer," she shares. "In the corsetry department, I was sent to meet stakeholders at Hickory to see if I was 'suitable.' Men dominated the corsetry industry, so being a woman in that space was groundbreaking."

Deb also confronts the stigma surrounding diabetes. "There's this misconception that diabetes is self-inflicted," she explains. "People assume it's caused by overeating or laziness, but that's not true. Education is key to breaking down these stereotypes."

Now retired from full-time retail, Deb channels her energy into helping others. She is a consultant for small businesses, assisting them in achieving growth and success. "I love seeing businesses thrive," she says. "My first client saw a 48% increase in sales in one month—that was such a rewarding moment."

Her involvement with Rotary has become a cornerstone of her life. "Rotary is my family," Deb says. "The people are incredible, and the work we do together makes a real difference. I also started the Geelong Art Show as a charity initiative, which has been a labour of love."

Deb's hobbies include art classes, though she humbly claims she "can't paint." Her works hang proudly in her home, a testament to her willingness to step outside her comfort zone. "Art has been a surprising joy," she admits. "It's about finding new ways to express myself."

When asked about her goals, Deb focuses on both personal and professional aspirations. "I want to live to see my grandchildren grow up and to continue supporting my kids, even though they're adults now," she says. "Professionally, I aim to leave a mark in retail by helping small businesses succeed."

Deb's message to the world is one of empowerment and action: "Don't let a disability or diagnosis stop you. Find what motivates you and pursue it with everything you've got. Disabilities don't define you—they're just part of the journey."

Participating in this project has been a meaningful experience for Deb. "It's about showing that disabilities come in many forms, visible and invisible. It's about inspiring others to take control of their lives and make the most of every opportunity."

Deb's story is a testament to resilience, advocacy, and the power of breaking barriers. Her journey reminds us that with determination and a supportive community, anything is possible.

Don't let a disability or diagnosis stop you. Find what motivates you and pursue it with everything you've got. Disabilities don't define you—they're just part of the journey.

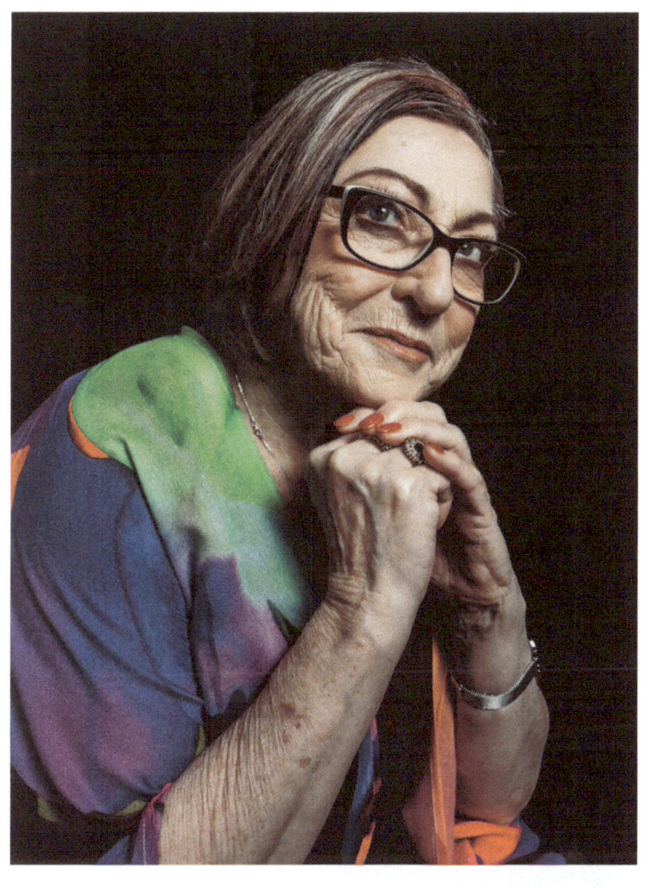
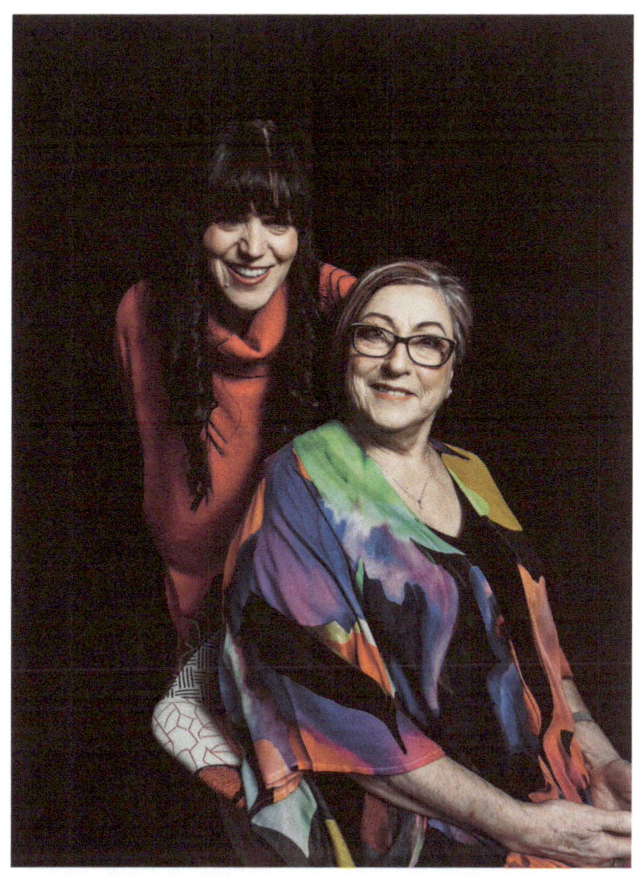
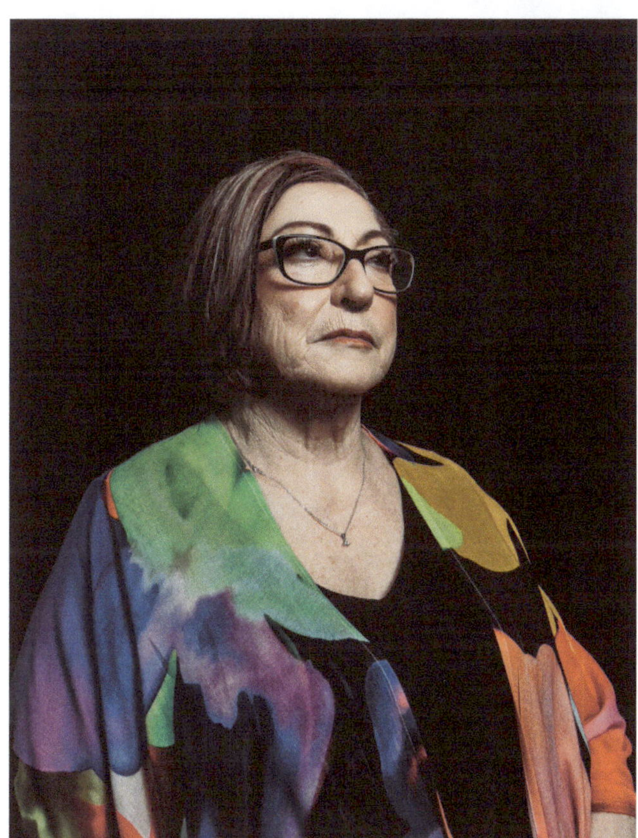
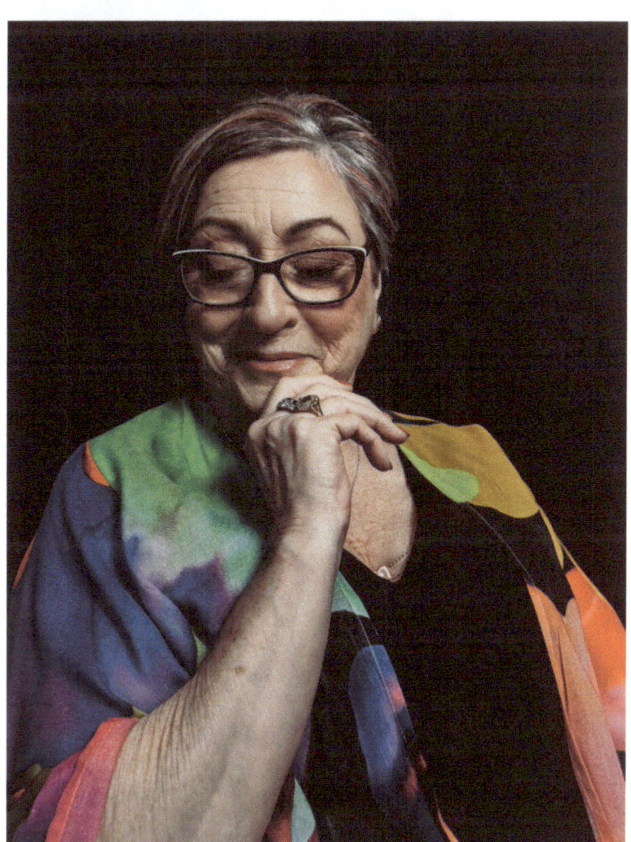

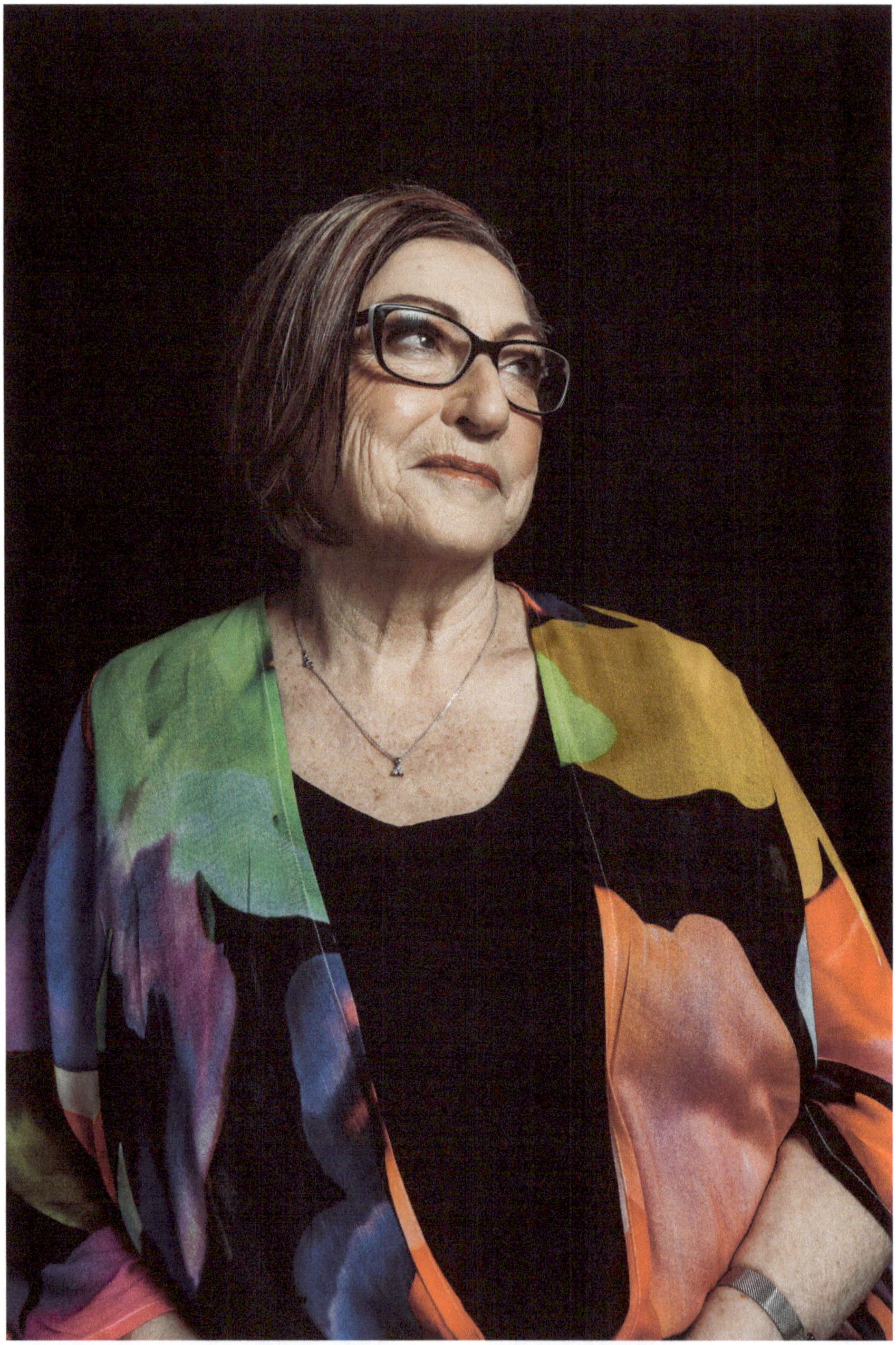

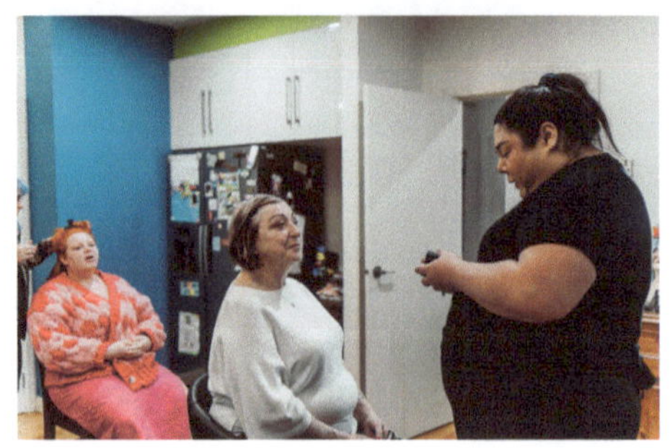

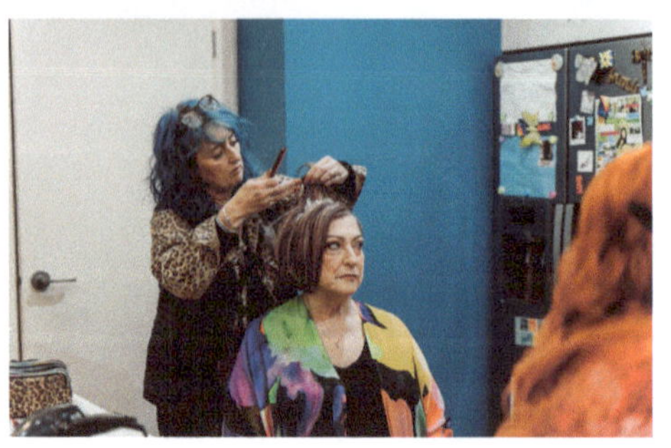

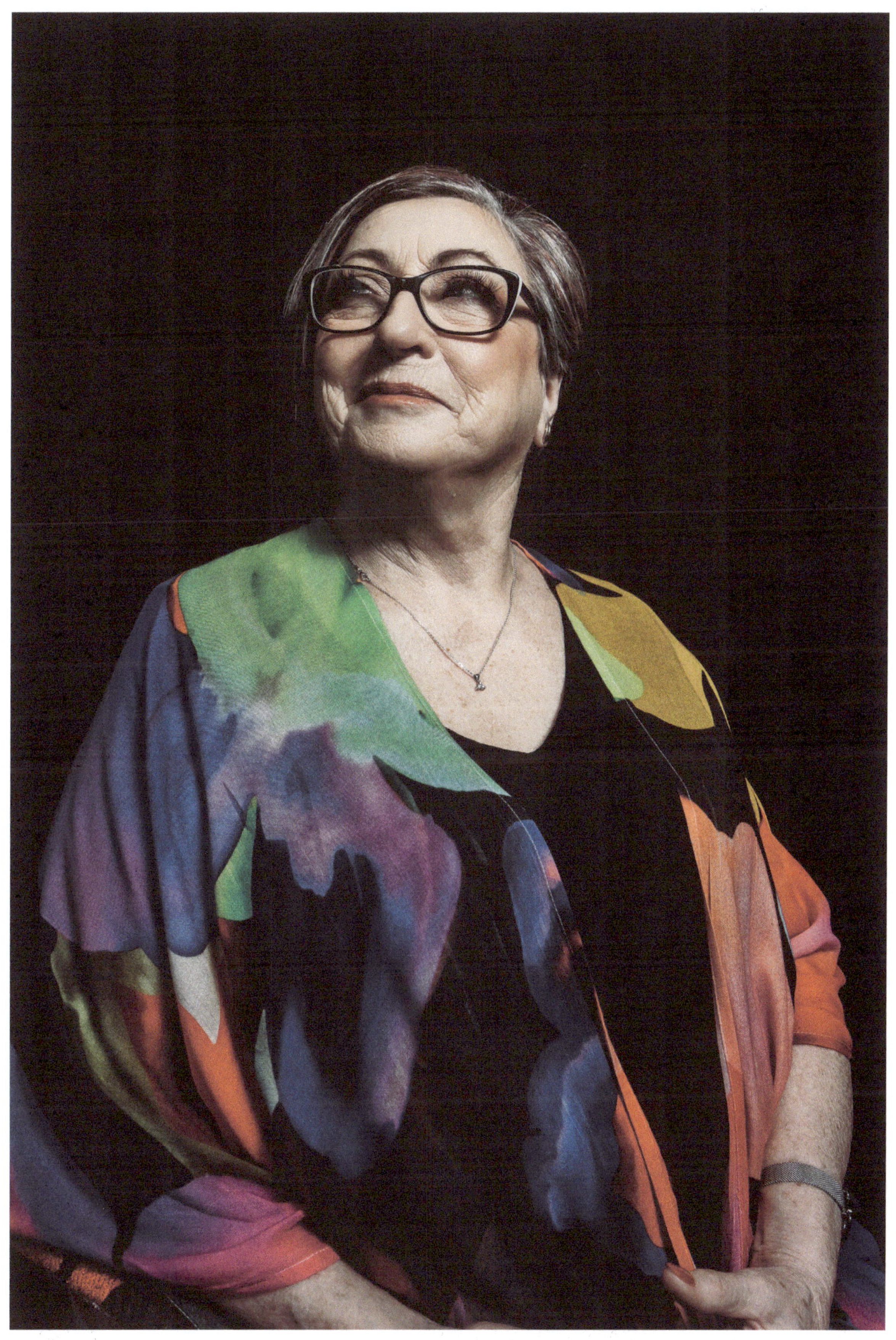

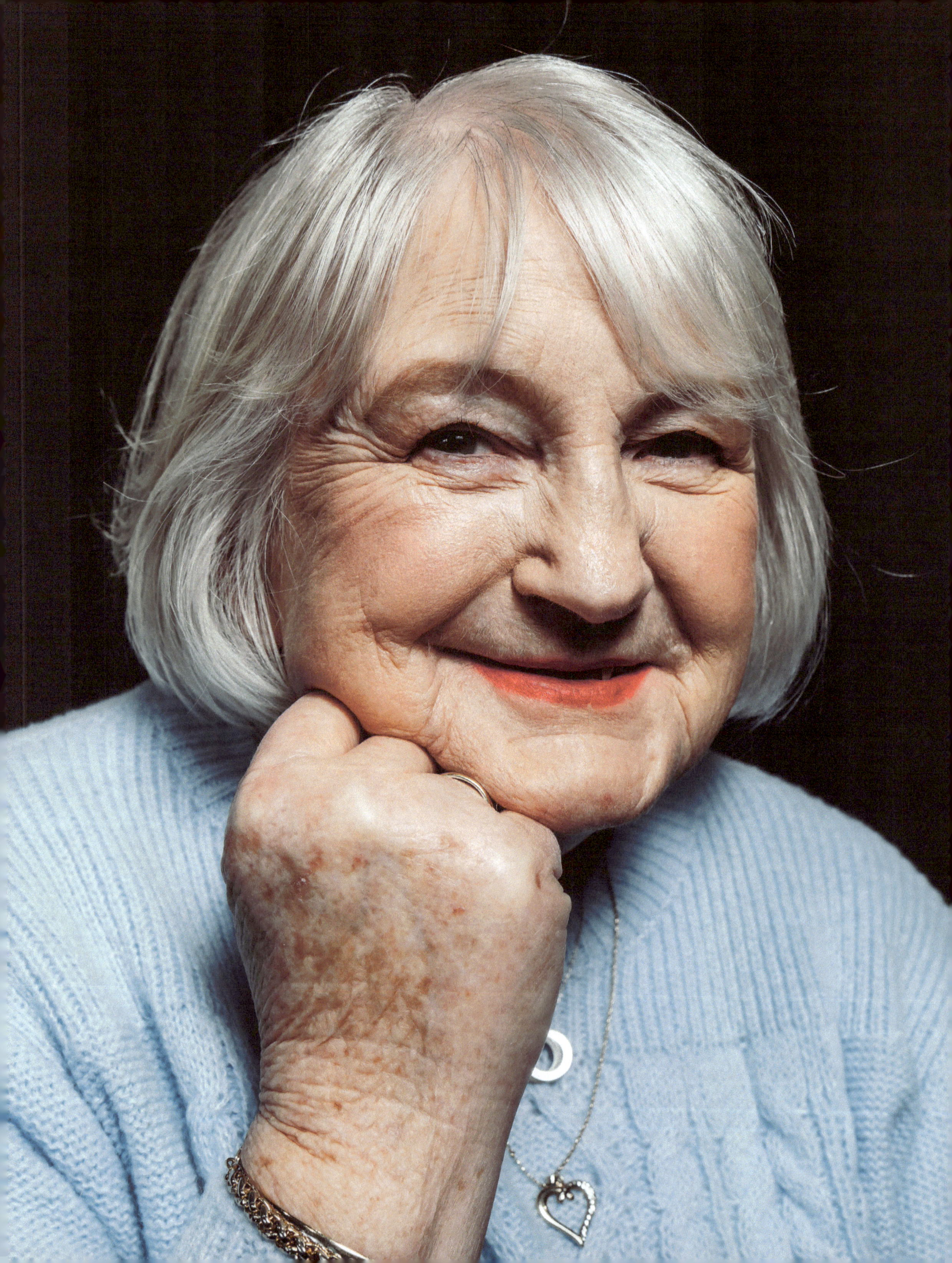

Diane Barclay

Laughter and Strength: A Philosophy of Going Under, Around, and Through Life's Walls

Diane is a proud Geelong native, is living proof that age and a diagnosis don't define a person. At nearly 75 years old, Diane continues to embrace life with humour, determination, and an unshakable spirit. Diagnosed with multiple sclerosis (MS) in 2003, Diane has found ways to adapt, thrive, and inspire others along the way.

"I've always been a housewife, but I've had various part-time jobs over the years," Diane recalls. "I've driven a tucker truck, cleaned schools and houses, and even did piecework sewing collars on shirts and zips on skirts. I loved that I could work from home and still be there for my kids."

Today, Diane fills her days with hobbies that bring her joy. "Knitting, crocheting, embroidery, and baking cakes are my passions. I don't love cooking meat, but cake decorating is a different story—it's creative and rewarding. And, of course, I've always got a good joke to tell."

Diane's humour is infectious, and she shares a joke wherever she goes, even if she sometimes fumbles with the punchline. "Laughter is so important," she says. "It helps you get through the tough times."

For Diane, breaking barriers means defying expectations and refusing to be boxed in by her disability. "People think someone with MS can't do certain things, but I've proven them wrong time and again," she says. "I've been on the back of a racing sidecar around the Broadford racetrack and travelled to Penrith and Tasmania on my husband's motorcycle. I also do all my gardening—though I leave the lawn mowing to someone else."

Her resilience is reflected in her message to others: "Don't let it take your life. MS might make things harder, but it doesn't mean you can't live. You just have to adapt and find new ways to do the things you love. Focus on what you can do, not what you can't."

Diane credits her daughter as a significant source of inspiration. "What she's achieved is incredible. Watching her has made me push myself further than I ever thought I could. She's a role model to me."

Participating in this project has been a step outside Diane's comfort zone. "I'm not usually one to do things like this, but I thought, why not? It's been wonderful, and I've enjoyed every moment."

Through her involvement in art classes, Diane has discovered a newfound love for painting. "I might need a little help getting started, but I've learned to embrace it. I even incorporated crochet doilies into some of my recent works—it's exciting to try new things."

Diane hopes her story will inspire others to keep pushing forward. "Life changes, and sometimes you have to find a new way to do things. But that doesn't mean you stop living. Whether it's through art, laughter, or just getting out of bed each day, there's always something worth doing."

Her final words are filled with gratitude: "Thank you to my family and everyone who's supported me along the way. You've helped me see that even when life is challenging, it's still beautiful."

“

Life changes, and sometimes you have to find a new way to do things. But that doesn't mean you stop living. Whether it's through art, laughter, or just getting out of bed each day, there's always something worth doing.

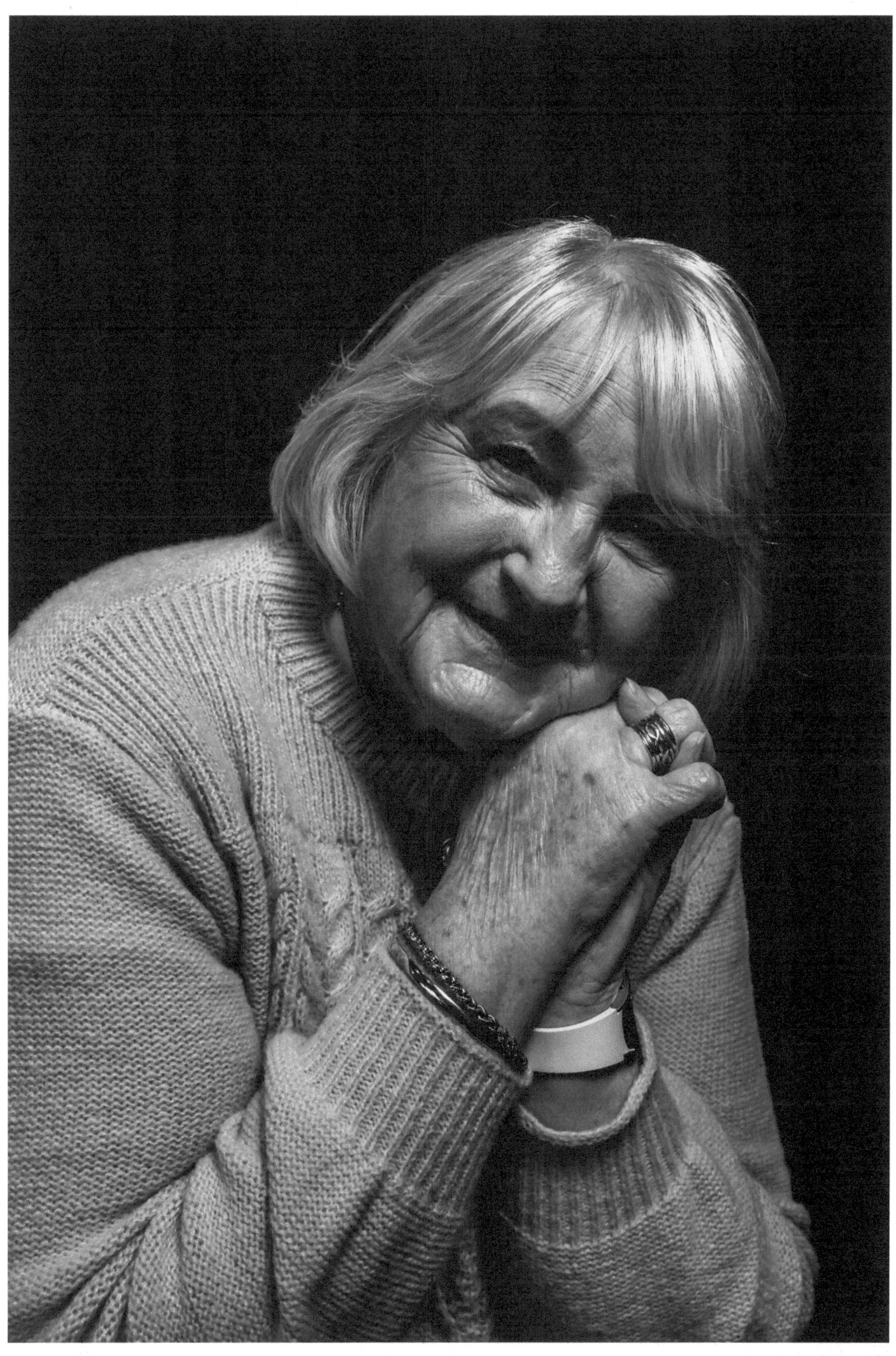

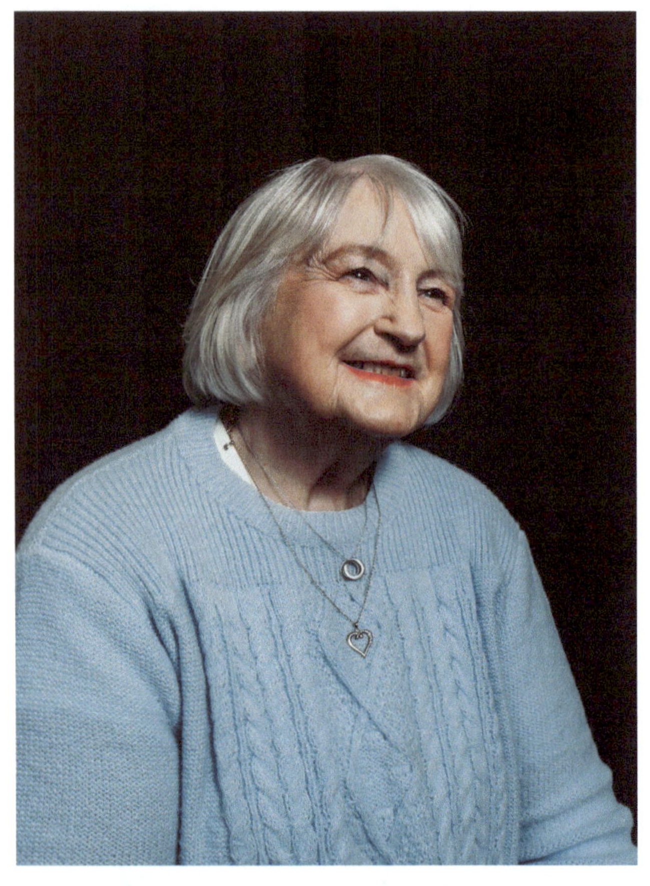
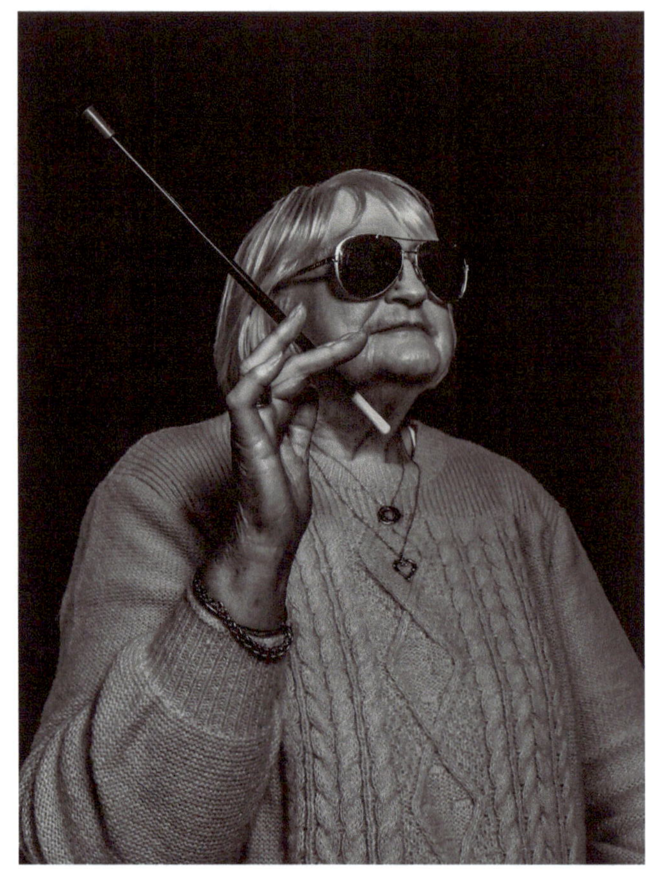
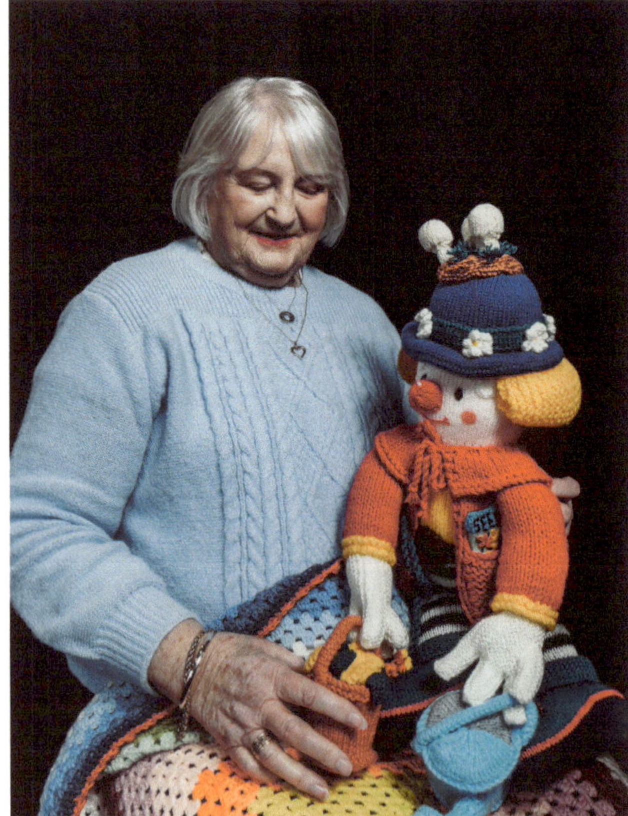
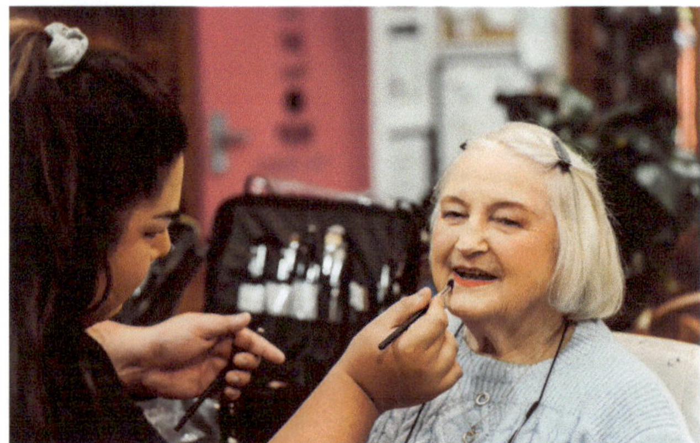
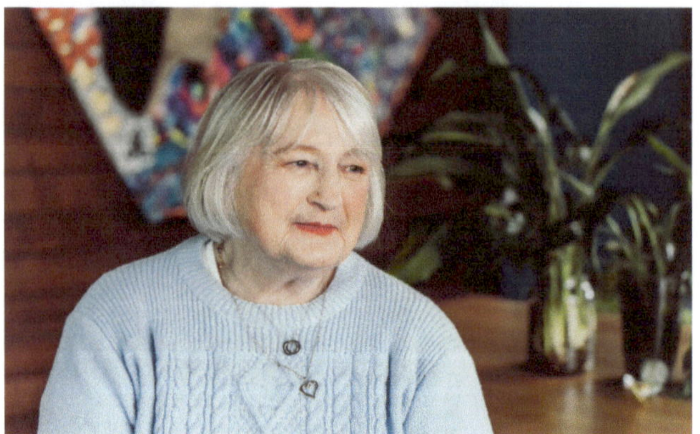

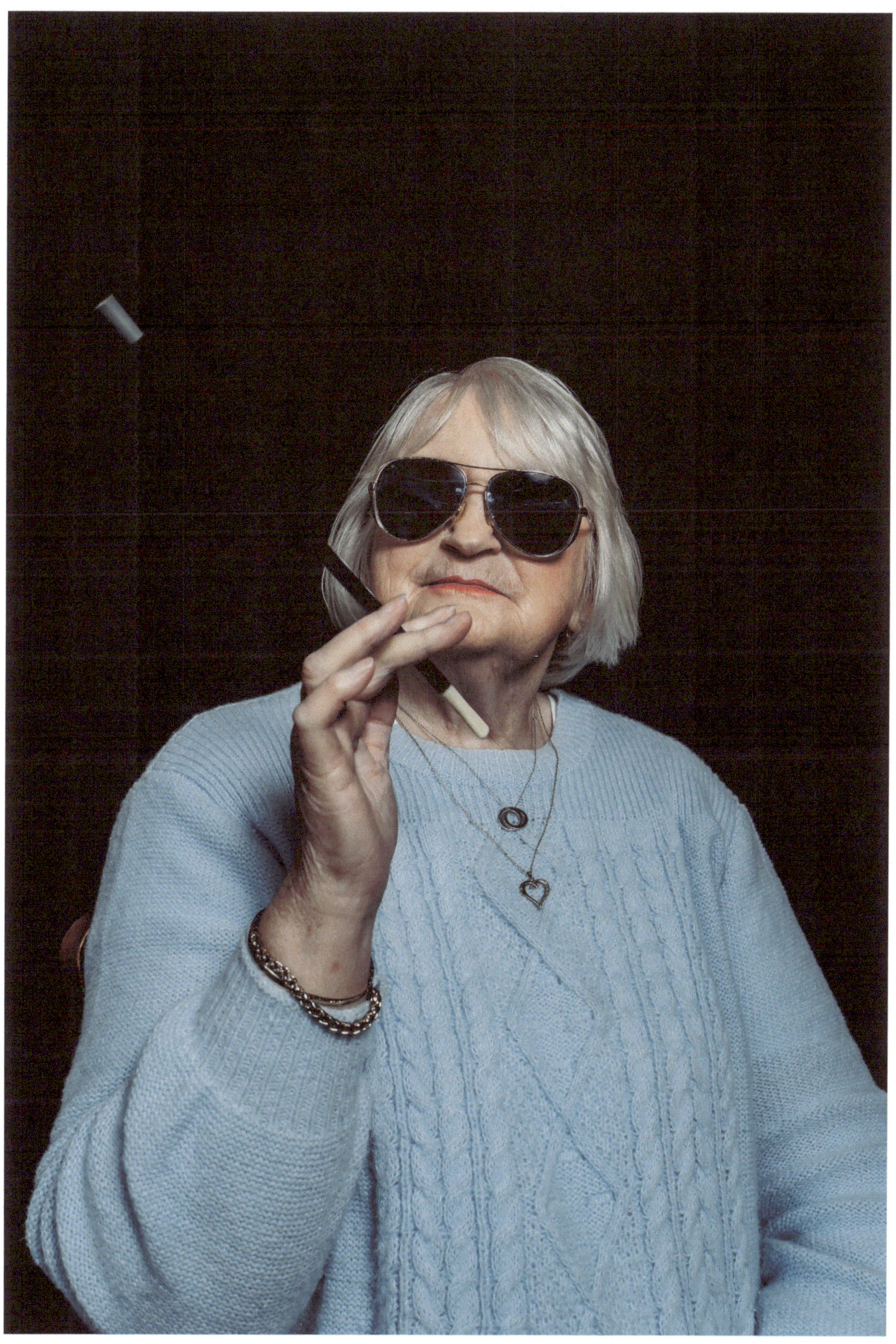

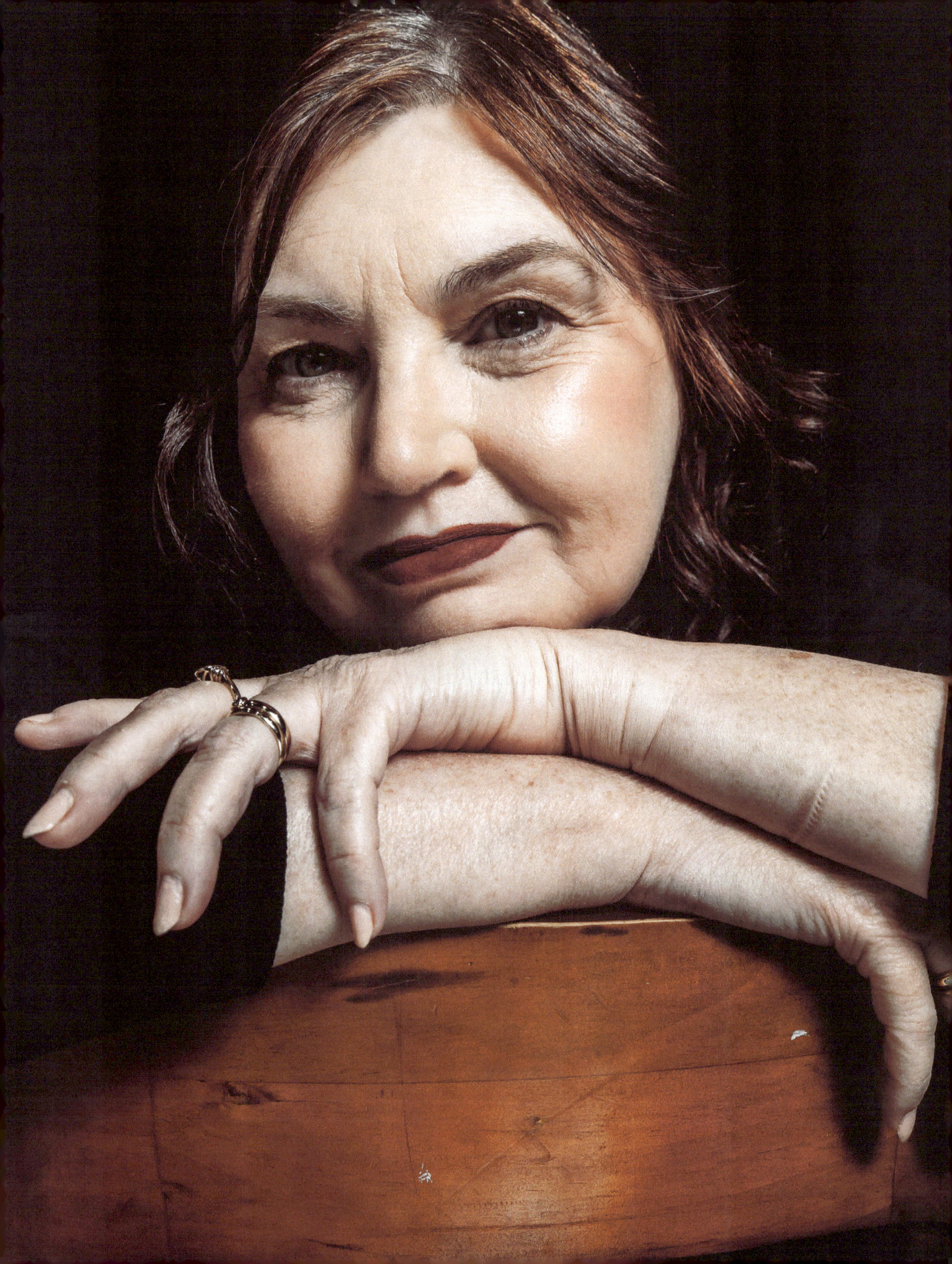

Donna Bolch

Burning Bright: Fight for Strength and Identity

Donna Bolch is a 52-year-old mother, wife, and artist who approaches life with humour, resilience, and a deep appreciation for the simple joys of family and creativity. Living with fibromyalgia and Functional Neurological Disorder (FND), Donna has faced a host of challenges, yet her journey is one of empowerment, advocacy, and finding purpose despite adversity.

Fibromyalgia and FND bring over 200 symptoms, including constant pain, cognitive issues, and seizures. "My whole body hurts 24/7," Donna explains. "There's burning, pins and needles, and a sense that my nervous system is firing on all cylinders all the time. It's a lot to handle." Diagnosed with fibromyalgia after a five-year journey of uncertainty, Donna initially spiralled into despair. "Hearing there was no cure was devastating. It felt like my life was over. But with medication, support, and a lot of inner work, I've learned to manage and accept it."

Acceptance has been key to Donna's growth. "It's not that I like having these conditions—I don't. But if you don't accept it, you spend all your energy fighting it. And with something like this, energy is precious."

Through it all, Donna's focus remains on being a positive role model for her two children. "Every day is a challenge, but I want my kids to see that no matter how big the obstacles, you can keep moving forward. Life is full of mountains to climb, but with determination, you can overcome them."

Art has become a significant outlet for Donna. "I love painting and using my art to express what living with fibromyalgia feels like. Some of my works illustrate the compounding symptoms, and sharing them has started conversations that bring awareness to the condition. Art has also introduced me to new friends and created a sense of community."

For Donna, breaking barriers means defying societal expectations and stereotypes around disability. "People often assume we can't do anything because of our conditions, but we can—and we do. It's about proving to ourselves and others that we're capable of much more than they realise."

Her support system has been a vital part of her journey. "My husband is incredible, as are my kids, my parents, and my sister. They're always there when I need them. And my friends and community have been amazing, too. They remind me that I'm not alone."

Donna is also a model and public speaker, using her platform to raise awareness and inspire others. “In 2022, I shared my life story on stage in front of 300 people, including my kids. It was nerve-wracking but so empowering. Hearing people say I was an inspiration made it all worthwhile.”

Participating in this project was an opportunity to push Donna out of her comfort zone and advocate for more research and awareness about fibromyalgia and FND. “These conditions affect so many people, especially women, yet they don’t get the attention they deserve. I hope this project sparks more conversations and drives change.”

Donna’s daily joy comes from family dinners around the coffee table, doing quizzes from the newspaper, and spending time with her husband and kids. “Those moments are sacred. They remind me what life is really about.”

When asked about her role models, Donna cites her family as her greatest inspiration. “My husband and kids make me want to be a better person every day. And if I had to pick a celebrity, it would be Lady Gaga. She has fibromyalgia too, and she’s shown that you can still achieve incredible things despite it.”

Donna’s message to the world is one of inclusion and action: “We’re here, and we have so much to contribute. Don’t forget about us when you’re planning events or spaces. Disability doesn’t mean we’re less—it just means we do things differently.”

Through her art, advocacy, and unwavering determination, Donna continues to break barriers and inspire others to live life fully, no matter the challenges they face.

We’re here, and we have so much to contribute. Don’t forget about us when you’re planning events or spaces. Disability doesn’t mean we’re less—it just means we do things differently.

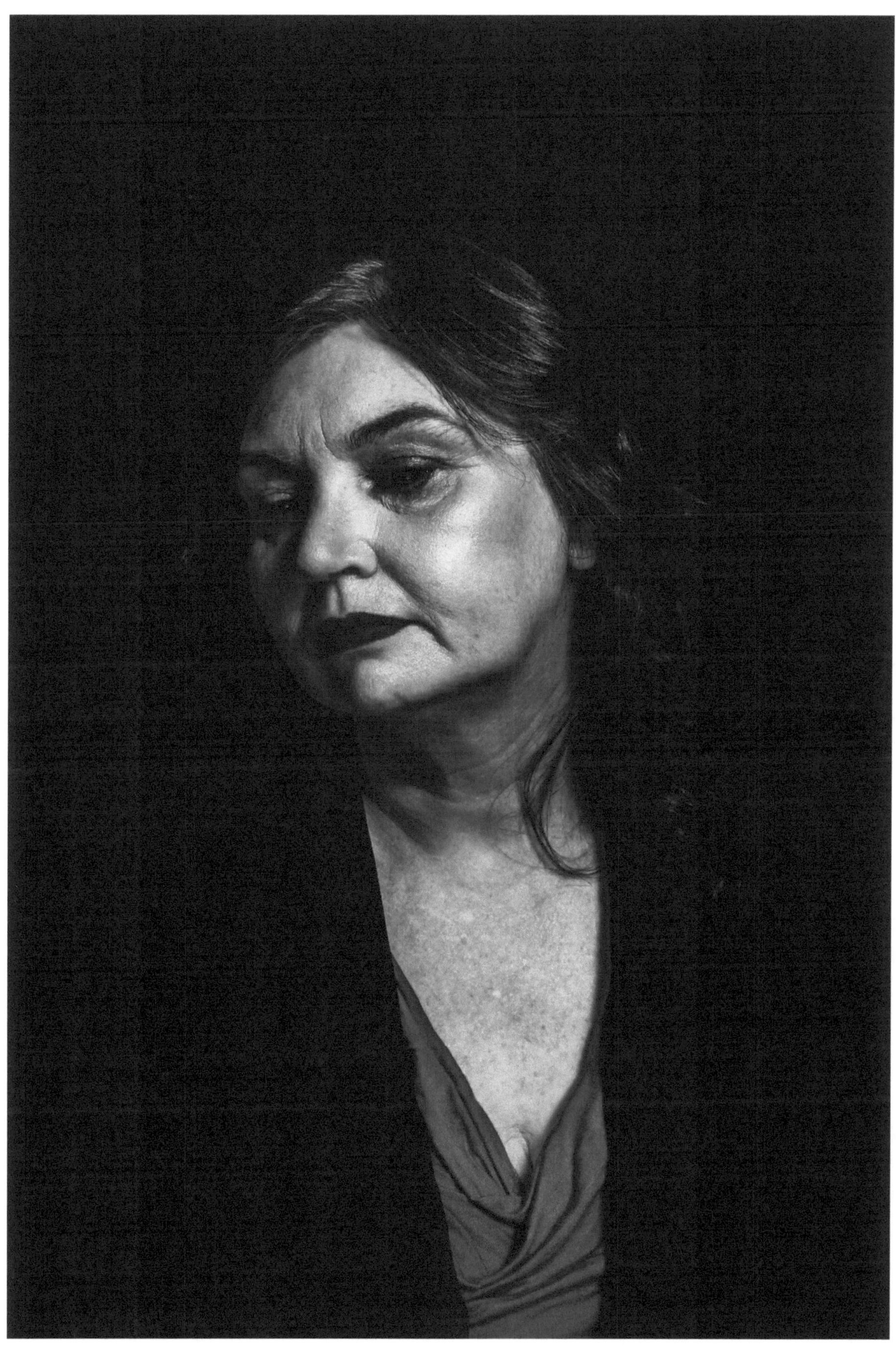

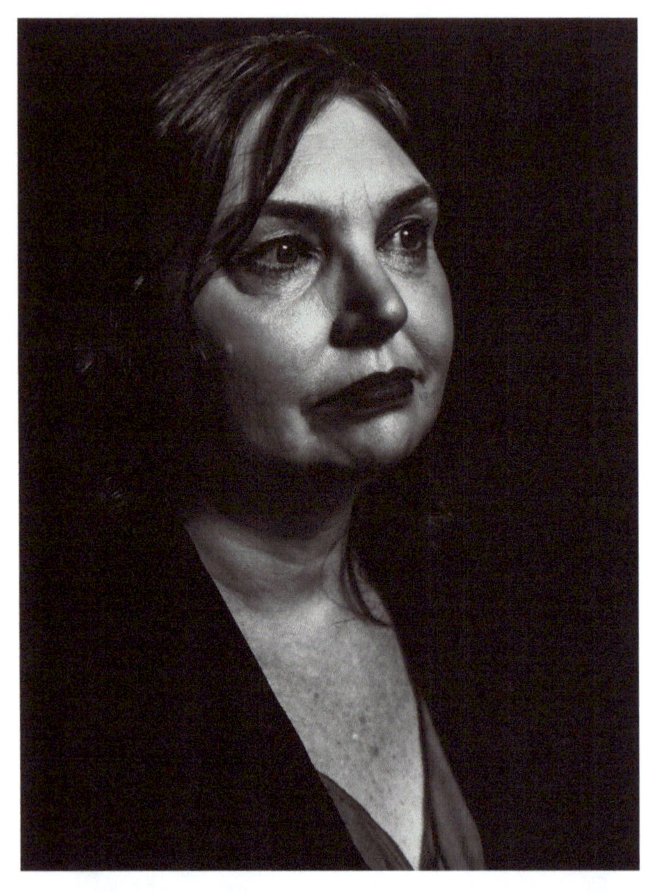

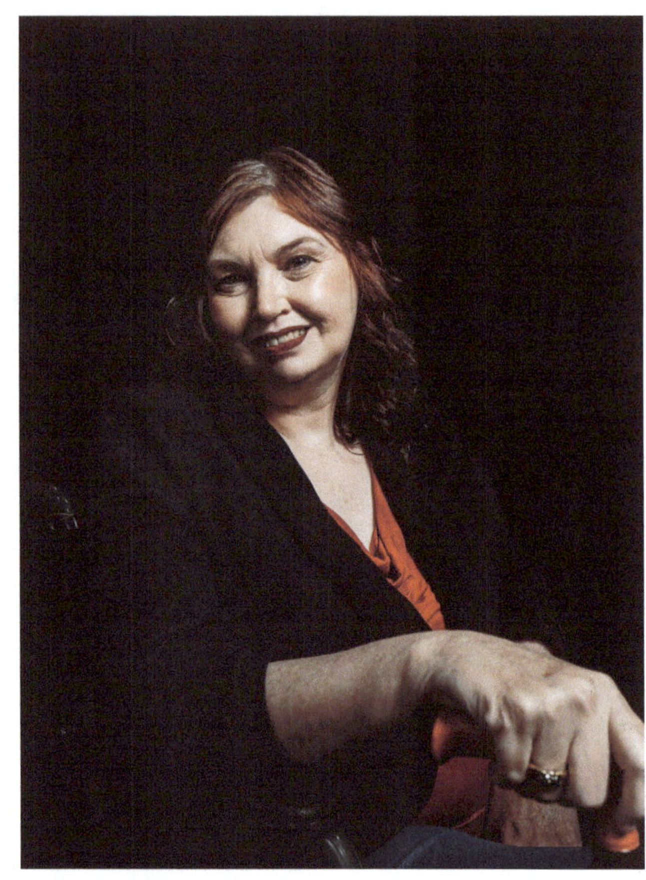

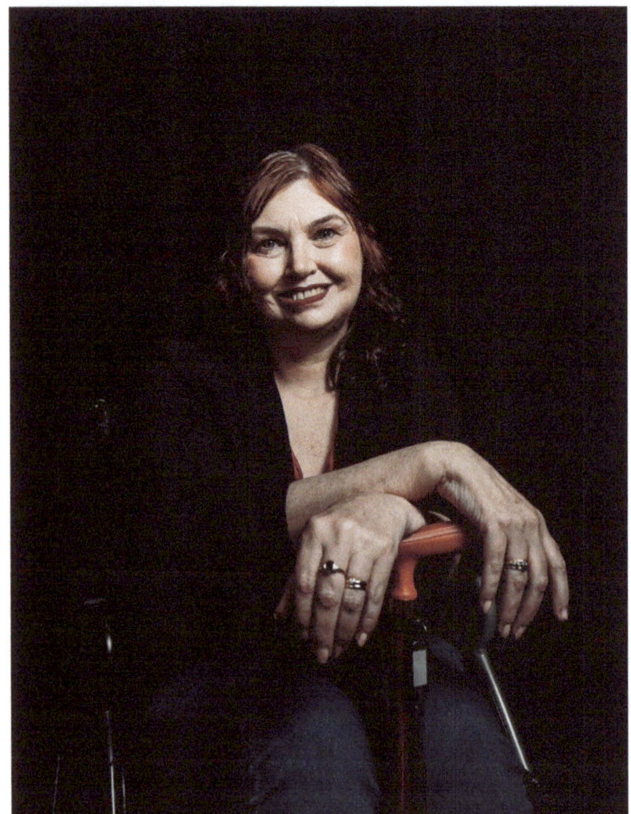

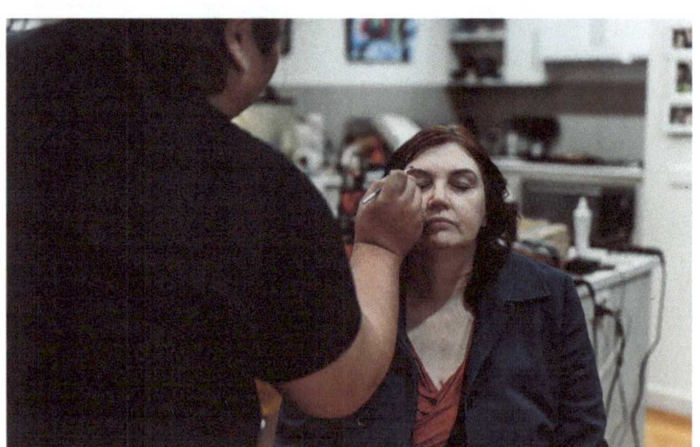

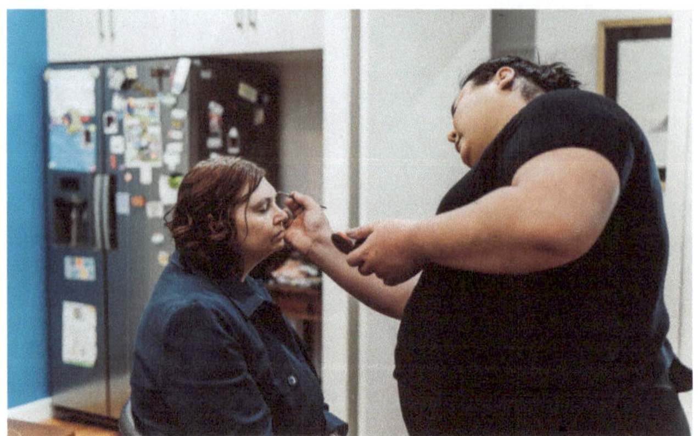

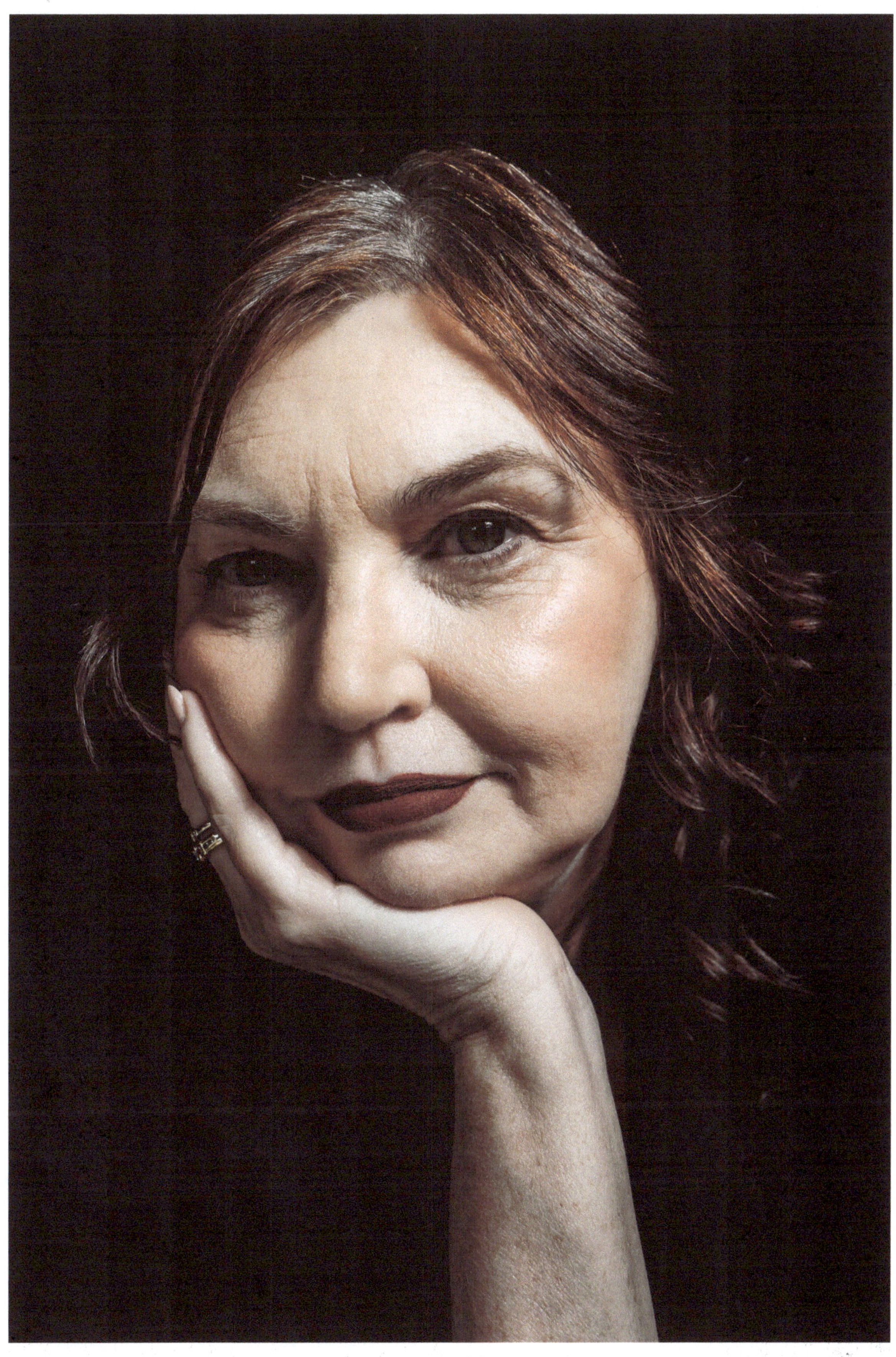

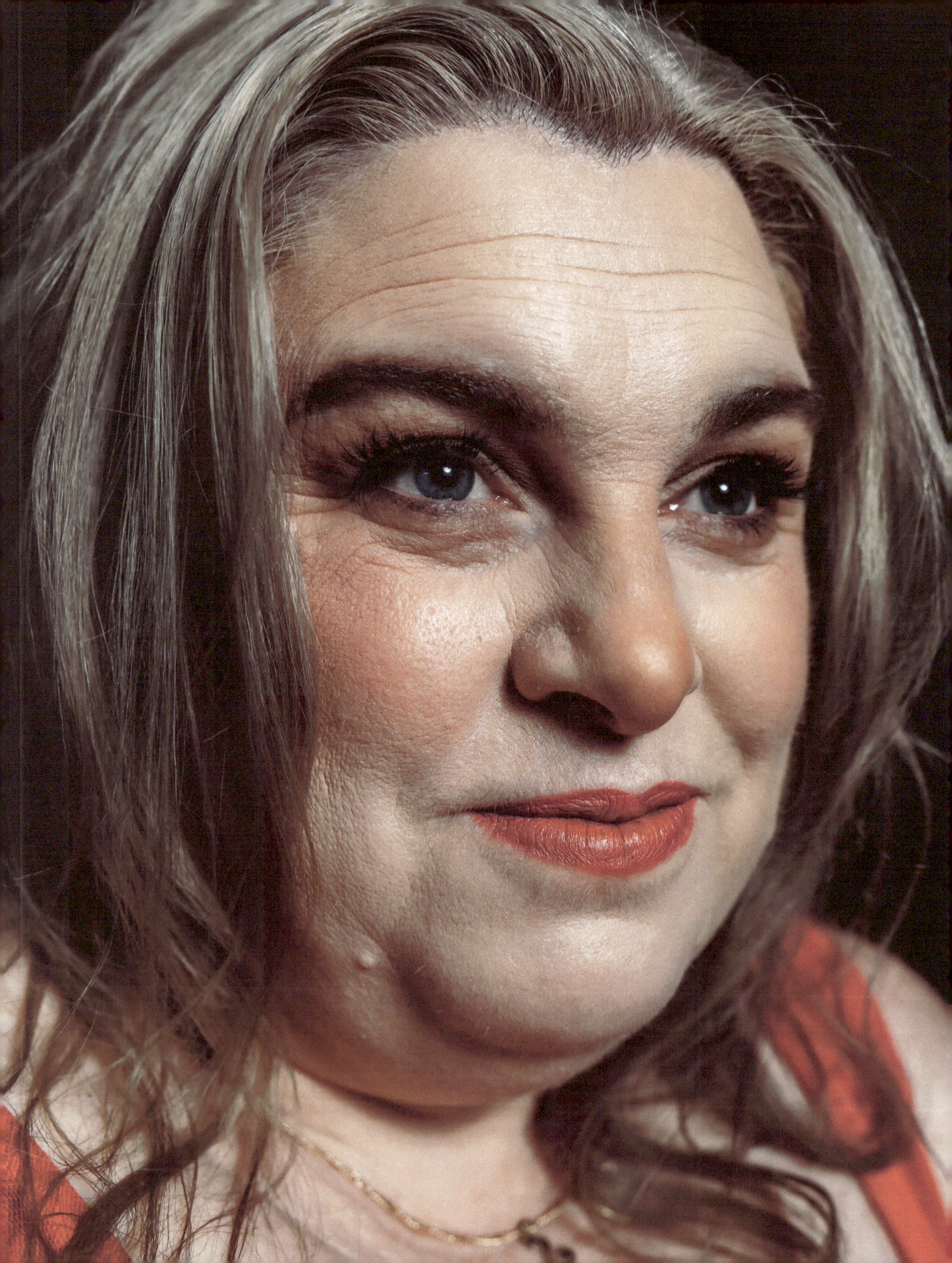

Fiona Demark

Finding a Way: A Journey of Going Under, Around, and Through Adversity

Fiona, originally from far western New South Wales, is a proud mother, artist, and photographer who has faced the challenges of disability with grace and determination. Diagnosed with Rod-Cone Dystrophy at a young age, she was told she might one day go blind—a prospect filled with uncertainty. Yet, Fiona has never let her disability define her or hold her back.

"I was lucky in a sense," Fiona shares. "My older sister had already been diagnosed, so when I came along, my parents were quick to recognise the signs. Resources were limited where we lived, so we often had to travel to Adelaide for medical care. But I've always approached life by making the best of what I have."

For Fiona, her disability has been both a challenge and a teacher. "Growing up in a small town, I just wanted to fit in. It took years to go from wanting to be like everyone else to embracing who I am. Now, I see my disability as part of what makes me strong and unique."

Breaking barriers has been a constant theme in Fiona's life. "It's about finding the obstacles, understanding them, and figuring out how to work around them. Sometimes, you can't go over a wall, but you can go under it or around it. It's about adapting and not giving up."

> *Disability doesn't mean you can't do things. It means you might have to do them differently.*

Fiona, a mother to two daughters aged 18 and 20, counts them among her proudest achievements. "They're incredible young women, and watching them grow into who they are has been a joy. They inspire me as much as I hope to inspire them."

An artist at heart, Fiona has always loved storytelling, which eventually led her to write a book reflecting on her teenage years and the challenges she faced. "Writing the book was a way to process my trauma and turn it into something meaningful. It's about the bumps along the road and how I made it out the other side."

When asked about her message to others facing challenges, Fiona is clear: "Disability doesn't mean you can't do things. It means you might have to do them differently. Be proud of who you are. Don't hide, and don't let anyone make you feel ashamed."

For Fiona, participating in this project is about breaking down misconceptions and showing that disability doesn't limit potential. "I want people to know that being different is nothing to be ashamed of. We all have something unique to offer."

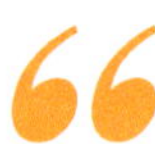

It's about finding the obstacles, understanding them, and figuring out how to work around them. Sometimes, you can't go over a wall, but you can go under it or around it. It's about adapting and not giving up.

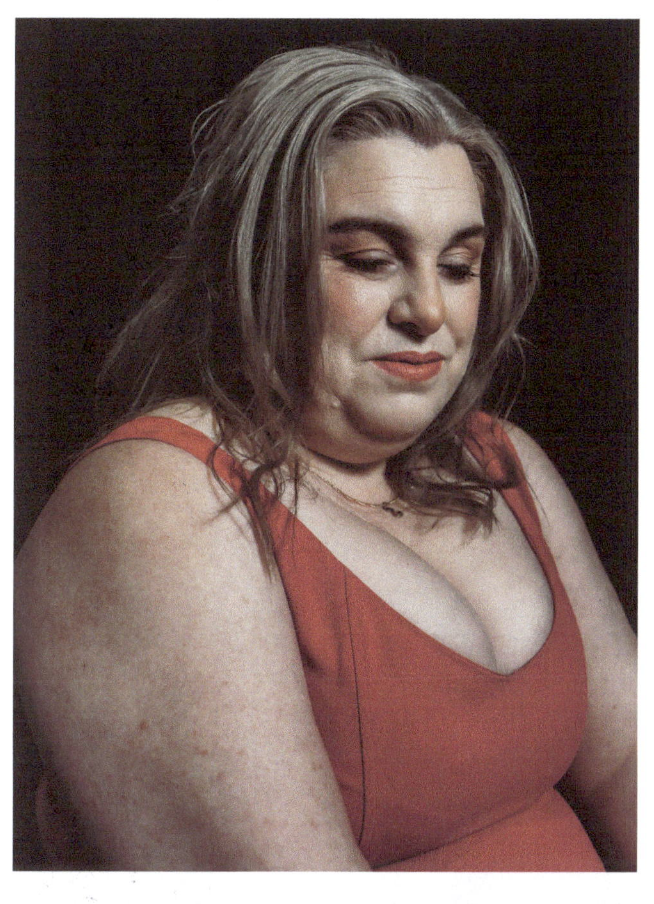

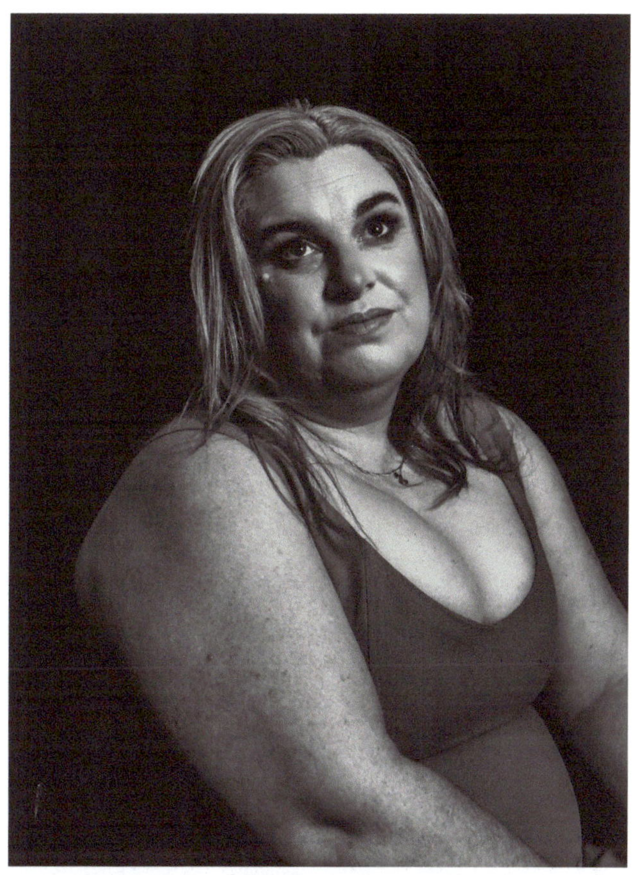

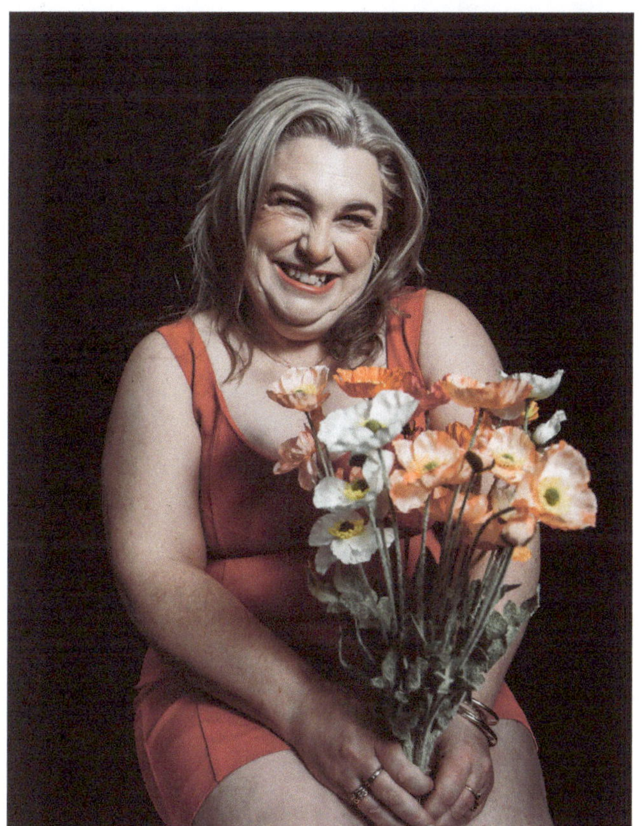

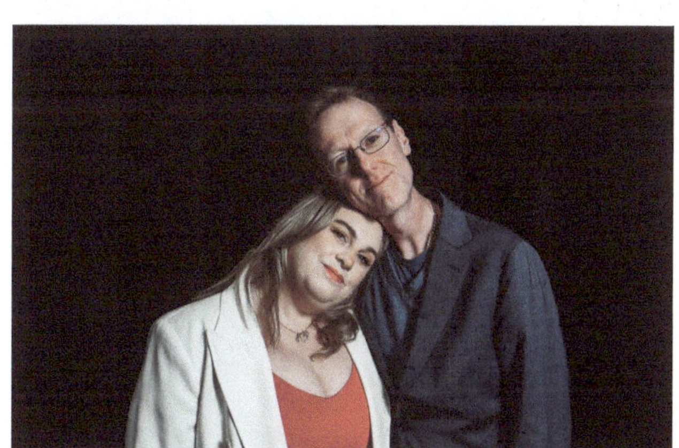

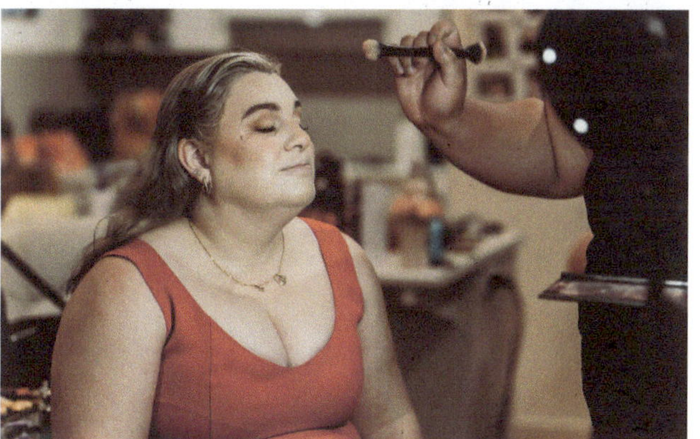

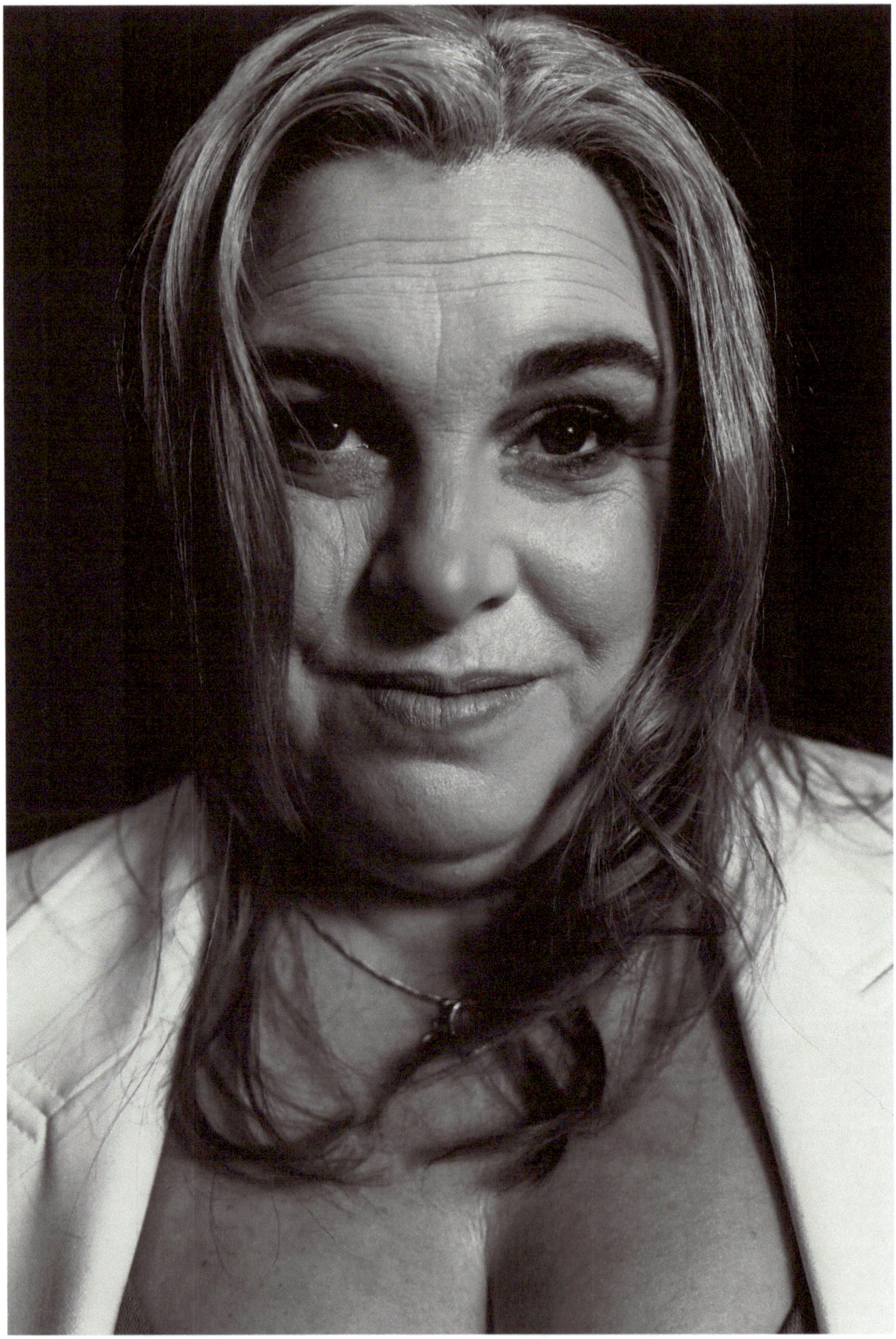

Be proud of who you are. Don't hide, and don't let anyone make you feel ashamed.

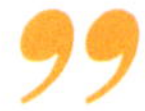

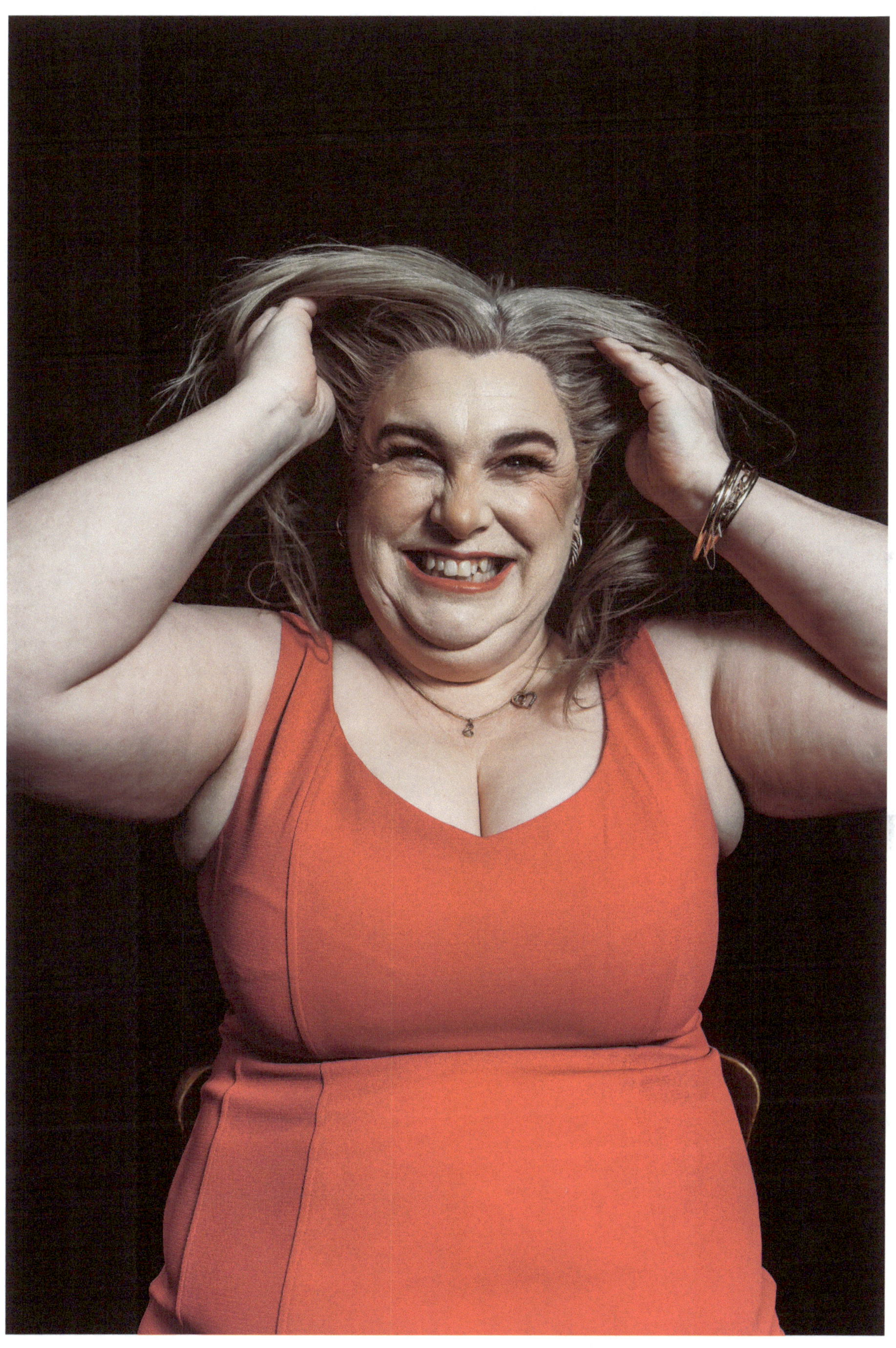

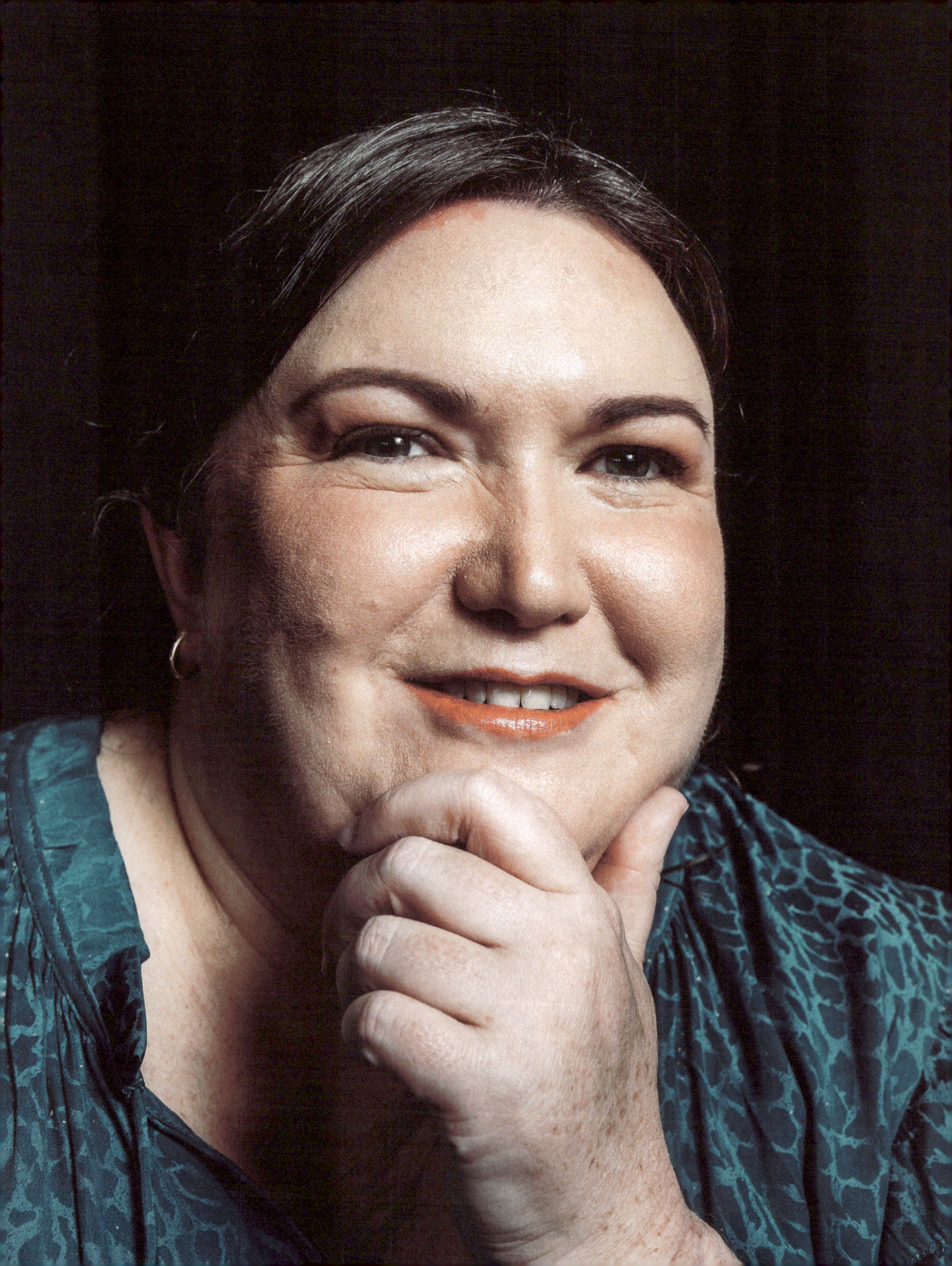

Jaclyn Davie

Finding My Voice: A Journey of Growth and Courage

Jaclyn Davie has lived in Geelong for 13 years, carving out a life full of resilience, creativity, and growth. Working full-time in the disability sector, Jaclyn's journey is marked by perseverance and a commitment to self-improvement, despite living with disabilities herself.

Jaclyn's challenges began early, shaping who she is today. "Learning to talk and finding my voice has been a long journey," she shares. "It's something I'm still working on, and doing this interview is a big step for me. It's a testament to how far I've come."

One of the pivotal moments in Jaclyn's life was getting her dog, Athlie. "Before I had her, I didn't leave the house much," she says. "But Athlie gave me a reason to go outside and start interacting with the community. She's been a game-changer."

Therapy has also been a cornerstone of Jaclyn's progress. "I've been in therapy for years, and it's been vital in helping me manage my mental health. It's not always easy, but having someone to talk to who's unbiased and supportive has made all the difference. It's helped me reach six years since my last hospital admission—a huge milestone for me."

It's about showing that it's okay not to be okay. Life doesn't stop because you have challenges. It's still possible to live a fulfilling life, even if it looks different than what others might expect.

When asked what breaking barriers means to her, Jaclyn says, "It's about showing that it's okay not to be okay. Life doesn't stop because you have challenges. It's still possible to live a fulfilling life, even if it looks different than what others might expect."

Jaclyn finds joy in her role as an aunt and in her artistic pursuits. For the past four years, she has attended JUZT Art Wellness classes, creating intricate sculptures adorned with diamond art. "I find so much peace and fulfillment in my art," she says. "It's a way for me to express myself and stay grounded."

Her proudest achievements include becoming more involved in the community and working full-time. "It's not easy balancing my own disabilities while supporting others in the disability sector, but it's rewarding. I've learned so much about empathy and resilience through my work."

Jaclyn also dreams of traveling again. "I used to travel on my own, but I stopped when I became unwell. I'm planning a trip to Perth with my nephews and sister this September, and it feels like such a big step forward."

Staying motivated is a daily choice for Jaclyn. "I don't want to go backwards," she says firmly. "It's not an option for me. I focus on what I can control and remind myself to keep moving forward, even if it's just a little bit at a time."

Her advice to others facing similar obstacles is simple but powerful: "Find what works for you. Build a support system, and don't be afraid to ask for help. Changing your mindset from being unwell to focusing on growth makes all the difference."

Jaclyn also hopes to dispel misconceptions about disabilities. "Working in the disability sector, I see how much people with disabilities are capable of, but society often underestimates us. Just because someone looks fine doesn't mean they're not facing challenges. We all have our own mountains to climb."

Participating in this project has been a big step for Jaclyn. "I'm not used to sharing my story, and I like to blend into the crowd. But I hope that by sharing my journey, I can inspire others to keep going, to ask for help, and to know they're not alone."

Her message to the world is heartfelt: "It's okay to go back sometimes, but always keep moving forward. Ride the wave and trust that you'll come out stronger on the other side."

Through her courage and determination, Jaclyn is breaking barriers, one step at a time. Her story is a reminder that resilience and creativity can pave the way to a brighter future.

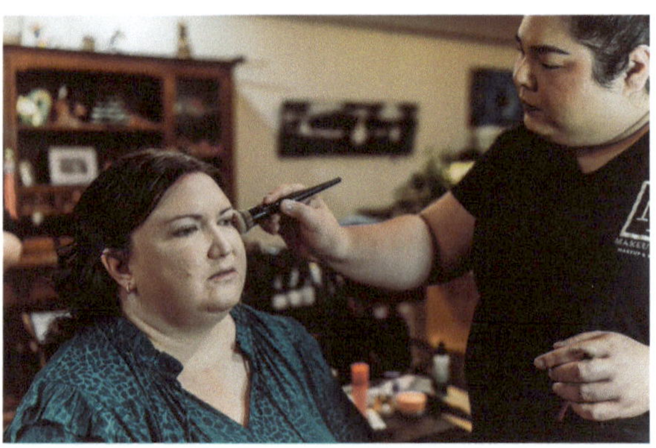

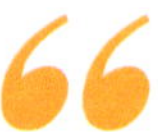

It's okay to go back sometimes, but always keep moving forward. Ride the wave and trust that you'll come out stronger on the other side.

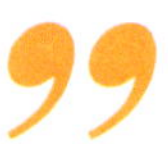

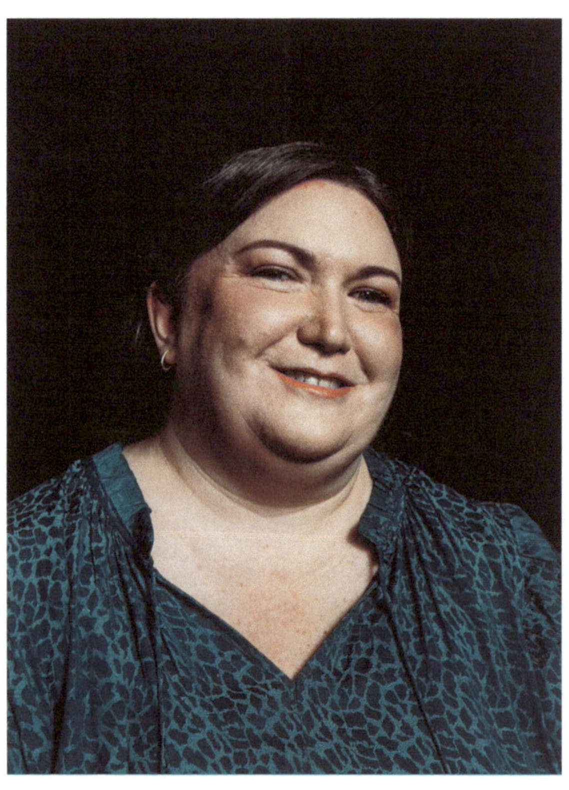

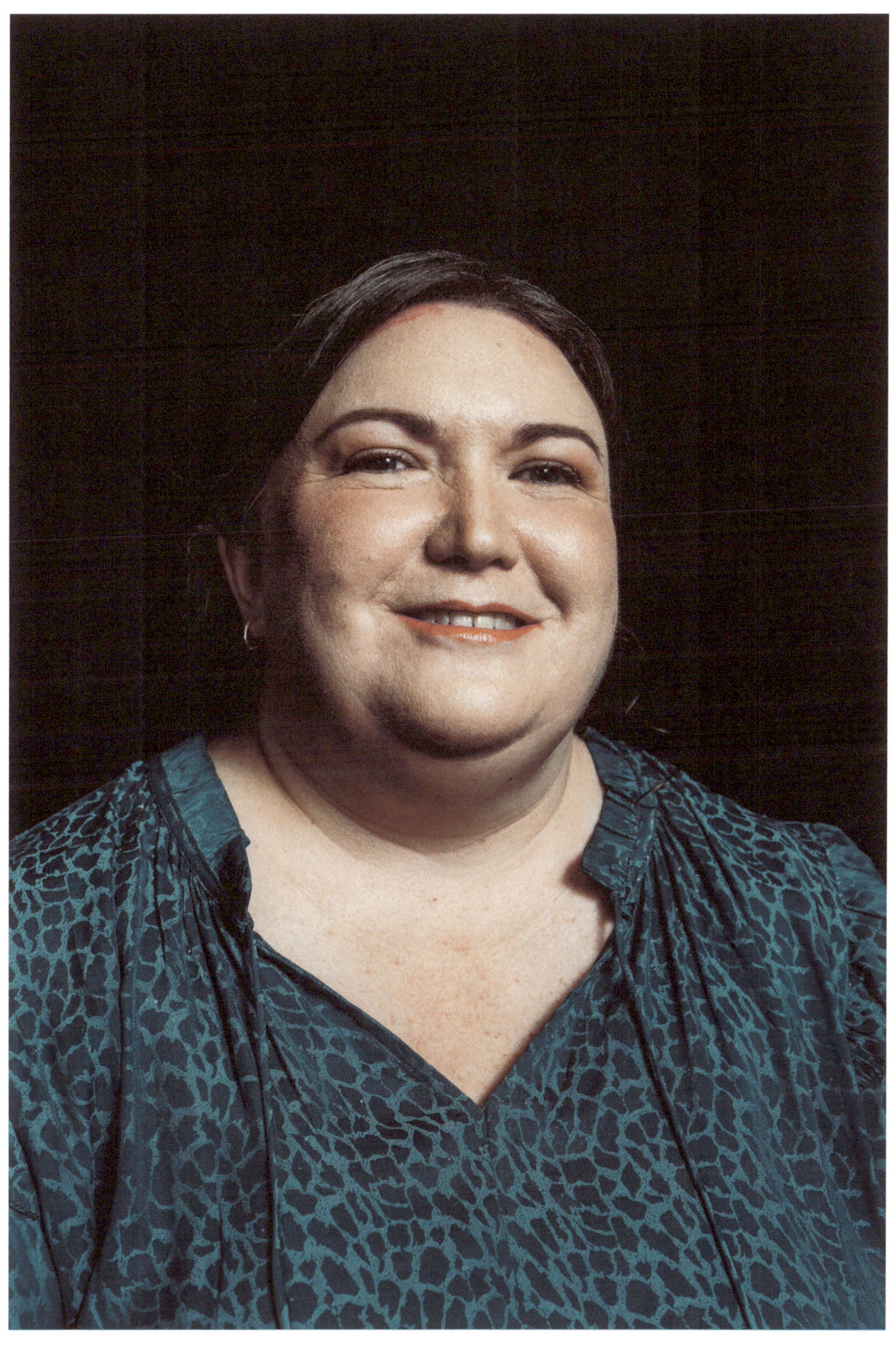

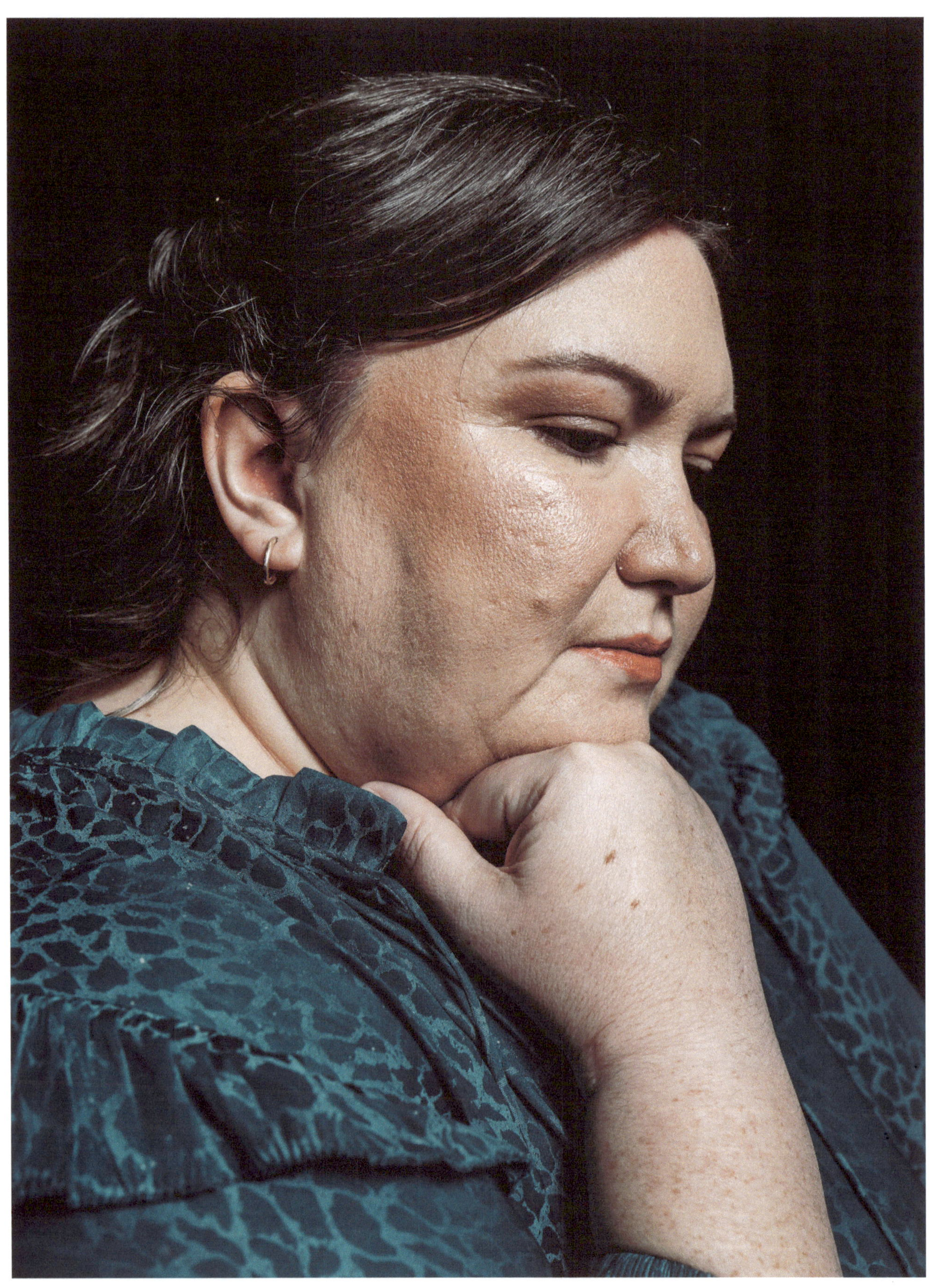

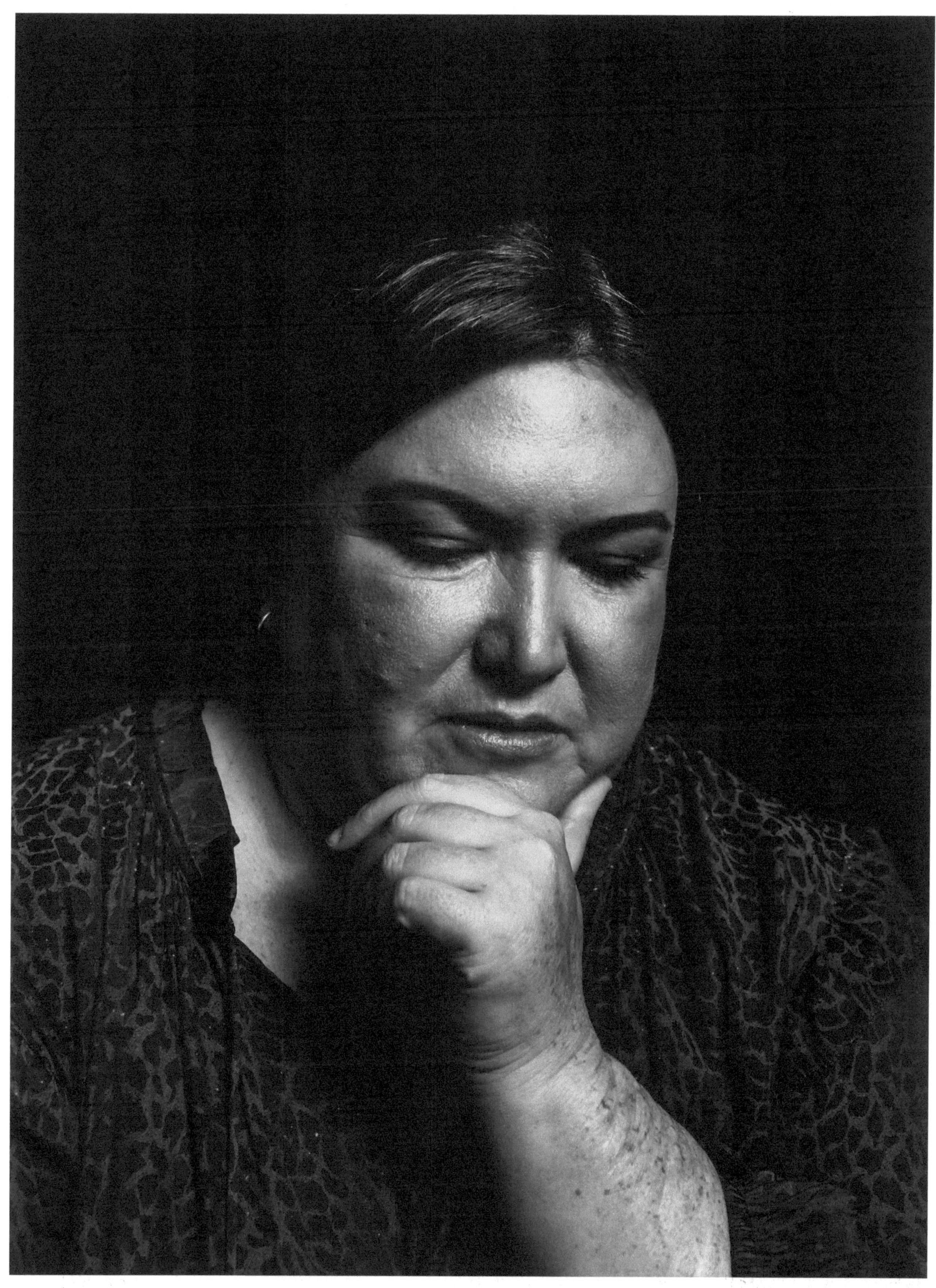

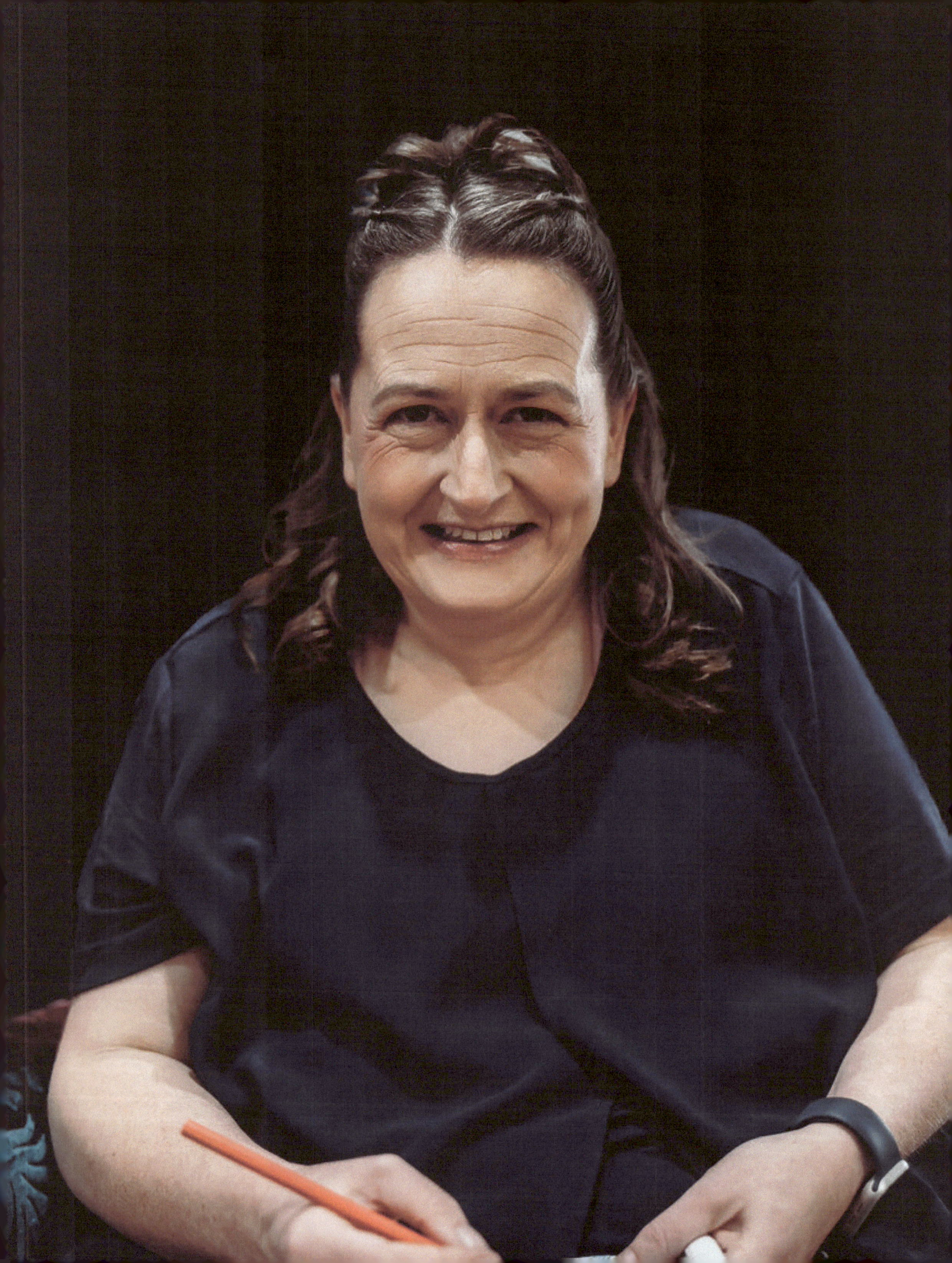

■ Jenni Strauch

Living Independently: A Journey of Creativity, Legacy, and Resilience

Jenni Strauch, a proud cat mum from Geelong, has a deep love for her nine-year-old feline companion, Sheldon. "He's been a big part of my family," she shares, beaming with pride. Sheldon has even inspired much of her artwork over the years. Alongside Sheldon, Jenni also cherishes her dog, Pansy, another muse for her creative endeavours.

For the past five years, Jenni has been attending art classes with JUZT Art, where she has become like family. "Art is one of my passions," she says, reflecting on her journey in exploring creativity and self-expression.

As Jenni approaches her 40th birthday, she celebrates her independence, supported by a strong network of family, friends, and NDIS services. "I wouldn't be able to live on my own without the support I have," she acknowledges. Her mum has been instrumental, ensuring her supports are in place, helping with banking, and, of course, looking after Sheldon when needed.

Beyond her artistic pursuits, Jenni has a lifelong connection to the Anglesea Surf Club. Since 1991, she has been involved with the Starfish Nippers program, which provides lifesaving skills and community for individuals with disabilities. "I'm the third generation in my family to be part of the surf club," she proudly explains. Her grandfather started the club, followed by her mum, aunt, and uncle. Now, Jenni continues the legacy, paving the way for the next generation.

Jenni credits her family, art teachers, and mentors for shaping her resilience and independence. She also honors the memory of her late father, who passed away two years ago. "I miss him so much, but I carry his lessons with me and share his stories with my niece and nephews."

I'm an example of how someone with an intellectual disability can live an independent life with the right support.

When asked why she chose to participate in this project, Jenni shares: "I'm turning 40 this year, and I wanted a beautiful portrait of myself. I also saw this as an opportunity to share my story. I'm an example of how someone with an intellectual disability can live an independent life with the right support."

With gratitude, she adds: "Thank you for this opportunity. It's been a joy to be part of this project."

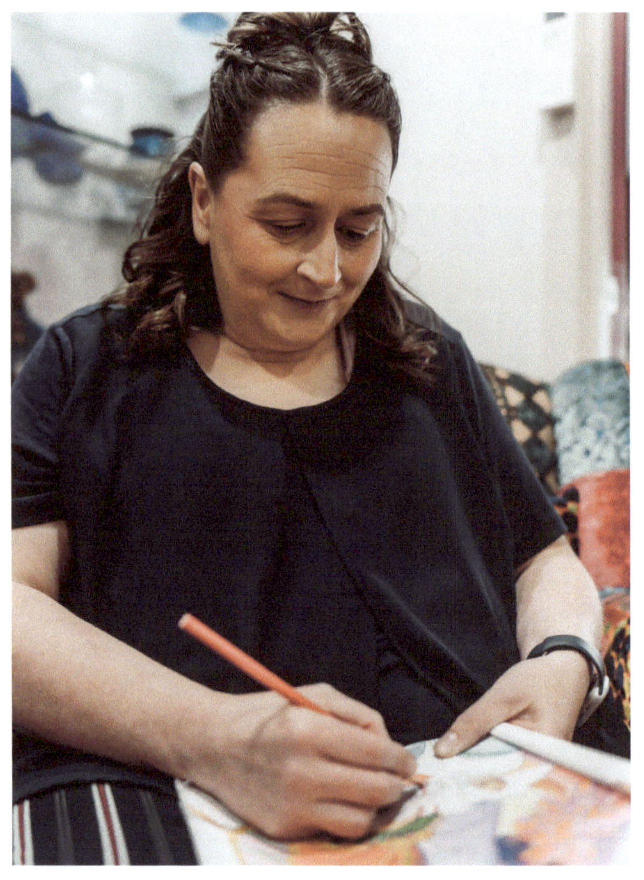
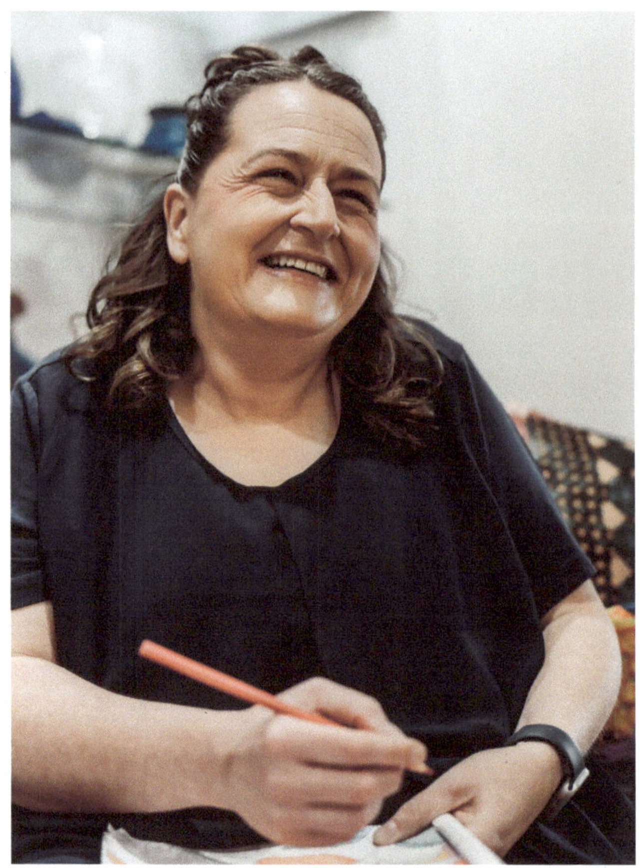
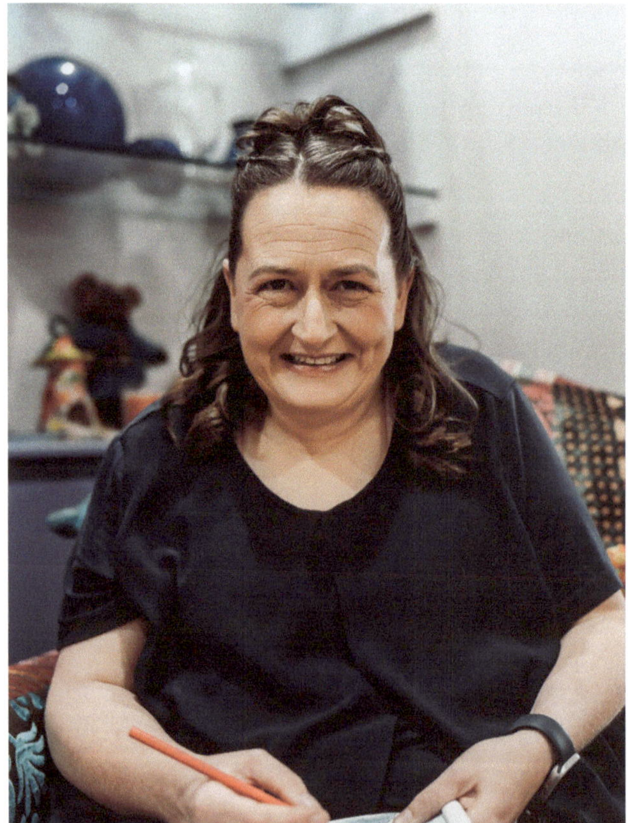
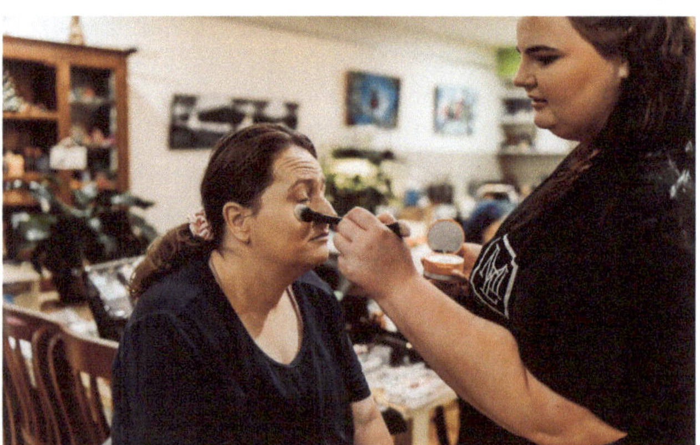
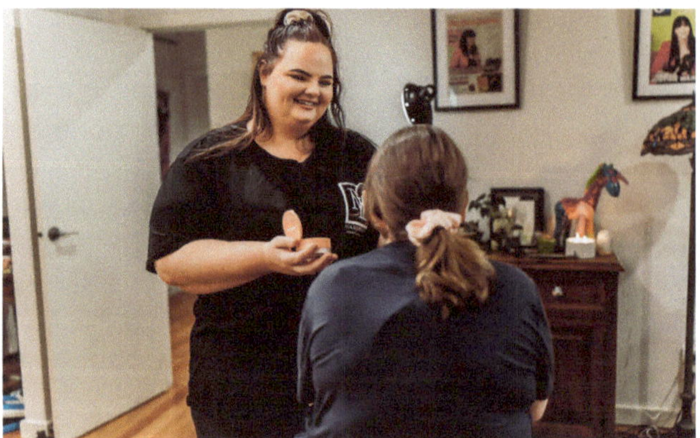

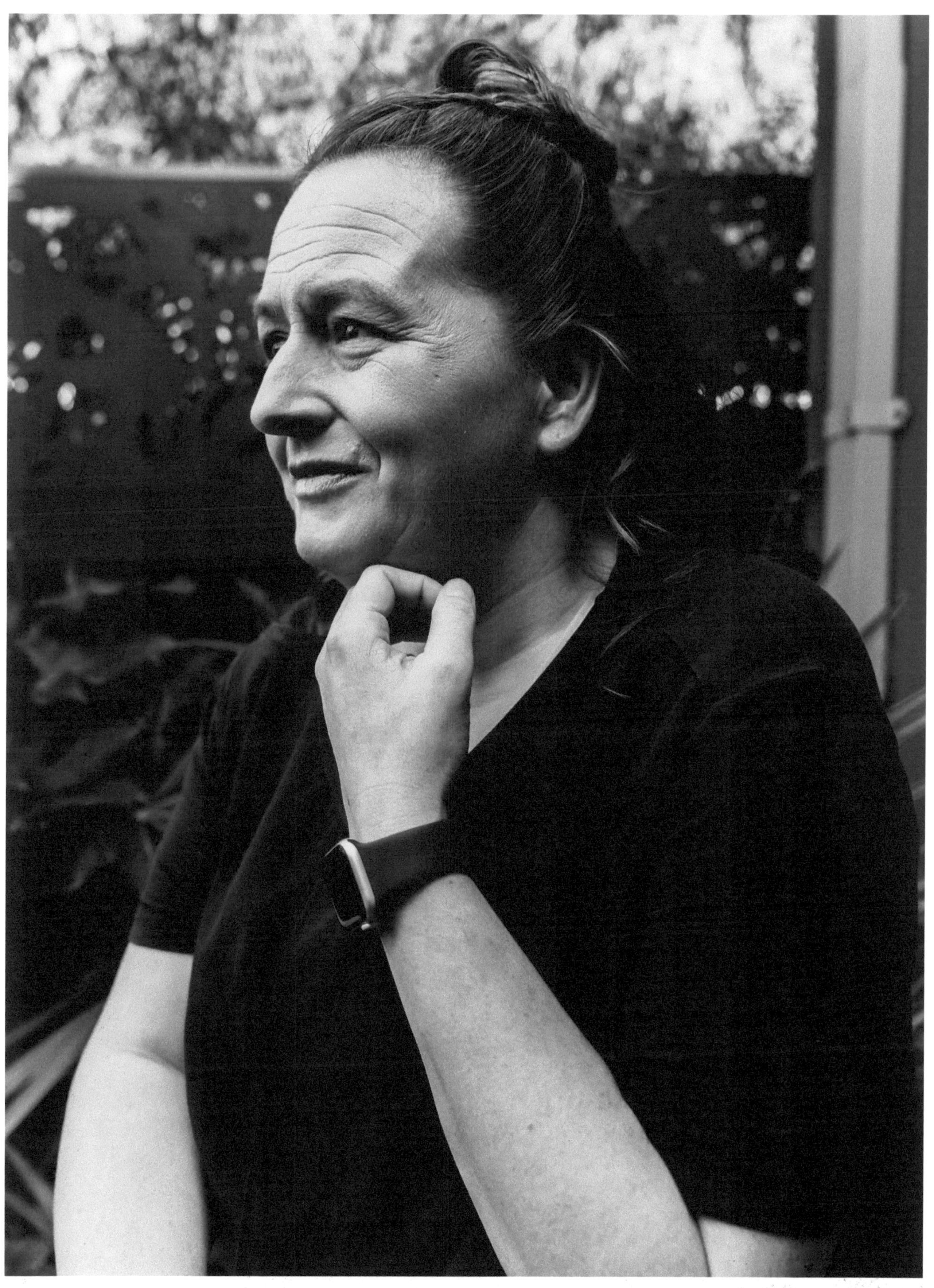

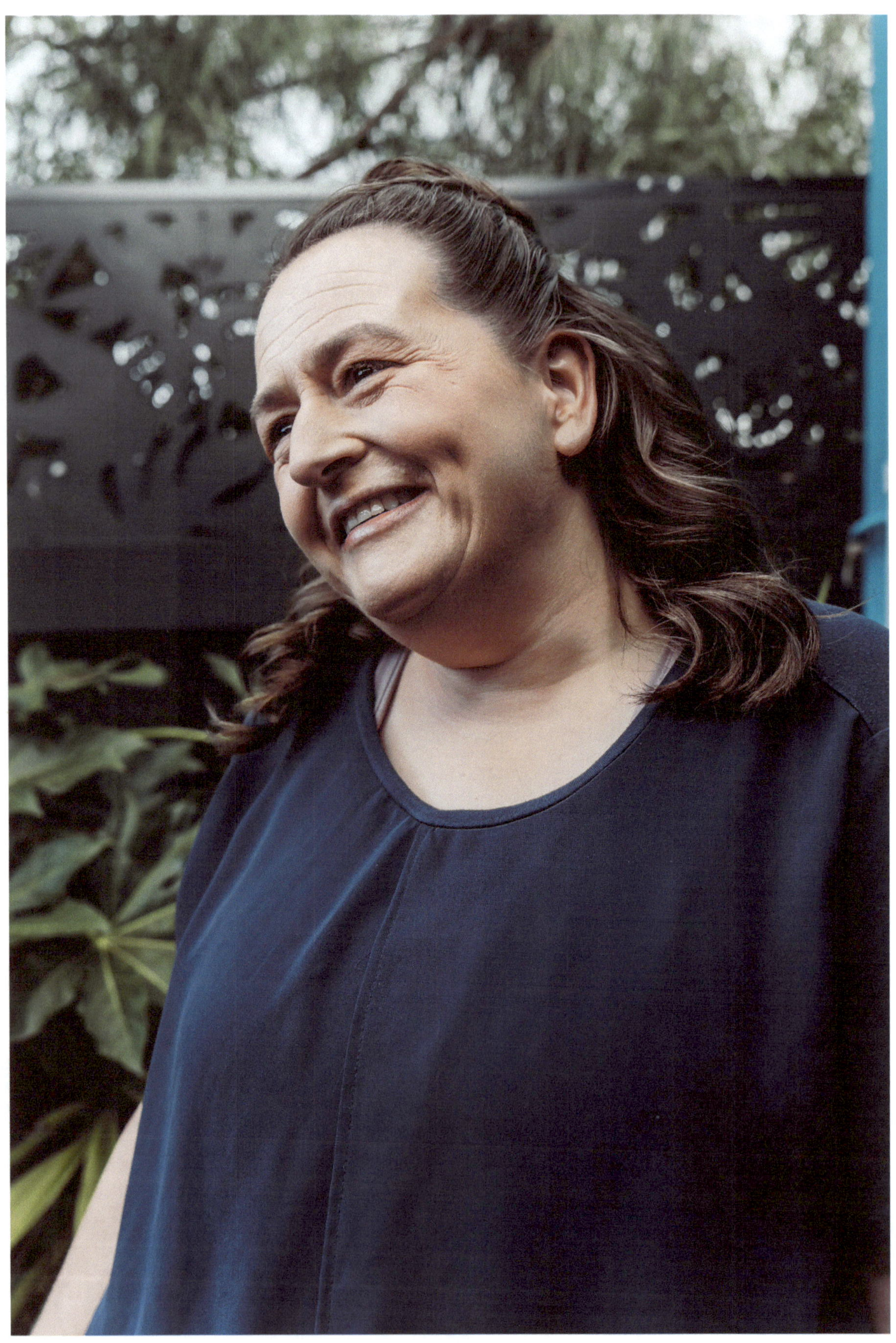

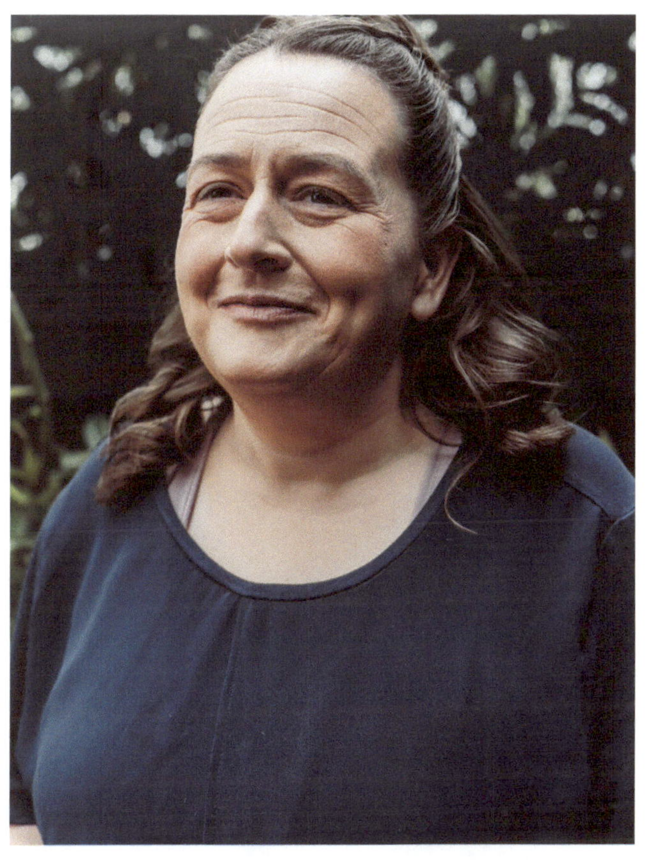
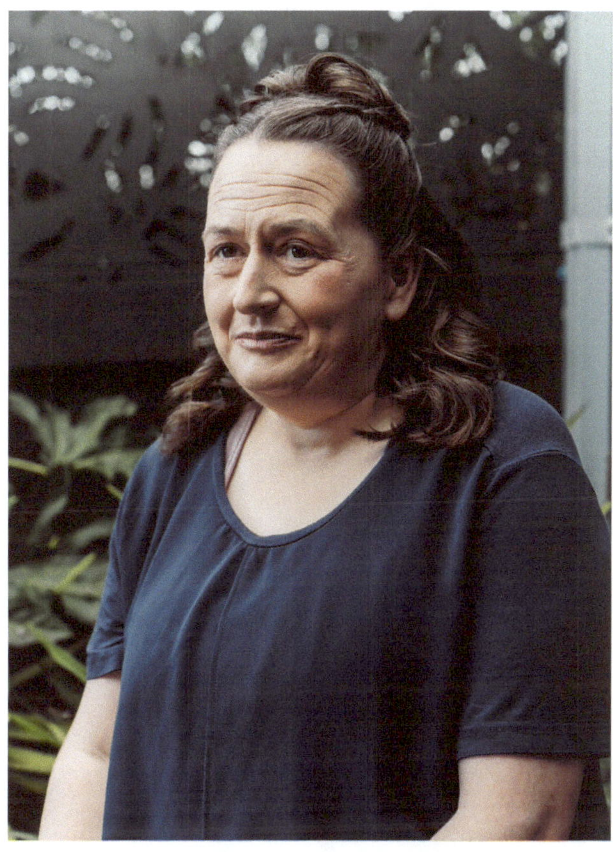
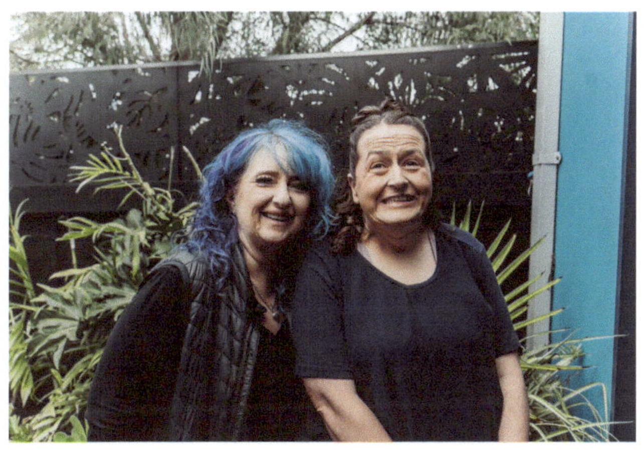
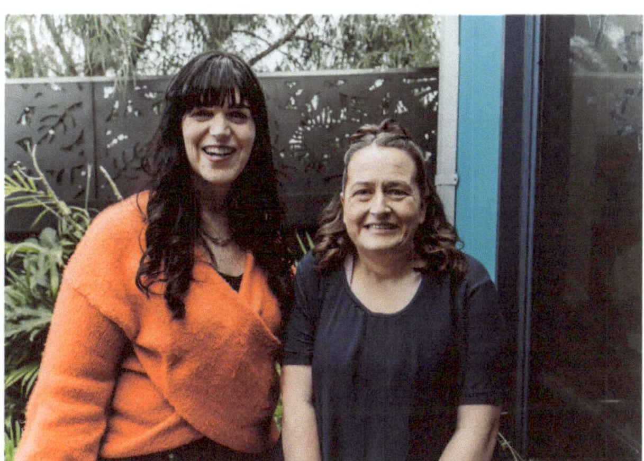

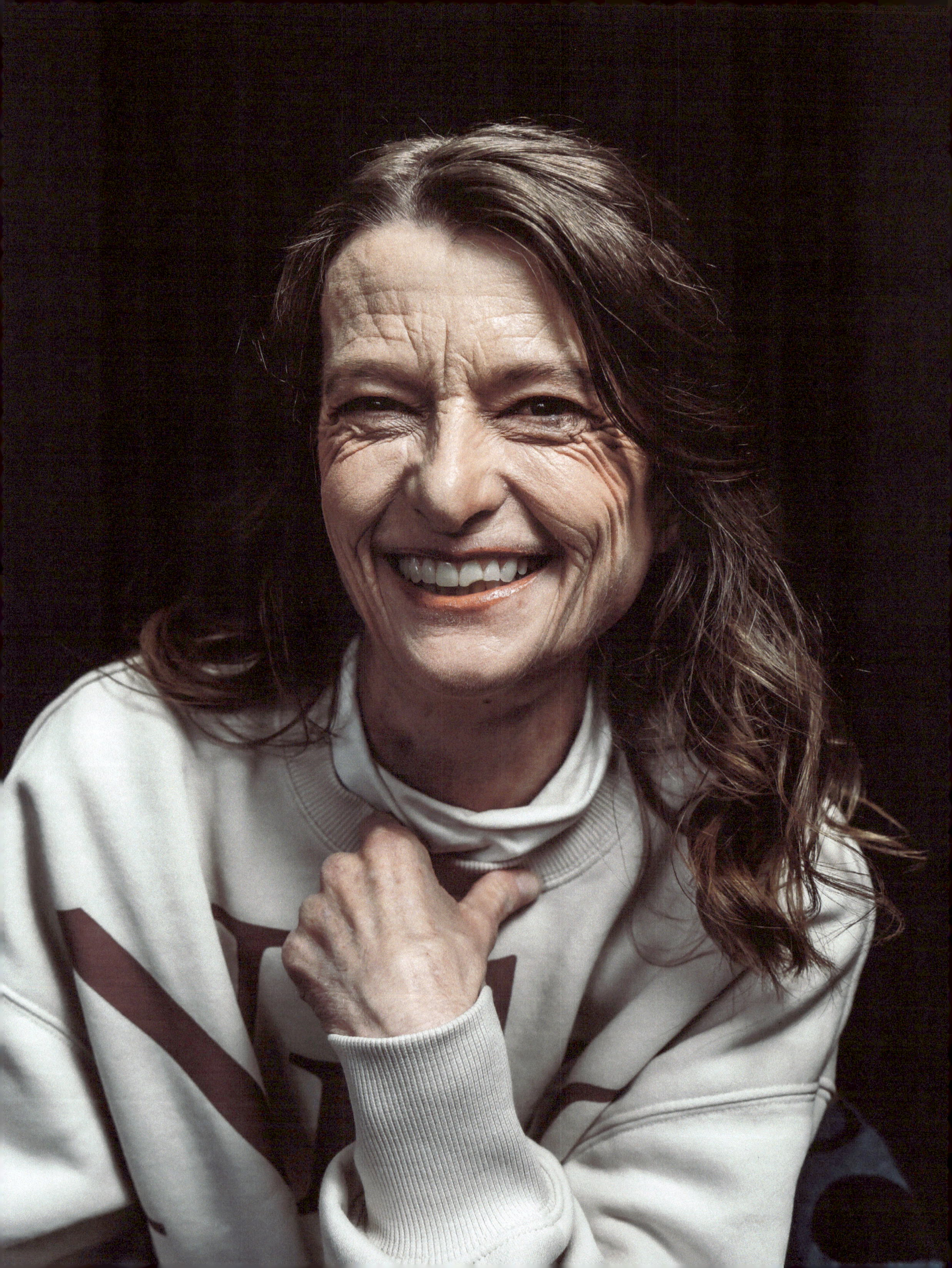

Jodie Buckley

Redefining Independence: A Journey of Strength, Family, and Resilience

At 49 years old, Jodie Buckley's journey has been marked by resilience, self-discovery, and an unwavering dedication to her family. A former baker and aged care worker, Jodie had to leave her career behind due to the progression of primary progressive multiple sclerosis (MS). Despite the challenges, she continues to adapt and grow, finding new ways to embrace life.

"Life's been tough," Jodie admits. "But we get through it. I've always worked hard, but when my mobility issues started making it impossible to continue, I had to adjust. It's been a process of figuring out what's next and coming to terms with how life looks now compared to a year or two ago."

Be kind to one another. You never know what someone is going through. It doesn't take much to be patient, offer a smile, or show a little compassion. We all need it sometimes.

Jodie's diagnosis of MS, a degenerative neurological condition, profoundly changed her life. "Primary progressive MS doesn't come with the ups and downs like some other types. It's constant. There's no getting better from the relapses—they're always there. It's tough, but in perspective, things could always be worse."

Despite her positivity, the journey hasn't been without its challenges. "The hardest part for me has been losing my mobility and the independence that came with it. I've resisted using aids for a long time, but I'm starting to realise they can actually give me back some of that independence. It's just hard to make that mindset shift."

Jodie's greatest sources of pride are her two daughters, aged 18 and 14. "They're my biggest achievement. I want them to grow up to be good people, and they are. Knowing they're happy and healthy makes me feel like I've done something right."

Her involvement in this project has been a step outside of her comfort zone. "I don't think of myself as brave," she says with a laugh. "But when this opportunity came up, I thought, why not? It's something different, and at this stage in my life, I'm willing to give new things a go."

Jodie has found solace and joy in activities like art classes and meditation. "I never thought I was artistic, but creating something with my hands has been so rewarding. It's helped me realise there's more to me than I thought. My latest project—a lifelike sculpture of my dachshund—is something I'm really proud of."

When asked about misconceptions surrounding disabilities, Jodie emphasises the importance of kindness and patience. "People might look at someone with a disability and think they're different, but we're all just human. Everyone has feelings, thoughts, and struggles, whether you can see them or not. A little kindness goes a long way."

Jodie credits her family and close friends as her greatest sources of support and inspiration. "My parents, my sisters, and my girls have been my rock. I'm so grateful for everything they've done for me. I hope they know how much they mean to me."

As she looks to the future, Jodie is focused on self-care and finding joy in the small things. "I'm learning to appreciate the moment—whether it's through art, spending time with family, or just taking a quiet moment for myself. My goals aren't big or flashy; they're about staying present and making the best of every day."

Her message to the world is heartfelt: "Be kind to one another. You never know what someone is going through. It doesn't take much to be patient, offer a smile, or show a little compassion. We all need it sometimes."

Jodie's strength and determination are evident in every step of her journey. "I might go down kicking and screaming," she says with a grin, "but I'll keep going. Life is tough, but it's also beautiful. You just have to find your way to see it."

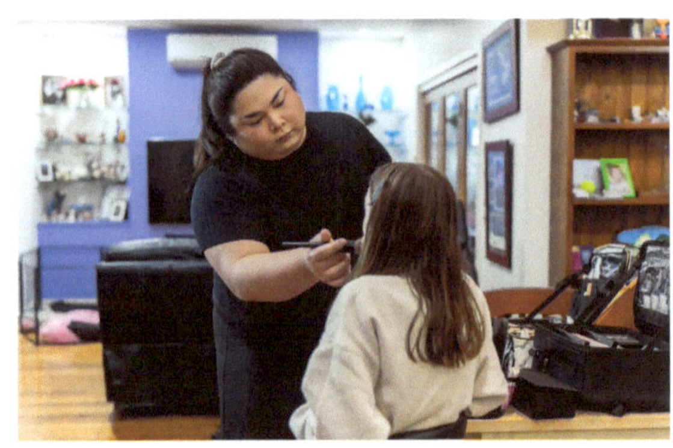

People might look at someone with a disability and think they're different, but we're all just human. Everyone has feelings, thoughts, and struggles, whether you can see them or not. A little kindness goes a long way.

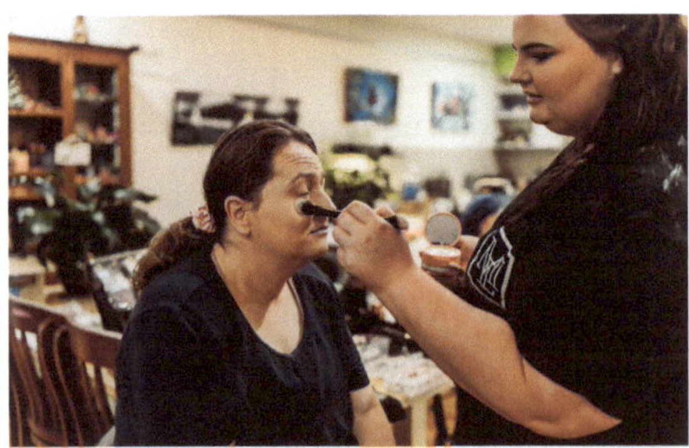

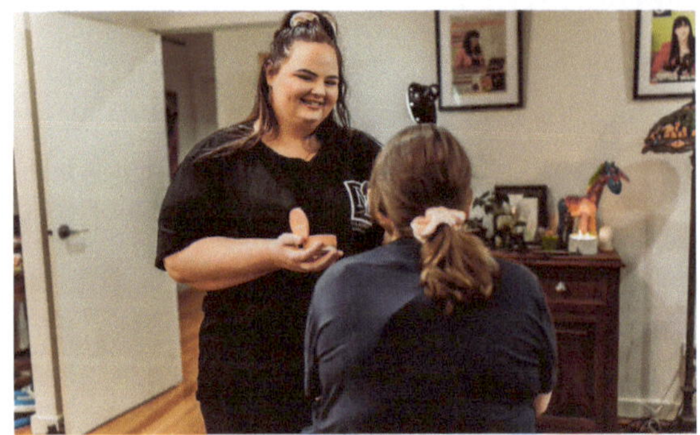

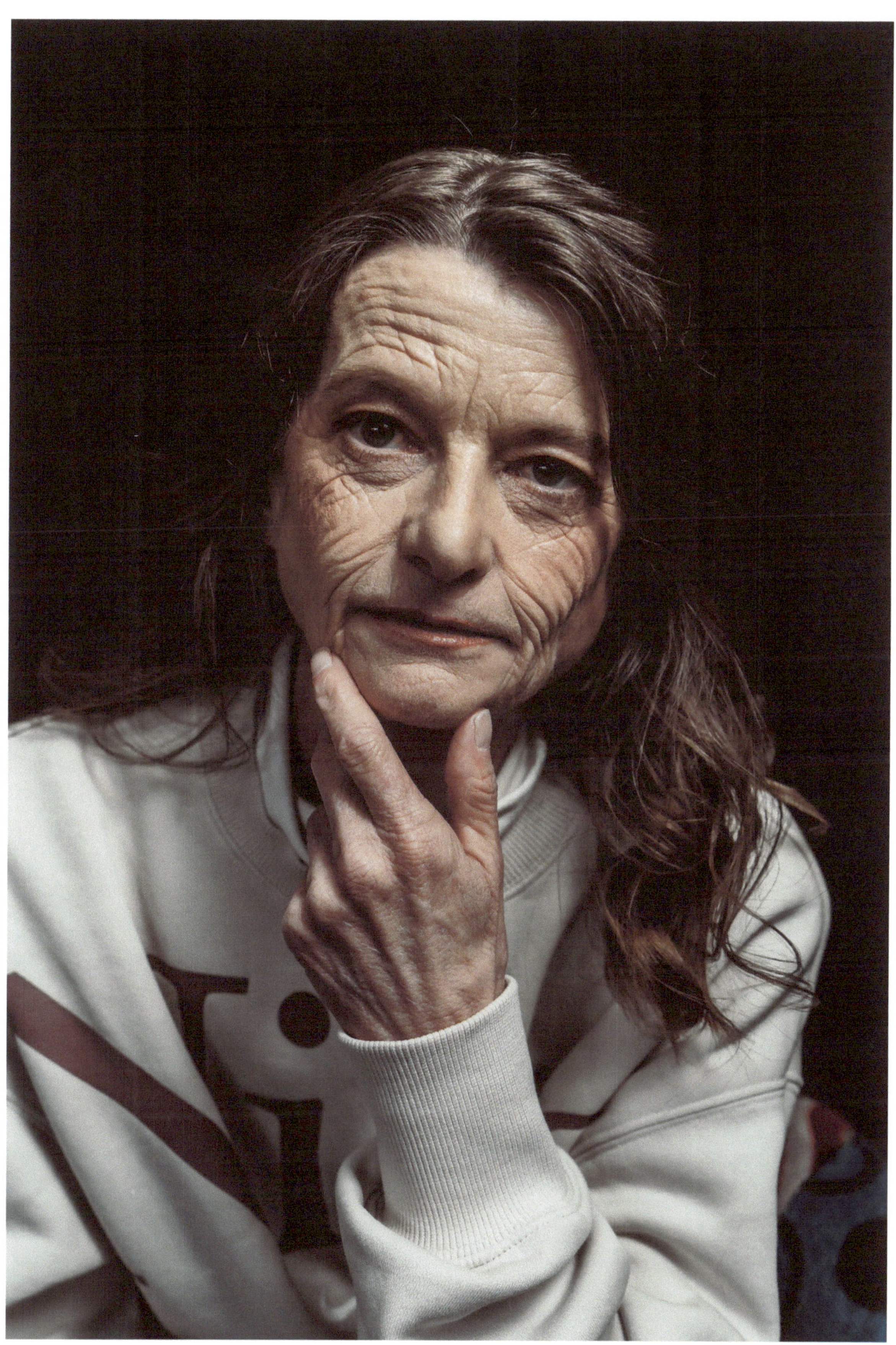

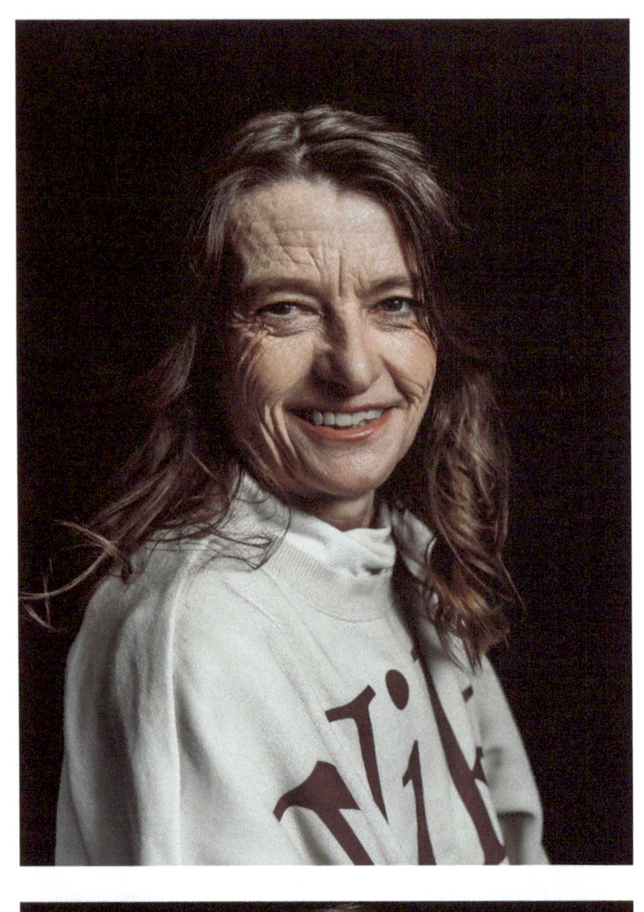

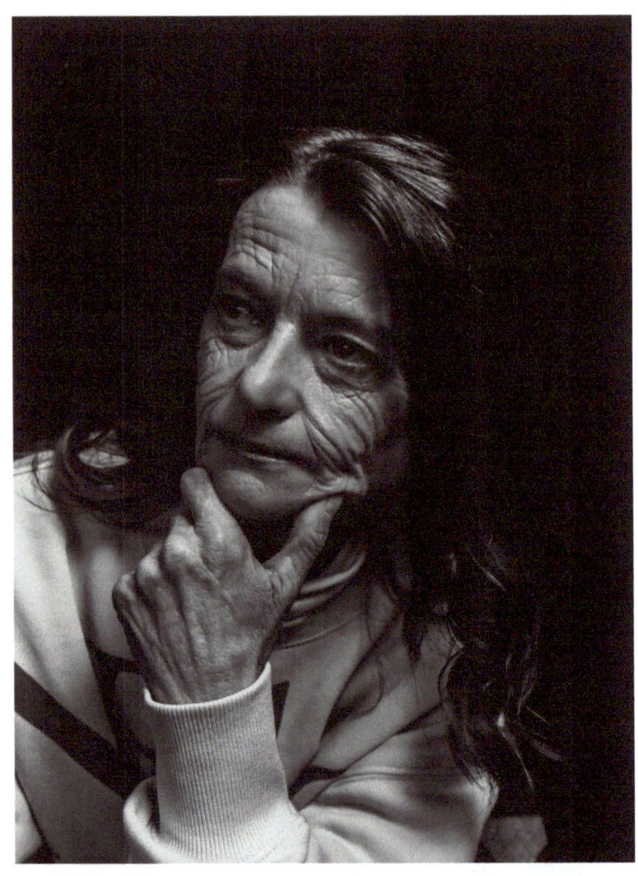

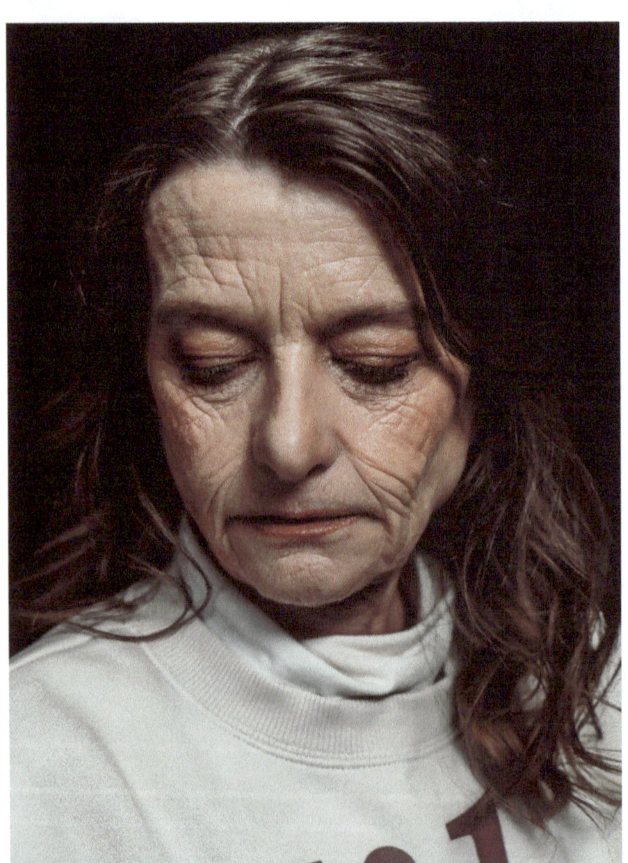

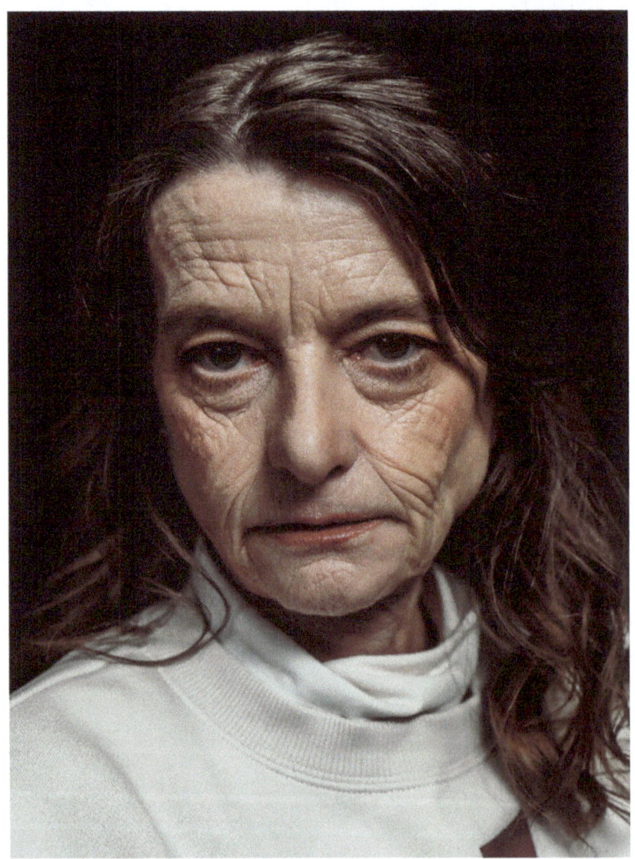

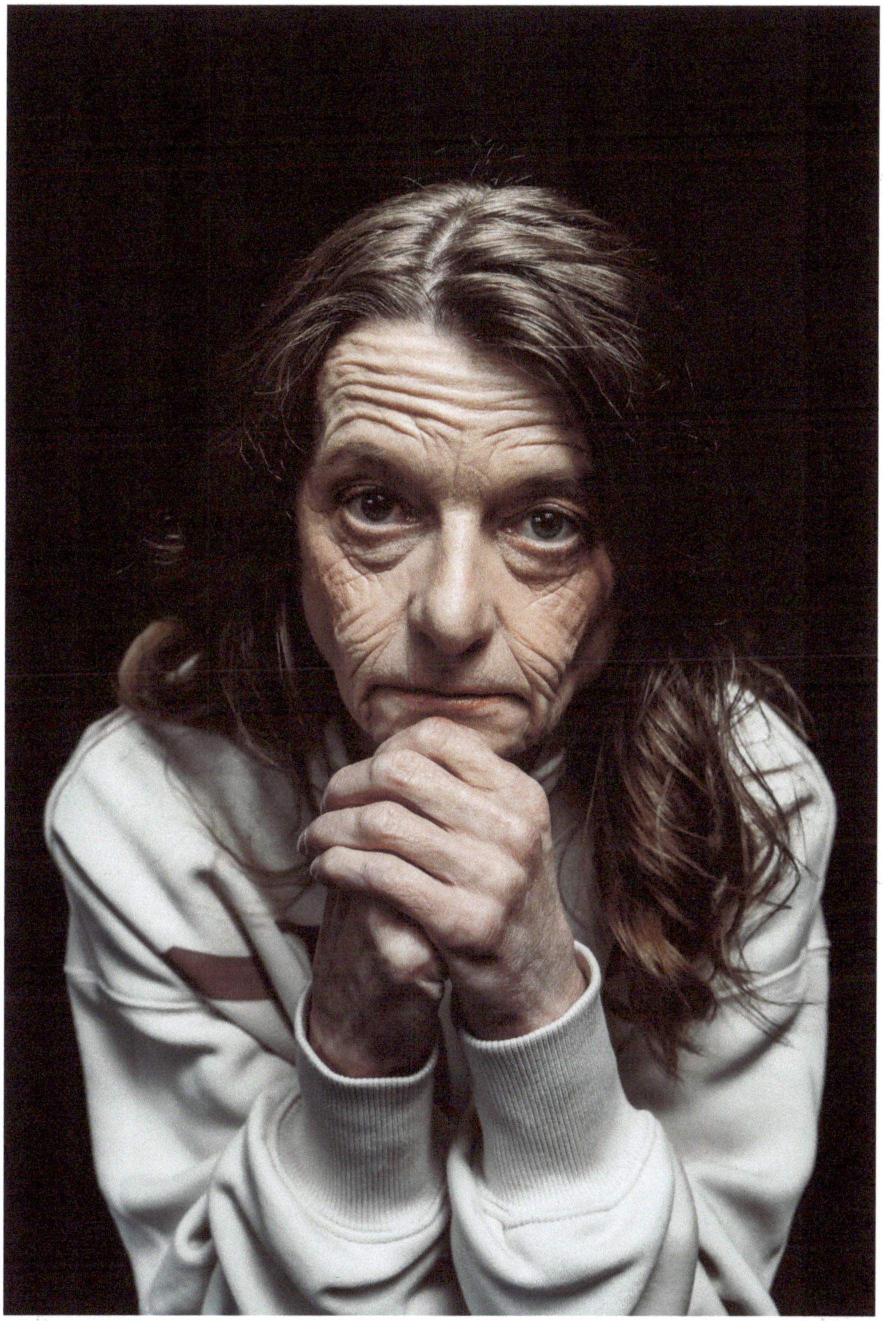

“

Life is tough, but it’s also beautiful. You just have to find your way to see it.

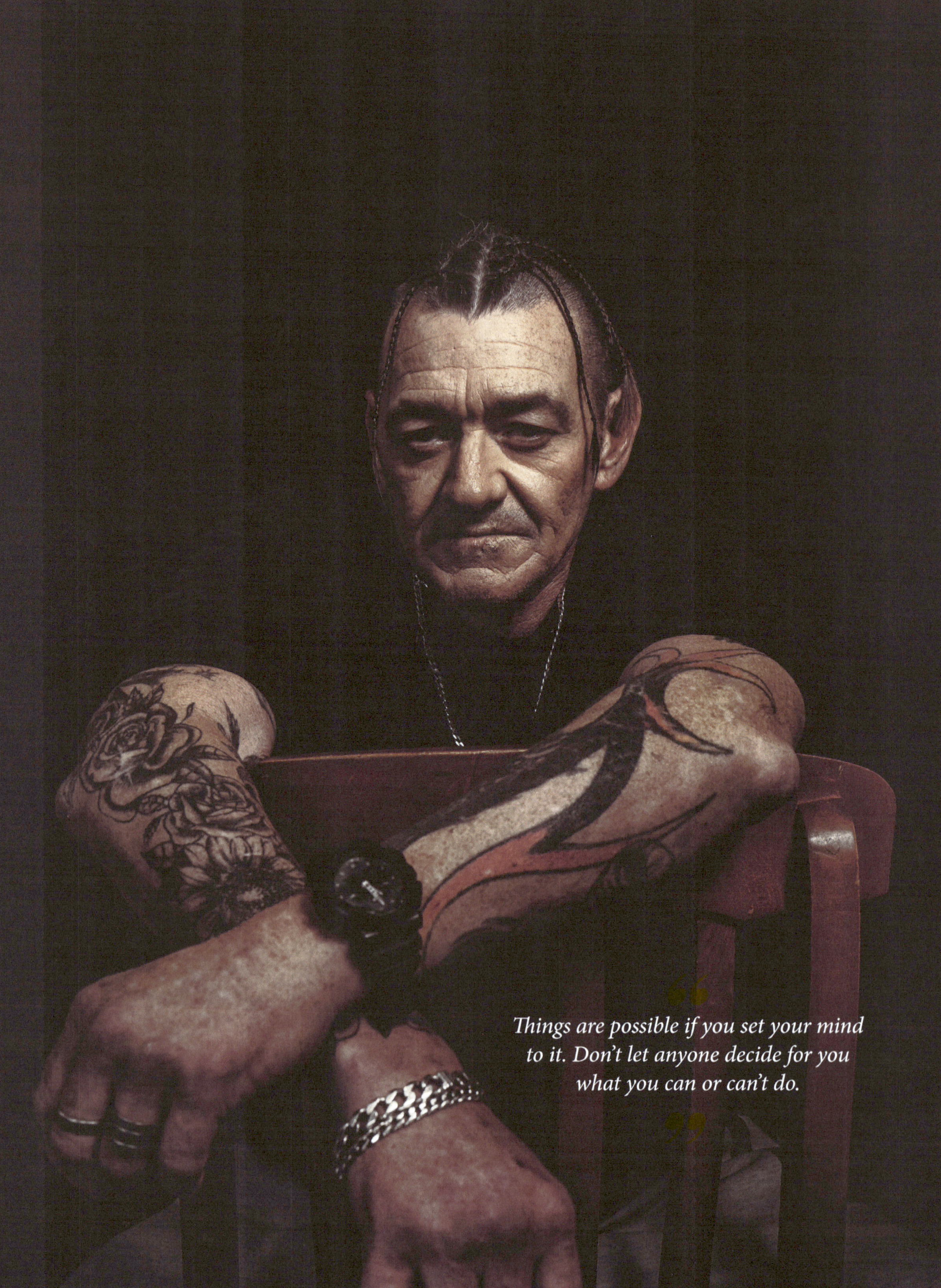
“
Things are possible if you set your mind
to it. Don’t let anyone decide for you
what you can or can’t do.
”

Joedy McMurray

Against All Odds: Determined Path to Independence

Joedy McMurray, a 51-year-old from Geelong, is a proud father of three and grandfather of five who has spent his life defying expectations and overcoming challenges. A former scaffolder and FIFO (fly-in-fly-out) worker in the mines, Joedy's world changed dramatically after a devastating freak accident in December 2016.

The accident left him with a spinal cord injury that doctors initially believed would prevent him from walking again. Diagnosed as an incomplete quadriplegic, Joedy faced overwhelming physical and emotional hurdles. Yet, with an unyielding mindset and determination, he defied the odds. "I was told I'd never walk again," Joedy recalls. "But I didn't want that to be my story."

Joedy's resilience is rooted in his love for his family. "Having my kids young, I always wanted to run around with them and now with my grandkids," he shares. This drive fuels his daily commitment to physiotherapy, pool exercises, and routines that keep his body moving. Winters in Geelong's colder climate exacerbate his pain, but Joedy remains steadfast. "It's hard, especially in winter, but I push through because it's worth it."

For Joedy, breaking barriers means challenging perceptions of what's possible with a disability. "I'm no freak, but I've seen with my own eyes that if you set your mind to something, you can make it happen," he says. His story serves as a reminder that disabilities come in many forms, not all visible. Joedy emphasises, "People often think disability means being in a wheelchair, but it's not always that simple."

One of Joedy's proudest achievements is his family. "My kids are my greatest accomplishment," he says, his face lighting up as he shares their ages, 32 to 28. Another goal he's actively pursuing is regaining his driver's licence. "Driving again will mean the world to me. I'll be able to pick up my grandkids and take them wherever I want without relying on public transport, support workers or NDIS taxis."

Joedy's determination extends beyond personal milestones. By participating in *Breaking the Barriers Through the Lens,* he hopes to inspire others to redefine their own possibilities. "This project is about showing what can be done. It's about resilience and focusing on what's possible, not what's holding you back."

Looking to the future, Joedy remains optimistic. "As long as I'm healthy, walking around, and spending time with my grandkids, I'm happy," he says with a smile. His journey exemplifies the power of resilience, community, and a mindset that refuses to accept limits.

Joedy's story is a testament to what can be achieved when determination meets action. His message is clear: "Things are possible if you set your mind to it. Don't let anyone decide for you what you can or can't do."

This project is about showing what can be done. It's about resilience and focusing on what's possible, not what's holding you back.

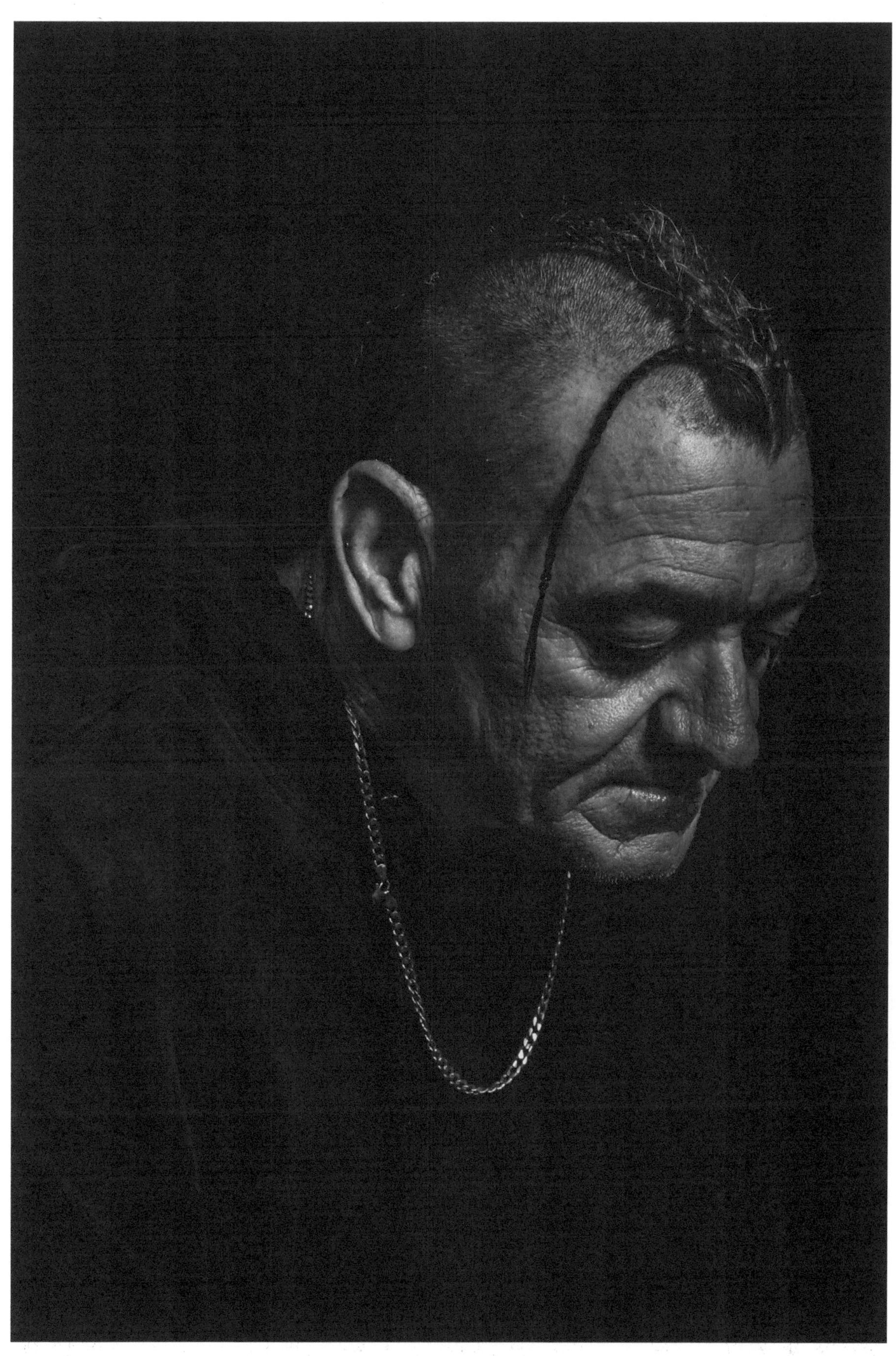

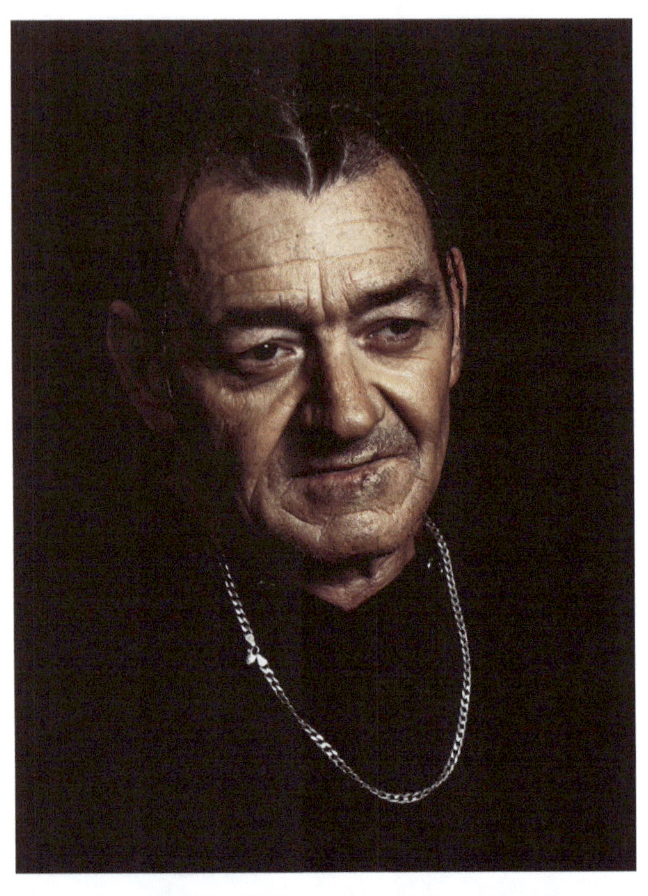
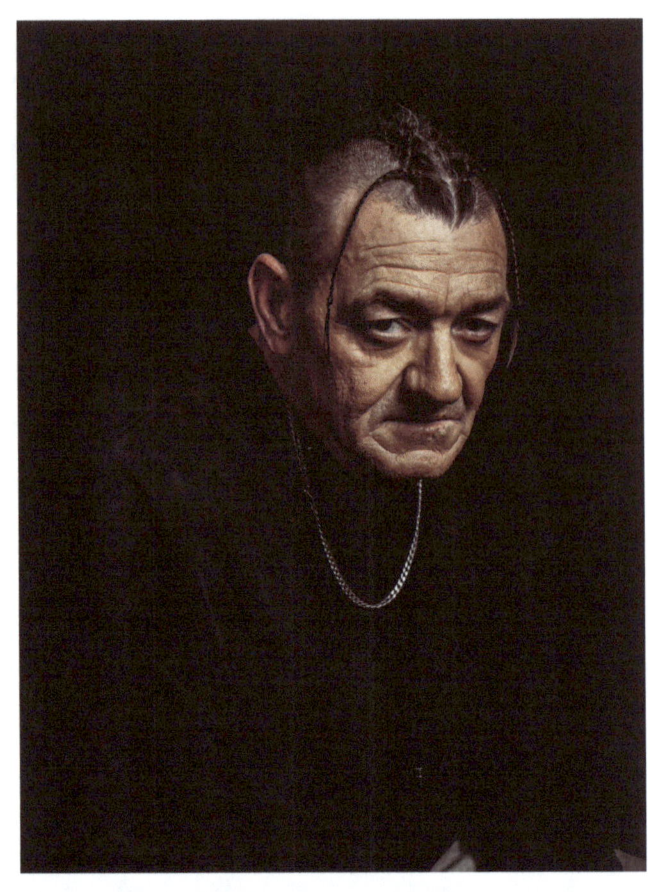
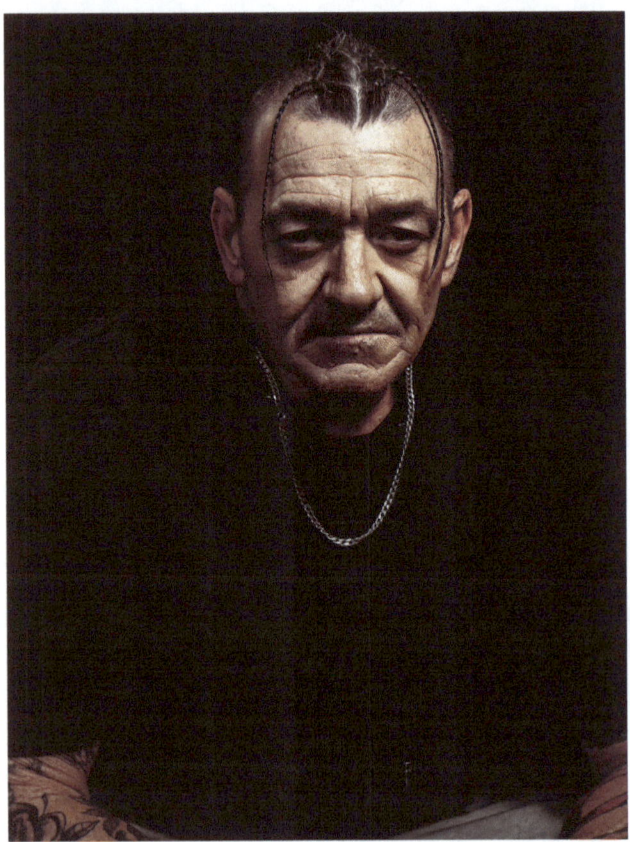
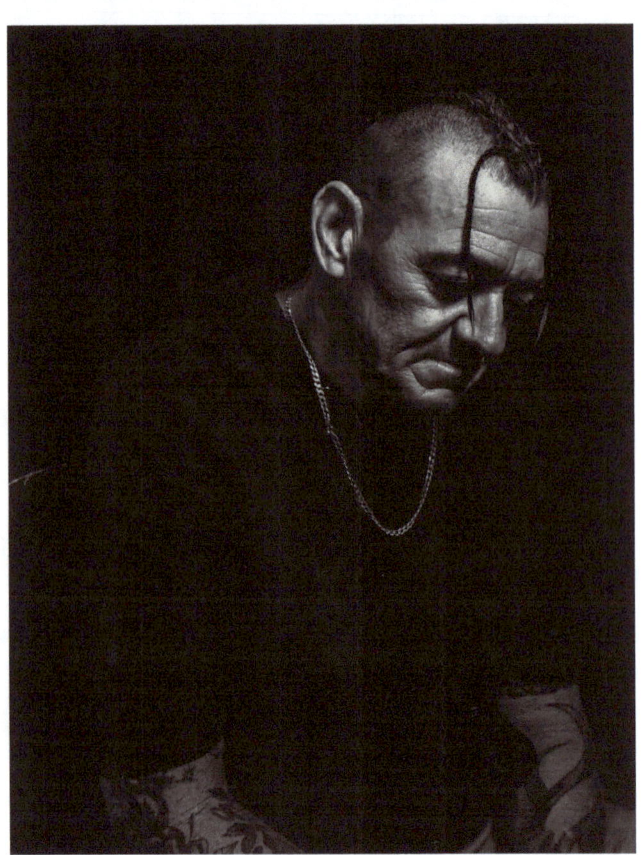

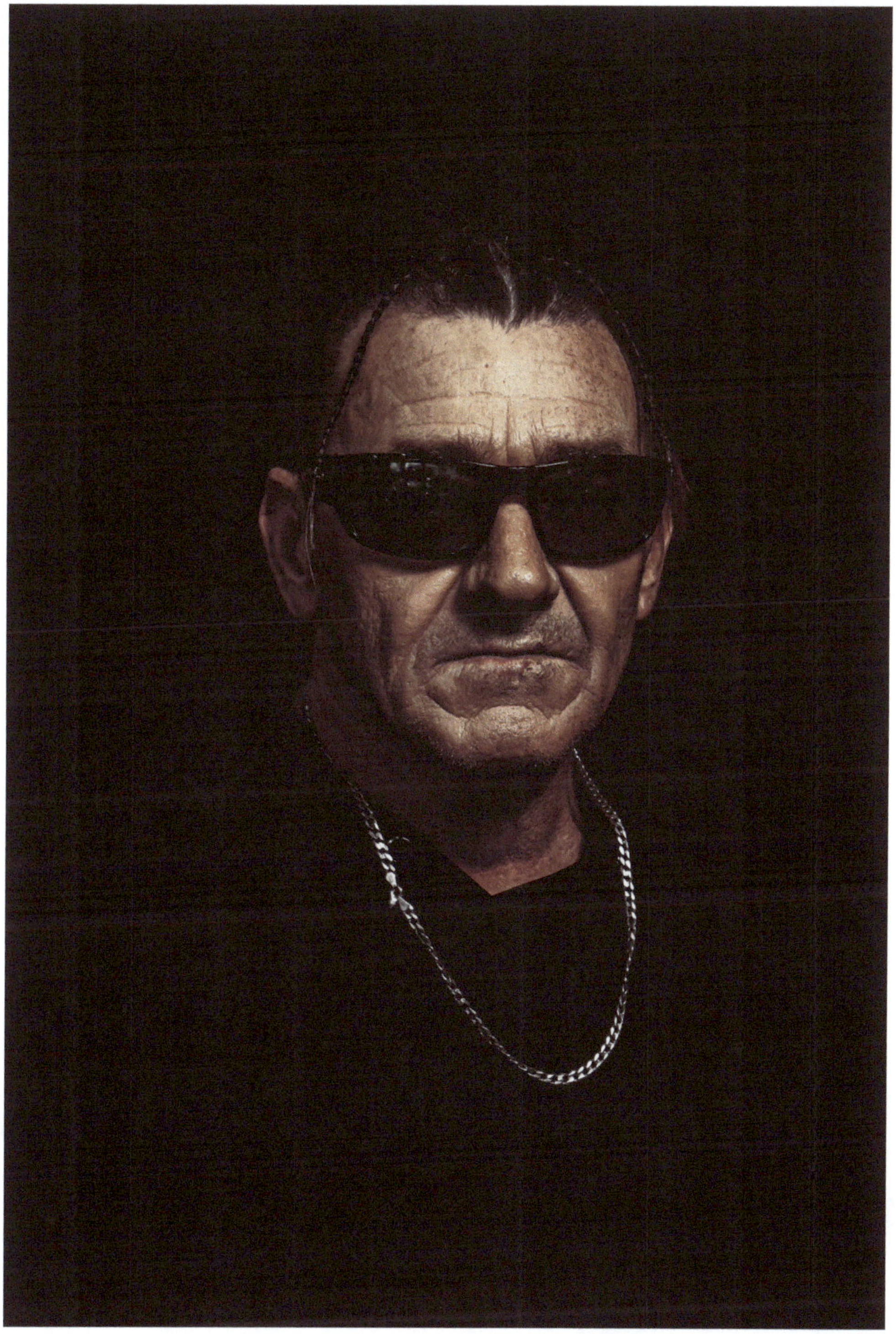

People often think disability means being in a wheelchair, but it's not always that simple.

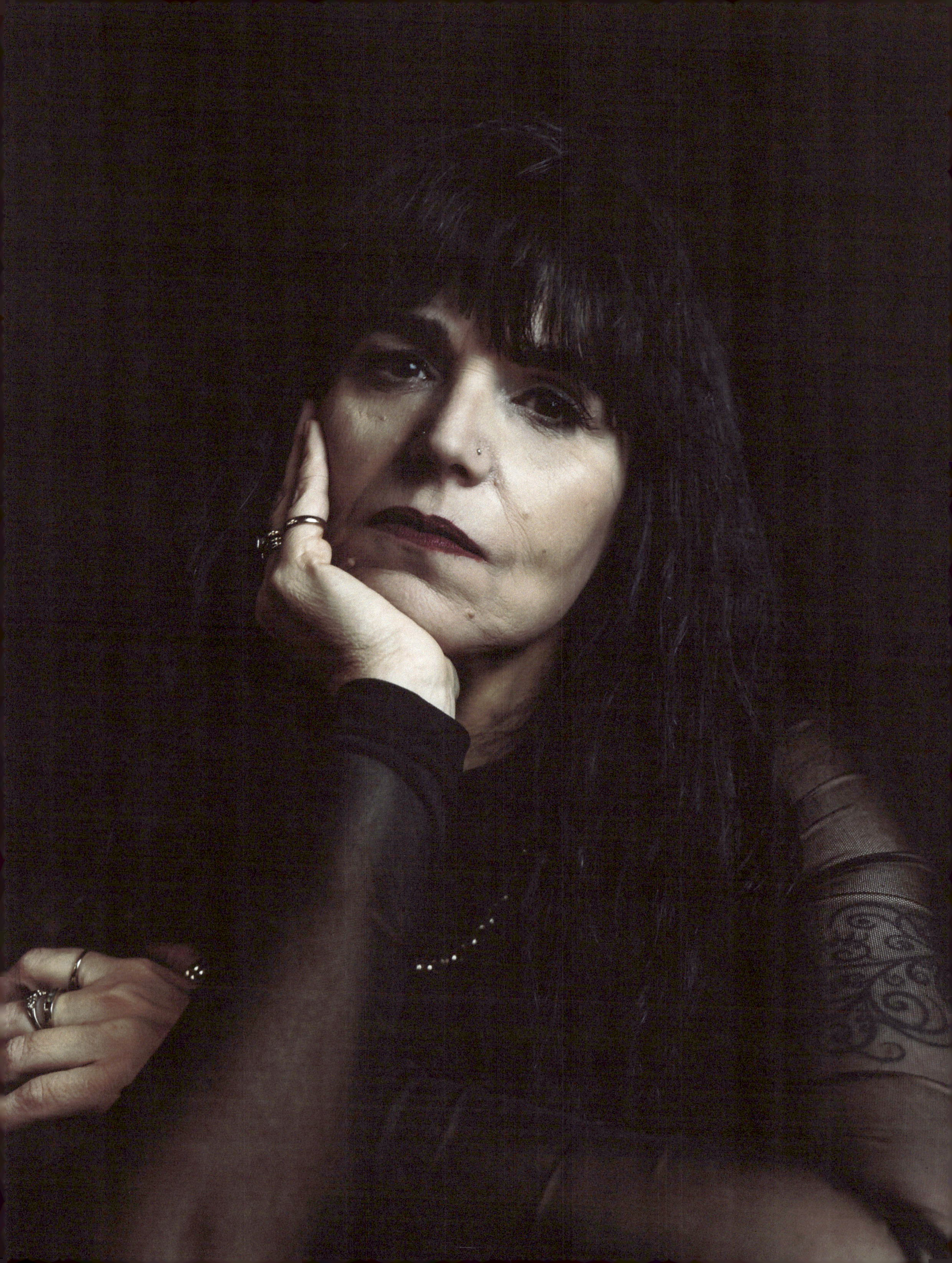

Justine Martin

Bouncing Forward with Moxie

Justine Martin is a living testament to the power of resilience, creativity, and determination. As the founder of Morpheus Publishing and Resilience Mindset, Justine has turned her personal challenges into platforms for advocacy, empowerment, and transformation, inspiring countless others to overcome their own barriers.

Born and raised in Geelong, Justine's life took a dramatic turn when she was diagnosed with multiple sclerosis (MS) and cancer, among other health challenges. "Being told I'd never work again was devastating," Justine recalls. "But I refused to let those diagnoses define me. Instead, I chose to adapt, grow, and push forward."

Resilience isn't about bouncing back; it's about bouncing forward. It's about using life's hardships as stepping stones to something greater.

Her experiences with adversity became the foundation of her mission. Justine founded **Resilience Mindset**, a coaching platform dedicated to teaching people how to navigate life's challenges and emerge stronger. "Resilience isn't about bouncing back," she explains. "It's about bouncing forward. It's about using life's hardships as stepping stones to something greater."

Through her work with Resilience Mindset, Justine delivers motivational speeches, workshops, and coaching sessions that help individuals and businesses thrive despite adversity. "I want to show people that no matter how tough things get, there's always a way forward," she says. "My journey with MS, cancer, and acquired brain injuries has taught me that strength comes from within, and with the right mindset, anything is possible."

In addition to Resilience Mindset, Justine is the driving force behind **Morpheus Publishing**, a company born from her passion for storytelling and advocacy. "Morpheus Publishing was created to give a voice to people who've faced adversity," she shares. "It's about sharing stories that inspire, educate, and empower."

Through Morpheus Publishing, Justine has helped many first-time authors, especially those with disabilities, bring their stories to life. "There's incredible power in sharing your journey," she says. "For those who've been told their stories don't matter, we're here to prove that they do."

Justine's own writing includes **MOXIE: How I Learnt to Harden the F* Up**,** her memoir that chronicles her journey of resilience and reinvention. She has also authored and illustrated children's books that promote inclusion and acceptance, such as **Same Same But Different** and **Finding Hope**, created for the charity Rivers Gift.

Breaking barriers is Justine's way of life. She is the first disabled person to win the prestigious **Geelong Business Leader of the Year Award.** She has garnered numerous accolades for her work, including recognition in disability leadership, coaching, and creative entrepreneurship. "Each award is a reminder that adversity doesn't limit us—it empowers us to achieve greatness," she says.

Adversity doesn't limit us—it empowers us to achieve greatness.

A passionate artist, Justine has also channelled her creativity into her art business, **JUZT Art,** where she uses painting as a therapeutic outlet. Her works have been showcased in exhibitions and have won awards, further proving that resilience can fuel creativity and success.

Justine's love for community is evident in every aspect of her life. Whether coaching clients, guiding authors or advocating for inclusivity, she is driven by a desire to make the world a better place. "I want to leave a legacy of hope," she says. "If my story can inspire even one person to keep going, then it's all been worth it."

Despite her health challenges, Justine is a force to be reckoned with. She competes as an all-abilities athlete in Strongman events, travels the world, and continues to grow her businesses while raising awareness about invisible disabilities. "Living with MS, cancer, and acquired brain injuries isn't easy," she admits. "But every day, I choose to show up, to adapt, and to thrive."

Her message to the world is one of empowerment: "Adversity doesn't define you—it refines you. Use your challenges as fuel for growth, and never stop striving for the life you want."

Justine Martin's story is one of transformation, resilience, and unyielding strength. Through her work with Resilience Mindset, Morpheus Publishing, and her art, she continues to break barriers and inspire others to live boldly, no matter the obstacles.

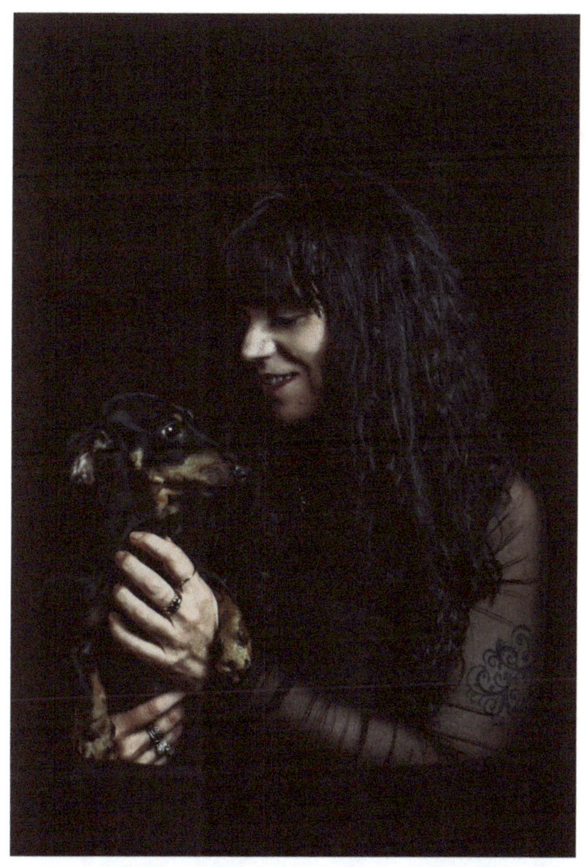

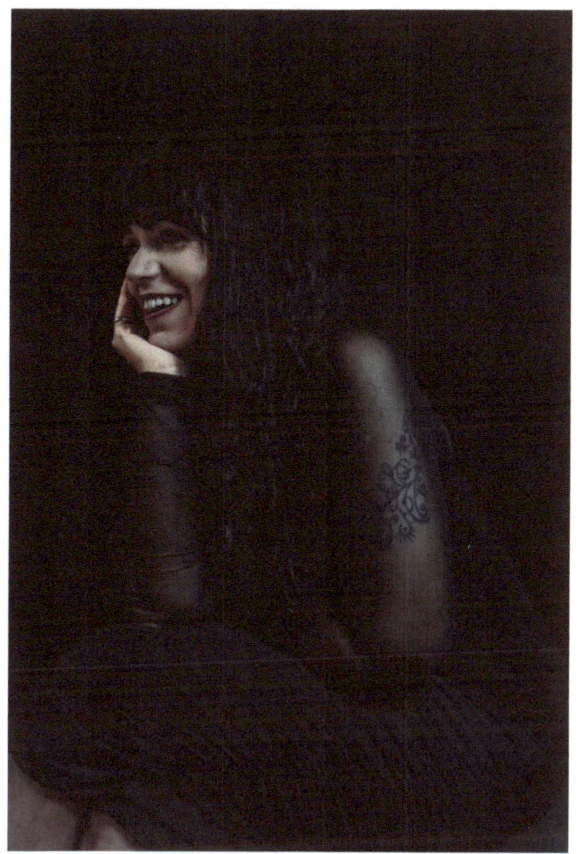

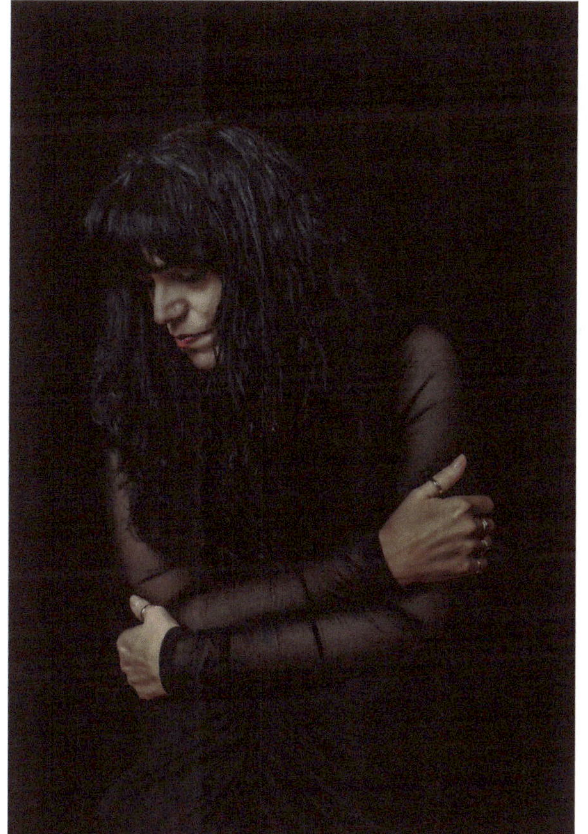

Adversity doesn't define you—it refines you. Use your challenges as fuel for growth, and never stop striving for the life you want.

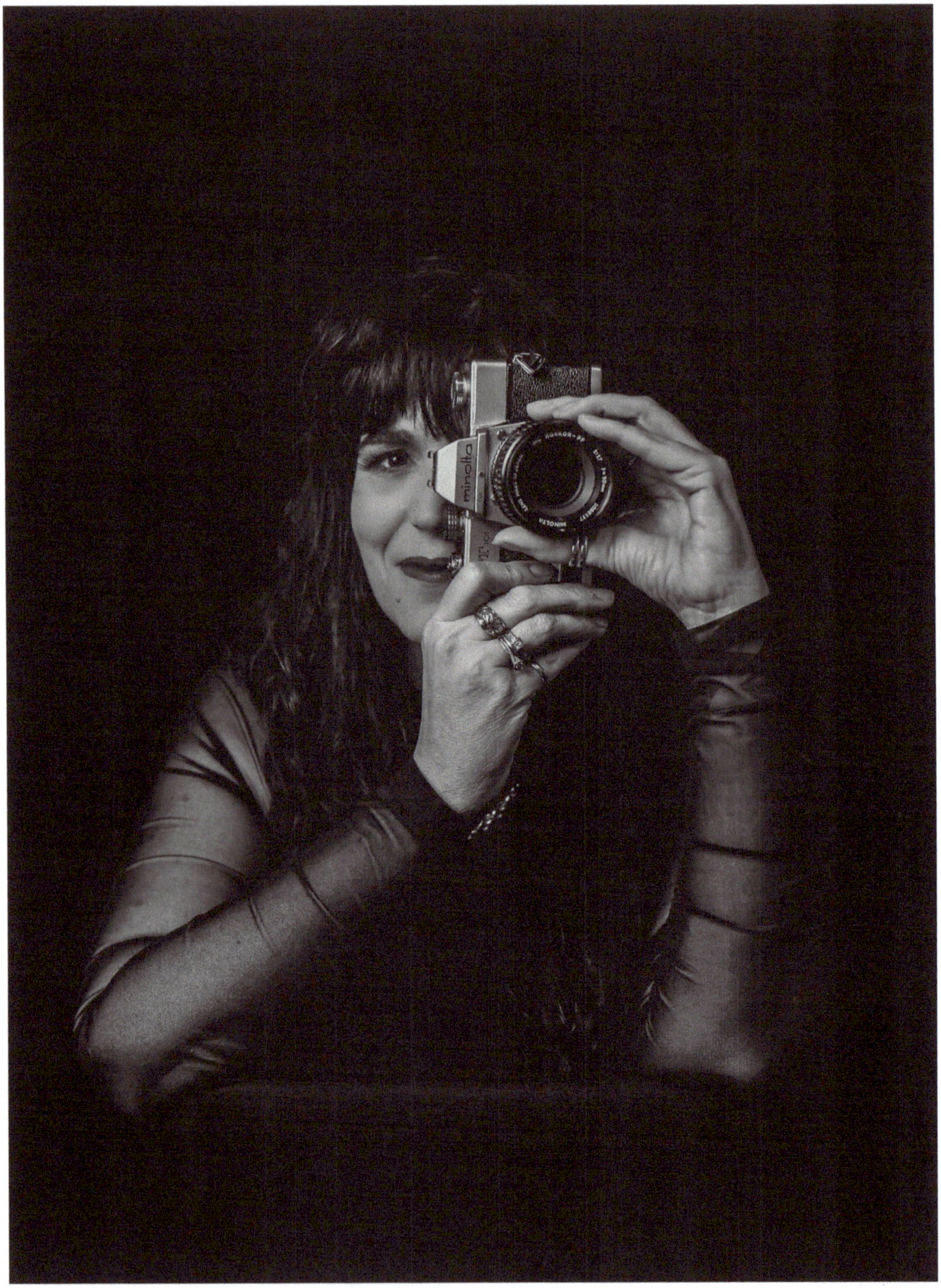

“

No matter how tough things get, there's always a way forward

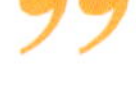

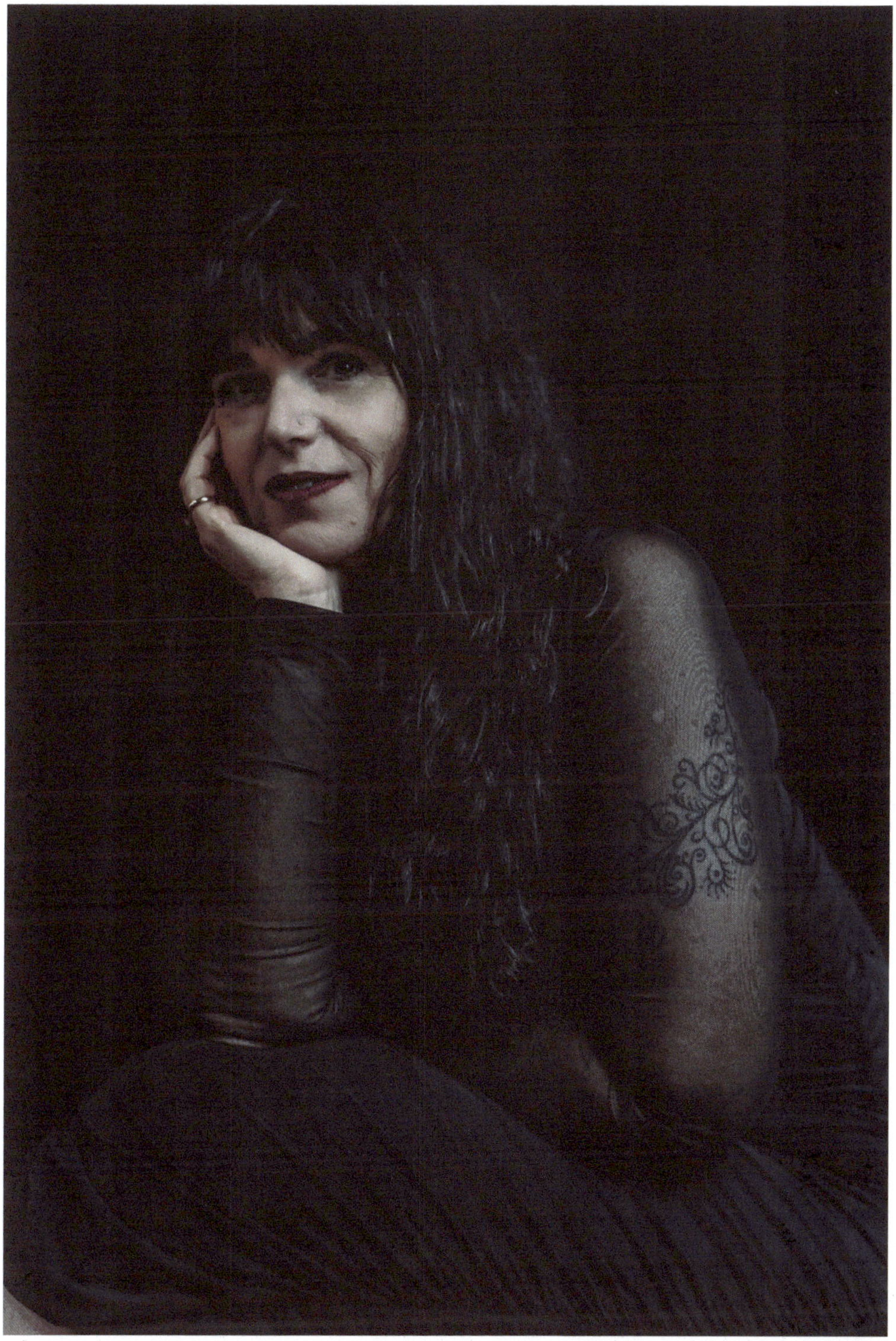

“

Every day, I choose to show up, to adapt, and to thrive.

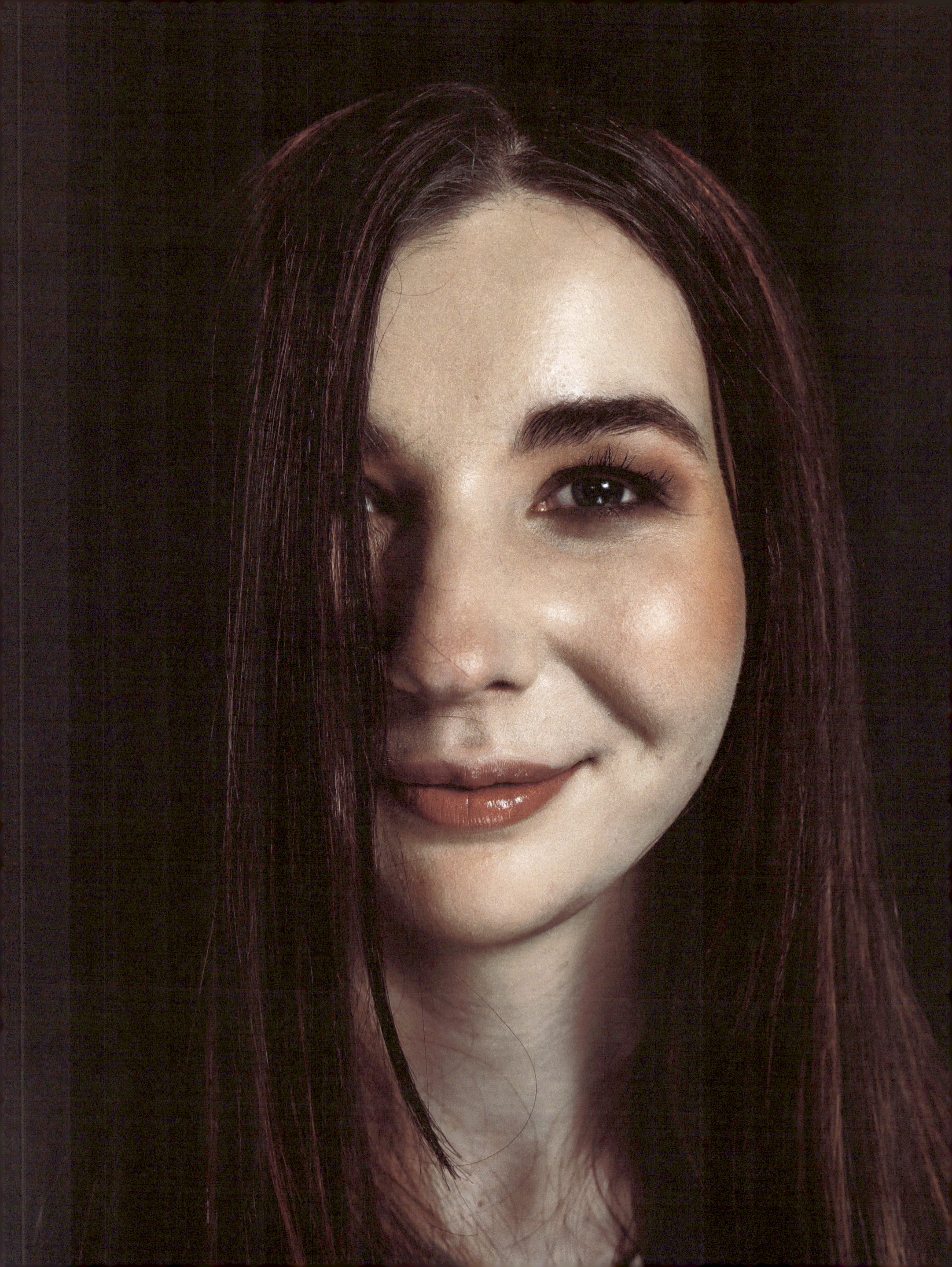

Lateisha Gizycki

Finding Strength Through Challenges

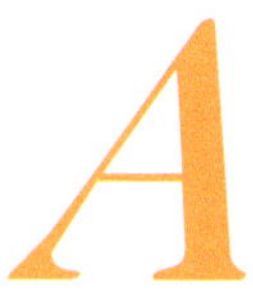

At just 26 years old, Lateisha is a beacon of determination, balancing her role as a childcare educator while pursuing her postgraduate diploma in early childhood education. Her journey is shaped by resilience and a commitment to self-discovery despite living with anxiety and depression.

"Being diagnosed with anxiety and depression late in primary school was a challenge," Lateisha shares. "It's something I've navigated through high school and into adulthood, but I'm figuring it out one step at a time."

Lateisha's ability to push through challenges is evident in both her personal and professional life. "Some days, staying focused is difficult," she explains. "My mind feels like a computer with too many tabs open. Completing assignments or staying on task can feel overwhelming, but I'm exploring strategies to manage, like creating structured to-do lists."

> *"You're not alone. It's okay to take your time, ask for help, and be yourself. Everyone is unique, and our differences are what make us special."*

Her resilience has been bolstered by a supportive network of family, friends, and colleagues. "At first, I felt alone, but over time, my loved ones have come to understand what I'm going through. Their encouragement has been invaluable, helping me feel more confident in my journey."

Travel has also played a pivotal role in Lateisha's growth. "Studying abroad in China for six months and visiting Bali recently were huge steps for me," she says. "Experiencing new environments has helped me grow more comfortable with change and the world around me."

Breaking barriers is deeply personal for Lateisha. "It's about not judging others and pushing past stereotypes. Sitting here today and sharing my story is a big step in breaking my own barriers," she reflects.

Looking to the future, Lateisha dreams of becoming a kindergarten teacher and travelling to Europe. "These are big goals," she admits with a smile. "But I'm determined to achieve them."

Creativity is another outlet that helps Lateisha stay grounded. "I love drawing, painting, playing the piano, and even singing karaoke despite my anxiety. Art helps me express myself and find peace."

Lateisha's message to others is one of hope and self-acceptance. "You're not alone. It's okay to take your time, ask for help, and be yourself. Everyone is unique, and our differences are what make us special."

Through her journey, Lateisha continues to inspire those around her with her resilience, creativity, and commitment to growth. Her story reminds us all that challenges can be opportunities for self-discovery and transformation.

"

It's about not judging others and pushing past stereotypes.

"

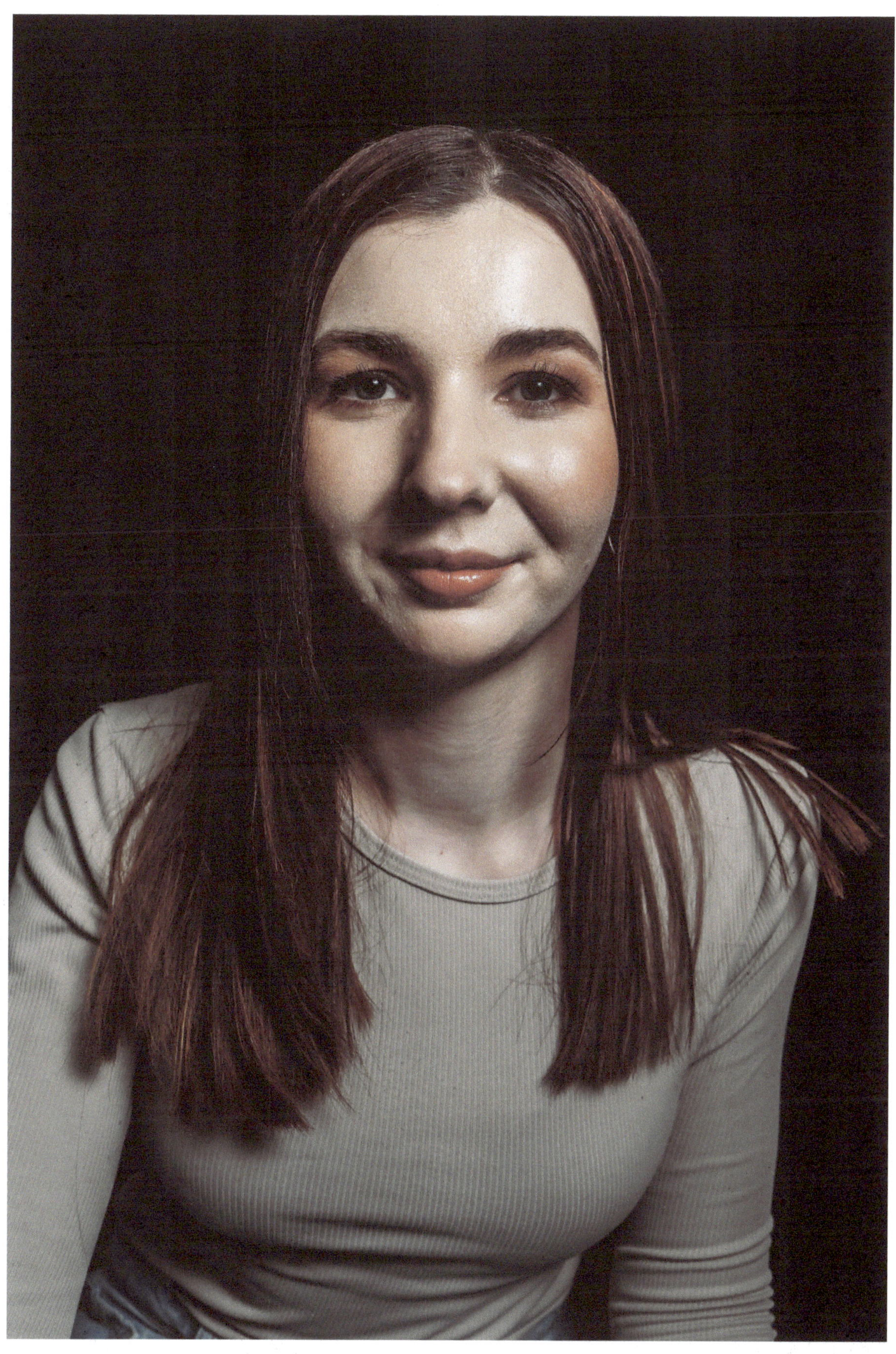

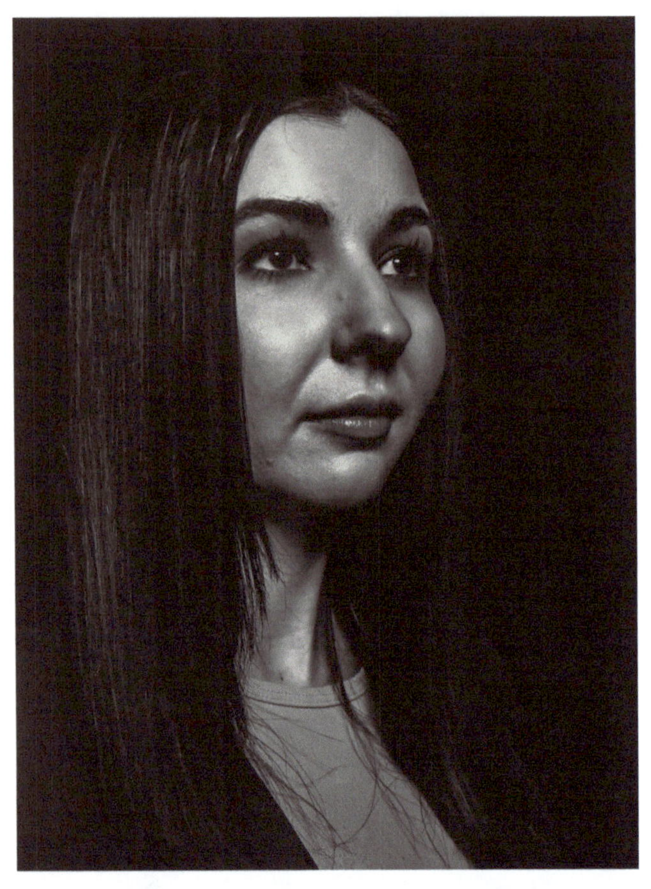
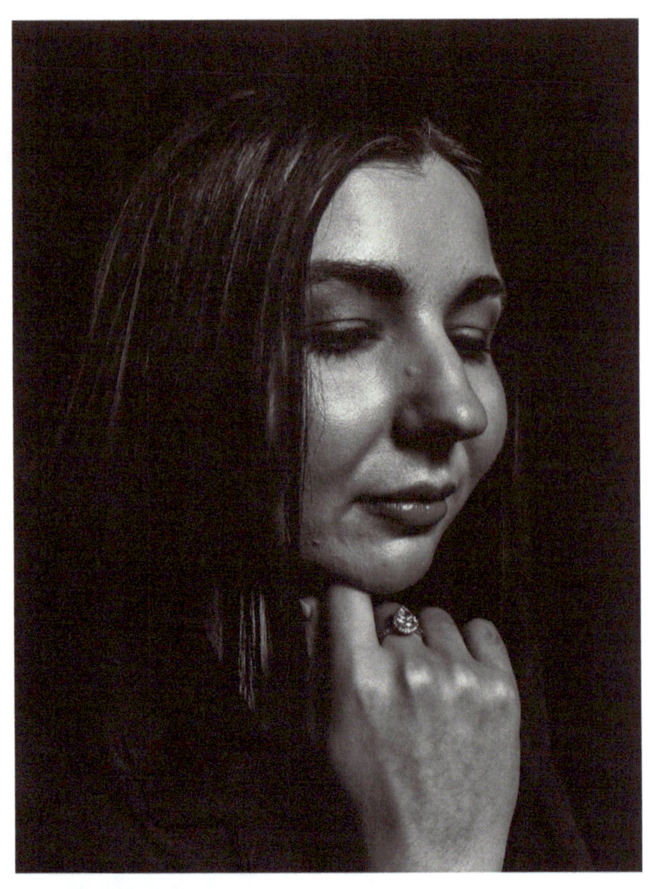
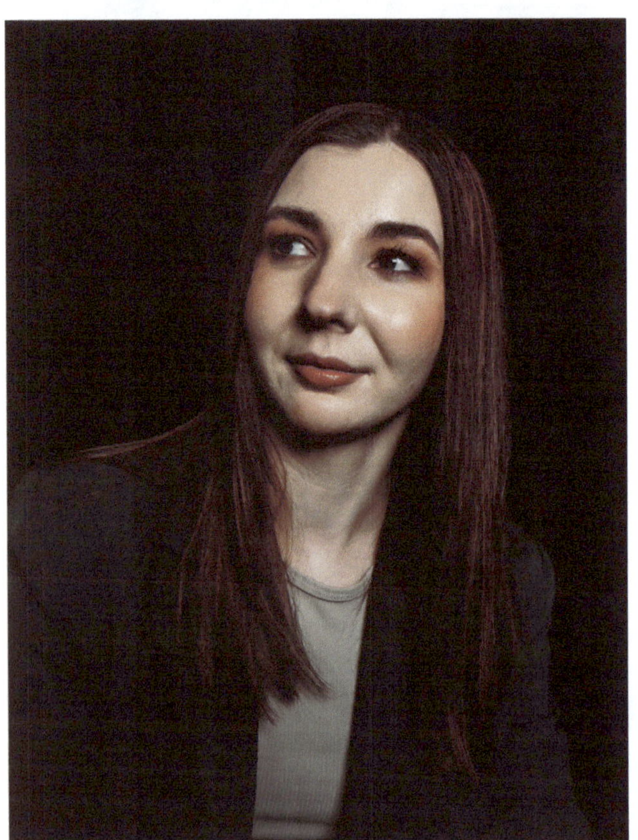
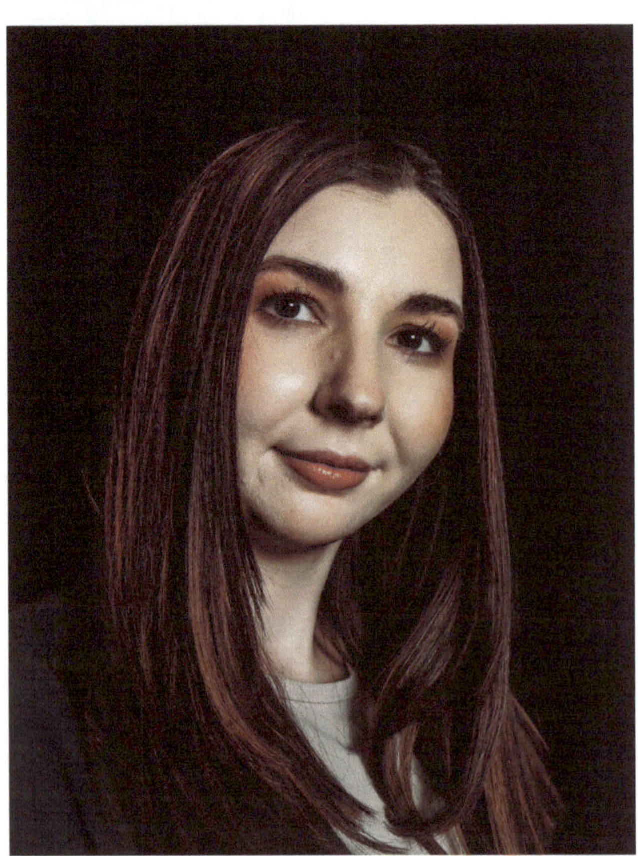

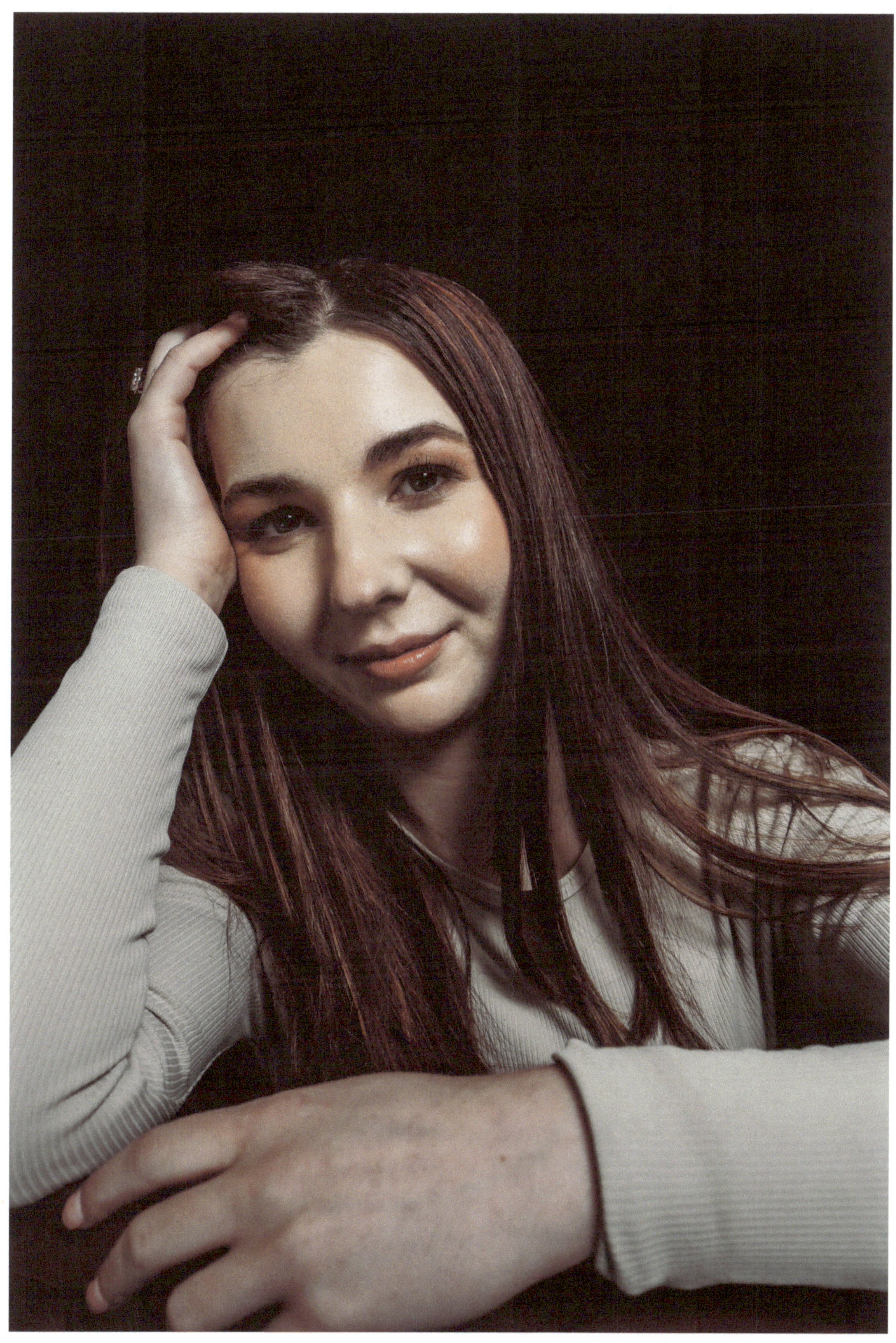

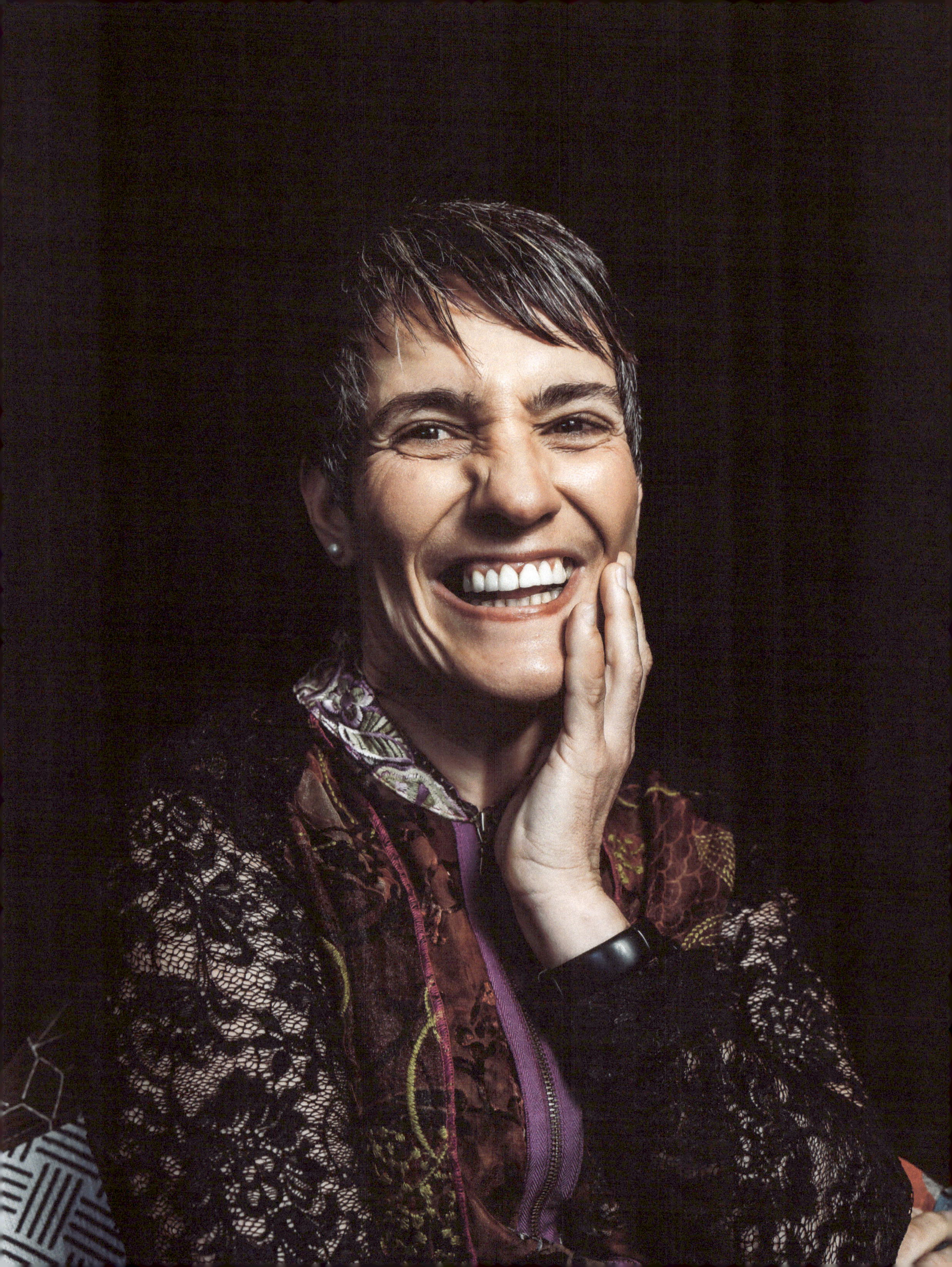

Nicole Spehar

Defying Expectations: A Pursuit of Strength and Independence

Nicole Spehar is a 44-year-old athlete, massage therapist, and advocate who has been defying expectations her entire life. Born with cerebral palsy, Nicole's journey is a testament to resilience, determination, and embracing one's abilities.

"I've had cerebral palsy since birth," Nicole shares. "It's all I've ever known. From a young age, I've been determined to succeed and do the best I can with what I have. That determination has carried me through many challenges."

Nicole's love for athletics began when she was 11 years old, and it has taken her around the world. "I've competed in Australia, Victoria, and even internationally. One of my proudest moments was winning a bronze medal in discus at the Pacific Games. Athletics has given me so much confidence and opened up opportunities I never thought possible."

Believe in yourself. Don't give up, and always give things a try. You never know what you're capable of until you push yourself.

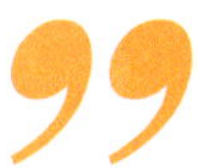

Over the years, Nicole has faced many challenges, including scepticism from others. "People doubted my ability to drive, but I didn't let that stop me. I told them, 'Give me a break, let me try. If I can't do it, I'll accept that—but don't decide for me.' That attitude has shaped so much of my life."

Nicole's achievements extend beyond athletics. She completed her VCE despite others doubting her abilities, and she now works as a massage therapist. "I've always loved proving people wrong when they say I can't do something. That word—'can't'—isn't in my vocabulary. There's always a way to adapt and modify."

Currently, Nicole is focused on her health and mobility. "A few years ago, I had a rolled disc in my back, which has affected my walking. I've been using a walker for over a year now, but my goal is to get off it and regain more independence. I'd also love to get back into running and continue competing in field events like discus and shot put."

When asked about societal inclusivity, Nicole reflects on the progress that has been made and the work that remains. "We've come a long way, but there's still a lot to do. It shouldn't be a question of whether a building is accessible—it should be a given. We need a world where everyone is included without question."

Nicole's advice to others facing obstacles is simple yet powerful: "Believe in yourself. Don't give up, and always give things a try. You never know what you're capable of until you push yourself."

Her involvement in this project is rooted in her desire to inspire others and promote inclusivity. "If sharing my story can encourage just one or two people to pursue their dreams or rethink accessibility, then it's worth it. Everyone has abilities—focus on what people can do, not what they can't."

Nicole credits her mum as one of her greatest inspirations. "She's always been my advocate, fighting for me to attend mainstream school and ensuring I had the opportunities I deserved. I've also been inspired by other athletes and mentors who've supported me on and off the track."

Looking ahead, Nicole hopes to continue making a difference in the disability sector. "I'd love to get more involved in advocacy, whether through speaking engagements or helping others navigate their own journeys. It's all about giving back."

Her message to the world is clear: "Don't look at the disability—look at the ability. Focus on what people can do rather than what they can't."

Nicole's story is one of resilience, positivity, and breaking barriers. "Life isn't always easy, but it's worth every challenge. We're all capable of so much more than we realise."

Don't look at the disability—everyone has abilities—focus on what people can do, not what they can't.

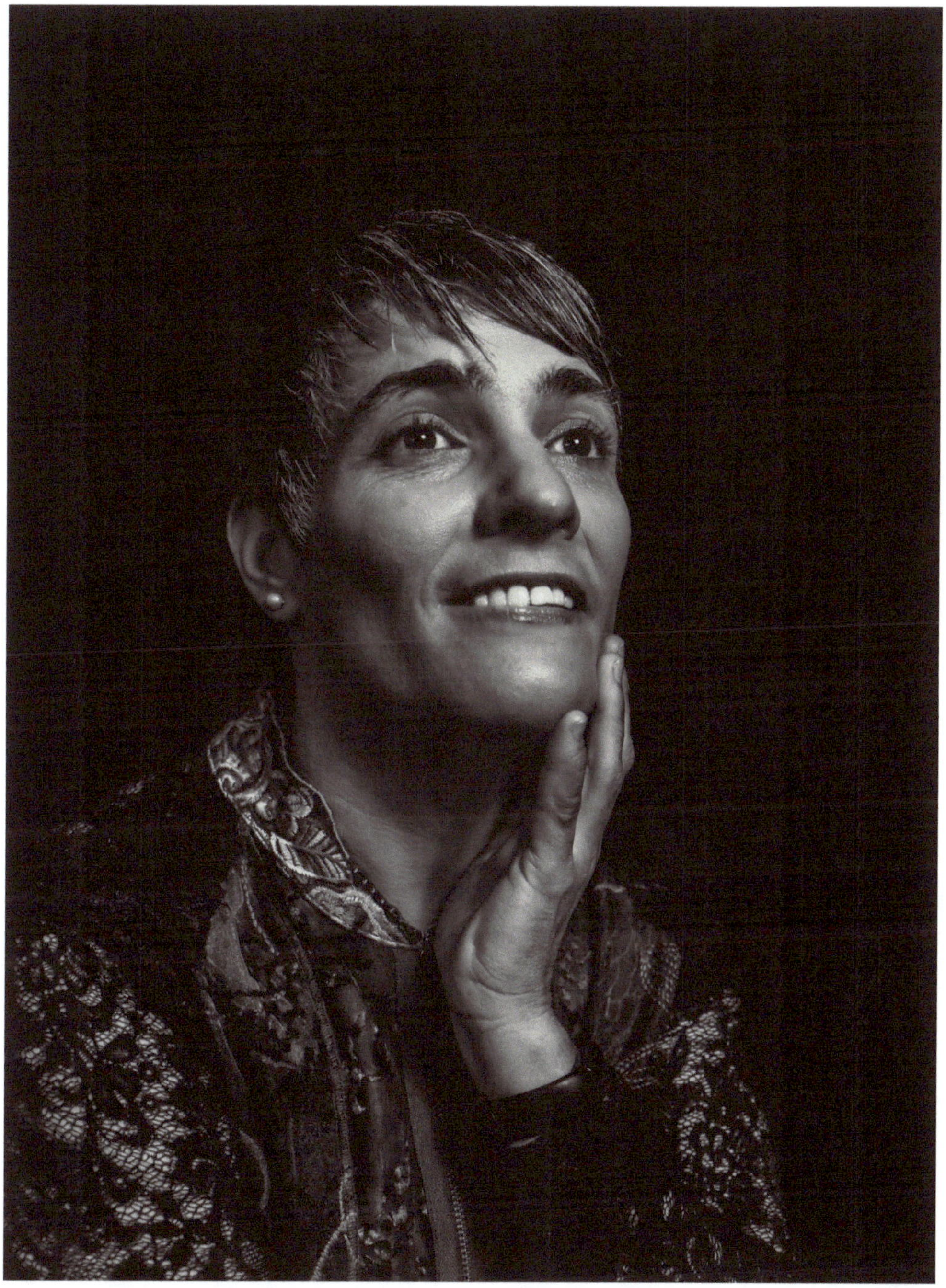

Give me a break, let me try. If I can't do it, I'll accept that—but don't decide for me.

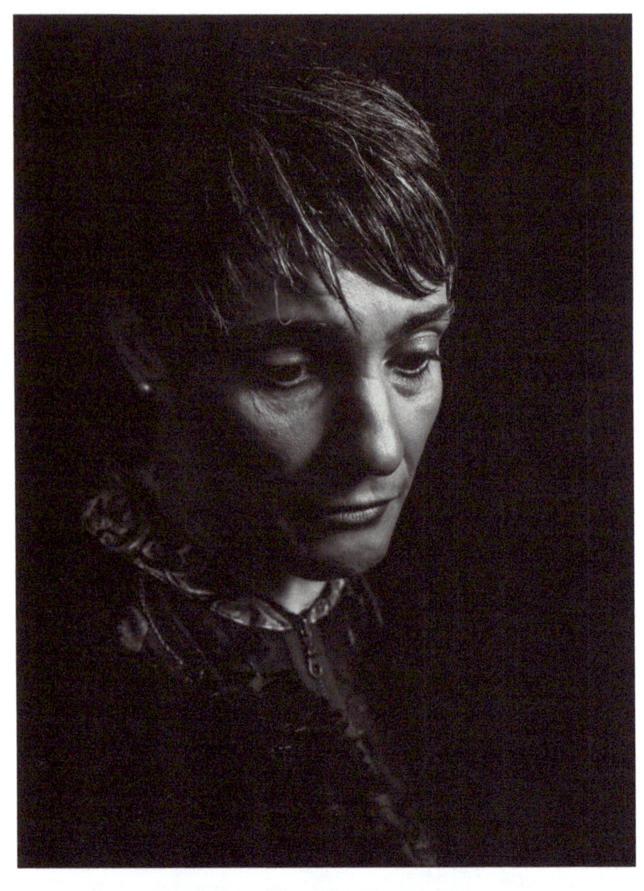
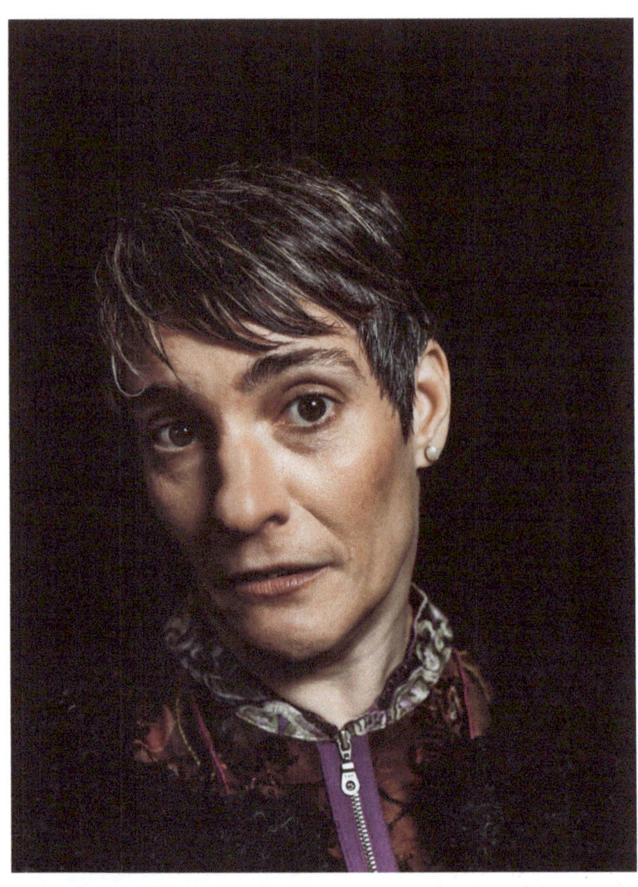
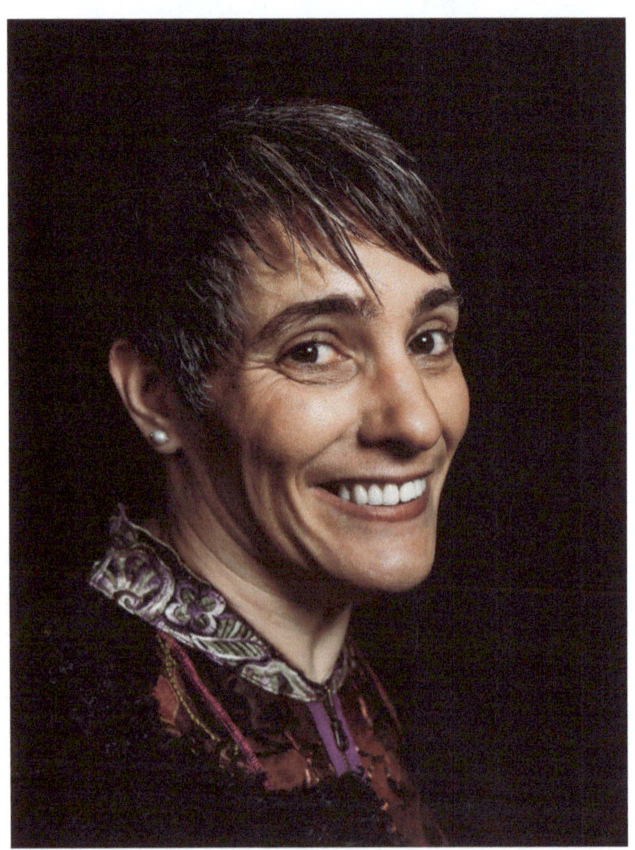
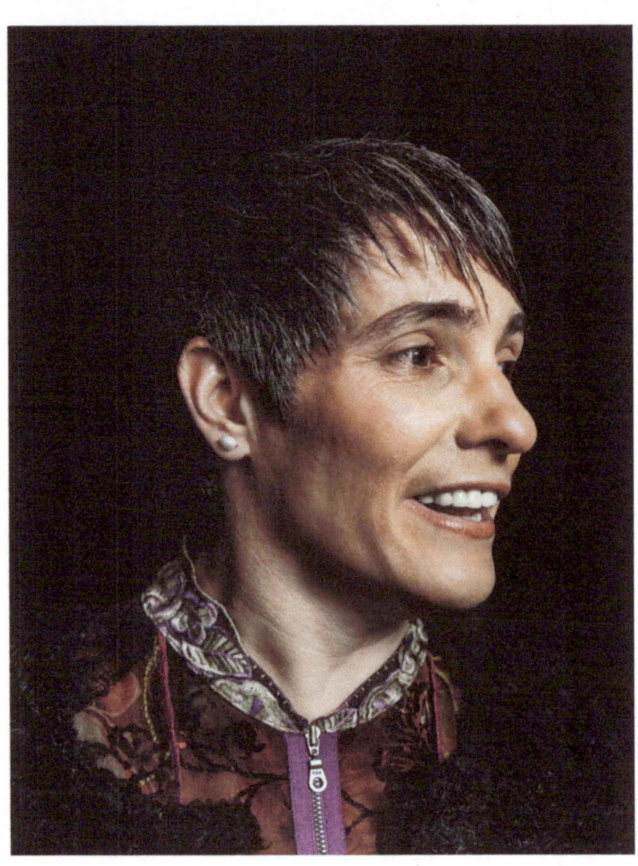

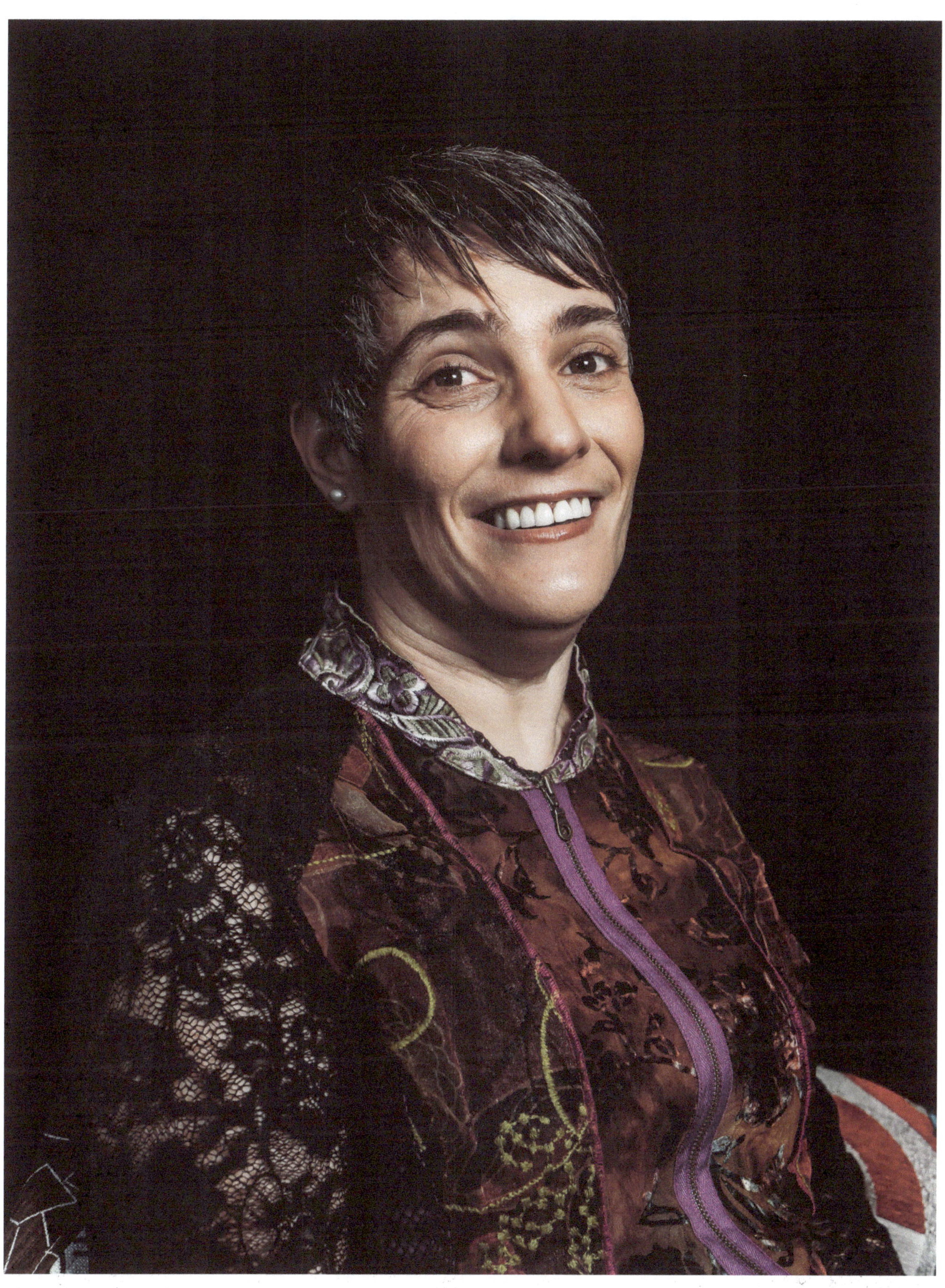

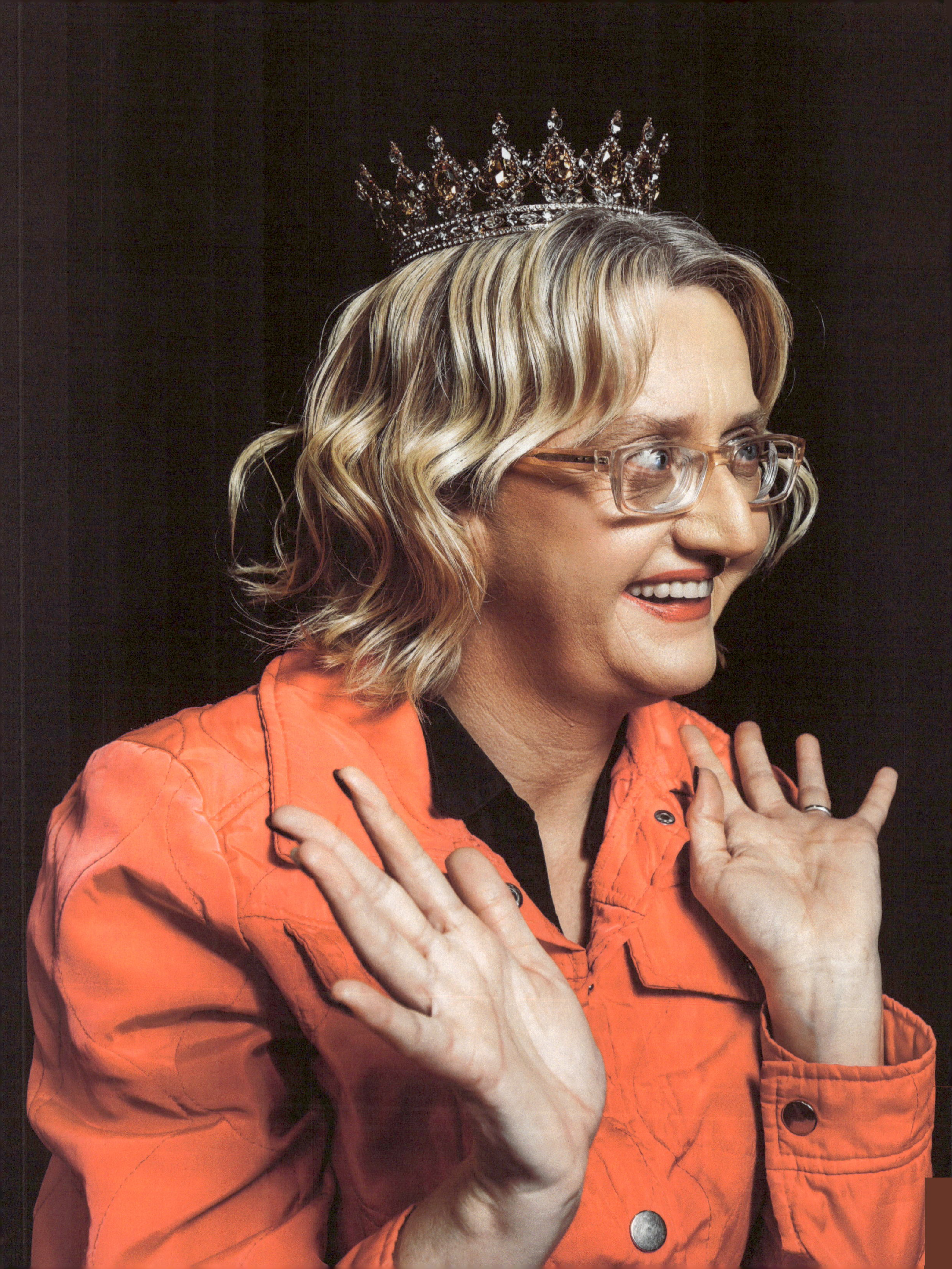

Raegan Cavagnino

Beyond Sight: Raegan's Journey of Resilience and Advocacy

Raegan Cavagnino is a woman of extraordinary resilience and determination. Born blind, she has navigated life with a spirit that refuses to be limited by her disability. From her early years to adulthood, Raegan has exemplified what it means to embrace challenges and turn them into opportunities for growth and advocacy.

Raegan's journey began with learning essential skills to navigate the world as a visually impaired individual. At the age of 15, she learned to type, a milestone that became a pivotal tool in her education and independence. "Typing opened up the world for me," she shares. "It gave me access to communication and learning in ways I couldn't have imagined before."

Her parents played an integral role in her early development, ensuring she was equipped with the skills and confidence to thrive. "I was fortunate to have parents who advocated for me and pushed for inclusion," she says. "They taught me that my blindness didn't define me—it was just one part of who I am."

> *"You are capable of more than you think. Don't let the world's perceptions limit your potential. Find your strengths, adapt, and keep moving forward."*

Throughout her life, Raegan has encountered and overcome societal misconceptions about blindness. "People often think blindness means helplessness," she reflects. "But that's far from the truth. Blindness has taught me adaptability, problem-solving, and resilience."

Breaking barriers is a theme that runs through every facet of Raegan's life. Whether it's navigating education, the workplace, or social environments, she has consistently challenged stereotypes and inspired others to see beyond her disability. "I've had to prove that I am capable, independent, and equal," she explains. "It's not always easy, but it's always worth it."

Raegan's involvement in *Breaking the Barriers Through the Lens* has been a meaningful experience. "This project is about visibility—not just in the literal sense, but in showing the world that people with disabilities are vibrant, capable, and full of potential," she says. "It's about sharing stories that challenge perceptions and foster understanding."

Technology has been a crucial enabler for Raegan, allowing her to live independently and stay connected with the world. "From screen readers to voice-activated devices, technology is a game-changer," she says. "It enables me to work, communicate, and explore life on my terms."

Raegan's hobbies and interests reflect her adventurous and creative spirit. She enjoys spending time with friends and family, engaging in community activities, and exploring new opportunities for growth. "Life is about adapting and finding joy in the journey," she says. "Blindness doesn't stop me—it simply pushes me to find different ways to achieve my goals."

Looking ahead, Raegan is committed to advocating for greater inclusion and accessibility for people with disabilities. "The world has come a long way, but there's still work to do," she says. "I want to be part of creating a society where everyone feels seen, valued, and empowered."

Her message to others is one of hope and perseverance: "You are capable of more than you think. Don't let the world's perceptions limit your potential. Find your strengths, adapt, and keep moving forward."

Through her advocacy, strength, and positive outlook, Raegan is breaking barriers and inspiring others to do the same. Her story is a reminder that true vision comes from seeing the possibilities within ourselves and others.

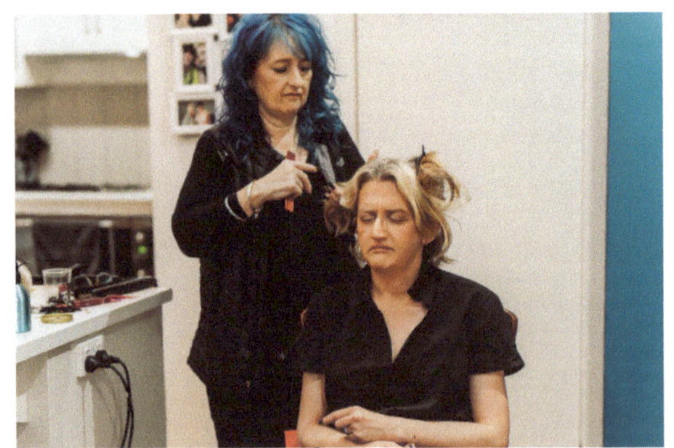

“*blindness didn't define me—it was just one part of who I am.*”

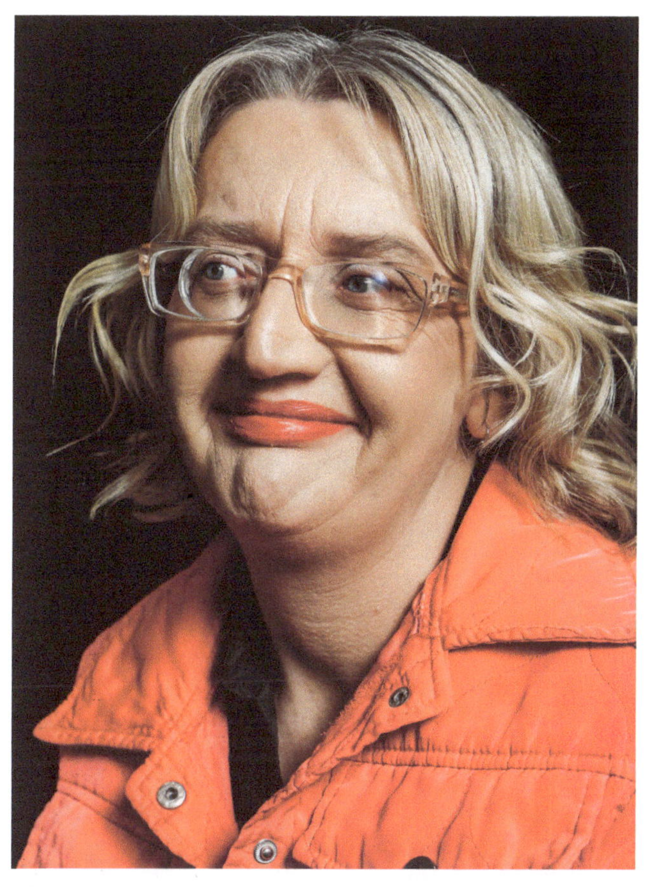
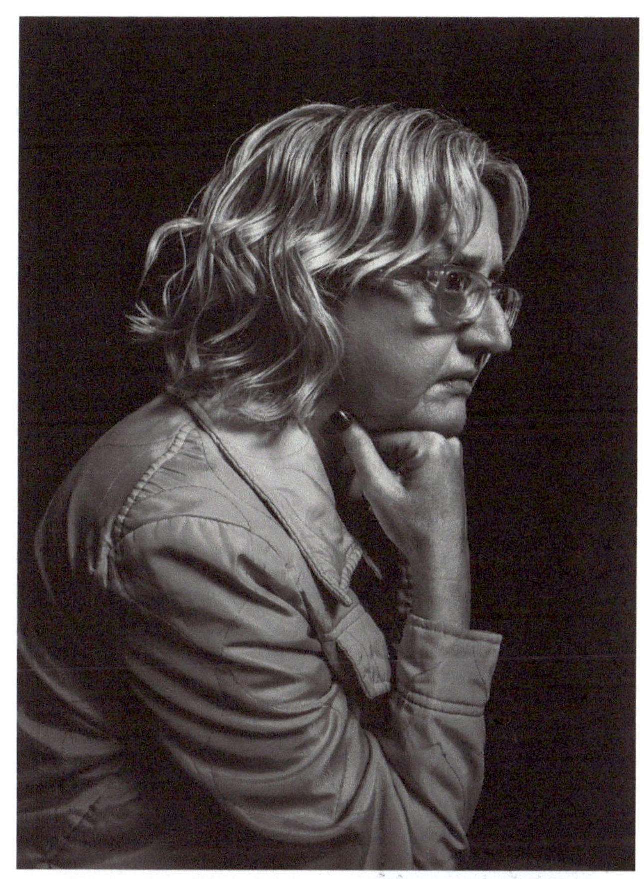
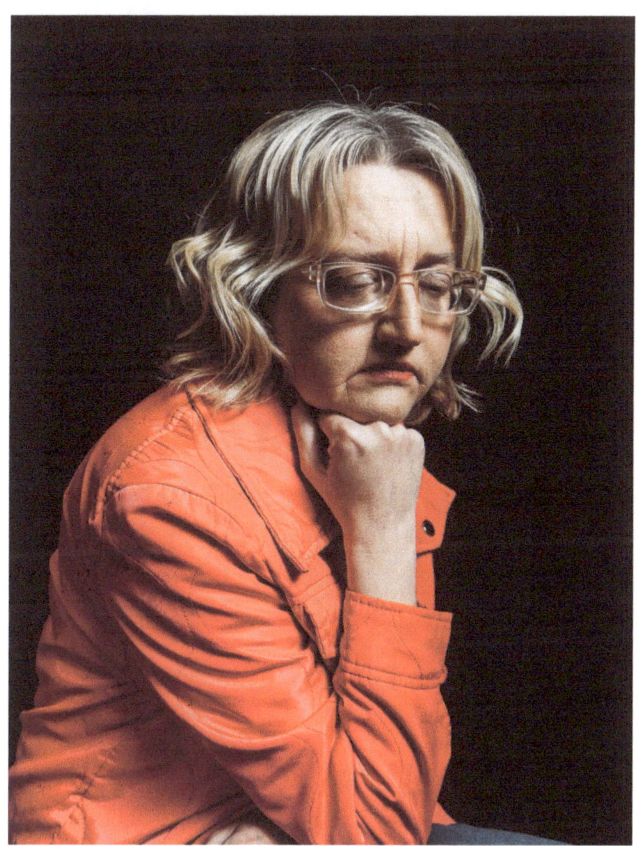
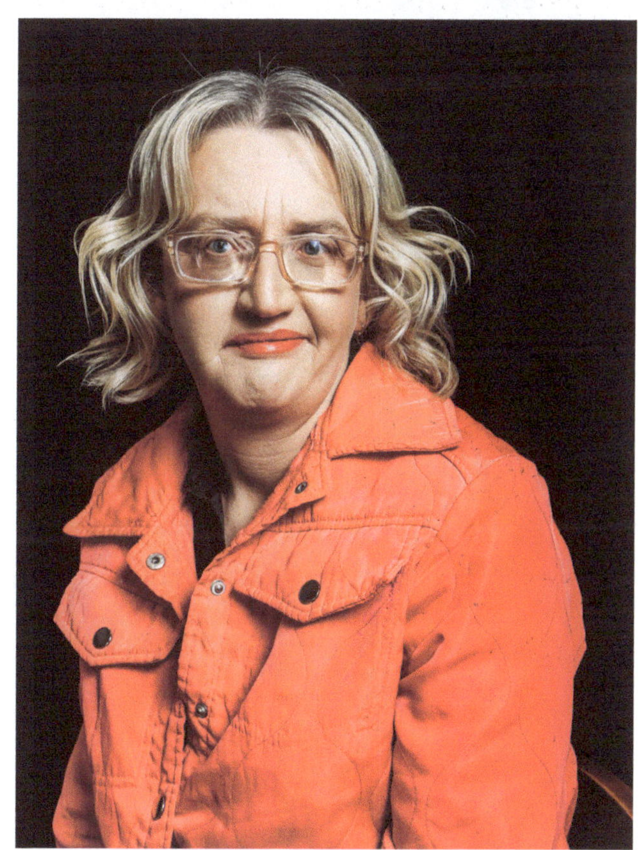

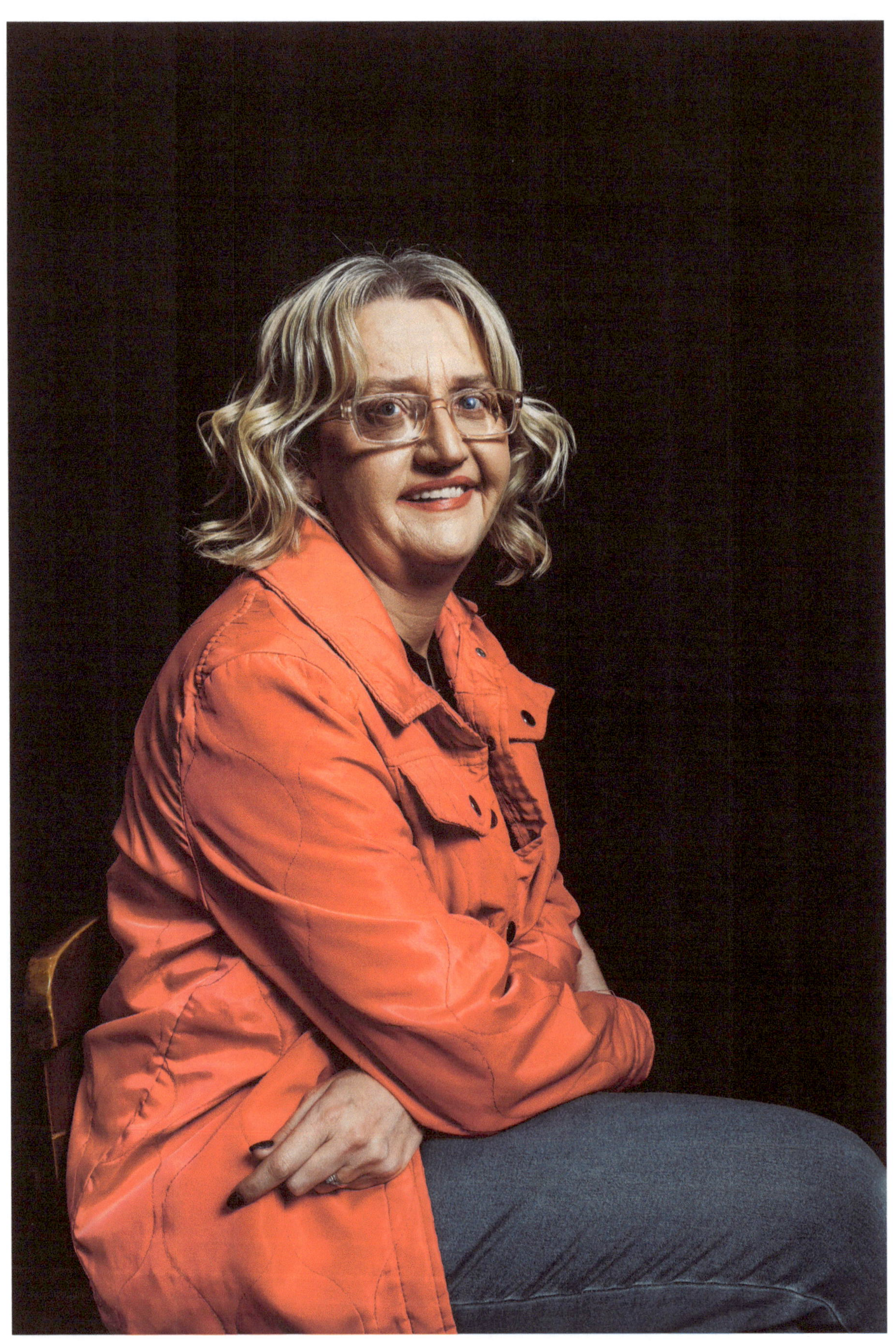

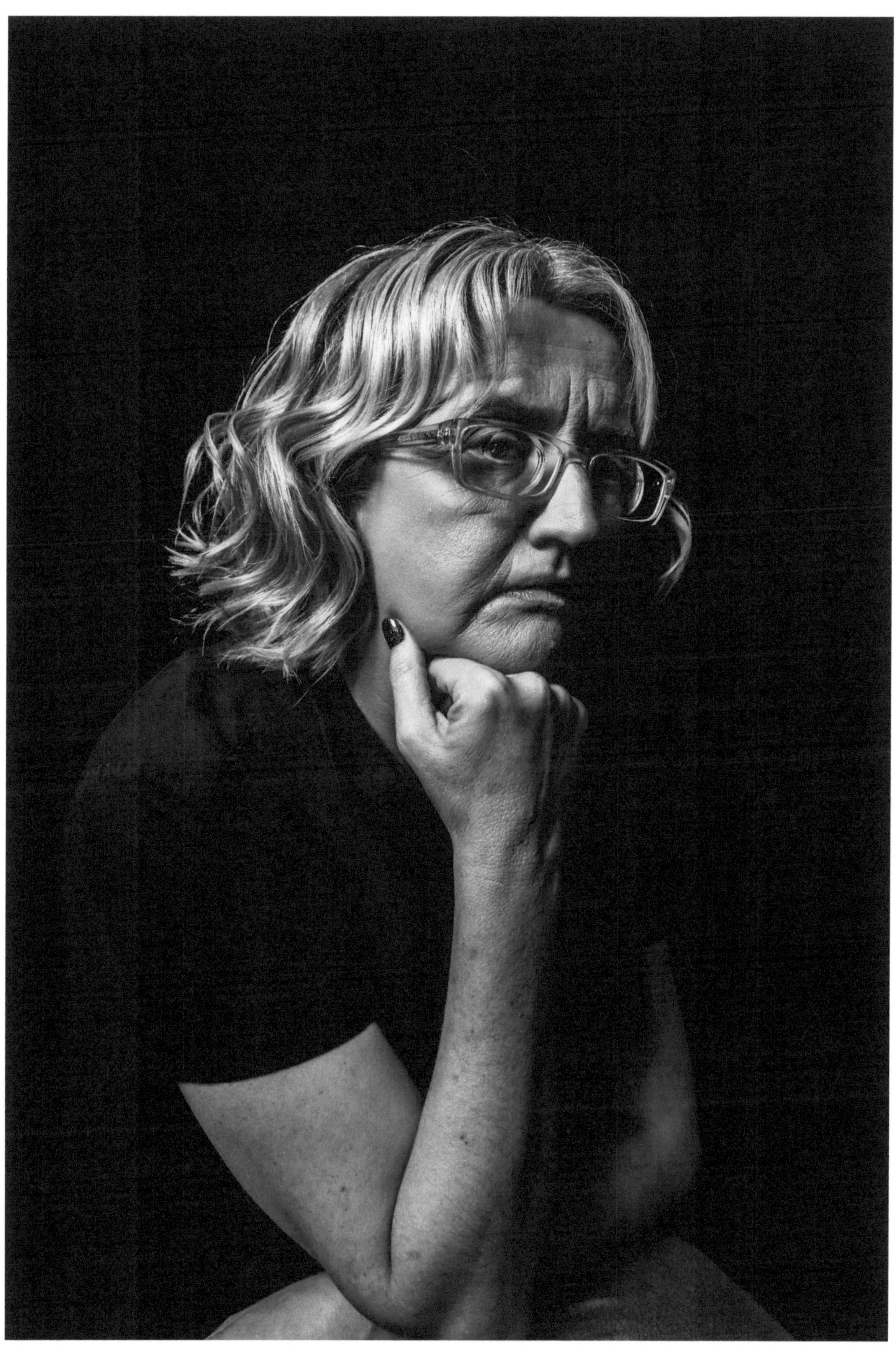

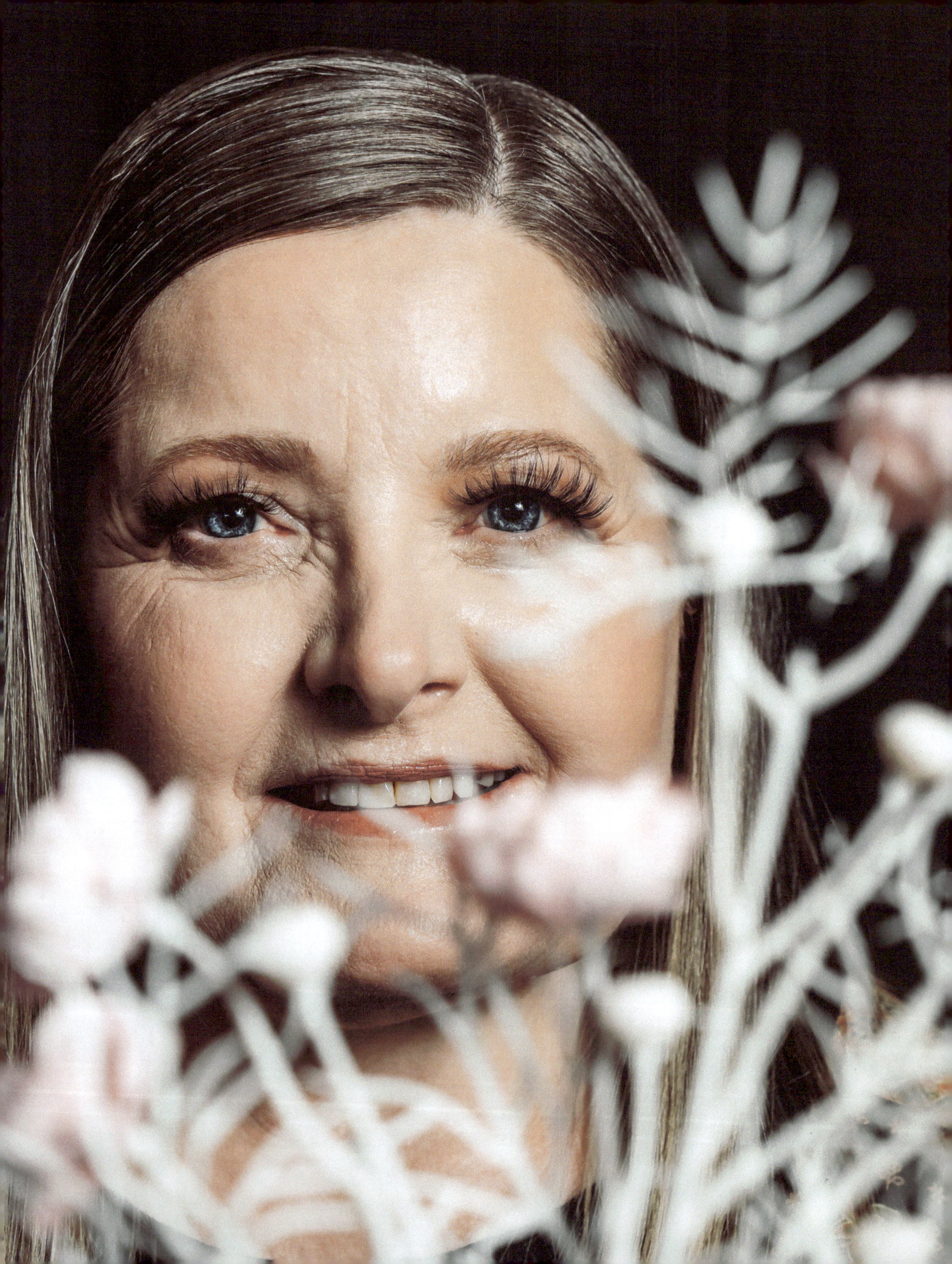

■ Sandy Johnston

Standing Tall: A Story of Overcoming Challenges with Grace

Sandy Johnston's journey is one of resilience, growth, and self-discovery. Born with Klippel-Feil Syndrome and Sprengel's Shoulder, Sandy's physical differences and chronic pain have been lifelong companions. Despite these challenges, she has chosen to live a full and meaningful life, reshaping barriers into stepping stones.

"My chronic pain has been with me since I was young," Sandy shares. "At first, I had a toxic relationship with it. Anger made it worse, so I had to consciously shift my narrative to find peace. Acceptance doesn't mean I like it, but it allows me to focus on living my life instead of fighting what I can't change."

One of Sandy's proudest achievements came as a teenager when she became an exchange student in the United States. "I didn't know where I would end up, but I spent a year at an American high school. Their culture of positivity was infectious, and I came back believing in myself in a way I never had before."

> *Surround yourself with empathetic people, dig deep, and embrace life as much as possible.*

However, life hasn't always been smooth. Sandy faced psychological abuse in a past relationship, an experience that nearly cost her and her children their safety. "I didn't even recognise it as abuse at first. Coercive control is so gradual and insidious. But when it became life-threatening, I had no choice but to leave and rebuild our lives from the ground up."

This period of recovery forced Sandy to confront difficult questions about self-worth. "Why didn't I value myself? Why didn't I like who I was? My disability made me feel different and less than others. It wasn't until I embraced self-love and acceptance that I could start to thrive. Now, I own who I am—unapologetically."

Today, Sandy uses her story to inspire and educate others about the complexities of living with disabilities. "Not all disabilities are visible, and everyone's challenges are unique. I want people to stop judging others by appearances. Disability isn't a dirty word, and it doesn't define who I am."

Sandy's advice to others is simple but profound: "Surround yourself with empathetic people, dig deep, and embrace life as much as possible. It's easy to withdraw when the challenges feel insurmountable, but participating in life, even in small ways, can make all the difference."

Through her involvement in this project, Sandy hopes to change perceptions. "I want to show that you can't always see a disability, and you certainly can't assume someone's abilities just by looking at them. Everyone's story is unique, and we all deserve understanding and compassion."

Sandy's strength and wisdom are a testament to the power of resilience and the beauty of self-acceptance. "It's not about perfection; it's about living authentically and fully, no matter what life throws your way."

"

Everyone's story is unique, and we all deserve understanding and compassion.

"

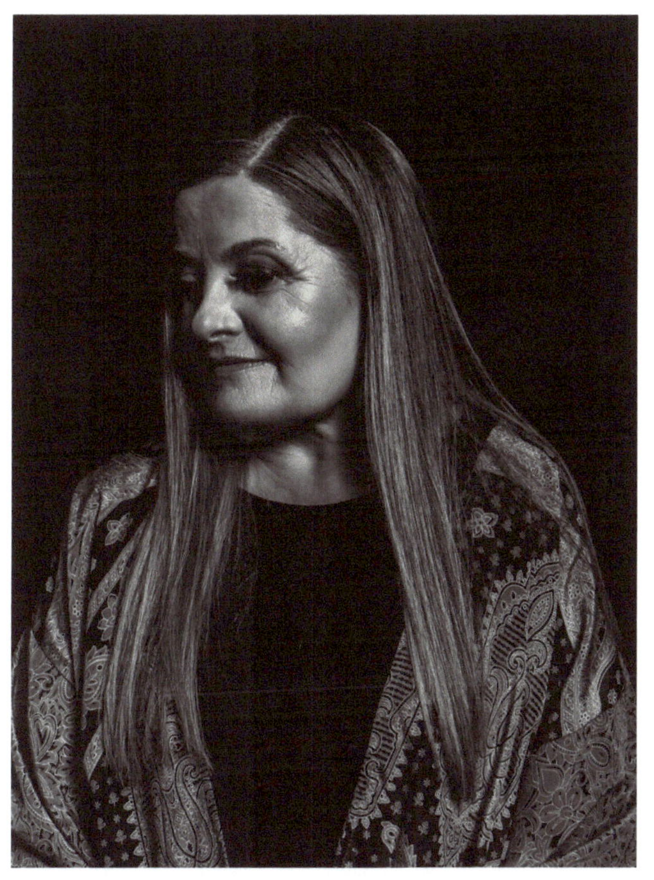

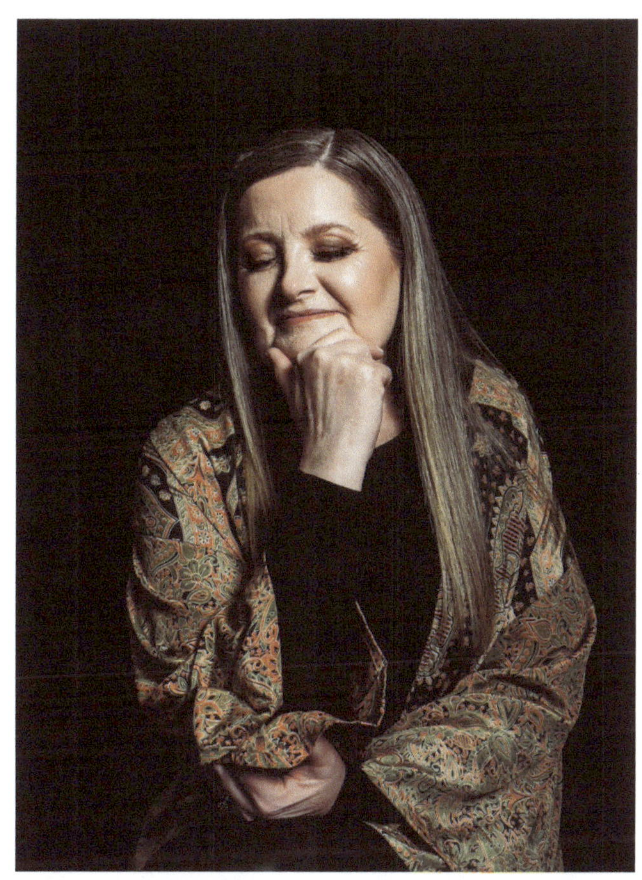

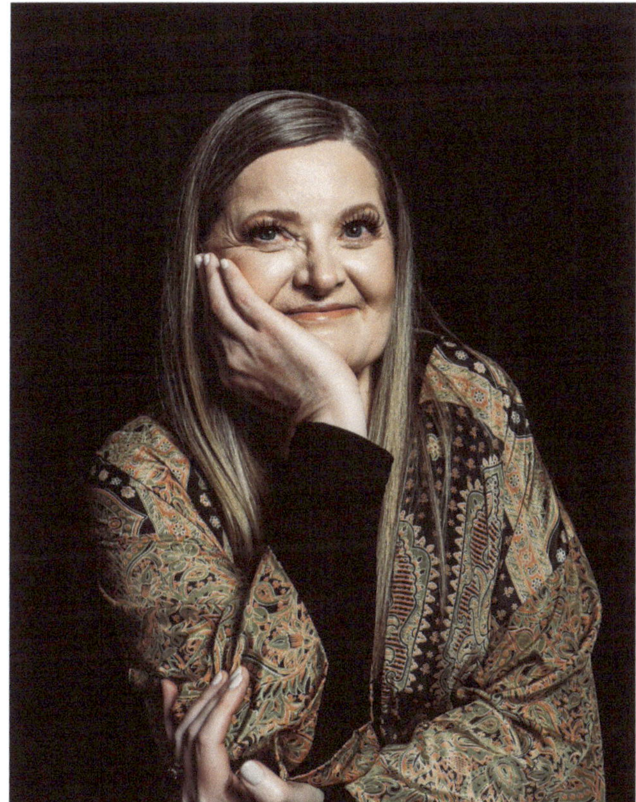

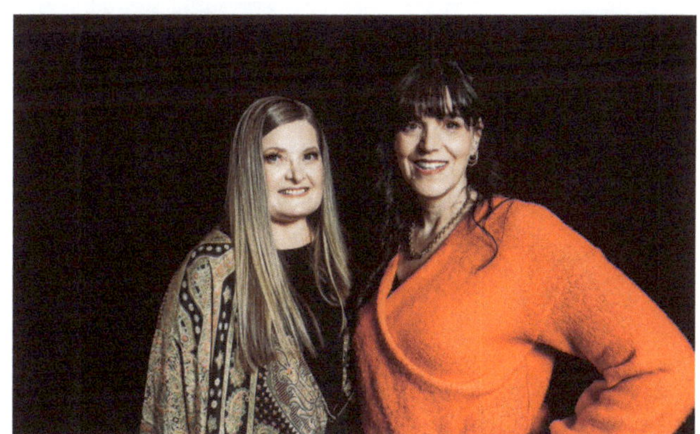

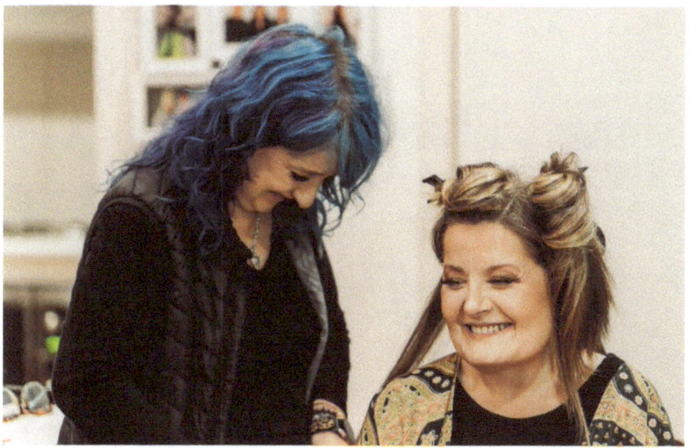

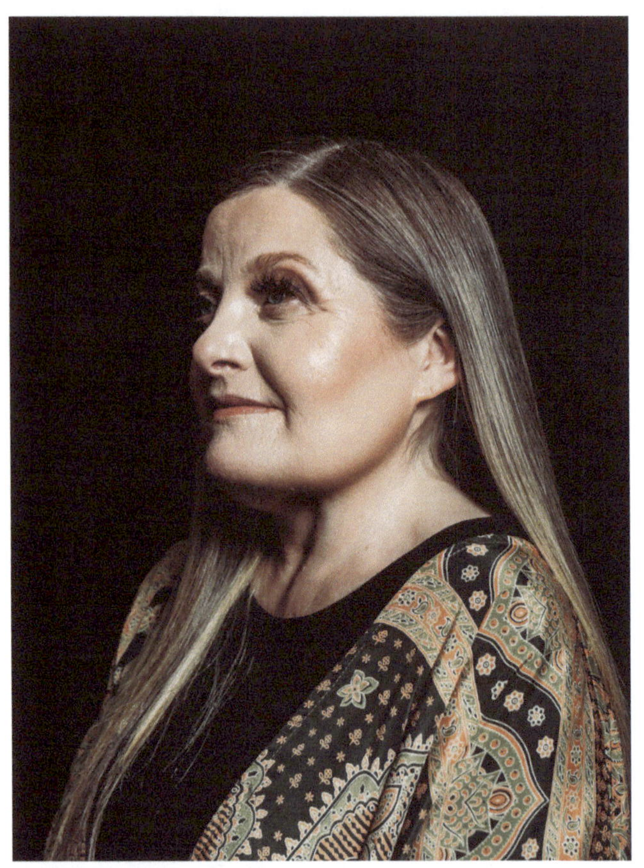

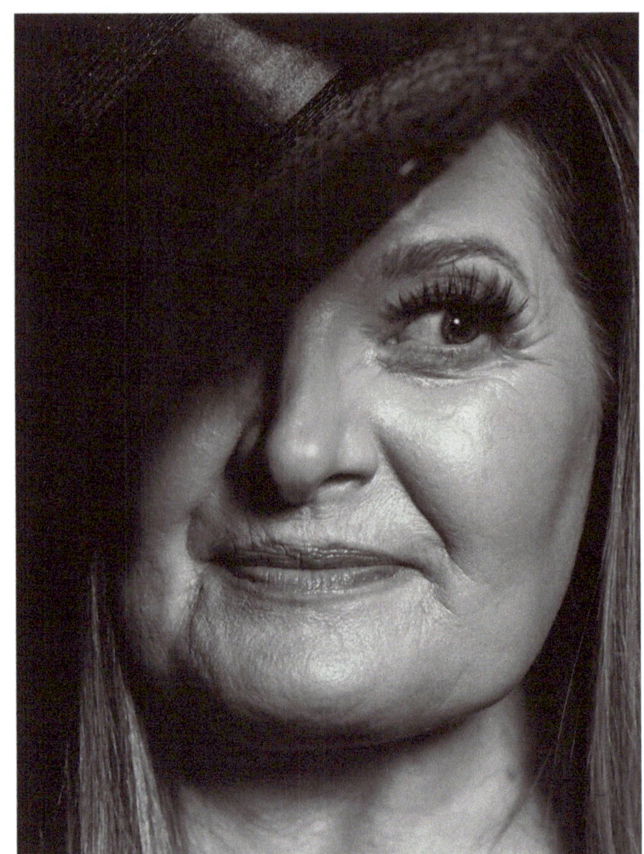

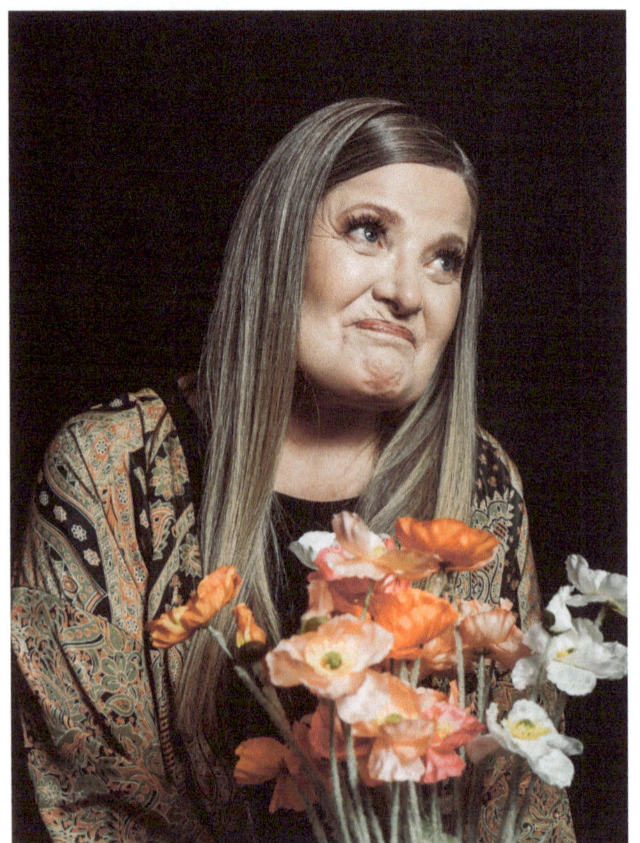

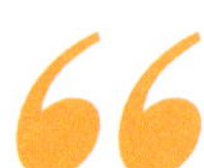

Participating in life, even in small ways, can make all the difference.

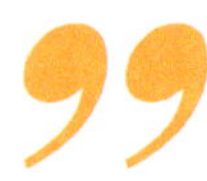

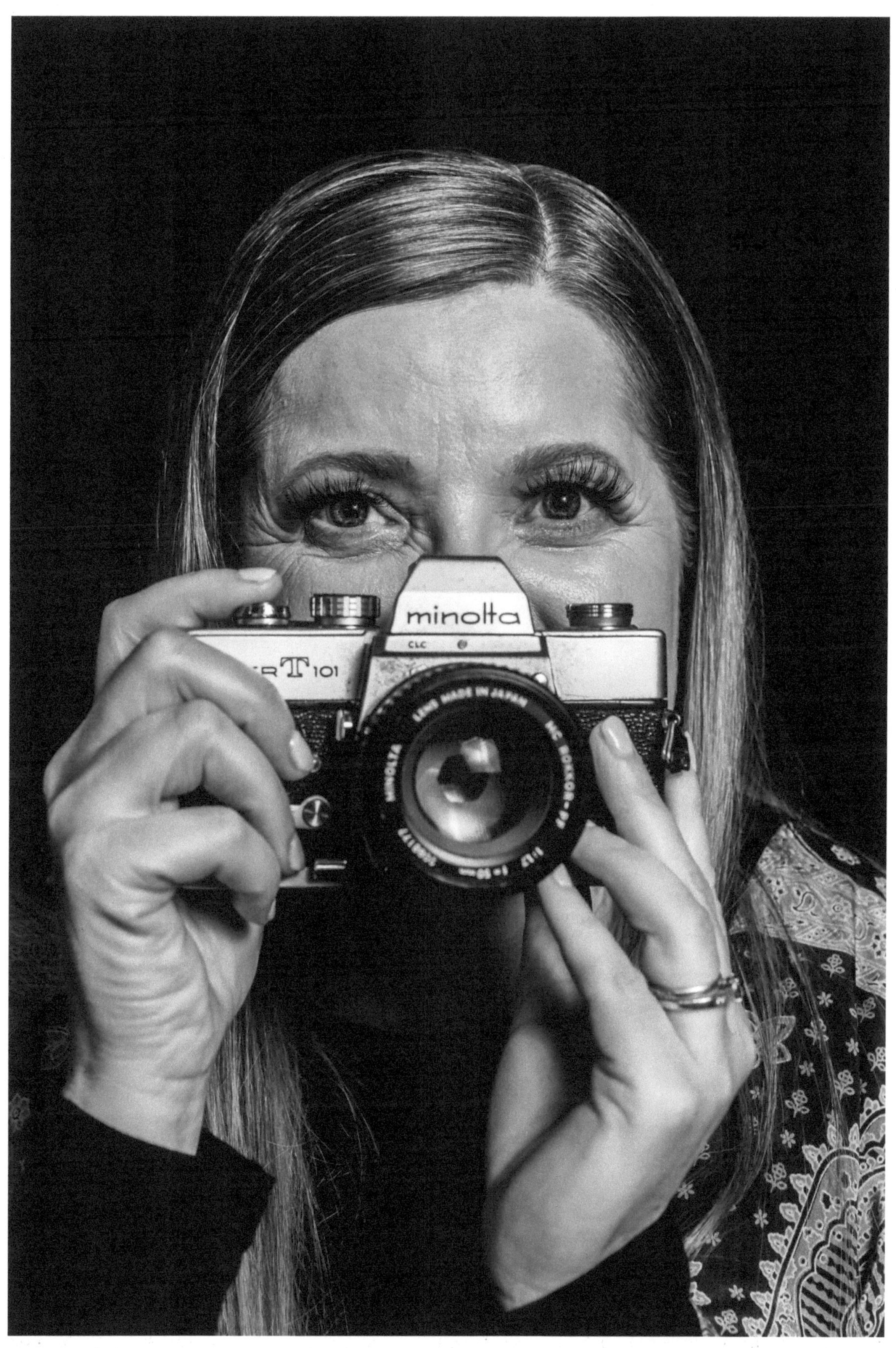
minolta
CLC

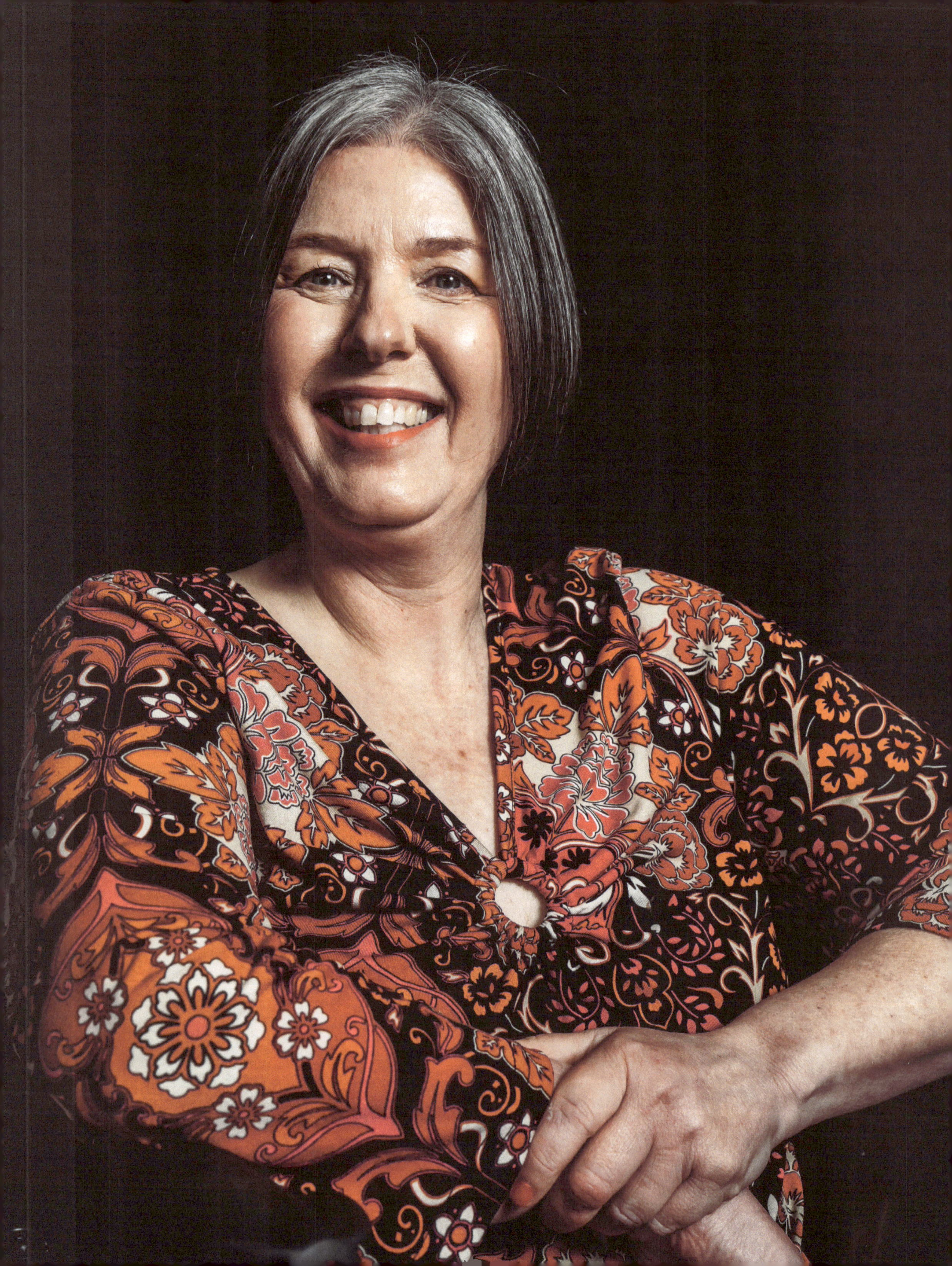

Tanya kay

Standing Tall: A Story of Overcoming Challenges with Grace

At 57 years old, Tanya Kayembodies resilience, adaptability, and a determination to find new ways of thriving despite the challenges of living with multiple sclerosis (MS). Diagnosed with relapsing-remitting MS just six years ago, Tanya's journey has been one of self-discovery, adjusting to a new normal, and learning to embrace life's changes with grace.

Reflecting on her diagnosis, Tanya recalls, "I wasn't surprised. In fact, I had suspected MS or something similar for years. The symptoms had been there—just one here and one there—for over two decades. But I was misdiagnosed with arthritis about 19 years ago. It wasn't until 2018 that I finally had an answer."

Living with MS has profoundly impacted Tanya's life. "It's affected every aspect of my daily life and activities," she shares. "I used to love playing tennis, badminton, and sewing, but mobility issues and fatigue have made those things impossible now."

> *Stay positive and motivated. Your state of mind is everything. Just do what you can for as long as you can, and keep moving forward.*

Tanya's current focus is on finding new hobbies and activities that align with her abilities. "I'm still exploring," she says. "One of my biggest hobbies at the moment seems to be going to appointments—physio, doctors, specialists. Managing MS becomes a full-time job."

Learning to adapt hasn't been easy, but Tanya has developed strategies to cope with the demands of MS. "Rest is a big part of my day," she explains. "I don't nap, but I need time to put my feet up and let my body recover. Fatigue is relentless, and it's not just physical—it's mental too."

One of Tanya's proudest moments was her first trip since becoming disabled. "I travelled to Queensland recently, and it was a huge deal for me. Using a wheelchair at the airport, organising logistics, and managing the physical toll of travel—it was all new and overwhelming. But I did it. It was empowering to break that mental barrier and prove to myself that I could still explore the world."

Driving is another milestone Tanya is tackling. "After a year of being unable to drive, I had to relearn with a left-foot accelerator and take multiple lessons. It took over a year to regain my restricted license, and now I'm working on building my confidence to drive in traffic again."

When asked about breaking barriers, Tanya explains, "It's about stepping out of my comfort zone and challenging myself to do things I didn't think I could. Being here today, sharing my story is part of that journey."

Tanya's message to others facing similar challenges is one of hope and perseverance. "Stay positive and motivated. Your state of mind is everything. Just do what you can for as long as you can, and keep moving forward."

Through her journey, Tanya has encountered misconceptions about MS and disabilities in general. "People often don't understand invisible symptoms," she says. "Even with visible mobility issues, I've had people doubt my diagnosis. It's frustrating, but it highlights the importance of education and awareness."

Participating in this project has been a meaningful experience for Tanya. "It's an opportunity to share my story and help others understand what living with MS is really like. Projects like this are so important for raising awareness and creating a more inclusive society."

Looking ahead, Tanya hopes to continue travelling and discovering new ways to enjoy life. "I'd love to take another trip, maybe interstate for now. I'm taking things one step at a time, finding joy where I can, and learning to adapt."

Tanya's journey is a testament to resilience and the power of breaking barriers. Her story inspires others to keep pushing forward, no matter the challenges they face.

Even with visible mobility issues, I've had people doubt my diagnosis. It's frustrating, but it highlights the importance of education and awareness.

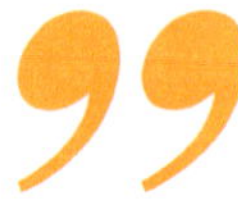

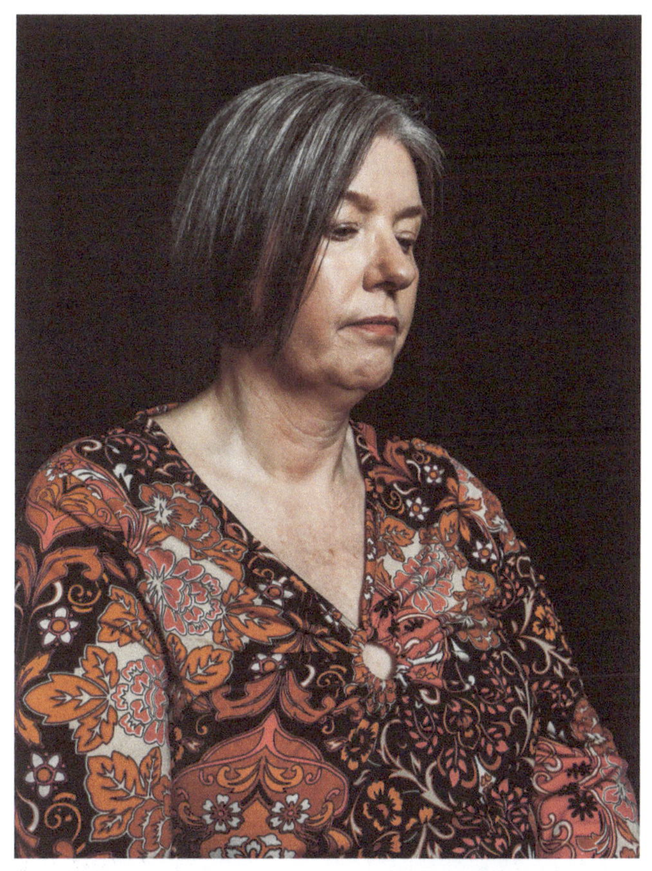
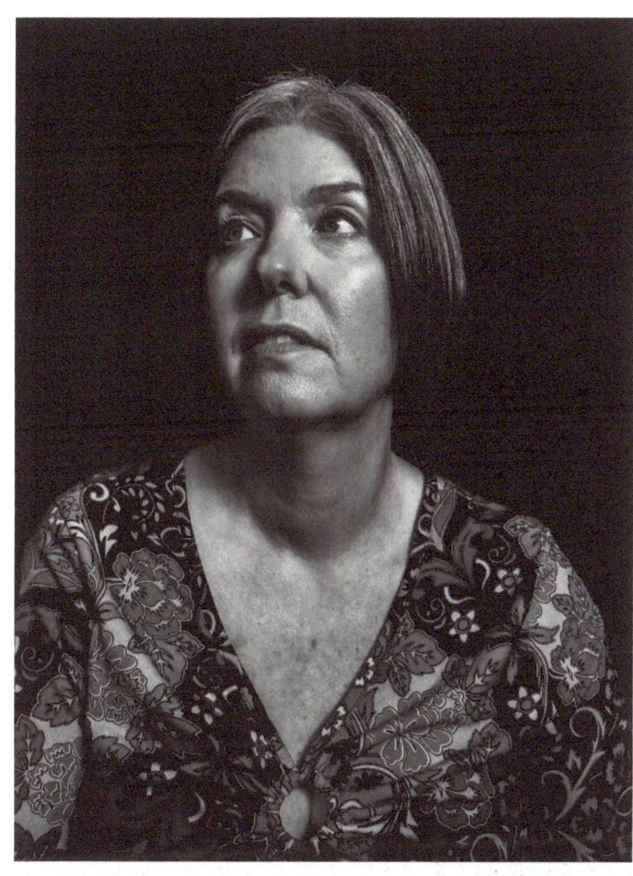
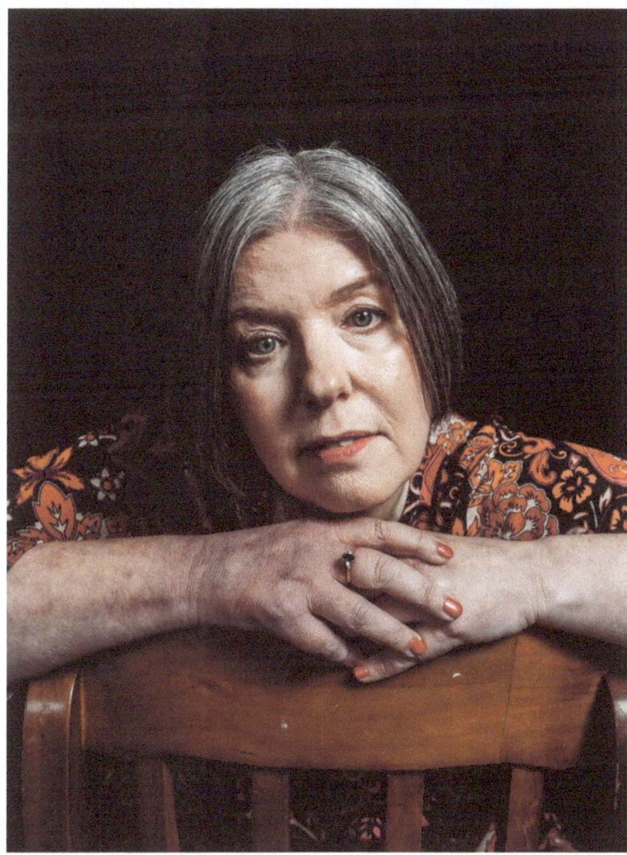
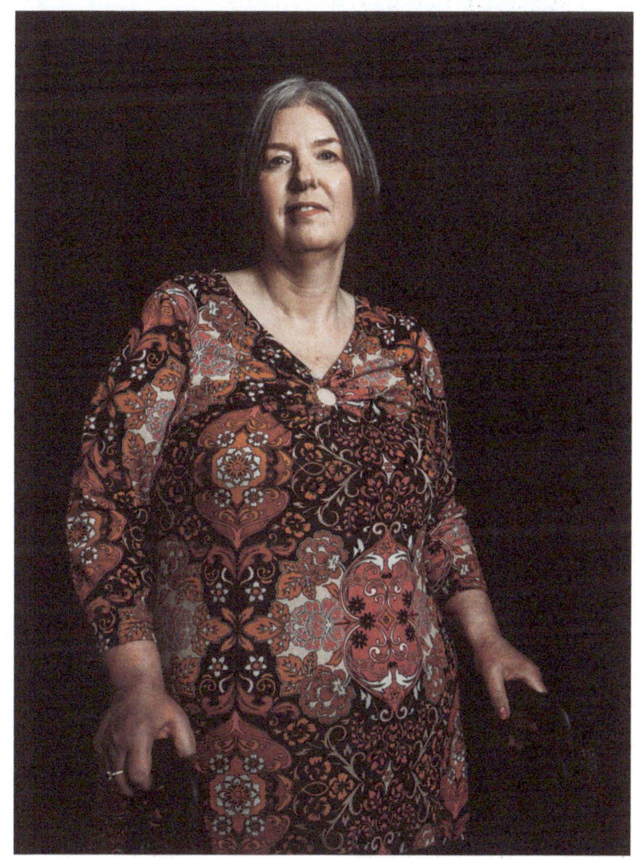

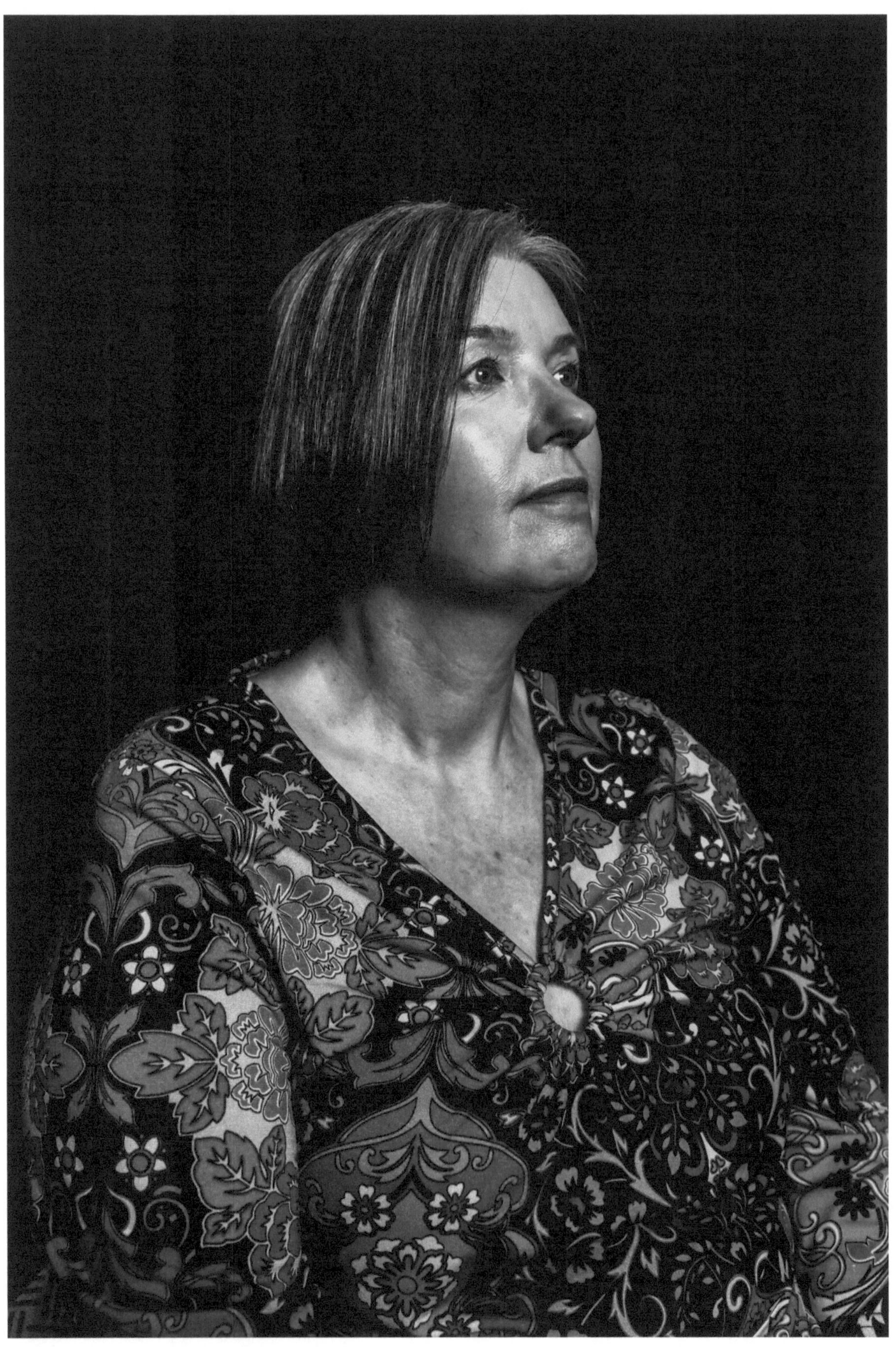

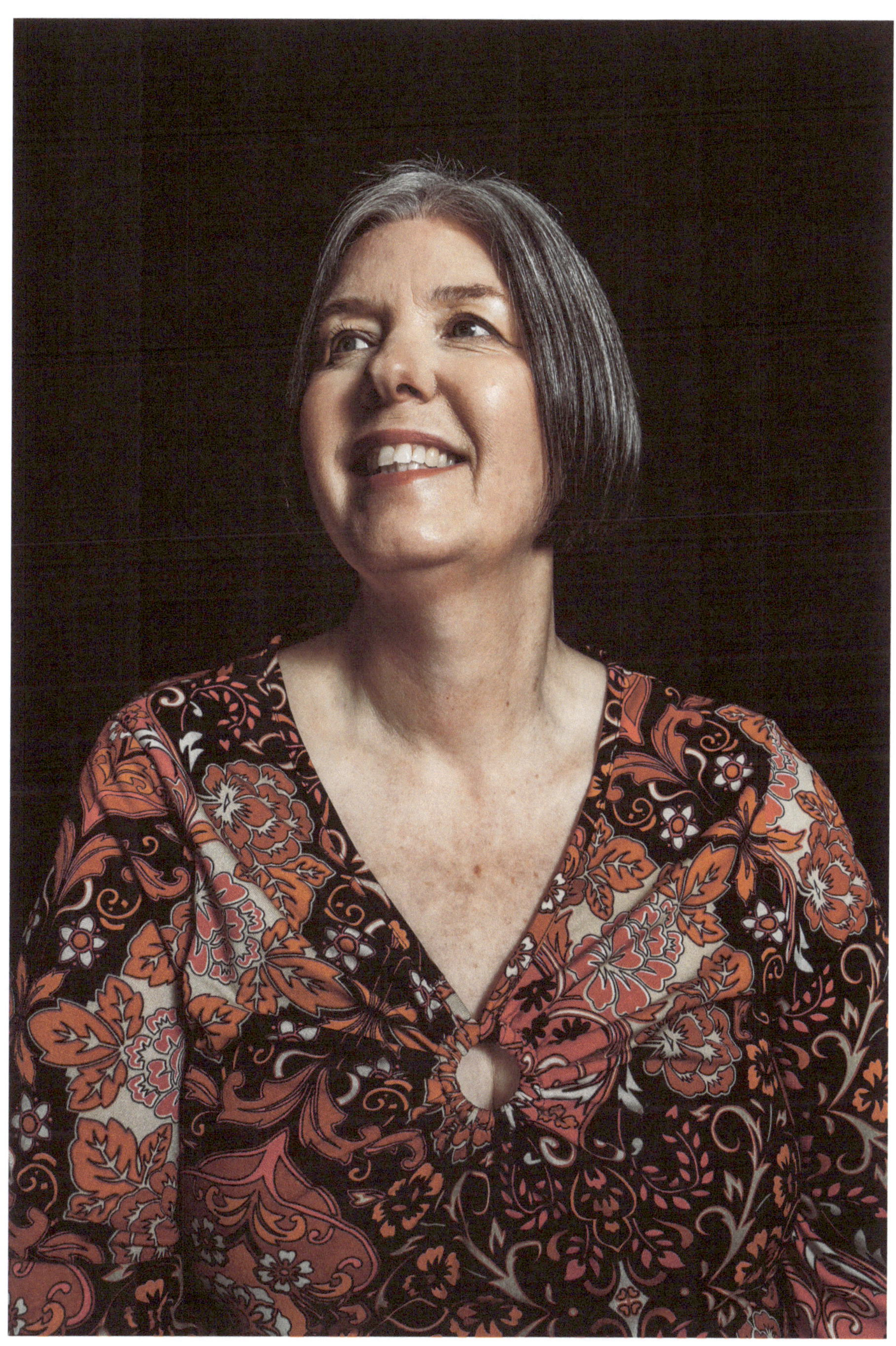

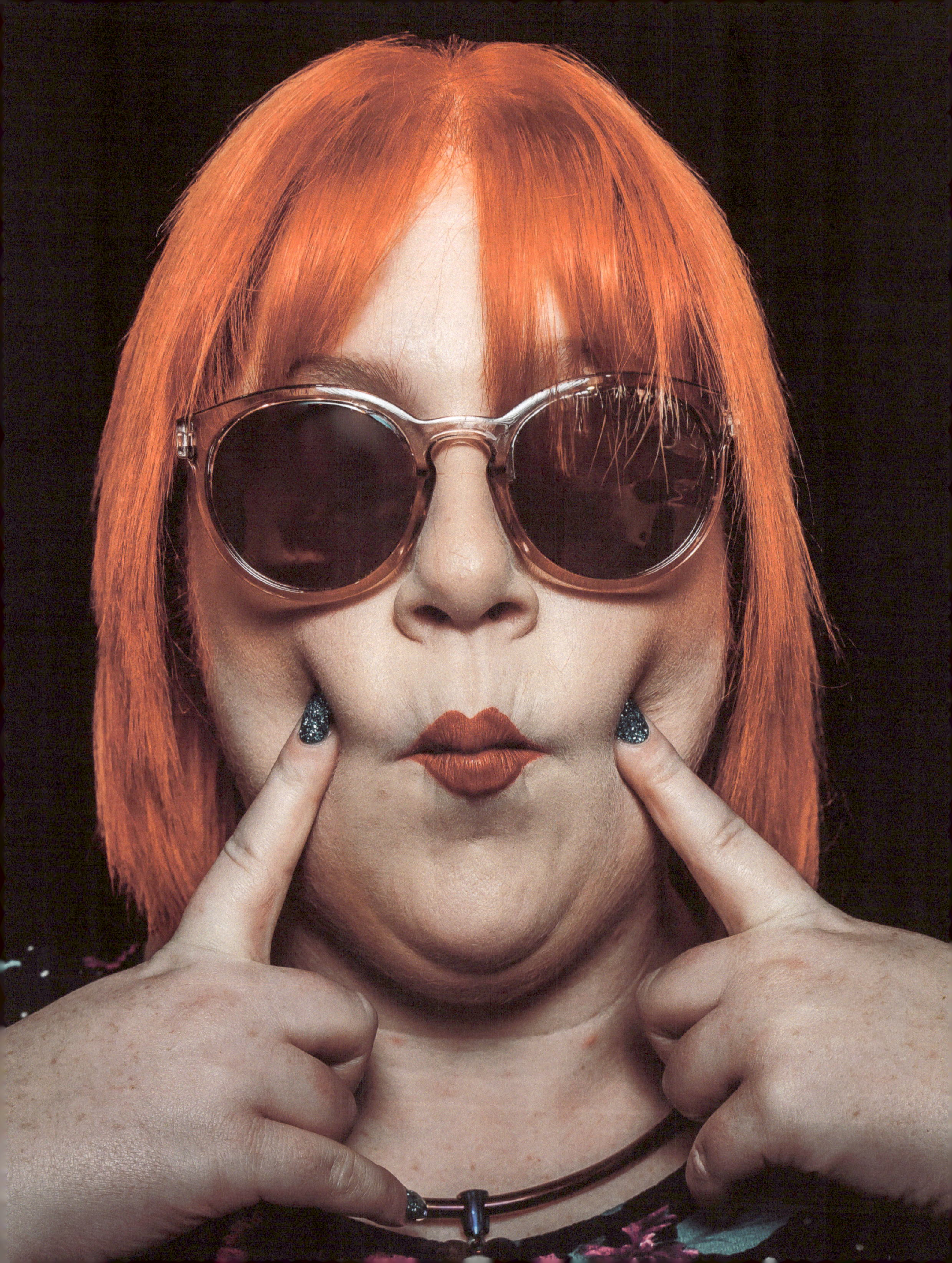

Temiekan Christensen

Embracing Identity and Creativity

At just 30 years old, Tem has already lived a life full of challenges, creativity, and triumphs. A proud mother of two young daughters, a talented photographer, and an artist at heart, Tem embodies resilience and self-discovery. Originally from Queensland, she has embraced life in colder climates and is creating a life filled with art, family, and personal growth.

Her experiences have shaped Tem's journey as someone with autism and ADHD. Diagnosed later in life, she reflects, "I've always known I was different, but having that diagnosis allowed me to understand myself better finally. It was like a light switch—finally seeing why I was the way I was." Additionally, she lives with lipoedema and lymphedema, conditions that come with their own set of challenges. "Finding clothes that fit properly or even just boots can be a struggle. But I've learned to adapt."

> *Don't change for other people. Be who you are because that's who you're meant to be. We all have something special to offer.*

Growing up in an environment marked by domestic violence, Tem faced immense obstacles, but she emerged stronger. "For 12 years, I lived in that world, and during that time, I was told my diagnoses were making me someone I wasn't. The truth is, I was just starting to embrace who I truly was."

Now, in a supportive relationship, Tem feels empowered to be her authentic self. "When I told my partner about my autism and ADHD, he just said, 'Okay, that's you. It doesn't change anything.' That kind of acceptance was overwhelming—it felt like I could finally be me without judgment."

Creativity has been a constant in Tem's life. As a professional photographer, she finds joy in capturing moments for others while expressing her own artistic vision. "Photography is my magic cape. When I'm behind the camera, I feel like a superhero—it gives me a sense of control and purpose."

Tem's crafting skills extend beyond photography. "I love making things, whether it's art pieces, custom shirts, or decals. Creating something from scratch brings me so much fulfilment, especially when I can share it with others."

Her biggest challenges revolve around managing daily routines and emotions. "Being autistic and having ADHD can make simple tasks like doing the dishes feel monumental. But with the help of my NDIS team and my partner, I've been learning to manage better. They've helped me set routines and understand my triggers, which has made a huge difference."

Participating in this project was a significant step for Tem. "For so long, I've hidden parts of myself because I feared being judged. But I don't want to hide anymore. I want to show people that I'm just me—no more, no less. It's about embracing who I am without shame."

Tem's proudest achievements include her daughters and finding the strength to leave an unhealthy relationship. "Standing up for myself and breaking free was one of the hardest things I've ever done, but it was also the most empowering. It taught me that I'm stronger than I think."

Her future goals are centred on turning her photography business into a full-time endeavour while continuing to explore her love of crafting. "I want to create a life where I can do what I love every day and provide for my family in a way that feels authentic to me."

When asked about her message to the world, Tem says, "Don't change for other people. Be who you are because that's who you're meant to be. We all have something special to offer."

Tem's story is one of transformation, creativity, and courage. Through her art and her voice, she is breaking barriers and showing the world the power of self-acceptance.

For so long, I've hidden parts of myself because I feared being judged. But I don't want to hide anymore. I want to show people that I'm just me—no more, no less. It's about embracing who I am without shame.

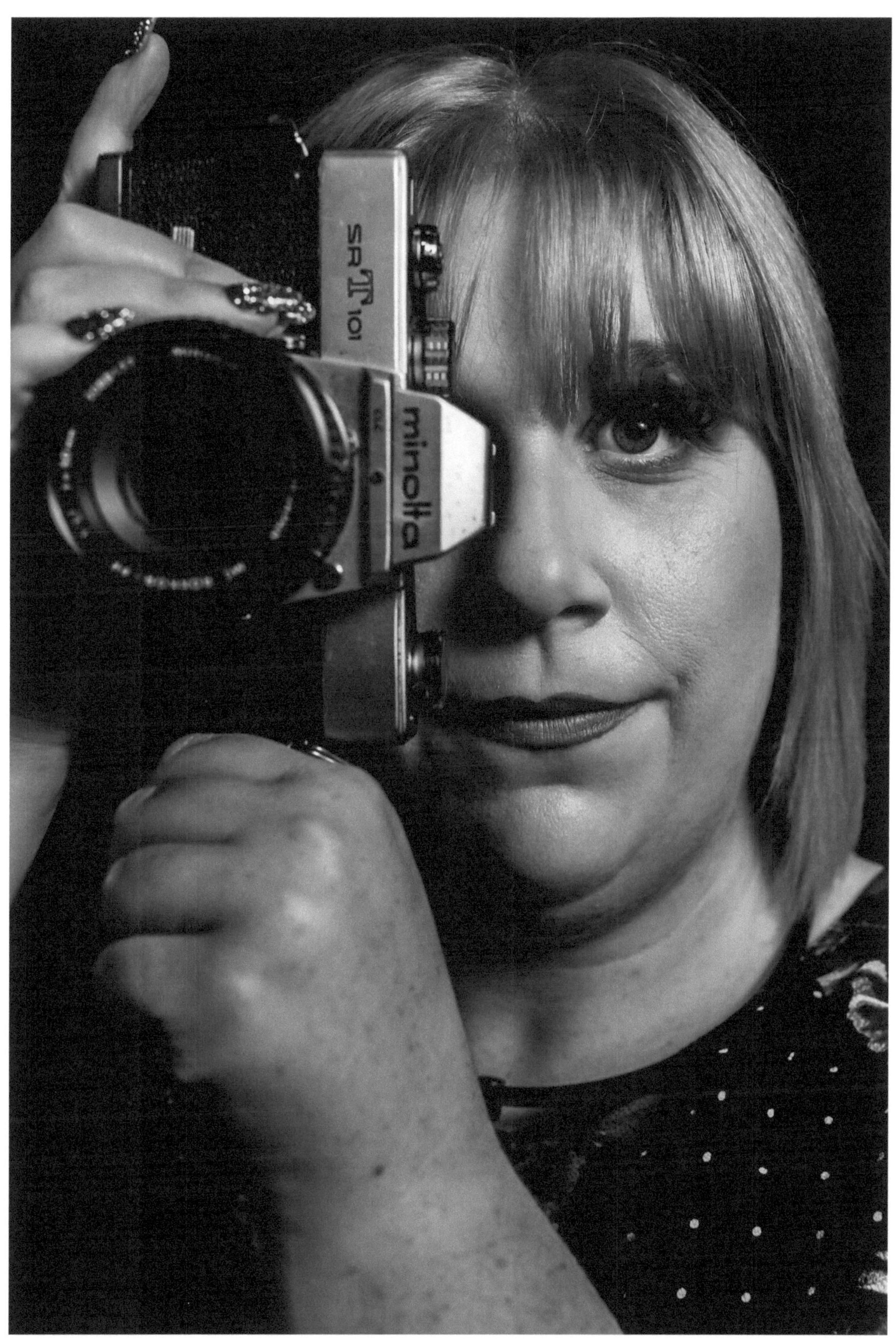
SR T 101
minolta

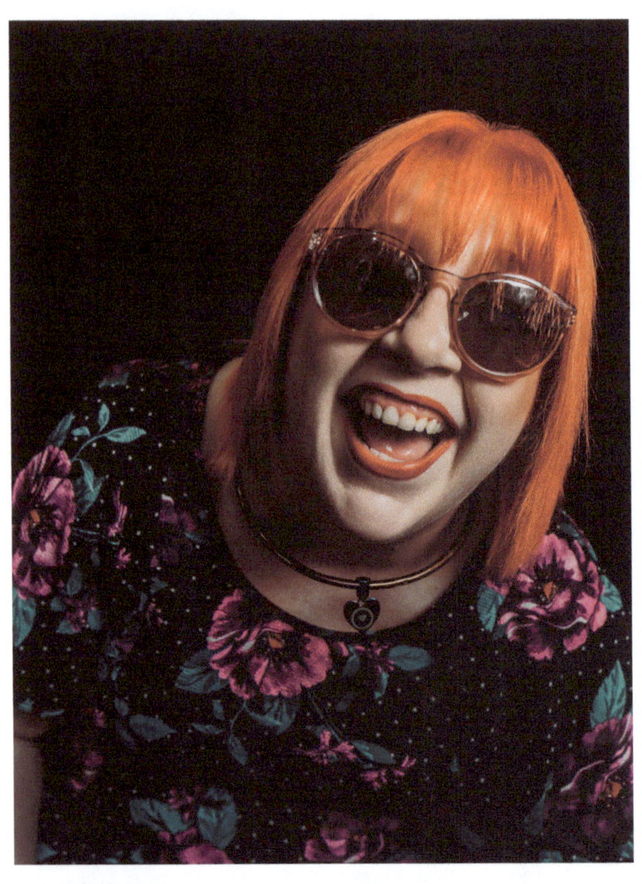
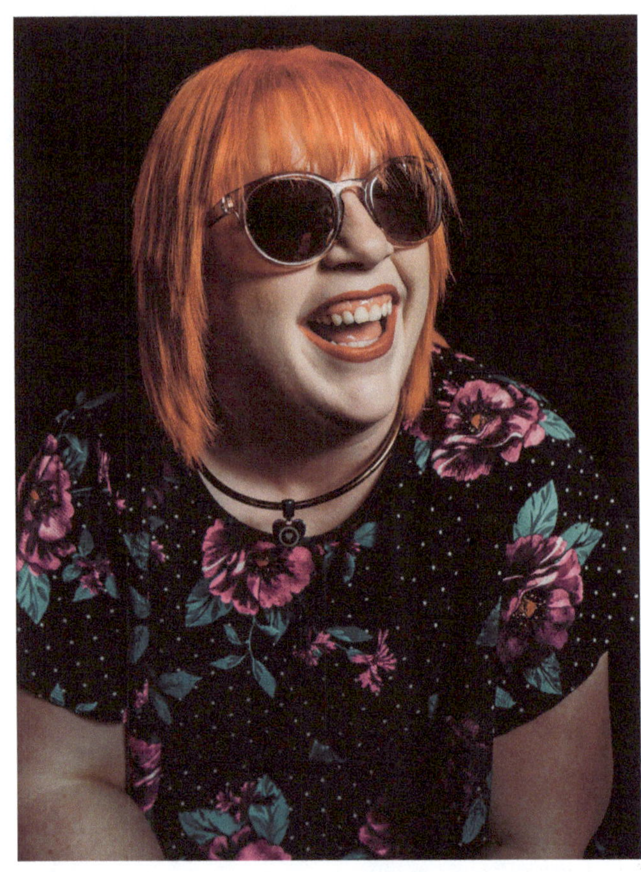
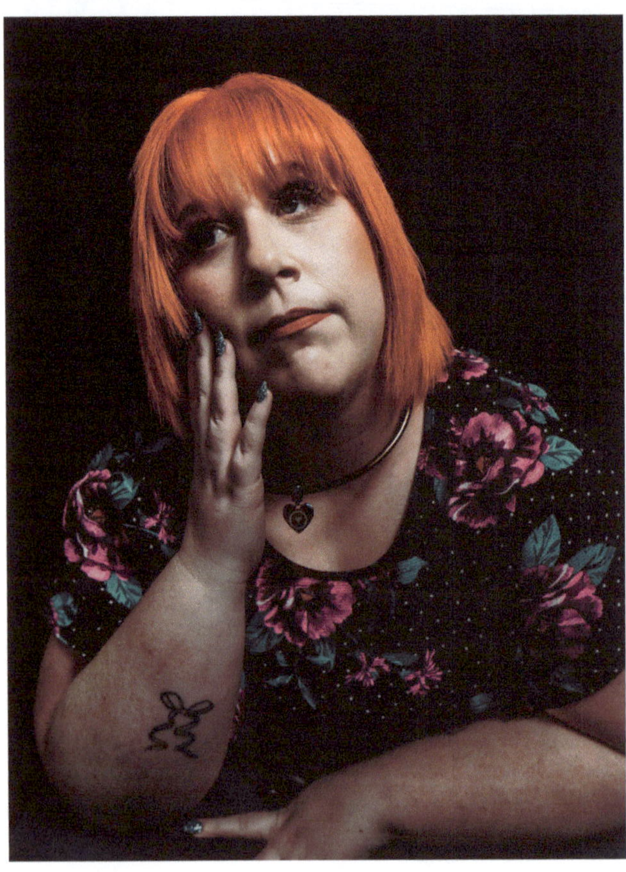
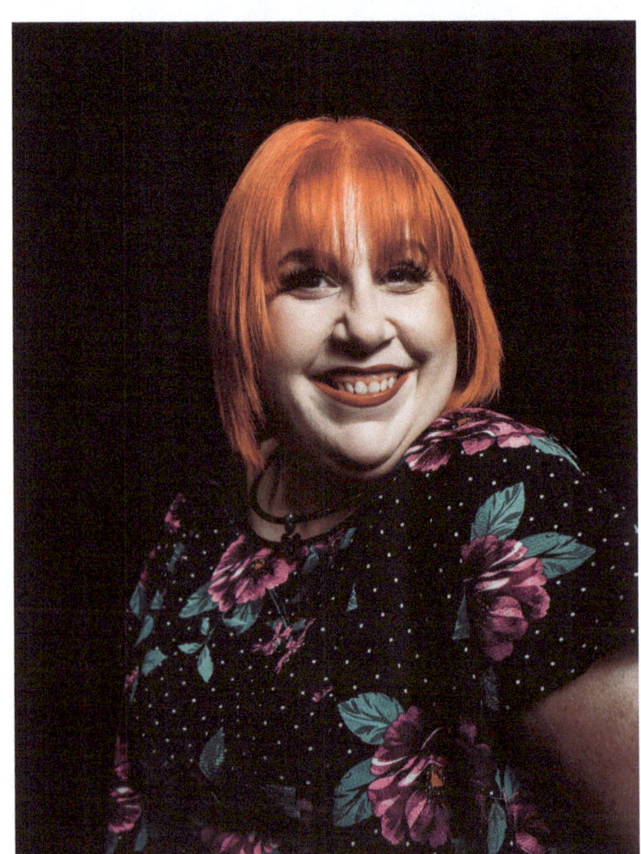

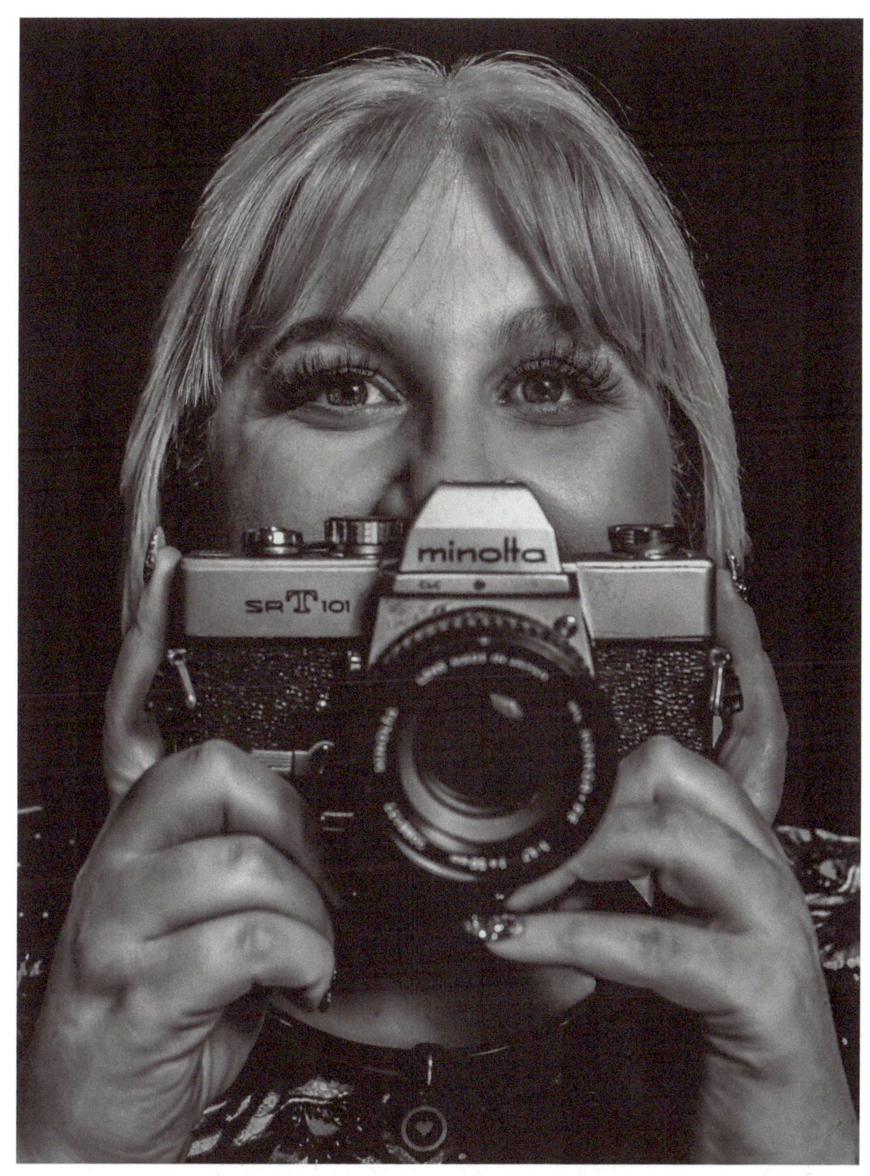
minolta
SR T 101

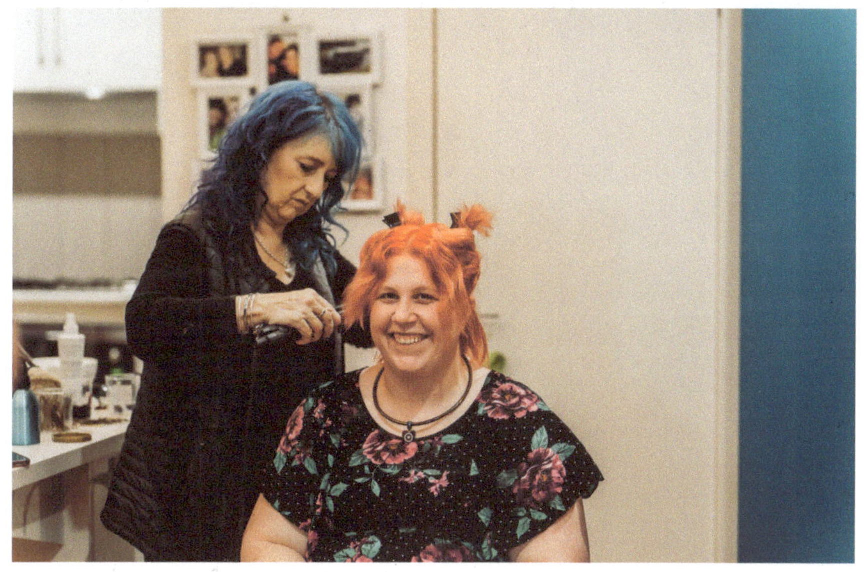

The Sponsors

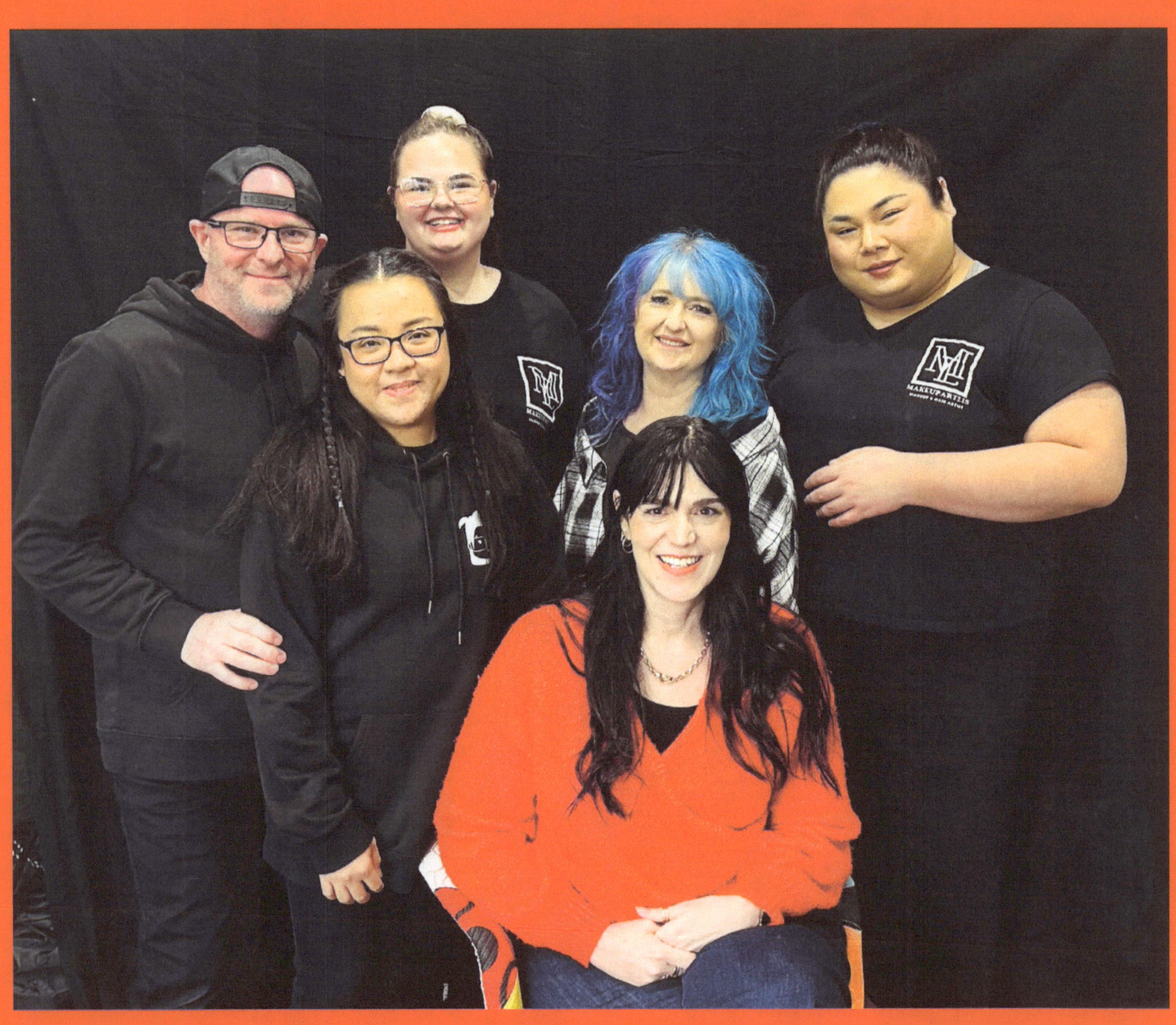

Strength comes from within, and with the right mindset, anything is possible.

Justine Martin

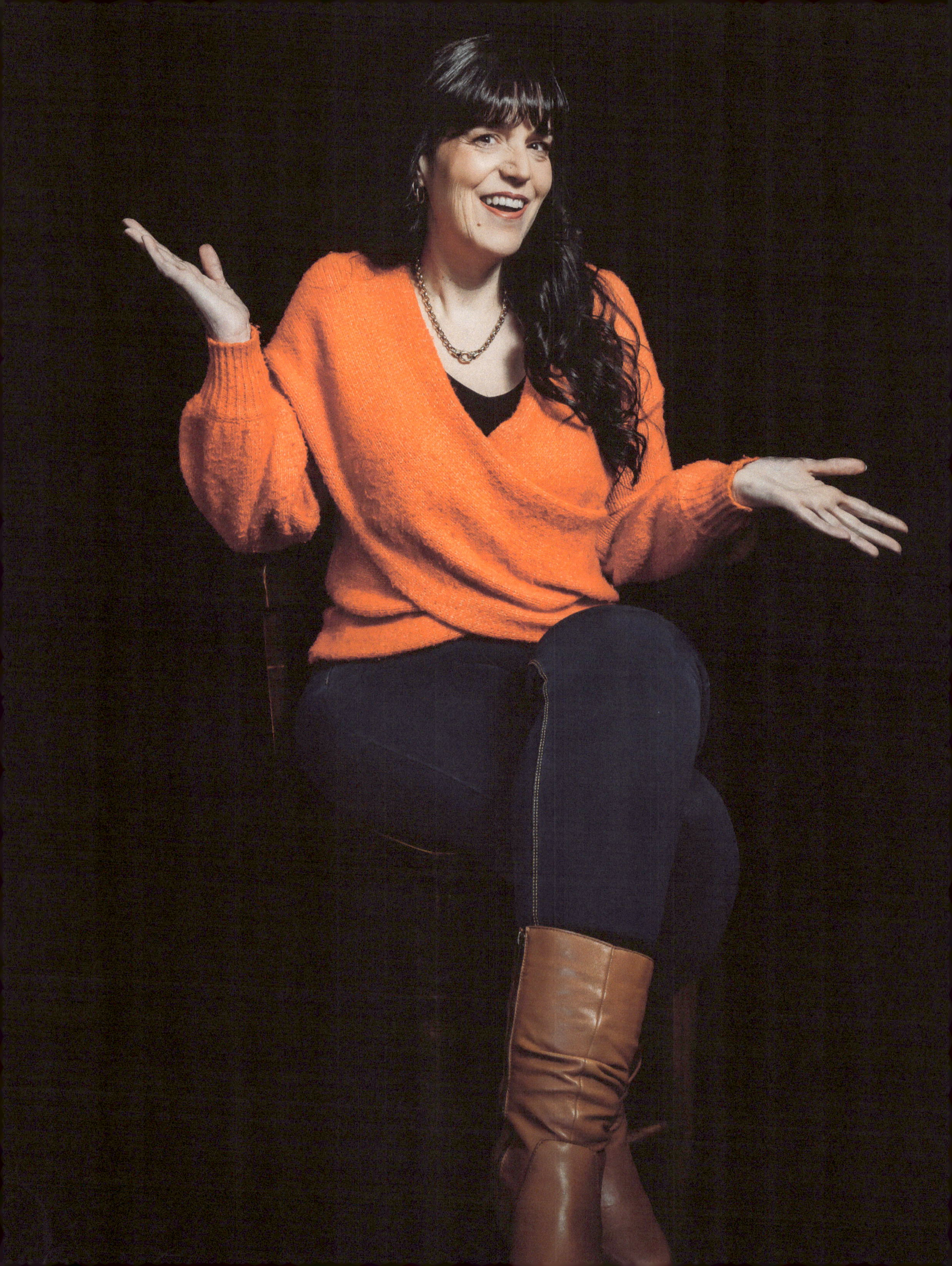

Justine Martin

Empowering Resilience and Storytelling

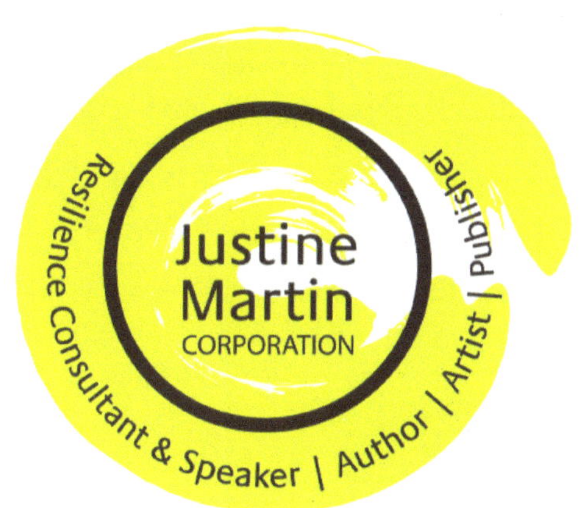

Justine Martin, the founder of **Resilience Mindset** and **Morpheus Publishing**, is proud to sponsor *Breaking the Barriers Through the Lens*. Through her businesses and personal journey, Justine embodies the spirit of the project, championing resilience, inclusivity, and the power of storytelling.

As someone who has faced significant health challenges, including multiple sclerosis (MS), cancer, and acquired brain injuries, Justine understands the importance of breaking barriers and redefining what's possible. "Sponsoring this project was a natural fit," she says. "It aligns perfectly with my mission to inspire others to overcome adversity and embrace their unique journeys."

Through **Resilience Mindset**, Justine has built a platform that empowers individuals and businesses to turn challenges into opportunities for growth. Her coaching, motivational speaking, and workshops teach the art of "bouncing forward" after setbacks. "Resilience is about adapting and thriving, even in the face of difficulty," she explains. "This project is a testament to that mindset, showcasing incredible stories of strength and perseverance."

With **Morpheus Publishing**, Justine provides a voice for individuals whose stories might otherwise go untold. "Everyone has a story that deserves to be shared," she says. "Through publishing, we help people turn their personal experiences into powerful narratives that inspire and educate. This aligns beautifully with the goals of *Breaking the Barriers Through the Lens*."

Justine's sponsorship goes beyond financial support; it reflects her personal commitment to inclusion and advocacy. Her artistic endeavours through **JUZT Art** have further showcased her creativity and determination. "Art and storytelling are powerful tools for connection and healing," she says. "This project beautifully combines those elements, creating a platform for people to share their truths."

Justine's sponsorship also underscores her belief in the importance of community. "Breaking barriers requires collective effort," she says. "Through initiatives like this, we're fostering greater understanding and creating a more inclusive world."

For Justine, *Breaking the Barriers Through the Lens* is more than just a project—it's a movement. "These stories need to be seen and heard," she says. "As a sponsor, I'm honoured to support this initiative and the incredible individuals whose stories are being shared."

Her message as a sponsor is clear: "Adversity doesn't define us—it refines us. By supporting projects like this, we can amplify voices, challenge misconceptions, and inspire others to see what's truly possible."

Through her businesses, advocacy, and sponsorship of *Breaking the Barriers Through the Lens*, Justine Martin continues to lead by example, breaking down barriers and empowering others to embrace their own resilience.

"

My story isn't about what I've been through—
it's about how I've chosen to rise above it.
Breaking barriers is about finding strength in
adversity, rewriting the narrative, and showing
others that resilience can transform lives.

"

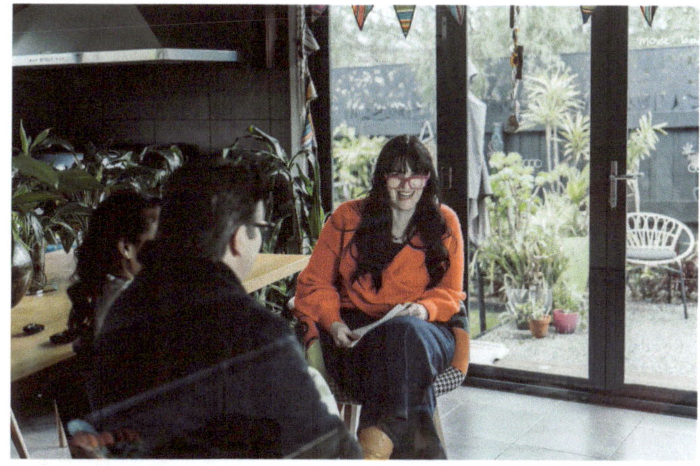

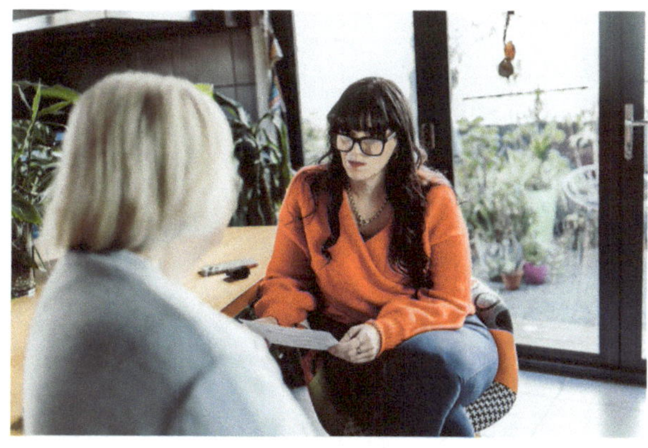

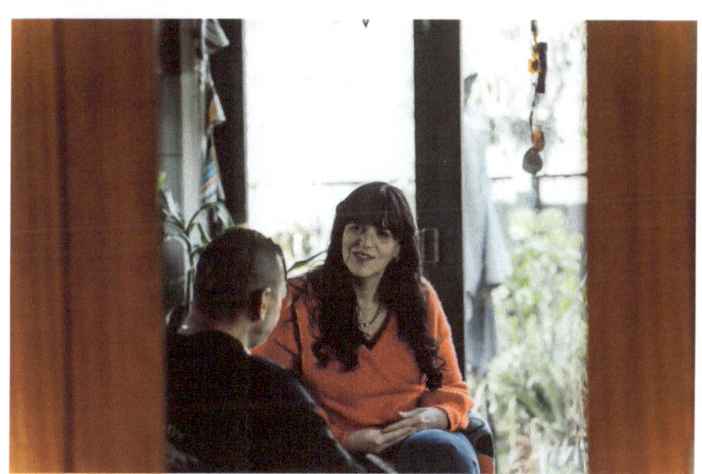

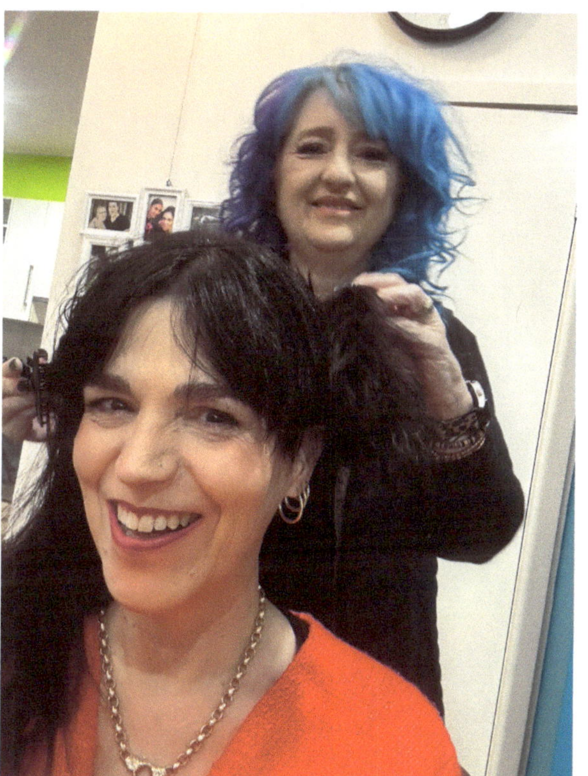

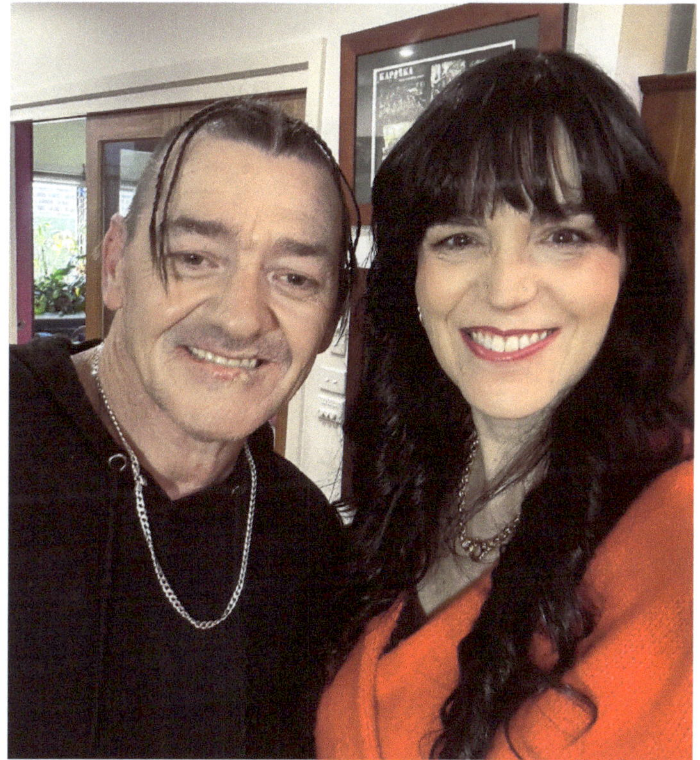

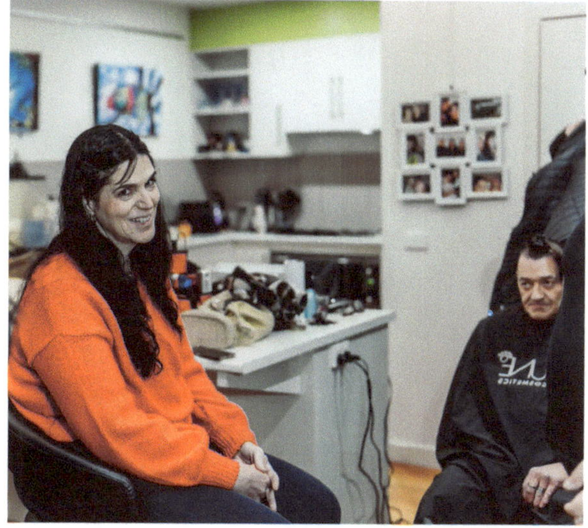

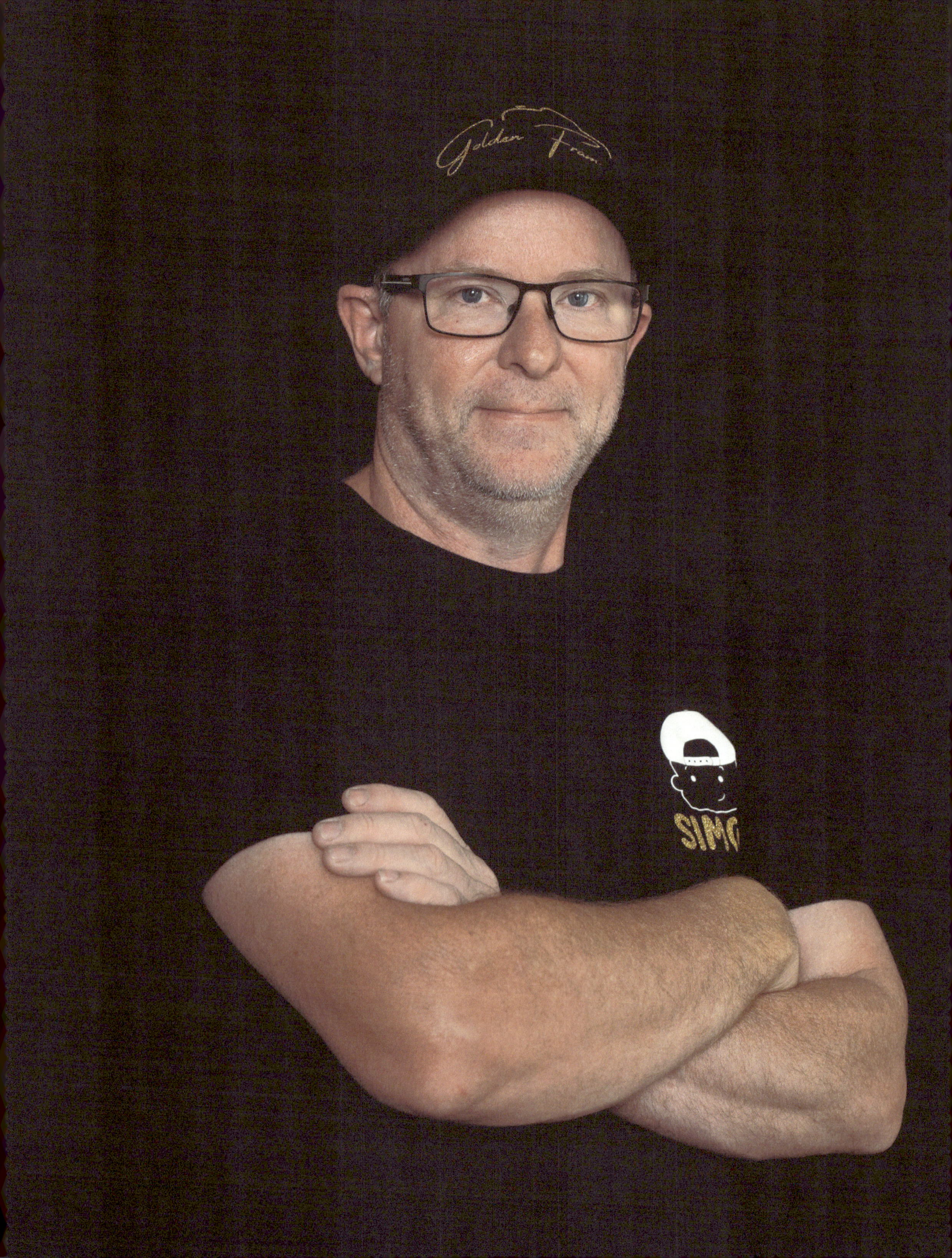

Simon and Julie's Story

SPONSOR: Golden Frame

Simon and Julie are the creative minds behind Golden Frame Productions, a business dedicated to capturing life's most meaningful moments through photography and videography. Together, they brought their talents to the *Breaking the Barriers Through the Lens* project, helping participants see themselves in a new light and contributing to a broader conversation about inclusion and resilience.

The idea for the project began with Simon. "I had this brainwave one day," he recalls. "I've been a wedding photographer for years, but I wanted to do something different—something that would showcase what I can do and tell a bigger story. I approached Justine with the idea of doing an exhibition, thinking it would be something small, maybe 10 photos in a little venue. But once I shared the idea, it quickly grew into something much bigger and more meaningful."

Julie, who manages videography for their business, adds, "It's been a transformative experience. I've learned so much about different disabilities, both visible and invisible, and about the incredible strength of the people we've worked with. Their stories are so inspiring."

The project brought together individuals from diverse backgrounds, all with unique experiences of disability. "I wanted to capture everyday people," Simon says. "But as we refined the idea, we decided to focus on individuals with disabilities. It's been amazing to hear their stories and see what they've achieved despite the challenges they face."

Julie reflects on the emotional impact of the project. "Seeing people come in scared or unsure and watching their transformation during the photo shoots was incredible. They'd arrive nervous, some even petrified, but by the end of the session, you could see their confidence shining through. Showing them their photos and seeing their reactions—it was priceless."

The project also pushed Simon and Julie out of their comfort zones. "As photographers and videographers, we're usually behind the camera, not in front of it," Julie laughs. "But this project required us to step up and share our journey as well. It was challenging but rewarding."

Simon's goal for the project was to show the world that anything is possible. "I wanted to share the message that anyone can achieve their goals if they put their mind to it. Disabilities don't define people; their determination and spirit do."

Julie adds, "The key takeaway from this project is the importance of inclusion and understanding. Every participant had a unique story and a positive message about creating a more accepting world."

The experience has also shaped how Simon and Julie approach their business. "This project has given us a deeper appreciation for the impact of our work," Simon says. "We're not just capturing moments; we're helping people see themselves in a new way."

Golden Frame Productions has grown significantly in recent years, thanks in part to their collaboration with Justine as a business coach. "When we started working with Justine, we were a small business doing a handful of weddings a year," Simon shares. "Now we're fully booked for the season and have even been nominated for several awards. It's been an incredible journey."

For Simon and Julie, the project is just the beginning. "We're already thinking about what's next," Julie says. "Whether it's more exhibitions, expanding into events, or finding new ways to tell people's stories, we're excited about the future."

Their message to the world is one of positivity and possibility. "Don't let anything stop you," Simon says. "You can achieve so much if you believe in yourself and are willing to step out of your comfort zone."

Julie adds, "Be kind and open-minded. The more we understand each other, the stronger our communities will be."

Through their artistry and dedication, Simon and Julie have helped participants of this project break barriers and shine. Their story is a testament to the power of creativity, collaboration, and compassion.

Everyone has a unique story and a positive message

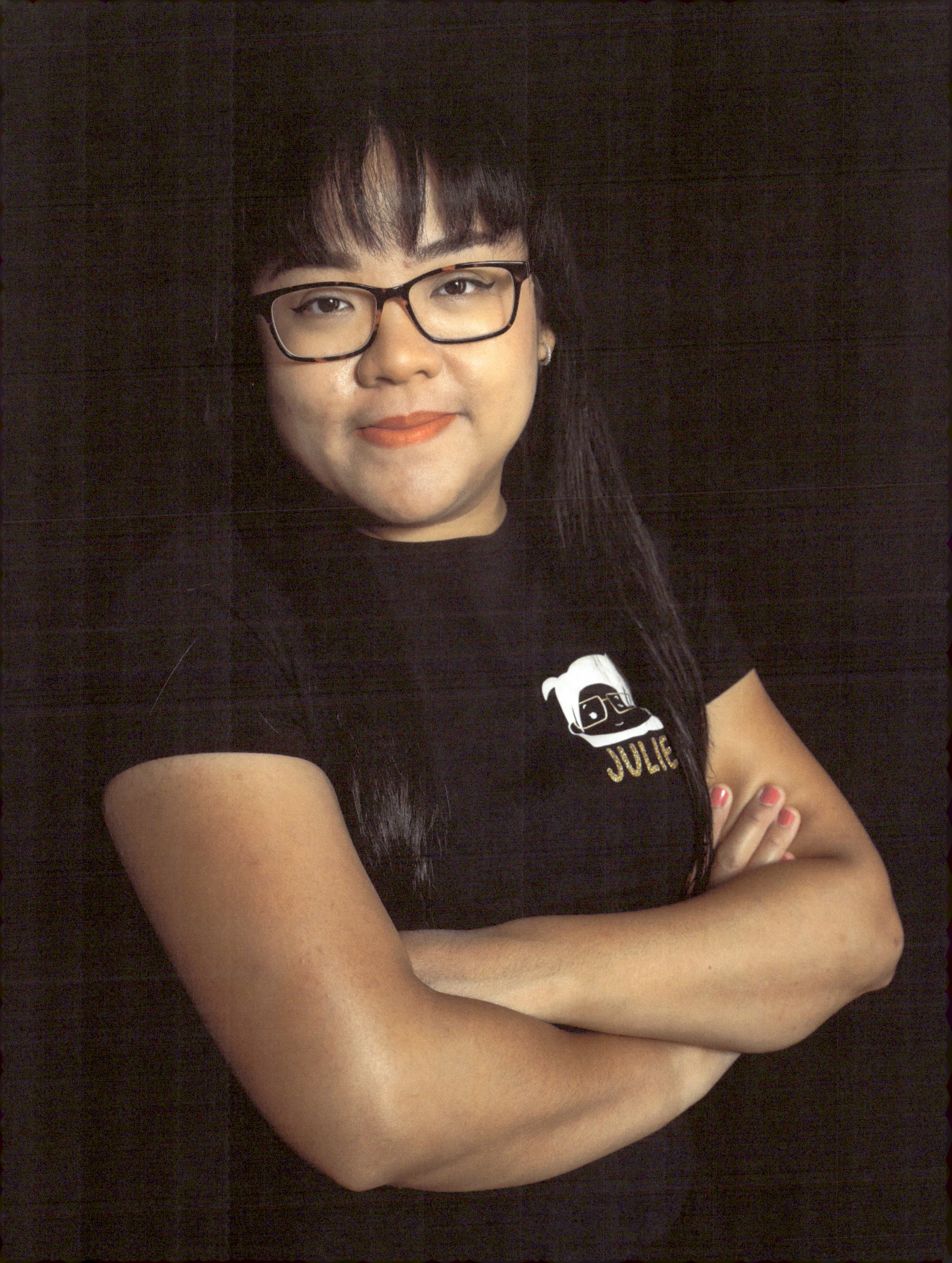
JULIE

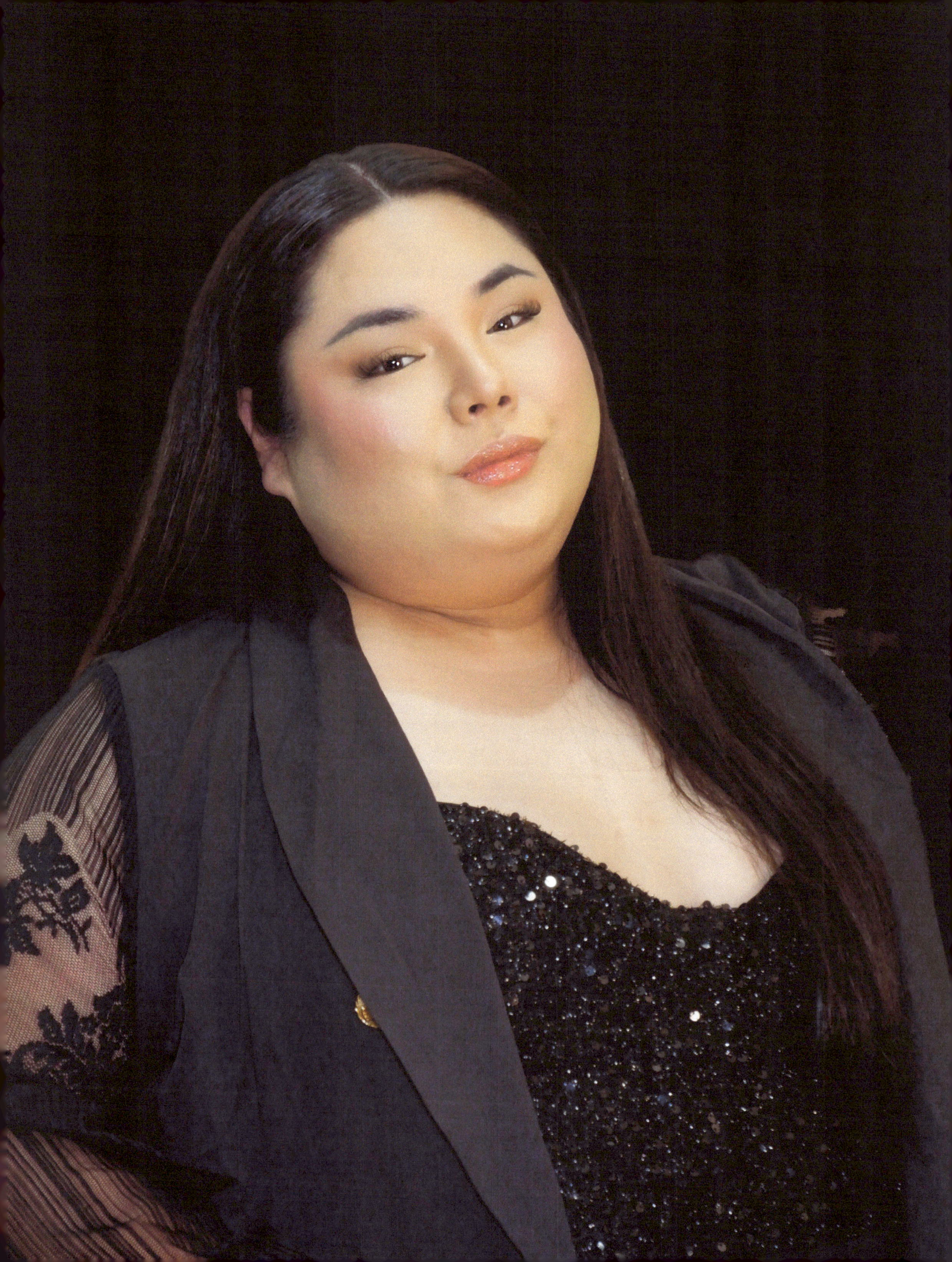

Lis Jamia and Eden Anderson

Supporting Beauty and Confidence

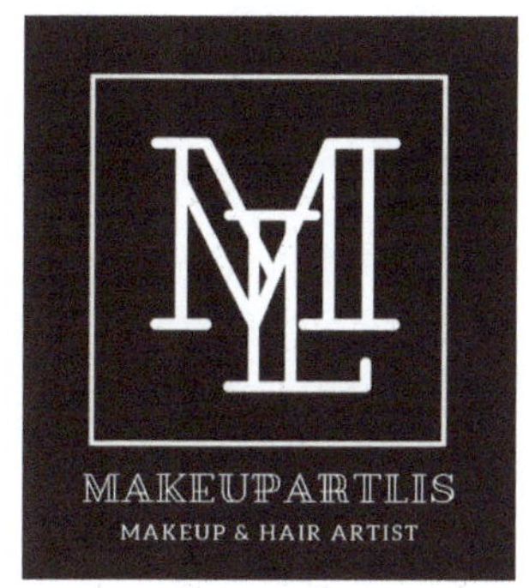

Lis Jamia and Eden are makeup artists who played a pivotal role in *Breaking the Barriers Through the Lens*, bringing their talents to support the participants of the project. Through their business, Liz and Eden specialise in makeup and hair for brides, special occasions, photoshoots, and even film and TV, helping people look and feel their best.

Lis explains how she got involved with the project: "I've worked with Simon, the photographer, on many weddings. When he mentioned the idea for this project and the need for makeup artists, I didn't hesitate. It felt like an incredible opportunity to support people with disabilities and contribute to something meaningful."

Eden, who recently joined Lis's team, reflects on the experience: "For me, the highlight has been the conversations and getting to know the participants. Hearing their stories and being able to empower them, even in a small way, has been really rewarding. It's about making them feel pampered, maybe in a way they wouldn't usually experience."

The project presented its own set of challenges, but Lis and Eden took them in stride. "Some participants had sensitive skin or other unique conditions we needed to work around," Lis shares. "It's been a learning curve for us, adapting our techniques to ensure everyone felt comfortable and beautiful."

Eden adds, "For some of the participants, this was their first experience wearing makeup. Seeing their reactions and how it made them feel—it's been amazing. It's given us a new perspective on how much beauty can empower and uplift."

One of the most rewarding aspects of their involvement has been the chance to challenge stereotypes and celebrate individuality. "Working with people with disabilities, I've realised that while some may see them differently, they're just as human as anyone else," Lis says. "Their stories, humour, and kindness have left a lasting impact on me."

Eden agrees, saying, "This project wasn't just about makeup—it was about connection and understanding. It reminded me how important it is to look beyond the surface and see the person."

The duo is grateful for the opportunity to be part of such a meaningful initiative. "It's been a fantastic experience, and we're honoured to have contributed," Lis concludes. "Projects like this remind us of the power of art and collaboration in breaking down barriers."

Through their artistry and compassion, Lis and Eden have helped participants shine, contributing not just to their appearance but to their confidence and self-esteem. Their involvement underscores the importance of community and the beauty of lifting others up.

"

Projects like this remind us of the power of art and collaboration in breaking down barriers.

"

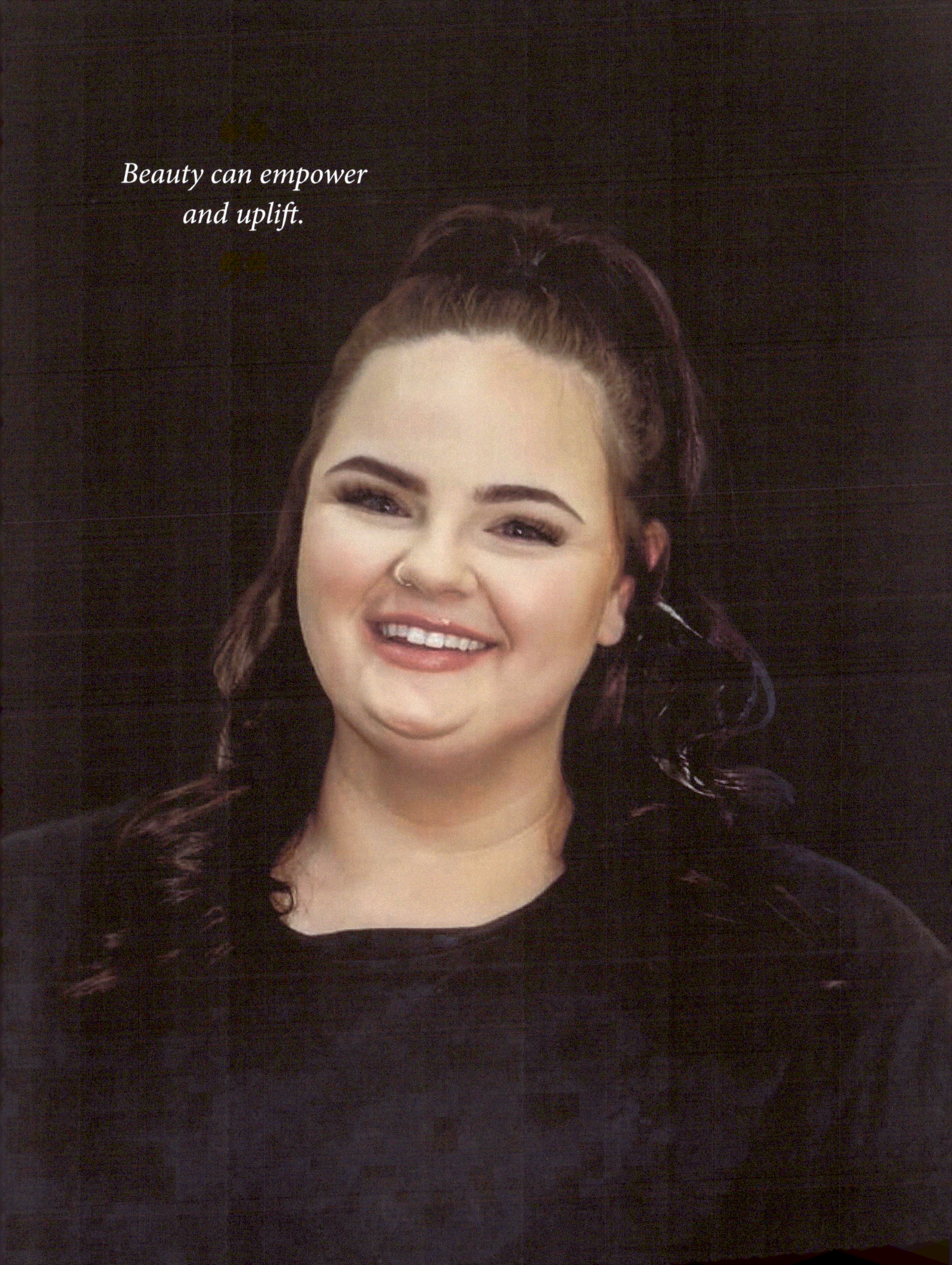
Beauty can empower
and uplift.

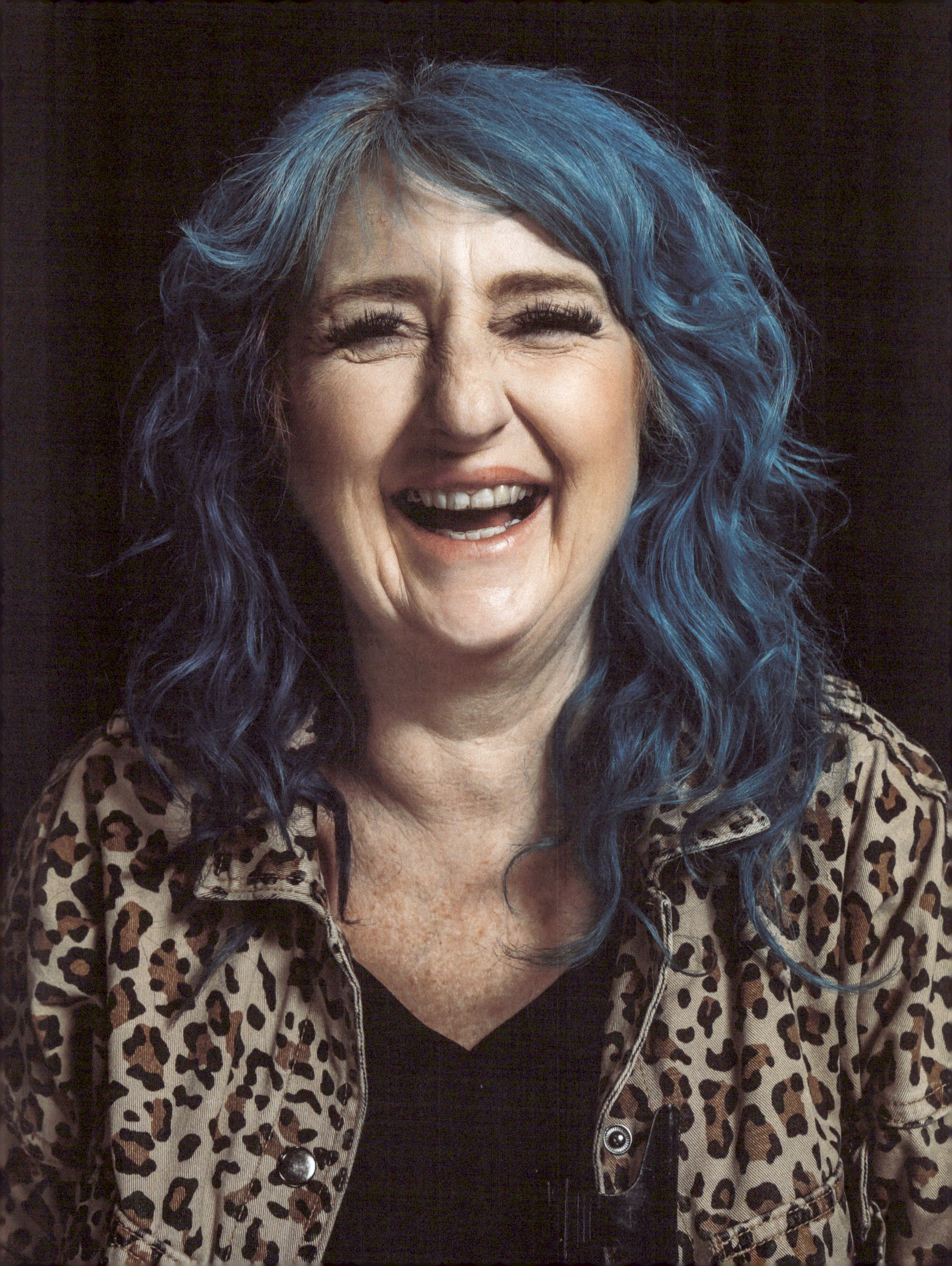

Joanne (Jo) Schwarzkopf

Finding Empowerment Through Creativity

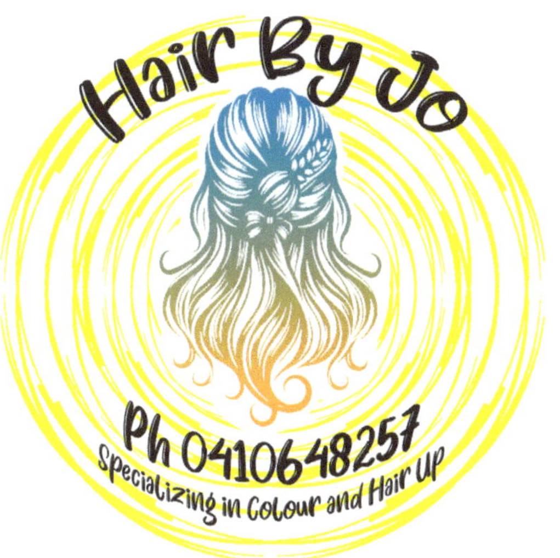

Joanne Schwarzkopf's journey with *Breaking the Barriers Through the Lens* has been a deeply transformative and rewarding experience. A former hairdresser turned support worker, Jo's life took an unexpected turn when a long-standing shoulder problem forced her to leave the profession she once thought defined her identity. However, her role in this project has not only reconnected her with her creative roots but also redefined her sense of purpose.

"I've had on-and-off shoulder problems for 15 years," Joanne shares. "It was so bad that I had to leave hairdressing. At the time, I thought my life was over. Hairdressing was who I was. Without it, I didn't know who I was going to be."

The project offered Joanne an opportunity to step back into the world of beauty and creativity, bringing her talent and experience to participants who might not otherwise have had the chance to feel like models. "To see people come in as one version of themselves and walk out empowered and glowing—it's the most rewarding feeling," she says. "It's like you're giving them a glimpse of their true potential."

Jo's husband also participated in the project, which made the experience even more special for her. "He was so nervous coming in, but by the end, he was saying, 'I'd do that again!' It was amazing to see him go through that transformation and be so proud of himself. His photos look incredible."

Despite being in pain during the project, Joanne refused to let it stop her. "If I were still working in the salon, I probably would have cancelled everything that day," she admits. "But there was no way I was missing out on this. It was history-making."

Her dedication didn't go unnoticed. "Even though you're dealing with your own disability, you gave up two weekends to be here," a team member told her. "Thank you for pushing through. Everyone loved having their hair done—it brought so much joy and confidence."

For Jo, the project wasn't just about styling hair. "It was about giving people an experience they might never have had," she explains. "Some participants may not have been able to afford this kind of experience or didn't have the confidence to walk into a regular studio. To see them leave with big smiles and their shoulders high—that's the magic of this project."

Jo also played a part in easing participants' nerves about being interviewed or filmed. "Many were scared at first," she says with a laugh. "But by the end, they'd say, 'Oh, that wasn't so bad!' Watching them gain confidence and feel empowered was incredibly rewarding."

Reflecting on her journey, Joanne is grateful for the opportunity to contribute to something so meaningful. "This project reminded me of why I loved hairdressing in the first place—it's about making people feel good about themselves. It's also shown me that even though life took me in a different direction, I still have so much to offer."

Her message to others is simple: "Don't let challenges define you. There's always a way to adapt, grow, and find new ways to use your talents. And remember, helping others often helps you rediscover yourself."

Through her creativity, dedication, and resilience, Joanne has not only helped participants feel seen and celebrated but has also reminded herself of the power of her craft. Her story is a testament to the transformative impact of breaking barriers and embracing new opportunities.

> “*Don't let challenges define you. There's always a way to adapt, grow, and find new ways to use your talents. And remember, helping others often helps you rediscover yourself.*”

DISCOVER BEAUTY AND EXPERTISE WITH JO SCHWARZKOPF

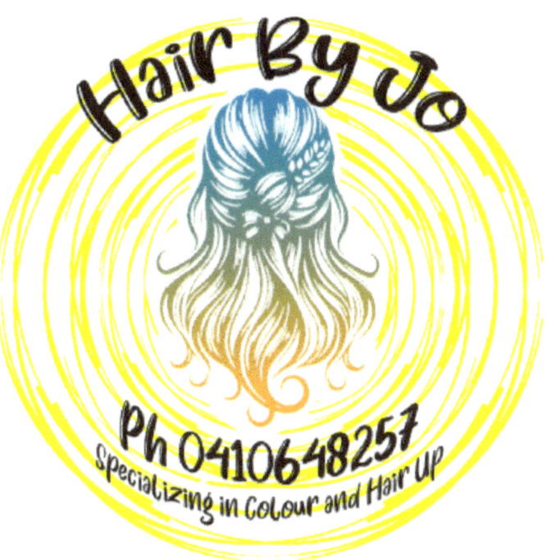

Hair & Beauty Specialist
Are you ready to transform your look and feel amazing? With over 35 years of experience in the hair and beauty industry, Jo is a trusted expert who combines skill, creativity, and a passion for helping you look and feel your best. From stunning hairstyles to enhancing your natural beauty, Jo offers a wide range of services tailored to your individual needs.

Hair Services
Jo specialises in all aspects of hairdressing, bringing expertise and artistry to every appointment. Whether you're looking for a chic new cut, a vibrant colour transformation, or a flawless hair-up style for a special occasion, Jo's attention to detail ensures you'll leave feeling confident and radiant.

- Hair Up Styles: Perfect for weddings, formals and special events.
- Expert Colouring: Customised colour services to enhance your unique style.

Brow & Lash Enhancements
Jo's skills extend beyond hairdressing, offering premium brow and lash services that will have you looking effortlessly polished. With a keen eye for detail and a commitment to perfection, Jo provides treatments that enhance your natural beauty.

- Brow Wax, Lamination & Tint: Shape, define, and perfect your brows.
- Lash Lift & Tint: Achieve longer, fuller-looking lashes with minimal maintenance.
-

Why Choose Jo?

- Over 35 Years of Experience: Trusted expertise honed over decades.
- Personalised Service: Every treatment is tailored to your unique needs.
- Passionate and Professional: Dedicated to creating looks that inspire confidence.
- Wide Range of Services: From hair transformations to brow and lash enhancements.

Whether you're preparing for a big event, looking for a fresh new style, or simply treating yourself to some well-deserved pampering, Jo is here to help you shine. With her friendly approach and unmatched expertise, you'll leave every appointment looking and feeling your absolute best.

Book Your Transformation Today!

- Contact Jo to schedule your personalised hair or beauty appointment.

Phone 0410648257

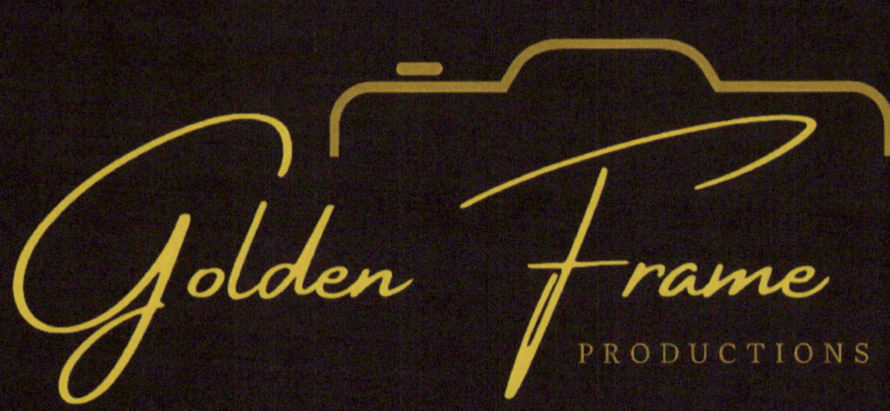

GOLDEN FRAME PRODUCTIONS

Simon and Julie Stein are an award-winning husband-and-wife team who balance their day jobs as a wood machinist and an early childhood educator with their shared passion for photography. In their spare time, they love heading out with their cameras on evenings and weekends to capture life's most meaningful moments.

As recognised professionals in their field, Simon and Julie specialise in documenting the heartfelt memories of couples making a lifetime commitment, surrounded by family and friends. In addition to weddings, they also enjoy photographing families and events, ensuring no special occasion is left undocumented. Based in the Geelong and Surf Coast region, they are happy to travel to your location to bring their expertise to your event. They provide all the shots you need—and plenty more you didn't even realise you wanted!

Their photography sessions are candid, laid-back, and fun. Simon and Julie take the time to get to know their clients, ensuring every session feels like celebrating with close friends who know exactly how to make you smile, laugh, and relax. With their award-winning approach, it's all about enjoying the moment while they capture memories to last a lifetime.

www.goldenframeproductions.com.au

hello@goldenframeproductions.com.au

@Golden Frame Productions

@goldenframeproductions_au

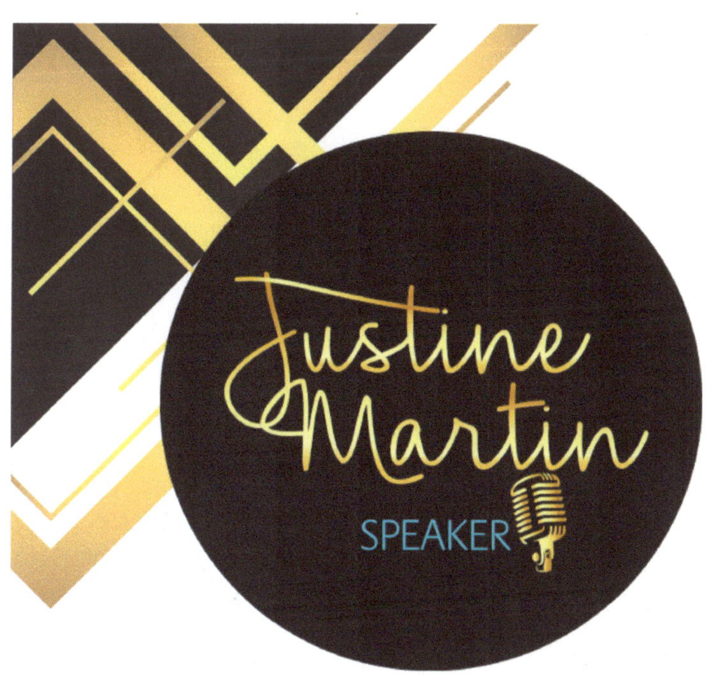

JUSTINE MARTIN SPEAKER

Justine Martin Speaker delivers powerful, transformative presentations that inspire, educate, and motivate audiences to embrace resilience and overcome life's challenges. Justine Martin, an award-winning international keynote speaker, artist, author, and resilience advocate, uses her extraordinary personal journey to connect with people on a profound level.

Justine's story is one of triumph over adversity. Having faced multiple sclerosis, cancer, and life-altering setbacks, she has emerged as a beacon of hope and strength. Through her engaging talks, Justine shares practical strategies for navigating change, building resilience, and turning obstacles into opportunities.

Her presentations are tailored to a wide range of audiences, from corporate teams and community groups to educational institutions and conferences. Justine is an expert at breaking down complex ideas into relatable, actionable steps, empowering her listeners to cultivate resilience and thrive in the face of life's challenges.

With her dynamic storytelling, captivating presence, and genuine authenticity, Justine Martin is more than just a speaker—she's a life-changer. Book Justine Martin Speaker today and inspire your audience to rise, thrive, and embrace the resilience mindset.

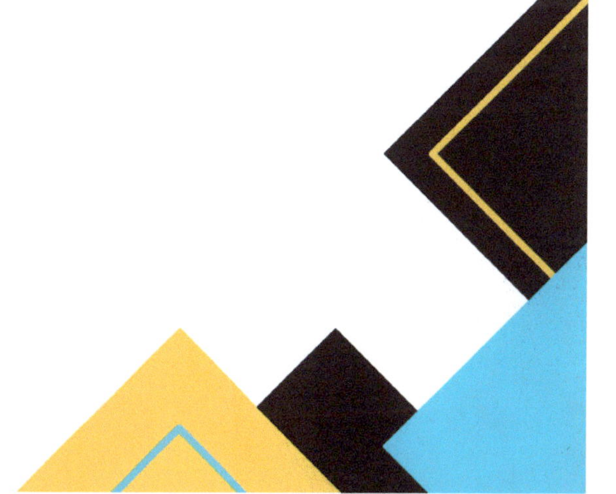

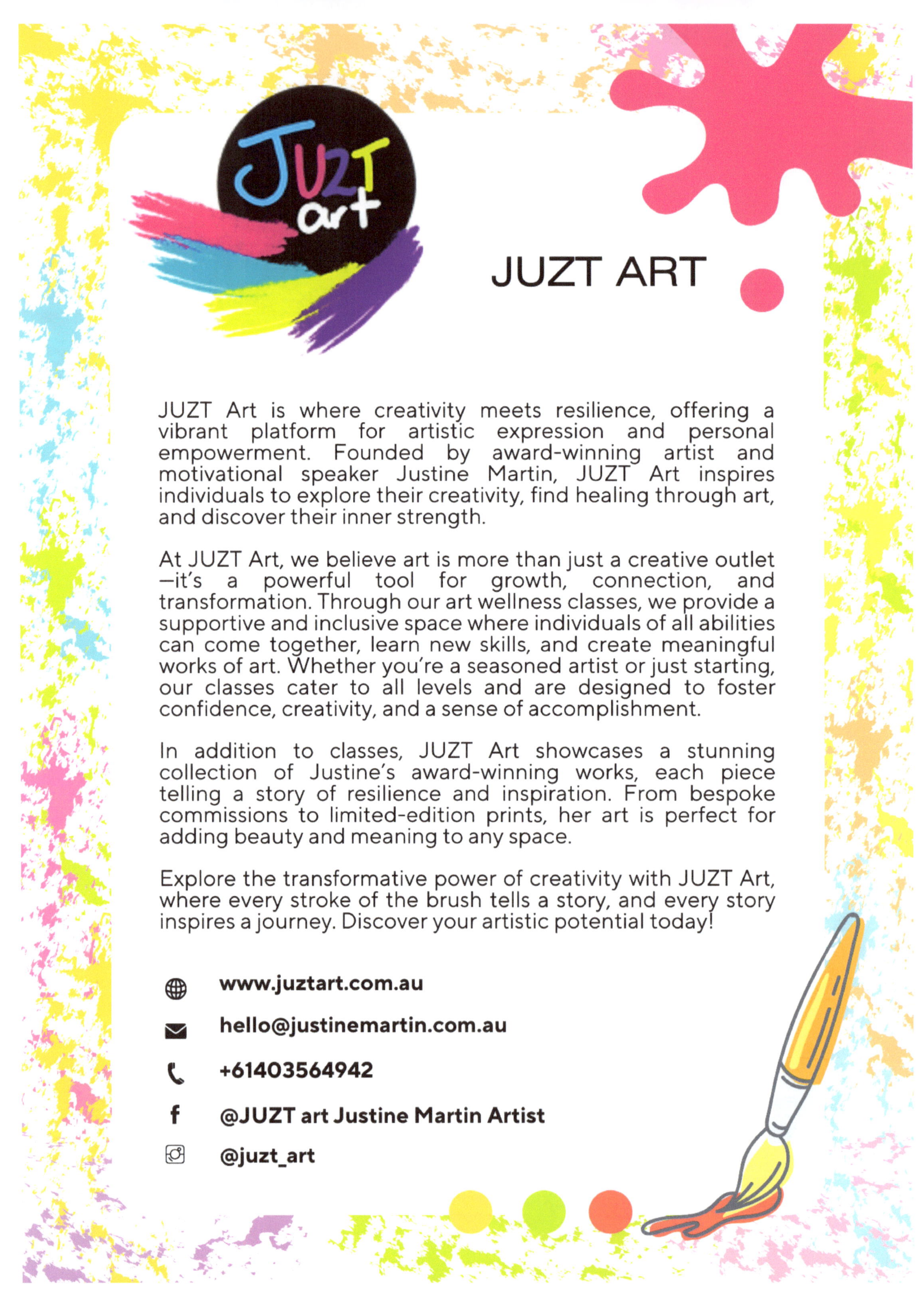

JUZT ART

JUZT Art is where creativity meets resilience, offering a vibrant platform for artistic expression and personal empowerment. Founded by award-winning artist and motivational speaker Justine Martin, JUZT Art inspires individuals to explore their creativity, find healing through art, and discover their inner strength.

At JUZT Art, we believe art is more than just a creative outlet—it's a powerful tool for growth, connection, and transformation. Through our art wellness classes, we provide a supportive and inclusive space where individuals of all abilities can come together, learn new skills, and create meaningful works of art. Whether you're a seasoned artist or just starting, our classes cater to all levels and are designed to foster confidence, creativity, and a sense of accomplishment.

In addition to classes, JUZT Art showcases a stunning collection of Justine's award-winning works, each piece telling a story of resilience and inspiration. From bespoke commissions to limited-edition prints, her art is perfect for adding beauty and meaning to any space.

Explore the transformative power of creativity with JUZT Art, where every stroke of the brush tells a story, and every story inspires a journey. Discover your artistic potential today!

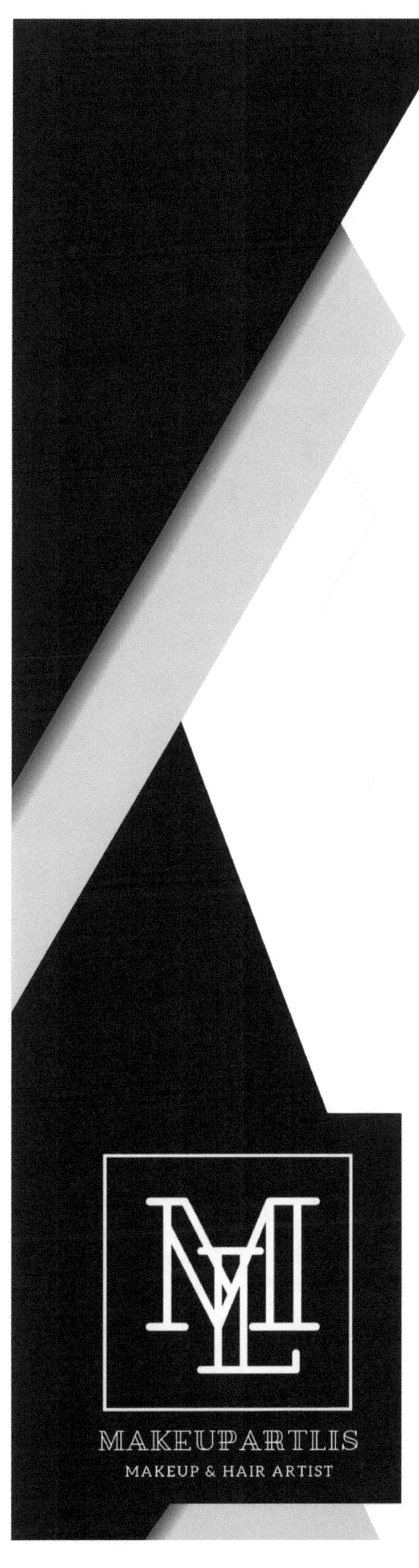

MAKEUPARTLIS

MAKEUPARTLIS is an award-winning makeup and hair studio that delivers high-quality services for weddings, special occasions, runway events, photoshoots, and film and TV productions.

Founded in 2019 by Lis Jaima, a passionate transgender makeup artist and hair stylist, MAKEUPARTLIS proudly embodies inclusivity and creativity. Lis is committed to fostering a welcoming environment and proudly declares that MAKEUPARTLIS is 101% LGBTQIA+ friendly.

At MAKEUPARTLIS, supporting diverse communities and advocating for equality are at the heart of everything we do. Regardless of who you are or how you identify, you will be treated with respect, kindness, and care. Our mission is to ensure that every client feels valued and leaves not only looking their best but feeling truly celebrated.

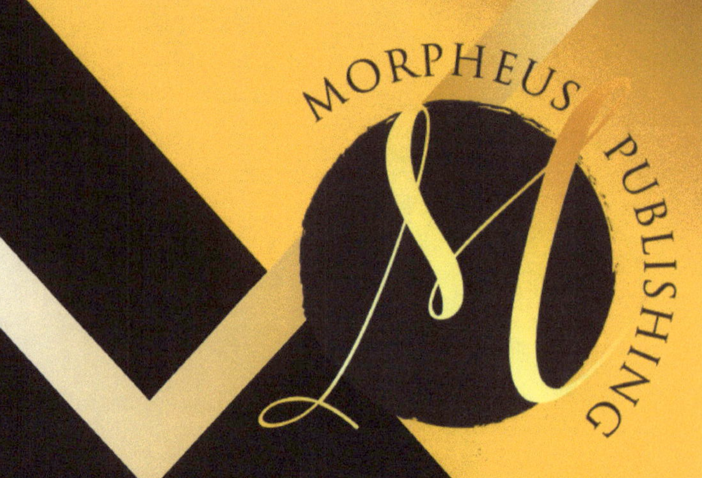

MORPHEUS PUBLISHING

Morpheus Publishing is where dreams take shape and stories come to life. Dedicated to empowering authors from all walks of life, we specialise in guiding individuals on their journey to becoming published authors. Whether you're a first-time writer or an experienced storyteller, Morpheus Publishing provides the expertise, support, and resources you need to bring your vision to the world.

Founded by award-winning author and resilience advocate Justine Martin, Morpheus Publishing is more than a publishing house—it's a community that celebrates creativity, diversity, and the power of the written word. We pride ourselves on working closely with our authors, offering tailored services, including editing, design, publishing, and marketing guidance, ensuring your book is not only published but positioned for success.

Our mission is to give every story the platform it deserves. From memoirs and fiction to self-help and children's books, we help turn your ideas into beautifully crafted books that inspire, educate, and entertain.

Take the first step towards achieving your publishing dreams with Morpheus Publishing, where your story matters, and your voice is heard. Together, let's create something extraordinary.

RESILIENCE MINDSET

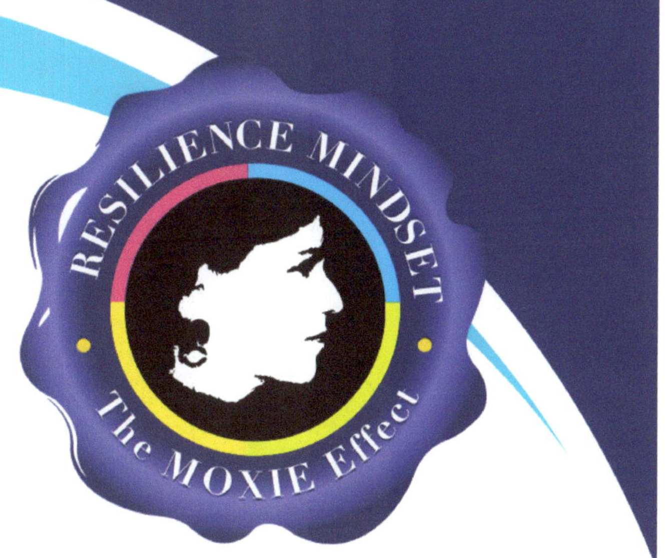

Resilience Mindset is your ultimate partner in overcoming life's challenges and unlocking your full potential. Founded by award-winning resilience advocate, motivational speaker, and coach Justine Martin, Resilience Mindset offers transformative coaching and programs designed to empower individuals to face adversity, embrace change, and thrive.

At Resilience Mindset, we believe that resilience is not just about bouncing back—it's about bouncing forward. Our tailored services include one-on-one coaching, group workshops, and motivational speaking, all aimed at equipping you with the tools and strategies to build confidence, overcome obstacles, and achieve your goals.

Whether you're navigating a personal or professional transition, dealing with unexpected setbacks, or simply looking to enhance your mental strength, Resilience Mindset provides a supportive and inspiring environment to help you thrive. With Justine's unique insights and lived experience, every session is a step toward creating a life filled with purpose, balance, and success.

Take control of your journey and cultivate the strength to rise above life's challenges with Resilience Mindset—because resilience isn't just a skill, it's a way of life.

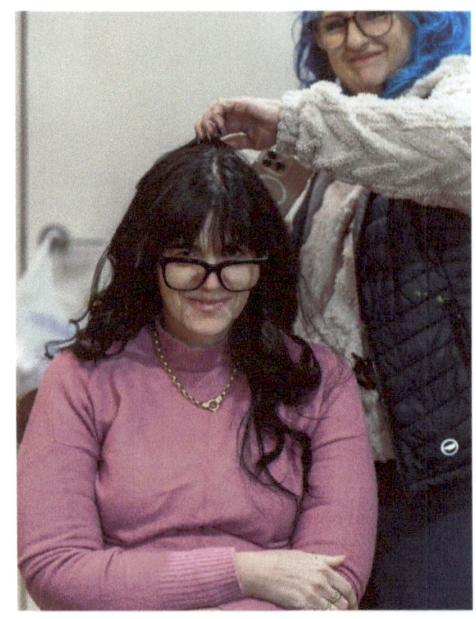

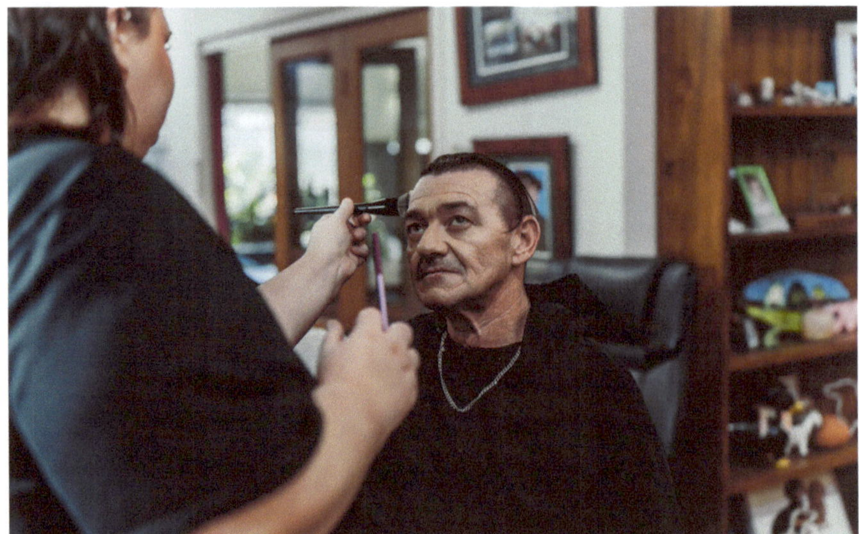

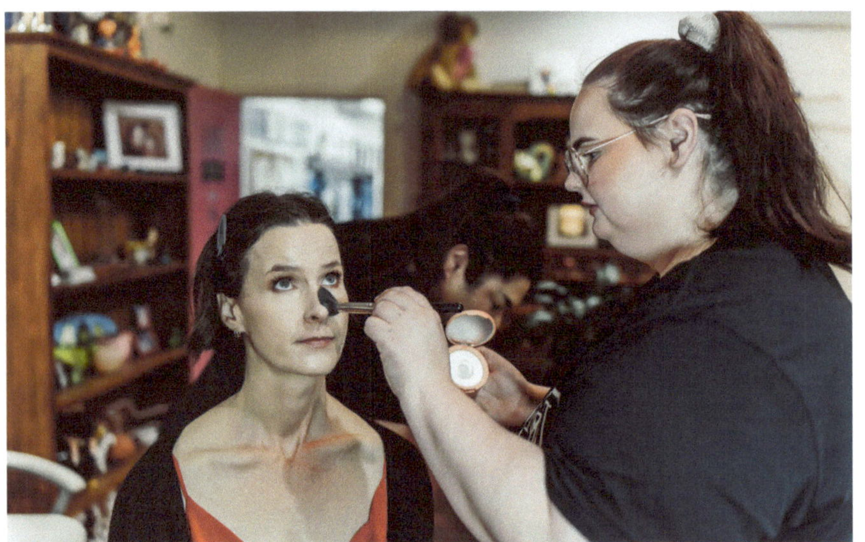

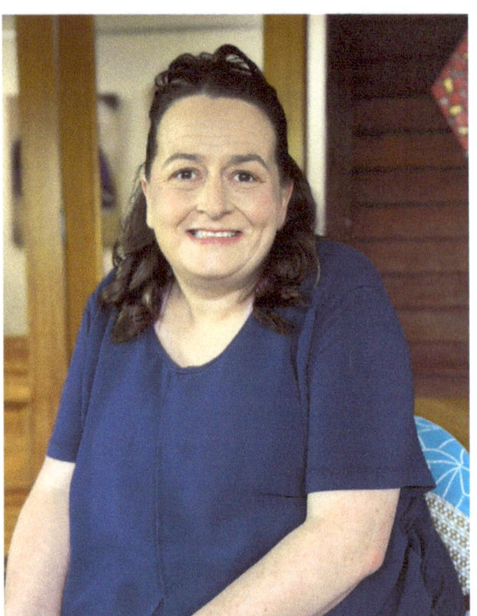

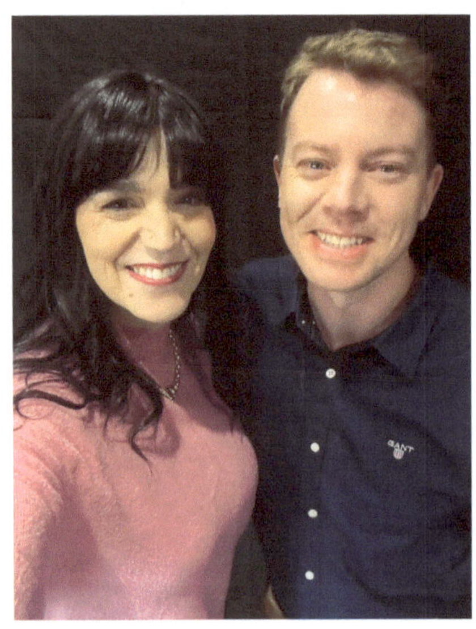

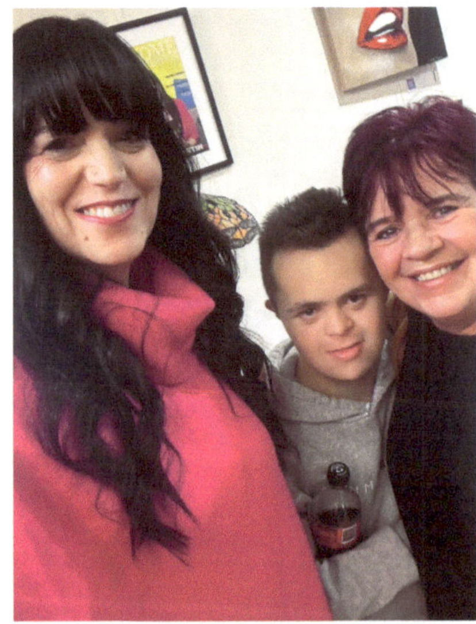

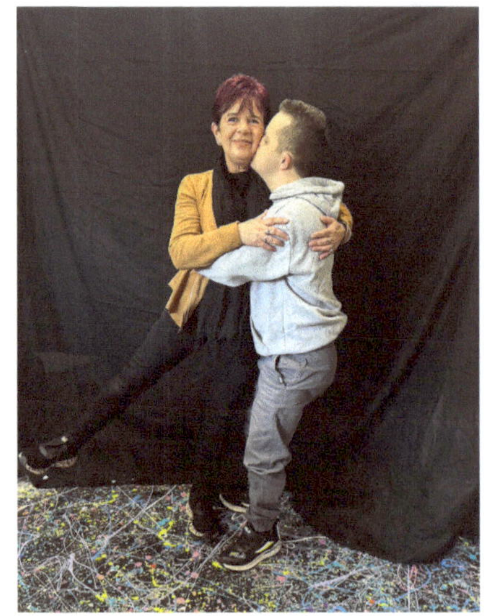

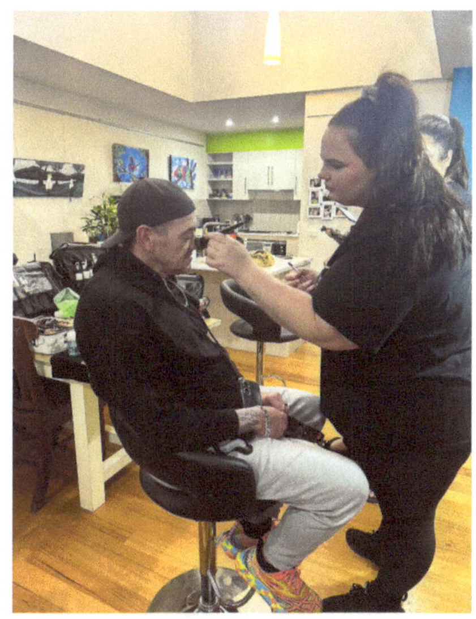

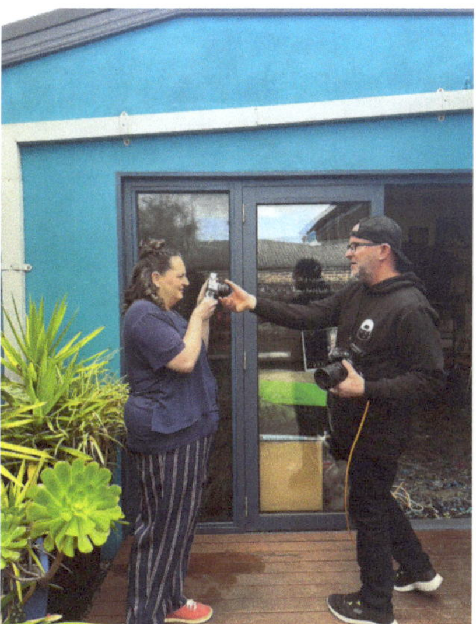

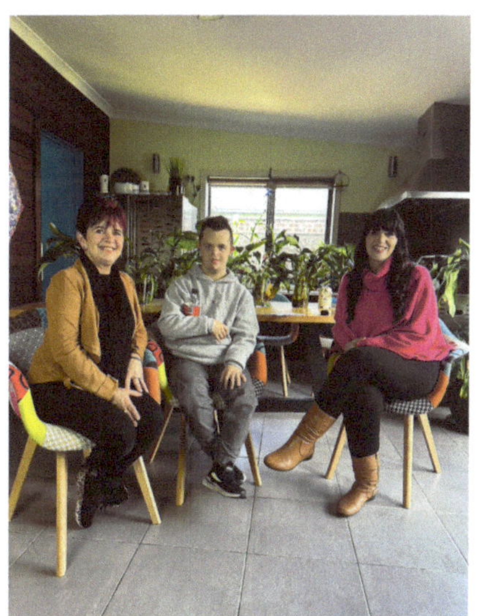

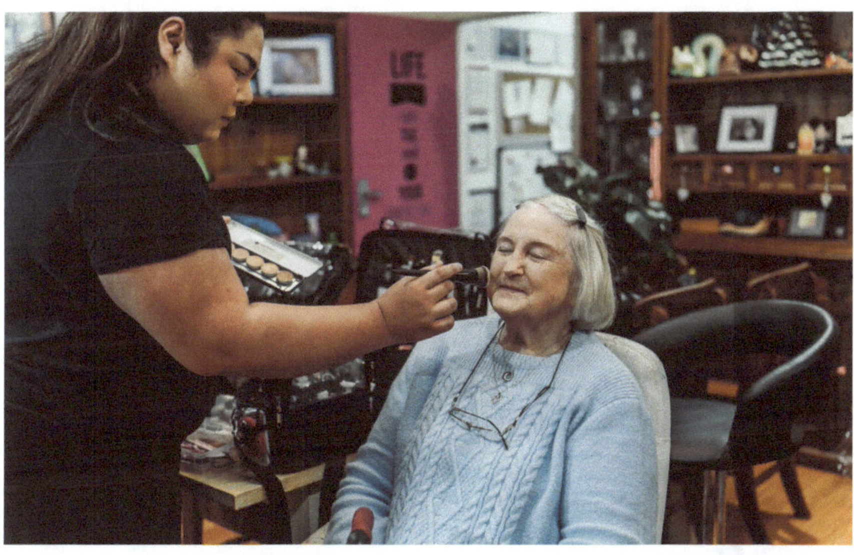
LIFE

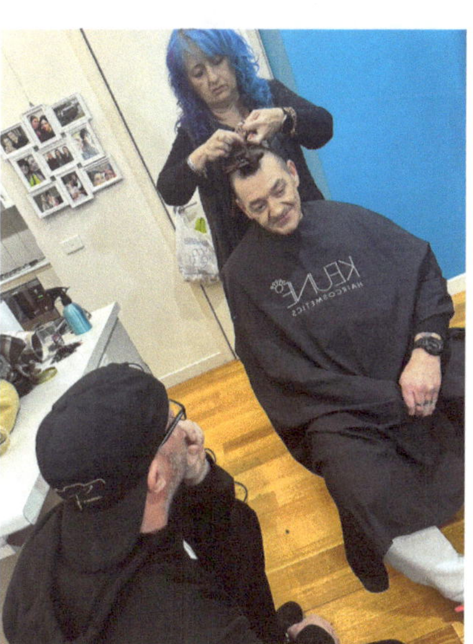

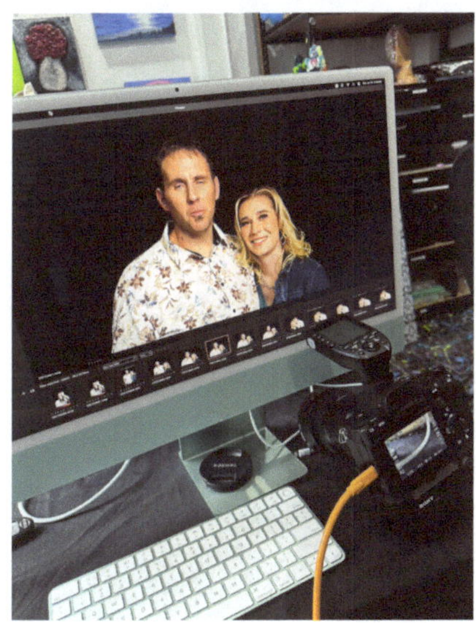

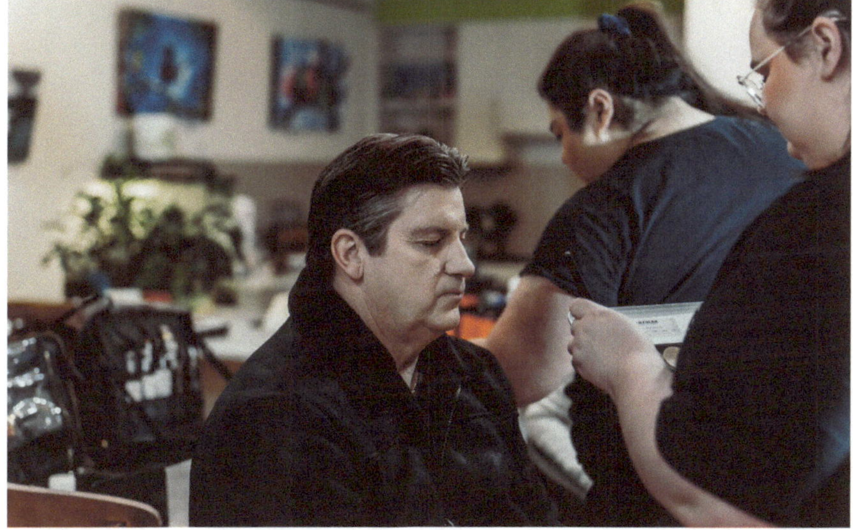

Breaking the Barriers Through the Lens is more than a project—it's a powerful reminder that every story has value, every voice matters, and resilience comes in many forms. Together, we're reshaping perceptions and celebrating the strength in diversity.

Justine Martin

www.ingramcontent.com/pod-product-compliance
Lightning Source LLC
LaVergne TN
LVHW070120110826
845147LV00002B/162